Supplier Collaboration with SAP® SNC

SAP PRESS is a joint initiative of SAP and Galileo Press. The know-how offered by SAP specialists combined with the expertise of the publishing house Galileo Press offers the reader expert books in the field. SAP PRESS features first-hand information and expert advice, and provides useful skills for professional decision-making.

SAP PRESS offers a variety of books on technical and business related topics for the SAP user. For further information, please visit our website: www.sap-press.com.

Butzlaff, Heinzel, Thome
Non-Standard Scenarios for SAP Supply Network Collaboration
2008, 150 pp.
ISBN 978-1-59229-195-3

Munirathinam, Potluri
Consultant's Guide to SAP SRM
2008, 511 pp.
ISBN 978-1-59229-154-0

Sethi
Enhancing Supplier Relationship Management Using SAP SRM
2007, 694 pp.
ISBN 978-1-59229-068-0

Karch, Heilig
SAP NetWeaver Roadmap
2005, 305 pp.
ISBN 978-1-59229-041-3

Mohamed Hamady, Anita Leitz

Supplier Collaboration with SAP® SNC

Bonn • Boston

ISBN 978-1-59229-194-6

© 2009 by Galileo Press Inc., Boston (MA)
1st Edition 2009

German Edition first published 2008 by Galileo Press, Bonn, Germany.

Galileo Press is named after the Italian physicist, mathematician and philosopher Galileo Galilei (1564–1642). He is known as one of the founders of modern science and an advocate of our contemporary, heliocentric worldview. His words *Eppur si muove* (And yet it moves) have become legendary. The Galileo Press logo depicts Jupiter orbited by the four Galilean moons, which were discovered by Galileo in 1610.

Editor   Eva Tripp
English Edition Editor   Jan Franke
Translation   lexsys Language Consulting
Copyeditor   Ruth Saavedra
Cover Design   Silke Braun
Cover Image   Getty Images/Andy Rouse
Layout Design   Vera Brauner
Production   Kelly O'Callaghan
Typesetting   Publishers' Design and Production Services, Inc.
Printed and bound in Canada

All rights reserved. Neither this publication nor any part of it may be copied or reproduced in any form or by any means or translated into another language, without the prior consent of Galileo Press GmbH, Rheinwerkallee 4, 53227 Bonn, Germany.

Galileo Press makes no warranties or representations with respect to the content hereof and specifically disclaims any implied warranties of merchantability or fitness for any particular purpose. Galileo Press assumes no responsibility for any errors that may appear in this publication.

"Galileo Press" and the Galileo Press logo are registered trademarks of Galileo Press GmbH, Bonn, Germany. SAP PRESS is an imprint of Galileo Press.

All of the screenshots and graphics reproduced in this book are subject to copyright © SAP AG, Dietmar-Hopp-Allee 16, 69190 Walldorf, Germany.

SAP, the SAP-Logo, mySAP, mySAP.com, mySAP Business Suite, SAP NetWeaver, SAP R/3, SAP R/2, SAP B2B, SAPtronic, SAPscript, SAP BW, SAP CRM, SAP Early Watch, SAP ArchiveLink, SAP GUI, SAP Business Workflow, SAP Business Engineer, SAP Business Navigator, SAP Business Framework, SAP Business Information Warehouse, SAP inter-enterprise solutions, SAP APO, AcceleratedSAP, InterSAP, SAPoffice, SAPfind, SAPfile, SAPtime, SAPmail, SAP¬access, SAP-EDI, R/3 Retail, Accelerated HR, Accelerated HiTech, Accelerated Consumer Products, ABAP, ABAP/4, ALE/WEB, BAPI, Business Framework, BW Explorer, Enjoy-SAP, mySAP.com e-business platform, mySAP Enterprise Portals, RIVA, SAPPHIRE, TeamSAP, Webflow und SAP PRESS are registered or unregistered trademarks of SAP AG, Walldorf, Germany.

All other products mentioned in this book are registered or unregistered trademarks of their respective companies.

Contents at a Glance

1	Introduction	15
2	Adaptive Supply Chain Network	19
3	Supplier Collaboration in a Model Company	29
4	Business Processes in SAP SNC 5.1	53
5	SAP SNC – Architecture	217
6	Integrating SAP SNC with Other SAP Solutions	243
7	Data Reorganization	257
A	Glossary	265
B	SAP Consulting Services Portfolio	271
C	The Authors	283

Contents

Preface 13

1 Introduction 15

    1.1   Who Is This Book For? 16
    1.2   How Is This Book Structured? 17

2 Adaptive Supply Chain Network 19

    2.1   Requirements 19
    2.2   Collaboration as a Key Function 23
    2.3   Supplier Collaboration 25

3 Supplier Collaboration in a Model Company 29

    3.1   Analysis of the Procurement Processes in a Model Company 29
            3.1.1   Analysis of Business Unit I 31
            3.1.2   Analysis of Business Unit II 34
            3.1.3   Analysis of Business Unit III 36
            3.1.4   Analysis of Business Unit IV 38
    3.2   Mapping the Analyzed Business Processes with SAP SNC 39
            3.2.1   Business Process Analysis of Business Unit I 43
            3.2.2   Business Process Analysis of Business Unit II 45
            3.2.3   Business Process Analysis of Business Unit III 47
            3.2.4   Business Process Analysis of Business Unit IV 49
            3.2.5   Planned System Landscape 50
            3.2.6   Next Steps 50

4 Business Processes in SAP SNC 5.1 53

    4.1   Generic Master Data 53
    4.2   Supplier Managed Inventory (SMI) 55
            4.2.1   Process Overview 55

		4.2.2	SMI-Specific Master Data	59
		4.2.3	Determining and Transferring Gross Demands and Stock Information	59
		4.2.4	Replenishment Planning Variant 1	61
		4.2.5	Creating the ASN for Replenishment Variant 1	64
		4.2.6	Goods Receipt	67
		4.2.7	Replenishment Planning Variant 2	69
		4.2.8	Creating Firm Receipts for Replenishment Variant 2	72
		4.2.9	Creating the ASN for Replenishment Variant 2	74
		4.2.10	Goods Receipt	76
		4.2.11	Monitoring Replenishment Planning with Supplier Managed Inventory (SMI)	76
		4.2.12	Calculating the Projected Stock in the SAP SNC System	77
		4.2.13	Maintaining Replenishment Service Profiles	78
		4.2.14	Assigning the Settings for Replenishment Planning	80
		4.2.15	Automatic Planning	81
		4.2.16	Downloading SMI Data	86
	4.3	Forecast Delivery Schedule Processing		89
		4.3.1	Process Overview	89
		4.3.2	Master Data Specific to Forecast Delivery Schedule Processing	91
		4.3.3	Creating and Sending the Forecast Delivery Schedule	91
		4.3.4	Confirming or Rejecting the Forecast Delivery Schedule	94
		4.3.5	Confirming Quantities and Dates/Times	95
		4.3.6	Creating and Publishing an ASN	97
		4.3.7	Goods Receipt and Proof of Delivery	99
		4.3.8	Monitoring Forecast Delivery Schedule Processing	100
	4.4	Purchase Order Handling		102
		4.4.1	Process Overview	103
		4.4.2	Master Data Specific to Purchase Order Handling	104

	4.4.3	Creating and Sending a Purchase Order	105
	4.4.4	Rejecting a Purchase Order	108
	4.4.5	Purchase Order Confirmation	108
	4.4.6	Approving the Purchase Order Confirmation	110
	4.4.7	Creating and Publishing an ASN	112
	4.4.8	Goods Receipt and Proof of Delivery	113
	4.4.9	Monitoring Purchase Order Handling	114
4.5	Subcontracting		116
	4.5.1	Process Overview	116
	4.5.2	Master Data Specific to Subcontracting	117
	4.5.3	Creating and Sending a Subcontract Order	118
	4.5.4	Rejecting a Subcontract Order	119
	4.5.5	Purchase Order Confirmation	119
	4.5.6	Approving the Purchase Order Confirmation	121
	4.5.7	Monitoring Subcontract Order Processing	121
4.6	Supply Network Inventory		122
	4.6.1	Process Overview	122
	4.6.2	Master Data Specific to SNI	124
	4.6.3	Integrating Customer Data	128
	4.6.4	Integrating Supplier and Partner Data	132
	4.6.5	Verifying Key Figures and Stock	133
	4.6.6	Monitoring and Making Adjustments	137
4.7	Work Order Collaboration		139
	4.7.1	Process Overview	140
	4.7.2	Master Data Specific to Work Orders	141
	4.7.3	Creating and Sending a Purchase Order	144
	4.7.4	Generating and Publishing a Work Order	145
	4.7.5	Confirming a Work Order	149
	4.7.6	Approving a Work Order Confirmation	151
	4.7.7	Updating a Work Order with Actual Data	151
	4.7.8	ASN and Goods Receipt	155
	4.7.9	Monitoring and Making Adjustments	156
4.8	Kanban		158
	4.8.1	Process Overview	158
	4.8.2	Master Data Specific to Kanban	160
	4.8.3	Sending a Kanban Request	165
	4.8.4	Creating an ASN	166

	4.8.5	Posting Goods Receipt	170
	4.8.6	Monitoring the Kanban Process	171
4.9	Delivery Control Monitor		173
	4.9.1	Process Overview	174
	4.9.2	Master Data Specific to the DCM	175
	4.9.3	Determining and Sending Stock Information	176
	4.9.4	Creating an ASN	177
	4.9.5	Posting Goods Receipt	181
	4.9.6	Monitoring Replenishment Planning with the Delivery Control Monitor	181
4.10	Dynamic Replenishment		183
	4.10.1	Process Overview	184
	4.10.2	Master Data for Dynamic Replenishment	185
	4.10.3	Transferring Customer Demands	186
	4.10.4	Maintaining Supplier Receipts	188
	4.10.5	Calculating and Checking Deviations	189
	4.10.6	Monitoring and Making Adjustments	193
4.11	ASN Processing		193
	4.11.1	ASN Processing	193
	4.11.2	Updating the ASN from Goods Receipt	198
4.12	Invoice Collaboration		200
	4.12.1	Process Overview	200
	4.12.2	Master Data Specific to Invoice Collaboration	205
	4.12.3	Creating and Publishing an Invoice	207
	4.12.4	Invoice Verification	209
	4.12.5	Optional: Publishing an Invoice Confirmation	209
	4.12.6	Invoice Processing and the Payment Run	209
	4.12.7	Creating and Publishing a Subsequent Debit or Credit	212
	4.12.8	Creating and Publishing a Credit Memo	213
	4.12.9	Creating and Publishing a Revaluation	214
	4.12.10	Monitoring Invoice Collaboration	216

5 SAP SNC – Architecture   217

5.1	Setting Up an SAP SNC System	217
5.2	System Landscape	220

	5.3	Basic Services	224
		5.3.1 Master Data Integration	224
		5.3.2 Validating Business Data	225
		5.3.3 Managing Exceptions	227
	5.4	Enterprise SOA Concepts	234
		5.4.1 From SOA to Enterprise SOA	234
		5.4.2 Enterprise SOA in Supplier Collaboration	235

6 Integrating SAP SNC with Other SAP Solutions 243

	6.1	Classifying SAP SNC into Various Supplier Collaboration Business Processes	243
	6.2	Collaboration Folders	246
	6.3	SAP NetWeaver Business Intelligence	248
	6.4	SAP Event Management	250
	6.5	SAP NetWeaver Portal	252
	6.6	SAP Advanced Planning & Optimization	253
	6.7	SAP Supplier Relationship Management	254

7 Data Reorganization 257

	7.1	Procedure	257
	7.2	Reorganizing Transaction Data	258
	7.3	Reorganizing Master Data	260
	7.4	Archiving Transaction Data	261

Appendices 263

A	Glossary		265
B	SAP Consulting Services Portfolio		271
	B.1	Implementing an SAP SNC Solution	271
	B.2	SNC02 – Strategic Roadmap Development for Supplier Collaboration	273
	B.3	SNC00 – Rapid SAP SNC Footprinting	274
	B.4	SNC01 – Introduction to Supplier Collaboration with SAP SNC	275
	B.5	SNC04 – Ramp-Up Application Hosting	277

	B.6	SNC05 – Supplier Backend Integration in the SAP SNC-SMI Process	279
	B.7	SNC06 – SAP SNC with SAP NetWeaver Portal	280
	B.8	SNC07 – Expert Solutions in SAP SNC	281
C	The Authors		283

Index 285

Preface

Production processes, from procuring raw materials to delivering the product to the end customer, are constantly changing. What were once linear supply chains with rigid processes are now becoming increasingly complex networks. As a result, industry faces the question of how to keep control of processes.

Transparency and collaboration between partners are crucial to gain a competitive advantage. Confrontation has been replaced by cooperation and collaboration with business partners as the prerequisites for success. With its *Supply Network Collaboration* (SNC) software solution, SAP aims to support the procurement collaboration process.

This book seeks to answer the question of *why* supplier collaboration is necessary. We show you *which types* of business processes the software can support and *which requirements* must be met for each of the business processes.

We could not have managed this challenge alone. Therefore, we want to express our gratitude to our colleagues, who have supported us not only in writing this book but also in so many other ways. In particular, we want to thank Dr. Markus Lenz, who offered his encouragement and helped us along the way as we developed the idea for this book. Our thanks go to Birgit Hecker and Tobias Weiblen for their contributions to this book, and Boris Kopp, Roman Palauro, and Bernhard Trebels for their joint efforts in developing the SAP SNC consulting services portfolio. It would not have been possible to provide descriptions of the business processes without the help of the SAP Global Marketing demo team. Last, but not least, we want to offer a special thanks to our families, who afforded us the time and space we needed, and our friends, who encouraged us to take the step of writing a book together.

Dr. Mohamed Hamady and **Anita Leitz**

What is this book about? Who is it intended for? How is the book structured, and what is the best way for you to read and interpret it? We answer these questions in the introduction.

1　Introduction

Collaboration means a number of individuals or a group of people working together. Different parties, for example, suppliers and customers, work together to solve complex problems and thereby create added value for the customer. To achieve this, efficient intercompany business processes are essential.

Collaboration

By opting for supplier collaboration, companies can improve their performance and increase profitability. Working together brings about strategic partnerships, whose goal it is to create a two-way competitive advantage through shared information and improved integration of business processes. The basis of any successful collaboration is mutual trust between the parties involved and a willingness to share information. However, it is also important to introduce *service-level agreements* (SLAs) and performance assessment tools so that the success of the collaboration can be reviewed.

Basics and objectives

Irrespective of the industry, supplier collaboration takes place at the following levels:

Levels of collaboration

- **Strategic level**
  Here, partners reach mutual decisions on strategic topics. Examples include binding agreements on production capacities, joint product design, and long-term pricing agreements.
- **Tactical level**
  This level might, for instance, involve sharing forecasting data, production plans, and transportation plans. The tactical level also relates to medium-term capacities, bills of material and stock on hand, material availability, and contracts.

- **Operational level**
  Over a short period, things such as purchase orders, production orders, invoices, and credit memos might be exchanged.

SAP Supply Network Collaboration

SAP Supply Network Collaboration (SNC) is a web-based component within *SAP Supply Chain Management* (SCM) that supports a number of business processes in supplier and customer collaboration. The global vision of adaptive supply chain networks is accommodated as part of supplier collaboration, in particular, in the areas of procurement planning, procurement processing, and billing. In this respect, collaboration takes place at both the tactical and operational levels.

This book provides you with a comprehensive explanation of the business processes and technical architecture of SAP SNC (Release 5.1). On the basis of a fictitious model company, you will become acquainted with the procurement processes that can benefit from supplier collaboration.

1.1 Who Is This Book For?

Target groups

The book is aimed at project managers and team members who are concerned with the optimization and implementation of supplier collaboration processes with SAP SNC.

It teaches you why collaboration not only makes sense but is actually needed, and which procurement processes are suitable for supplier collaboration. Taking a fictitious company as an example, we show you which business scenarios in SAP SNC can be used to map given procurement processes. In addition, information about the system architecture is provided, which should be taken into account when setting up an SAP SNC system.

Basic knowledge of logistics and procurement business processes and a grounding in the materials management and production planning areas in SAP ERP are required to understand this book.

1.2 How Is This Book Structured?

The book consists of seven chapters:

Chapter 2 Adaptive Supply Chain Network begins by discussing the difficulties faced by global companies in the increasingly interconnected world of business. The chapter describes why collaboration is essential and what measures can help improve a company's ability to perform and react in the supply chain. It highlights the special significance of collaboration with business partners and explores supplier collaboration with SAP SNC.

Chapter 3 Supplier Collaboration in a Model Company analyzes the procurement processes of a company and maps these business processes with the SAP SNC solution.

Chapter 4 Business Processes in SAP SNC 5.1 describes the supplier collaboration business processes provided in SAP SNC 5.1. The individual processes and their steps are explained in detail. You are given an overview of the generic and scenario-dependent master data.

Chapter 5 SAP SNC – Architecture details the architectural considerations to take into account when setting up and integrating an SAP SNC system. We provide an overview of the basic services that are possible with supplier collaboration based on SAP SNC.

Chapter 6 Integrating SAP SNC with Other SAP Solutions deals with the possibility of integrating SAP SNC with other SAP products. Examples are used to show which SAP systems are beneficial to achieve comprehensive supplier collaboration.

Chapter 7 Data Reorganization provides details about the tools used to reorganize transaction data and master data.

Appendix A contains a glossary of important terms. Appendix B SAP Consulting Services Portfolio is aimed primarily at customers who want to initiate a project in the area of supplier collaboration with SAP SNC. SAP Consulting offers a number of best practice consulting services for this purpose.

Different demands draw companies into a mesh of requirements and actions. Collaboration shores up the logistics network and is fast becoming essential in the fight to stay competitive. SAP has developed solutions that enable you to integrate collaboration into your business processes.

2 Adaptive Supply Chain Network

This chapter opens with a discussion of the requirements placed on an *adaptive supply chain network* based on the concept of *supply chain management* (SCM). Section 2.2 Collaboration as a Key Function then explores the meaning of collaboration with customers, suppliers, and partners. Section 2.3 Supplier Collaboration deals with aspects of supplier collaboration, with particular focus on supplier integration from a logistics and production processes perspective.

2.1 Requirements

Global competition and changing consumer behavior are leading to new challenges for the logistics processes in companies. Not only are processes continuously gaining in complexity, but the number of involved partners is also increasing steadily. One way to meet these challenges is through better collaboration.

Aims of supply chain management

One aspect of global competition is the growing trend toward production outsourcing, which companies must cope with using stronger network ties. This increasing globalization also impacts purchasing and procurement. Along the entire process chain, from the supplier of the raw material to the customer who receives the end product, logistics is steadily becoming more complex. A greater willingness to adapt, accommodate, and collaborate is needed at all stages along the supply chain.

Impact on purchasing

Supply networks	The resulting structure, with its many distributed partners, bears a closer relation to a network than a chain. For this reason, the term *supply chain* is becoming less common and is frequently replaced by *supply network*.

Certain external factors have a particular bearing on the supply network:

Risks during transportation	Lengthier procurement and transportation times increase risks in logistics. The geographical spread of partners opens the door to greater variety in transportation lanes and procurement options. This situation also contributes to the vulnerability of the network to deficiencies and delays.
Challenges in production	The planning and lifecycles of products are becoming shorter, and end customers want variable, configurable products. An equally high degree of flexibility is expected when it comes to deliveries. All of this puts customers under great pressure to get products to the market in their desired form.
Cost factors	The power of low-cost producers to displace traditional suppliers is growing, and high fuel prices are prompting companies to seek cheaper distribution alternatives. Furthermore, price wars are forcing companies across the board to streamline production and lower warehouse stock levels that could be critical for the entire delivery network.
Customer retention	Although customer loyalty to products and brands is falling, customers nevertheless expect customer service to improve. Companies that cannot execute their logistics processes efficiently lose even more customers as a result of these conflicting circumstances.

In addition to these external factors, issues within the company can complicate procurement logistics processes.

Lack of a consistent procurement strategy	A standard procurement strategy is often lacking in companies, which prevents them from living up to new challenges. A misconstrued decentralization concept, in which every branch office has responsibility for its own procurement activities, has unfavorable results:

- Despite sharing matching requirements, the different branch offices or business segments of the company procure different assortments.

- No standard invitations to tender or outline agreements with suppliers exist. As a consequence, price differences are identified for the same article at the same supplier.
- Conditions are not applied across the board.
- Several suppliers are responsible for supplying the same product.
- The day-to-day procurement of direct materials is extremely time-consuming.

Therefore, it can be said that procurement processes are often not standardized. Business processes for the same situation are handled differently in the branch offices with the same suppliers. This results in data maintenance that is intensive both in terms of time and cost, and therefore is also error-prone. To give a practical example, a company might receive a confirmation fax for each order from supplier A. However, when the company deals with supplier B, it is normal to receive notification by telephone if the requested deadline cannot be met. The lack of an established, automated, real-time communication channel means communication with suppliers is not transparent.

Lack of standardization

The fact that a common, integrated system platform for procurement and purchasing only exists to a limited extent also impairs other business steps, because there is a lack of consolidated information about purchase volume and no standardized means of accessing controlling data concerning company-wide expenditure.

The solution to these problems lies in the creation of adaptive supply chain networks. These adaptive supply chain networks must be flexible enough to continuously identify changing circumstances and react rapidly. Seamlessly combining planning, production, procurement, and distribution, they offer a complete overview of the supply chain.

Adaptive supply chain network

This enables fast decision-making. Such adaptive supply chain networks are the key to logistics collaboration.

Collaboration in procurement makes it easier to remain competitive because close cooperation between partners facilitates the process of optimizing the process chain. When customers and suppliers share information, supply risks are reduced and bottlenecks identified early on. The creation of such strategic partnerships, along with the accompanying

Collaboration in procurement

willingness to offer partners an insight into one's own processes, enables closer integration of processes. All involved parties stand to benefit from such close cooperation.

Dynamic supply chains

The particular challenge here lies in the fact that the supply chain is not a static system, but a dynamic, ever-changing network. The trend toward outsourcing, greater variety, and shorter product lifecycles is making the supply chain increasingly complex.

In its broadest definition, supply chain management is aimed at the integration, planning, optimization, and control of industrial value chains and the corresponding cash, information, and material flows. The goal is to look beyond company boundaries when tracing these processes. Activities focus on meeting customer requirements while simultaneously optimizing costs in the supply chain.

Supply chain management is particularly effective at improving the performance of the supply chain and thereby also its ability to react quickly to unforeseen events, such as fluctuations in demand.

Adaptive supply chain network

To safeguard these goals, SAP SCM 2007 supports the adaptive supply chain network, which is characterized by the following measures (see Figure 2.1).

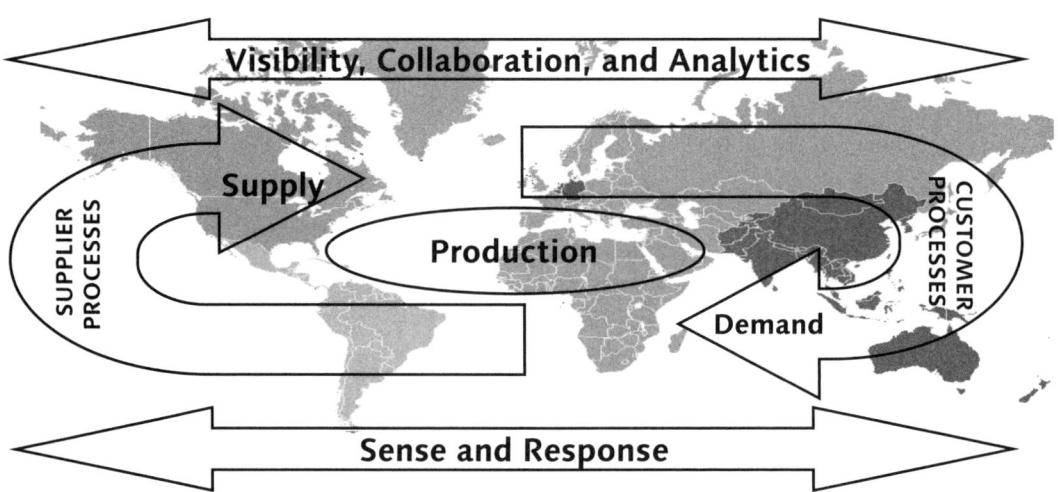

Figure 2.1 Adaptive Supply Chain Network

- **Synchronized requirements and receipts**
  The bidding, procurement, production, planning, and distribution processes become integrated company processes. As this occurs, they become linked to each other at strategic, tactical, and operational levels. The trend is moving away from restricting planning to internal processes and toward taking into account dependencies across the entire company.

- **Control of requirements, quotations, and capacity**
  To enable companies to react in real time to changing market demands, closer integration of planning and control activities is sought. The aim here is to improve sales order processing and contribute to increased customer satisfaction on the one hand, while also enabling status tracking at order, product, and execution level.

- **Transparency, collaboration, and analytics**
  The transparency that has now been created in the current and planned requirement, receipt, and capacity situation of the involved companies allows for quick reactions to changes that occur at short notice. An end-to-end information flow must be established here to enable the required interaction with customers and suppliers.

Furthermore, analytical functions based on real-time data are required to support the decision-making process and to monitor strategic, tactical, and operational goals. These functions should be used to analyze and assess collaborative efforts so that weaknesses can be identified and rectified.

2.2 Collaboration as a Key Function

When collaboration is used as an approach to managing the adaptive supply chain network, all of the participants must show a willingness to be open with each other. The aim here is to agree on ways to manage logistical processes with customers and suppliers. This achieves gains in both flexibility and transparency. To reduce the complexity and effort involved in implementing intercompany collaboration processes, collaboration with business partners should be realized on the basis of recognized process and technology standards. This also makes it possible

Collaboration with business partners

2 | Adaptive Supply Chain Network

to integrate business partners with greater speed and flexibility in a dynamic, ever-changing network. As soon as the collaboration processes between business partners have been implemented and are stable, the focus should shift to rooting out and fixing exceptional situations and bottlenecks.

Collaboration with SAP SNC

SAP SNC supports collaboration with customers, suppliers, and contract manufacturers (see Figure 2.2).

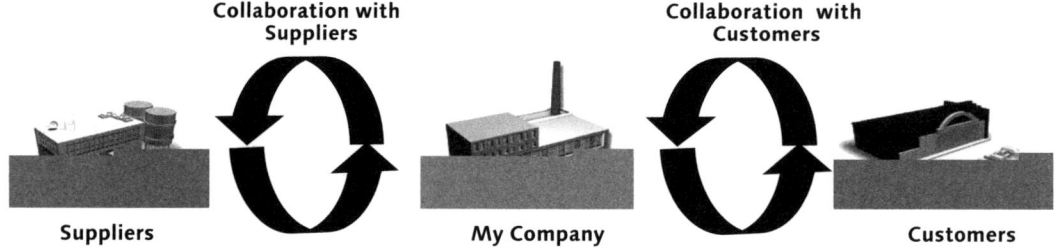

- Gross Demands
- Stock on Hand
- Outsourced Manufacturing
- Delivery Schedule
- ASNs (including packaging information)
- Min/Max or Days of Coverage
- Proof of Delivery
- Invoicing Collaboration

- Forecasting & Promotion
- Consumption/Sales History
- Shipment Schedule
- Purchase Order
- Inventory Balances

Figure 2.2 Collaboration with SAP SNC 5.1

SAP SNC provides business partners with relevant information concerning internal production and logistics processes and enables further coordination. Business partners interact with the SAP SNC platform using a web-based interface and by connecting their systems with *SAP NetWeaver Process Integration* (PI).

In addition, the standard version contains predefined collaboration processes that can be configured and implemented in a short space of time.

Benefits of collaboration

All in all, collaboration with business partners based on SAP SNC is expected to bring gains in logistical performance. For example, it can bring about increased forecast accuracy for future requirements, lower levels of (safety) stock, and a reduction in stockouts. Figure 2.3 shows the benefits of collaboration from customer and supplier perspectives.

This book takes a closer look at supplier collaboration business processes with SAP SNC 5.1.

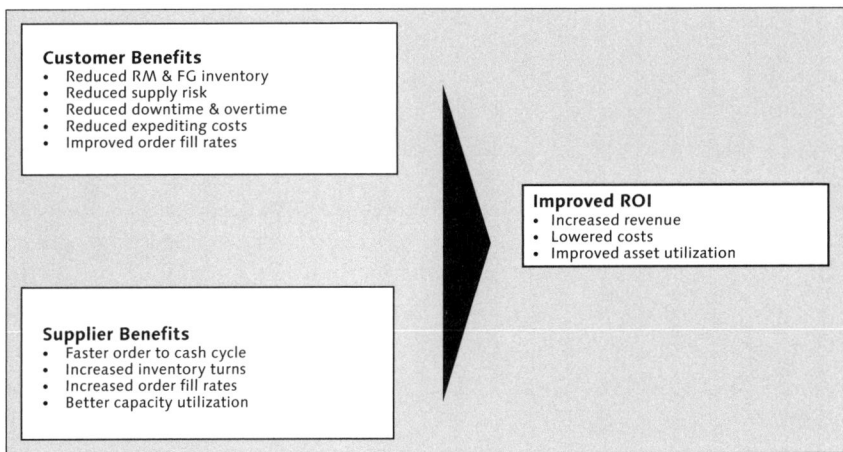

Figure 2.3 Benefits of Collaboration on the Basis of SAP SNC 5.1

2.3 Supplier Collaboration

In its broadest sense, supplier collaboration involves designing and running purchasing and procurement processes (see Figure 2.4). *Strategic purchasing* deals with long-term relationships with suppliers.

Classifying supplier collaboration

Design and product lifecycle management is concerned with matters of cooperation on the part of suppliers, particularly during the product development phase and *make-or-buy* decisions.

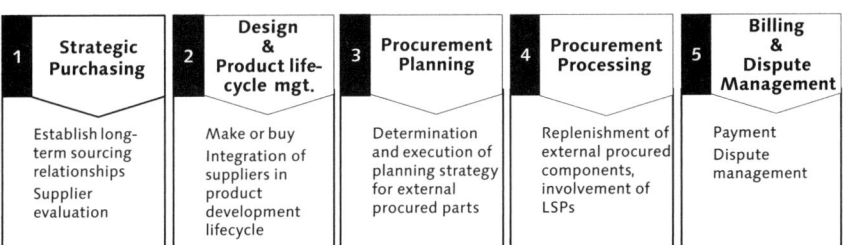

Figure 2.4 Classification of Supplier Collaboration Processes

Procurement planning and processing involves planning external procurement and source determination, and may also be concerned with the actual execution of procurement.

Billing and dispute management incorporates the steps for payment processing and any associated subsequent adjustments.

Supplier collaboration, as set out in SAP SNC 5.1, can be allocated to the procurement planning and processing area. For the purposes of replenishment planning and control, the business processes in SAP SNC support different variations of collaboration with suppliers.

If your company stages gross demands and stock, you can give responsibility for replenishment planning and control of selected products to your supplier. Alternatively, you have the option of planning replenishment yourself and coordinating replenishment control with your supplier. In both cases, you and your supplier can view the progress of replenishment planning and control in SAP SNC and obtain information about exceptional situations.

Supplier collaboration with SAP SNC represents a further stage in the development of supplier integration, especially in respect to the functional scope and intensity of integration (see Figure 2.5). The information channels commonly used until now to interact with suppliers—fax, email, telephone, or mail—are no longer sufficient to live up to the heightened demands on supplier collaboration. Supplier integration is also often established by means of the local ERP or SCM system using *electronic data interchange* (EDI) or WEB-EDI. The high financial cost of this type of integration limits its area of application to strategic suppliers.

Figure 2.6 provides a broad overview of the components in supplier collaboration with SAP SNC 5.1 developed on the basis of the SAP NetWeaver technology platform. SAP SNC 5.1 is composed of the following business processes that are based on common basic services:

- **Supplier Managed Inventory (SMI)**
  SMI supports replenishment planning by the supplier on the basis of a minimum or maximum supply or day's supply.

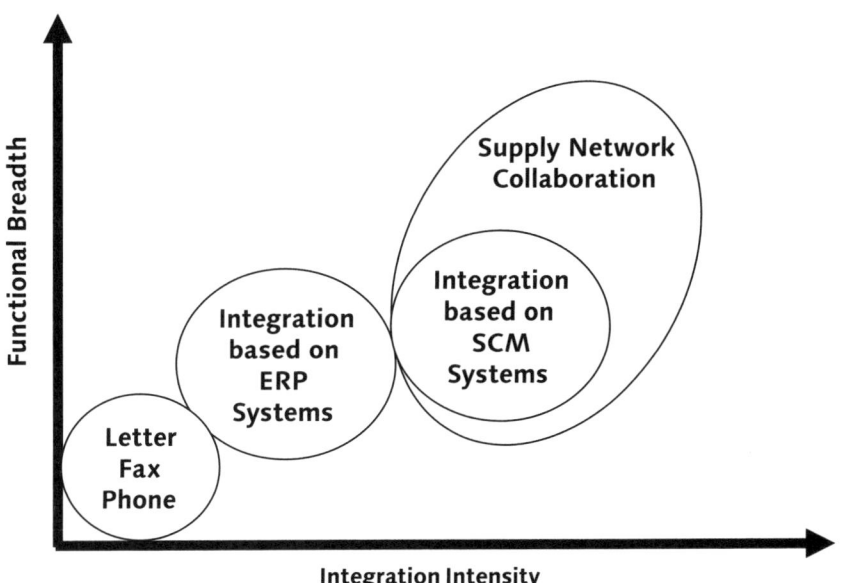

Figure 2.5 Vendor Integration Development Stages

- **Forecast delivery release process**
  Forecast delivery release process supports replenishment planning when it is performed by a customer on the basis of a purchase scheduling agreement.

- **Purchase order process**
  Purchase order process supports replenishment planning when it is performed by a customer on the basis of a purchase order.

- **Subcontracting**
  Subcontracting makes it possible to process subcontract orders. Subcontractors are able to confirm their component consumption.

- **Supply Network Inventory**
  Supply Network Inventory calculates and shows the projected stock for products and components in the customer, supplier, and partner locations.

- **Work order collaboration**
  Work order collaboration supports collaboration with outsourced production areas.

- **Kanban**
  This business process supports kanban production control with external suppliers.
- **Inbound delivery control**
  Inbound delivery control supports minimum and maximum replenishment control by the supplier.
- **Dynamic replenishment**
  Dynamic replenishment enables the comparison of customer planned and firm demands and supplier receipts.
- **Invoice collaboration**
  Invoice collaboration allows invoices and credit memos to be processed between customers and suppliers.

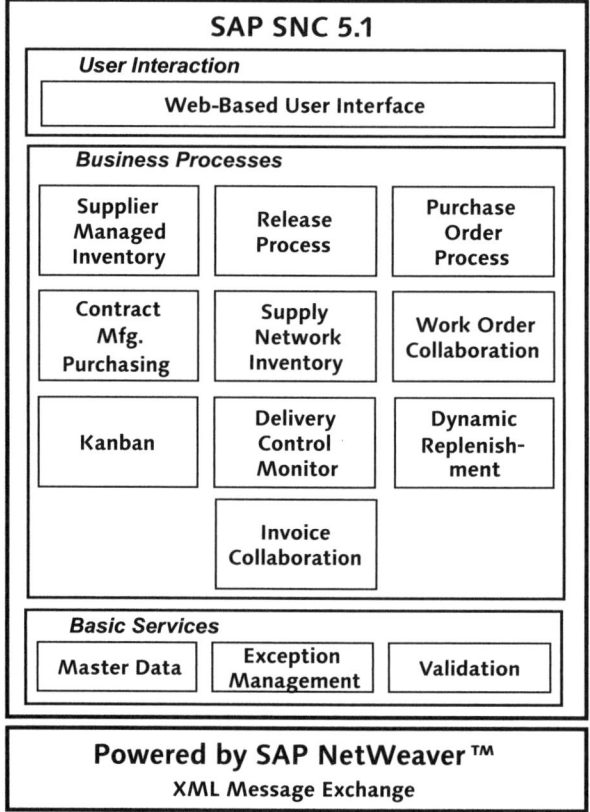

Figure 2.6 Supplier Collaboration with SAP SNC 5.1

This chapter describes the procurement processes of a model company. First, the strengths and weaknesses of the individual subprocesses are analyzed. Next, the processes used for procurement handling in the separate business units are mapped to the scenarios in SAP SNC.

3 Supplier Collaboration in a Model Company

In this chapter, we explore the strengths and weaknesses of the procurement processes in place at a model company. This analysis lays the foundation for further investigation to identify which business processes in SAP SNC could help optimize supplier collaboration in the individual business units.

3.1 Analysis of the Procurement Processes in a Model Company

Our fictitious model company, the global industrial group A.M.H.L. Industries, boasts a large product portfolio. A.M.H.L. consists of four major business units. Business Unit I produces custom-built parts for luxury cars made to the specifications of the vehicle owners. Business Unit II manufactures ball bearings that are used in a range of industries. Business Unit III is a supplier of electronic parts for the entertainment industry, and the smallest, Business Unit IV, produces mounting and assembly materials that are procured solely by the other three business units.

Model company

Innovative strength, accelerated improvement of company processes, and a focus on internationalizing market cultivation activities are seen as essential to achieving ongoing net sales growth and expanding market share.

3 Supplier Collaboration in a Model Company

As a strategically important measure to optimize company processes, drastic improvements to the *supply chain* beyond the company's own boundaries are needed, and supplier collaboration is expected to be a major contributor to achieving this goal. To this end, the procurement processes of each business unit will be examined in detail, with the aim of establishing whether and to what extent the SAP SNC solution can bolster and optimize procurement processes across the organization and which business processes it would make sense to implement.

Weaknesses The analysis of procurement processes reveals that all four business units are pursuing their own procurement strategies, because procurement responsibility is decentralized and lies with the individual units. As a result of these heterogeneous procurement structures across the enterprise, general weaknesses can be identified:

- In spite of identical requirements in terms of the quality and composition of raw materials, different materials are purchased.
- Many suppliers are used for the same products.
- Outline agreements with suppliers are not negotiated consistently.

These weaknesses have far-reaching consequences:

- Different conditions, and therefore different prices, have been agreed upon with the same vendors.
- Because no consolidated information concerning purchase volumes is available, the company cannot take advantage of quantity discounts.
- Purchasing different raw materials of the same quality results in unnecessary rises in levels of stock on hand.
- Because minimum quantities must be purchased that cannot be consumed before the shelf life expiration date, large quantities end up having to be disposed of each year.

Due to the company's development, as well as the acquisition and merging of some divisions, business units I and IV each have their own ERP systems, whereas business units II and III use one common ERP system. A single ERP system for all business units is planned. To achieve this, the intention is to begin by performing a release upgrade of the system used by business units II and III in the coming three years and then integrate business units I and IV.

For the purpose of simplifying the analysis, we have divided the procurement processes into five subprocesses (see Figure 3.1).

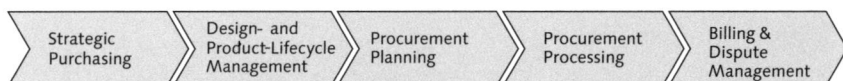

Figure 3.1   Procurement Process Subprocesses

3.1.1 Analysis of Business Unit I

Approximately 90% of the required, externally procured components and raw materials are custom produced according to drawings. These are custom-built car parts manufactured only at the express request of customers. The number of suppliers used is relatively high, whereas the order quantities remain very low in each case. The complexity of the production of the purchased materials is reflected in the stringent approval process. In some cases, the suppliers are small-scale operations with no more than 10 employees. Due to a lack of IT resources, invoices produced using a typewriter are by no means unusual. For about 3% of materials, requirements are known at least three months in advance. This information is faxed once a week to selected suppliers with whom close working relationships have existed for many years.

Business Unit I

Strategic Purchasing

Strategic purchasing is not particularly well developed. It is relatively difficult to negotiate outline agreements in light of the large number of suppliers and small quantities of products, which are very often produced according to specific plans. Long-standing business relationships arise from the fact that a supplier possesses special expertise in particular production techniques.

Design and Product Lifecycle Management

A high degree of consultation between the customer and the suppliers is required for the custom production of individual parts. Drawings and other production documents are sent to the suppliers on a regular basis. Requests for changes for procedural or customer-specific reasons require customers, suppliers, and the production plant to invest a lot of time and engage in a high level of communication. Numerous telephone conversations, faxes, and on-site meetings are necessary.

Procurement Planning

For most materials, procurement planning is dictated by the project manager determining which suppliers come into consideration on the basis of the production techniques needed. Automatic planning is triggered for a small number of materials.

Procurement Processing

Purchase orders are posted to the supplier together with the drawings. If orders are urgent, the purchase orders are faxed in advance, and some suppliers also receive purchase orders by email. There is no standard procedure for the supplier to confirm the requested delivery date. Similarly, there is no way of confirming that the material has been sent.

In addition to the actual purchase orders, the supplier receives demand forecasts for certain materials. Such information provides nothing more than a forecast and is subject to change at any time.

Billing and Dispute Management

The suppliers issue an invoice based on the delivered quantity. Any incorrectly delivered or defective materials are returned with a note to the supplier.

Summary   Business Unit I has identified the fact that strategic purchasing is practically nonexistent as a particular weakness. Supplier evaluations and the strategic selection of suppliers according to particular criteria take place only at a very rudimentary level.

Design and product lifecycle management is a very important part of supplier collaboration, but the process has not been optimized and should be standardized to a greater extent.

Procurement planning and processing also demonstrate very few standardized processes that could reduce manual effort. A handful of long-standing employees know the individual processes, which might differ from supplier to supplier. An analysis of suppliers showed that there are no main suppliers. In fact, 80% of sales are achieved with 70% of the suppliers (see Figure 3.2).

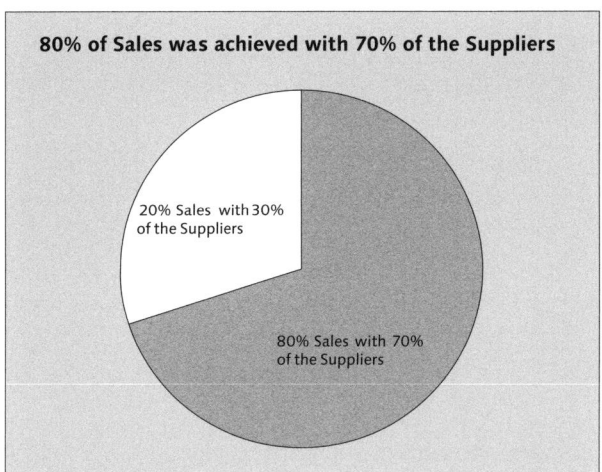

Figure 3.2 Sales and Supplier Analysis for Business Unit I

The analysis of procured materials revealed that 90% of parts have to be custom made on a specific basis (see Figure 3.3).

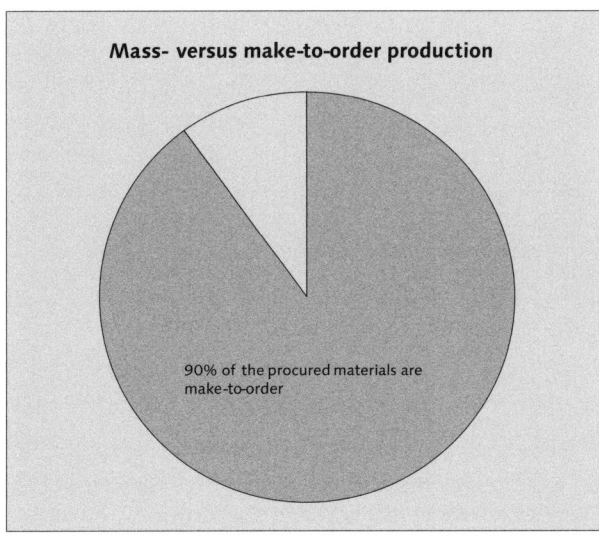

Figure 3.3 Proportion of Procured Parts that Are Custom Productions

3.1.2 Analysis of Business Unit II

Business Unit II manufactures ball bearings for the automotive, high tech, aviation, and aerospace industries. The analysis of the procurement processes in Business Unit II showed that outline supply agreements governing quantities and the time frame for acceptance have been concluded with approximately 80% of all suppliers. Demand forecasts of up to one and a half years can be guaranteed. Some suppliers receive demand forecasts electronically in different types of systems. In return, the supplier provides automatic notification when a material has been sent.

Strategic Purchasing

Long-term supplier relationships are secured by concluding outline agreements. Suppliers are evaluated annually.

Design and Product Lifecycle Management

More than 90% of ordered materials are commodities that are available on the market from a number of manufacturers. Collaboration in design and product lifecycle management is not developed.

Procurement Planning

Source determination takes place automatically on the basis of outline agreements for the bulk of procured parts. For a smaller number of materials that are commodities, inquiries are sent to potential suppliers, and bids are requested on a regular basis. Quota arrangement rules are used to define the percentage of individual materials to be procured from each supplier.

Procurement Processing

Most suppliers receive an e-mail once a week outlining the fixed daily release quantities for the next two weeks. Similarly, the expected weekly requirements are provided to the suppliers up to 6 months in advance for information purposes. This information is sent to a small number of suppliers electronically, and these same suppliers also send electronic notifications when goods have been sent.

Billing and Dispute Management

Business Unit II successfully implemented self-billing about one year ago. This means procured materials are no longer paid for on the basis of invoices from the supplier, but are paid using data from the goods receipt.

Over the past few years, Business Unit II has endeavored to manage procurement processes more efficiently in a variety of ways. By concluding outline agreements consistently and providing early notification of requirements, the unit has been able to negotiate price reductions of up to 3%.

Summary

In-house costs are reduced through use of electronic data exchange. However, this exchange is only operational with a relatively small number of suppliers that have the technical capability to send and receive data.

In addition to the gains made in logistical efficiency, the business unit has succeeded in simplifying financial processes by converting to self-billing.

The unit is currently looking for solutions to further simplify processes for certain selected materials and suppliers. For local suppliers based within an hour's traveling distance from the plant, plans are centered on a simple solution based on a control cycle. This would mean materials would no longer have to be planned as part of the *material requirements planning* (MRP) run. A variety of proposals are being looked at here.

The degree of automation in data exchange is shown in Table 3.1. A distinction is made on the basis of the number of suppliers, in total and as a percentage, with which data exchange is fully automated, partly automated, and not automated.

	No. of Suppliers	Fully Automated Processes (Backend - Backend)	Partly Automated Processes	No Automated Processes
Total	500	0	15	485
In %	100	0	3	97

Table 3.1 Degree of Process Automation in Business Unit II

3 | Supplier Collaboration in a Model Company

3.1.3 Analysis of Business Unit III

Business Unit III In Business Unit III, only a small proportion of the electronic parts for the entertainment industry are still produced in-house. More than 75% of the semi-finished and finished parts are procured by means of subcontracting. The components needed for this are acquired in a number of ways:

- They are provided by the business unit itself.
- The components are planned and ordered by the business unit but delivered directly to the subcontractor from the component supplier.
- Some components are procured and paid for by the subcontractors themselves.
- Some outline agreements between the business unit and the component supplier provide for subcontractors to release materials themselves.

Figure 3.4 provides a graphical overview of the sources from which subcontractors procure their components.

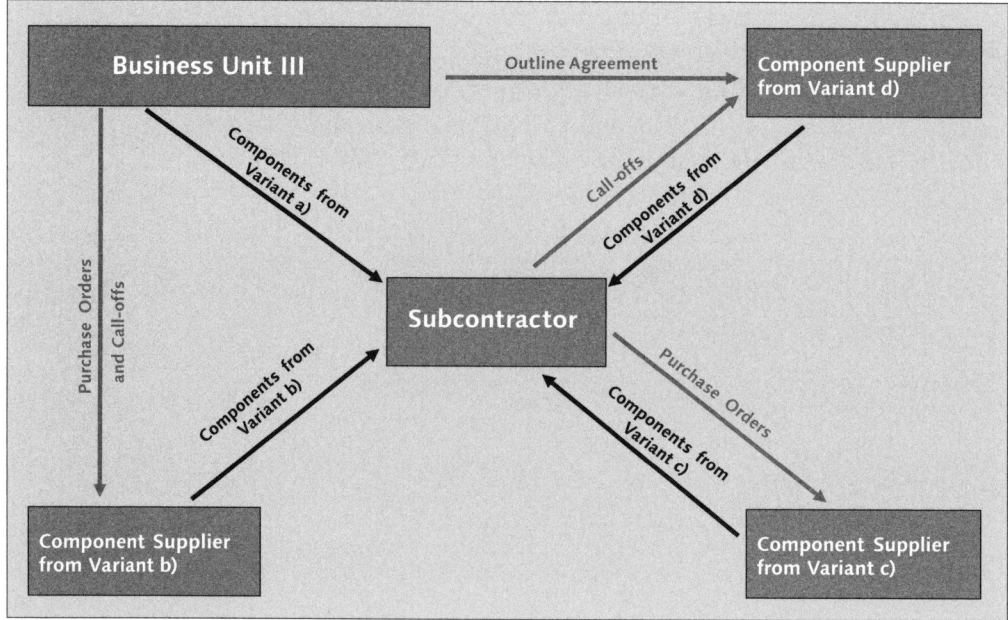

Figure 3.4 Component Sources of Subcontractors

Strategic Purchasing

Strategic purchasing does not go much beyond negotiating time quotas with subcontractors. Closer relationships are maintained with some subcontractors who, despite having been spun off from the business unit a few years ago, are still located on the plant premises.

Design and Product Lifecycle Management

In some cases, the finished products are complex, and the parts provided for them are custom made. It is therefore vital that the customer, business unit, subcontractor, and subcontracting component supplier work closely together here.

Procurement Planning

In procurement planning, the business unit defines in detail with the subcontractor which product is to be produced within the agreed time quota.

Procurement Processing

Some subcontractors have been granted access to the internal ERP system to make it simpler to work with the business unit. In such cases, subcontract orders are modeled in the system as production orders that are confirmed by the subcontractor. The subcontractor also posts goods receipts of subcontracting components directly. This necessitates a high level of effort on the part of the business unit's IT team. They have to ensure that the SAP logon access software is kept up to date on the subcontractor's PCs and that the authorization concept is strictly observed.

Billing and Dispute Management

An agreement is in place with most of the suppliers that invoices should be issued on a monthly basis.

A great deal of manual effort is required in the design phase to ensure consultation between the parties, namely, customer, subcontractor, and subcontracting component supplier. The business unit is looking for a

Summary

way to improve this process, on the one hand to shorten the consultation period, and on the other to minimize the number of errors. They want to automate and standardize activities as much as possible.

Having outsourced most of its products, the business unit already has considerable experience with supplier collaboration in procurement processing. Unfortunately, the traditional processes in SAP ERP are not sufficient to satisfactorily model such extensive use of subcontracting. Alternatives are being investigated as a matter of urgency to simplify subcontracting processes, increase the visibility of production at the subcontractor, and replace the *workarounds* in the SAP ERP system. In particular, the business unit no longer wants to allow suppliers to access its ERP system in the future.

3.1.4 Analysis of Business Unit IV

Business Unit IV is the smallest of the four units. It is responsible only for creating products that are further developed or sold in the other three business units.

The articles it produces are mainly series production parts with relatively constant consumption levels. Stock is transferred between business units I–III and IV using the *kanban pull principle*. This procedure is already used to interact with most suppliers, but is not yet supported by a system.

Figure 3.5 shows the kanban pull principle. The supplier is only asked to supply a new material when that material is withdrawn by the customer.

Figure 3.5   Kanban Pull Principle

Strategic Purchasing

Strategic purchasing has not been developed and consists mainly of selecting the lowest bid from the different suppliers. Contracts are then concluded and reviewed annually.

Design and Product Lifecycle Management

The parts to be procured are commodities that are required continuously over longer periods. Design and product lifecycle management can therefore be disregarded.

Procurement Planning

Procurement planning is mainly performed by assessing on a yearly basis whether the customer requirements of business units I–III are met with the existing supplier contracts, and whether the kanban control cycles, with the number of containers and quantities, are still current.

Procurement Processing

Procurement planning is managed using kanban with the suppliers. This takes place manually and is not supported by a system.

Billing and Dispute Management

An agreement exists with 75% of suppliers that invoices are settled monthly.

In general, the business unit does not see much room for improvement but would like a system to support procurement processing.

Summary

3.2 Mapping the Analyzed Business Processes with SAP SNC

After performing an analysis, A.M.H.L. opts to conduct a detailed investigation of the procurement process and map it to the business scenarios in SAP SNC as its first priority. It is hoped that supplier collaboration will bring the greatest improvements in procurement planning. To this end, questionnaires about materials and suppliers are evaluated to establish which business processes within the SAP SNC solution could help optimize supplier collaboration for each business unit.

Analysis of potential

The analysis of potential revealed that the use of an optimized, group-wide procurement processing solution could lower purchasing and IT costs by up to 20%. To achieve this, purchasing processes would be automated and the information flow optimized. In addition, in the future there would be just one, central platform with an integrated system landscape for all business units.

To determine whether and to what extent the business processes would match the processes in SAP SNC, the first step was to perform a supplier analysis in each business unit.

A questionnaire was created to analyze the top 30% of suppliers who did the most business (see Table 3.2).

Supplier No.	Yes	No
1. Does a long-standing relationship (longer than three years) exist with this supplier?		
2. Is an EDI connection in place with this supplier?		
3. Is closer cooperation planned with this supplier?		
4. With the exception of fixed purchase orders and releases, are planned requirement quantities over a longer period communicated to this supplier?		
5. Is this supplier expected to take on greater responsibility in the future?		
6. Is the move time short (less than three hours)?		

Table 3.2 Sample Questionnaire for Supplier Analysis

Next, the materials that these suppliers procure were looked at in detail (see Table 3.3).

Material No.	Yes	No
7. Is this material required on a regular basis?		
8. Are these requirements known about well in advance (more than three months)?		
9. Is the material a custom production or production according to a drawing?		
10. Is the material procured from more than one supplier?		
11. Is the material a subcontracted material for which components are delivered by the customer?		
12. Is this material always available from the supplier?		

Table 3.3 Sample Questionnaire for Material Analysis

After the suppliers and materials had been evaluated, the results were mapped to the existing processes in SAP SNC (see Table 3.4).

The process was as follows:

If a question was answered "yes" by the majority, the processes that met the criterion particularly well were rated positively (+).

If a question was answered "no" by the majority, the processes that would meet the criterion were rated negatively (–).

Legend for the Following Tables		
PO	=	Purchase order handling
DR	=	Dynamic replenishment
SA	=	Scheduling agreement processing
SMI	=	Supplier managed inventory
DCM	=	Delivery control monitor
SC	=	Subcontracting
WO	=	Work order
SNI	=	Supply network inventory
KB	=	Kanban

3 | Supplier Collaboration in a Model Company

Question	PO	DR	SA	SMI	DCM	SC	WO	SNI	KB
1. Does a long-standing relationship exist with this supplier?									
2. Is an EDI connection in place with this supplier?									
3. Is closer cooperation planned with this supplier?									
4. Are planned requirement quantities over a longer period communicated?									
5. Is the supplier expected to take on greater responsibility?									
6. Is the move time short?									
7. Is this material required on a regular basis?									
8. Are these requirements known about well in advance?									
9. Is the material a custom production?									
10. Is the material procured from more than one supplier?									
11. Is the material a subcontracted material?									
12. Is this material always available from the supplier?									

Table 3.4 Mapping of Results to Business Processes in SAP SNC

3.2.1 Business Process Analysis of Business Unit I

One of the findings of the analysis of suppliers was that the suppliers with whom conventional communication takes place tend to have long-standing business relationships (see Table 3.5).

Number of Suppliers Investigated: 80	Yes (%)	No (%)
1. Does a long-standing relationship (longer than three years) exist with this supplier?	80	20
2. Is an EDI connection in place with this supplier?	0	100
3. Is closer cooperation planned with this supplier?	80	20
4. With the exception of fixed purchase orders and releases, are planned requirement quantities over a longer period communicated to this supplier?	3	97
5. Is this supplier expected to take on greater responsibility in the future?	10	90
6. Is the move time short (less than three hours)?	1	99

Table 3.5 Result of Supplier Investigation for Business Unit I

Supplier investigation

The evaluation of materials showed once again that due to the production of single components, materials are rarely required on a regular basis (see Table 3.6).

Number of Materials Investigated: 250	Yes (%)	No (%)
7. Is this material required on a regular basis?	15	85
8. Are these requirements known about well in advance (more than three months)?	5	95
9. Is the material a custom production or production according to a drawing?	90	10
10. Is the material procured from more than one supplier?	10	90
11. Is the material a subcontracted material for which components are delivered by the customer?	0	100
12. Is this material always available from the supplier?	5	95

Table 3.6 Result of Material Investigation for Business Unit I

Material investigation

3 | Supplier Collaboration in a Model Company

Business process analysis

The results of the questions about suppliers and materials were mapped to the business processes in SAP SNC. Only processes with a positive or neutral rating were highlighted in gray. These processes are particularly suitable for implementation in SAP SNC (see Table 3.7).

Question	PO	DR	SA	SMI	DCM	WT	WO	SNI	KB
1. Does a long-standing relationship exist with this supplier?		+		+					
2. Is an EDI connection in place with this supplier?								−	
3. Is closer cooperation planned with this supplier?		+		+			+	+	
4. Are planned requirement quantities over a longer period communicated?					−				
5. Is the supplier expected to take on greater responsibility?	+		+	−					
6. Is the move time short?					−				
7. Is this material required on a regular basis?	+		−	−		+			−
8. Are these requirements known about well in advance?	+		−	−					
9. Is the material a custom production?	+		−	−	−	+	+		−
10. Is this material procured from more than one supplier?	+	+	+	−	−	+	+		
11. Is the material a subcontracted material?	+	+	+	+	+	−	−		
12. Is this material always available from the supplier?	+	+	+		−	+	+	+	−

Table 3.7 Mapping of Results for Business Unit I to the Processes in SAP SNC

Results

The main argument in favor of purchase order handling is that the orders are for small, irregular custom productions. For a select number of suppliers, the business unit wants to provide forecasts that are likely to become orders for selected materials. *Dynamic replenishment* (DR) would tie in well with this goal.

The low and irregular procurement quantities and the custom productions are notable factors that go against scheduling agreement processing, *supplier managed inventory* (SMI), the delivery control monitor, and the kanban process.

Business Unit I does not currently place subcontract orders externally. However, given that the materials are more than suitable for such a business process, it would be worthwhile to consider introducing this practice for certain products in the future.

The main argument against using the functions of the supply network inventory (SNI) Monitor is that a certain number of the suppliers are small-scale operators that would struggle to automate the transfer of data about current stock and requirements.

These small-scale operators, some of whom still create their invoices with a typewriter, should create their invoices in SAP SNC in the future.

3.2.2 Business Process Analysis of Business Unit II

The evaluation of suppliers and materials returned the following results (see Tables 3.8 and 3.9).

Number of Suppliers Investigated: 95	Yes (%)	No (%)
1. Does a long-standing relationship (longer than three years) exist with this supplier?	70	30
2. Is an EDI connection in place with this supplier?	15	85
3. Is closer cooperation planned with this supplier?	70	30
4. With the exception of fixed purchase orders and releases, are planned requirement quantities over a longer period communicated to this supplier?	95	5
5. Is this supplier expected to take on greater responsibility in the future?	65	35
6. Is the move time short (less than three hours)?	15	85

Table 3.8 Result of Supplier Investigation for Business Unit II

Material investigation

Number of Materials Investigated: 420	Yes (%)	No (%)
7. Is this material required on a regular basis?	85	15
8. Are these requirements known about well in advance (more than three months)?	80	20
9. Is the material a custom production or production according to a drawing?	2	98
10. Is the material procured from more than one supplier?	30	70
11. Is the material a subcontracted material for which components are delivered by the customer?	0	100
12. Is this material always available from the supplier?	15	85

Table 3.9 Result of Material Investigation for Business Unit II

Business process analysis

When mapping the questions to the business processes, the conclusion was reached that the subcontracting scenario bore no relevance, because this business unit does not procure any materials on a subcontracting basis.

All other scenarios were deemed to be relevant in principle. However, Business Unit II has been working with outline agreements and forecasts for many years. For this reason, it would like to continue to collaborate with suppliers on this basis. With regard to long-standing suppliers from which certain products are procured exclusively, the business unit wants to further step up cooperation by transferring planning responsibility to these suppliers. The SMI process would be ideally suited to this purpose. Furthermore, the unit wants to make more use of the delivery control monitor for multiple deliveries per day from a small number of suppliers located within an hour's distance.

Results

A packaging distribution center that supplies goods three times a day to meet requirements was selected as a pilot supplier. The packaging materials are always available at the distribution center. The current stock would be transferred using the delivery control monitor, which would trigger replenishment in Business Unit II.

Because Business Unit II has been using self-billing for over a year, the payment status of the credit memos should also be displayed in SAP SNC.

Electronic data exchange, *business-to-business* (B2B), will still be supported. This offers the advantage that exceptions will now be visible in SAP SNC (see Table 3.10).

Question	PO	DR	SA	SMI	DCM	SC	WO	SNI	KB
1. Does a long-standing relationship exist with this supplier?			+	+	+				
2. Is an EDI connection in place with this supplier?	+		+					+	
3. Is closer cooperation planned with this supplier?		+	+	+	+		+		
4. Are planned requirement quantities over a longer period communicated?		+	+	+					
5. Is the supplier expected to take on greater responsibility?					+				
6. Is the move time short?						+			
7. Is this material required on a regular basis?			+	+					
8. Are these requirements known about well in advance?			+	+					
9. Is the material a custom production?			+	+					
10. Is this material procured from more than one supplier?			+	+					
11. Is the material a subcontracted material?							−	−	
12. Is this material always available from the supplier?			+	+					

Table 3.10 Mapping of Results for Business Unit II to the Processes in SAP SNC

3.2.3 Business Process Analysis of Business Unit III

The evaluation of suppliers and materials returned the results shown in Tables 3.11 and 3.12. What is particularly striking in this business unit is that the production of 90% of articles is outsourced and there is a strong desire for closer cooperation.

Supplier investigation

Number of Suppliers Investigated: 30	Yes (%)	No (%)
1. Does a long-standing relationship (longer than three years) exist with this supplier?	40	60
2. Is an EDI connection in place with this supplier?	10	90
3. Is closer cooperation planned with this supplier?	70	30
4. With the exception of fixed purchase orders and releases, are planned requirement quantities over a longer period communicated to this supplier?	15	85
5. Is this supplier expected to take on greater responsibility in the future?	40	60
6. Is the move time short (less than three hours)?	15	85

Table 3.11 Result of Supplier Investigation for Business Unit III

Material investigation

Number of Materials Investigated: 120	Yes (%)	No (%)
7. Is this material required on a regular basis?	60	40
8. Are these requirements known about well in advance (more than three months)?	80	20
9. Is the material a custom production or production according to a drawing?	30	70
10. Is the material procured from more than one supplier?	65	35
11. Is the material a subcontracted material for which components are delivered by the customer?	90	10
12. Is this material always available from the supplier?	5	95

Table 3.12 Result of Material Investigation for Business Unit III

Business process analysis

Business Unit III works almost exclusively with subcontractors. Because the system currently supports this process to an unsatisfactory degree and there are numerous sources of errors due to the lack of transparency, the unit sees a lot of scope for improvement here. In particular, it wants to replace the current solution, whereby the supplier confirms production data in the unit's own backend system, with order processing in SAP SNC as soon as possible.

Purchase order handling is to be introduced for parts provided. Business Unit III will, however, wait until Unit I has implemented this process to benefit from its experiences.

Outline agreements are in place for some parts provided. Because subcontractors perform releases from these outline agreements themselves, this process will not be mapped in SAP SNC at this time (see Table 3.13).

Question	PO	DR	SA	SMI	DCM	SC	WO	SNI	KB
1. Does a long-standing relationship exist with this supplier?									
2. Is an EDI connection in place with this supplier?								+	
3. Is closer cooperation planned with this supplier?									
4. Are planned requirement quantities over a longer period communicated?				−					
5. Is the supplier expected to take on greater responsibility?				−					
6. Is the move time short?					−				
7. Is this material required on a regular basis?			+	+					
8. Are these requirements known about well in advance?			+	+	+				+
9. Is the material a custom production?	+					+	+		
10. Is this material procured from more than one supplier?	+		+			+	+		
11. Is the material a subcontracted material?						+	+	+	
12. Is this material always available from the supplier?					−				

Table 3.13 Mapping of Results for Business Unit III to the Processes in SAP SNC

3.2.4 Business Process Analysis of Business Unit IV

Because Business Unit IV uses kanban to manage almost all of its procurement activities and this is now to be supported by a system, a detailed investigation of suppliers and materials was deemed unnecessary.

3.2.5 Planned System Landscape

Because some suppliers supply materials to more than one business unit and the different ERP systems are to be merged into one in the future, the decision was made to use a common platform. Electronic exchange between business units and a selected number of suppliers will continue, and the data exchanged and any exception messages will also be visible in SAP SNC (see Section 5.3 Basic Services).

System landscape — Figure 3.6 offers an impression of how the system landscape with the different ERP systems of the individual business units and SAP SNC might look.

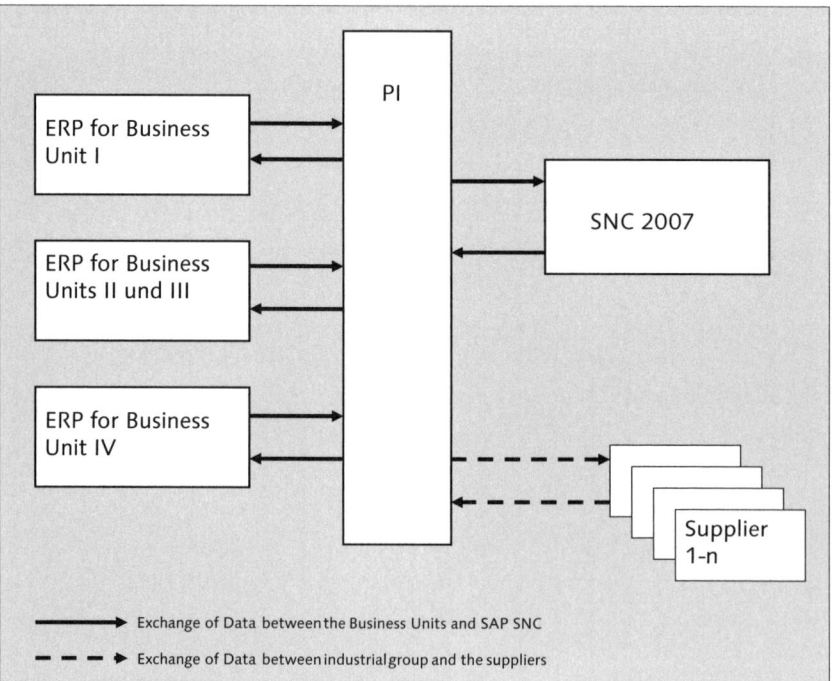

Figure 3.6 Planned System Landscape in the Company

3.2.6 Next Steps

Other projects in the area of supplier collaboration are prioritized. The order is determined both by strategic relevance and expected value added (see Figure 3.7).

Project prioritization

Once the various procurement handling processes in SAP SNC have been implemented successfully in the four business units, the next step is to optimize collaboration in the area of product lifecycle management. One particular aim here is to improve the way documents are exchanged. A separate project will be set up for this purpose.

The company also wants to be able to gather consolidated purchasing volume information across all business units in the future, with a view to establishing a stronger starting position for negotiating prices.

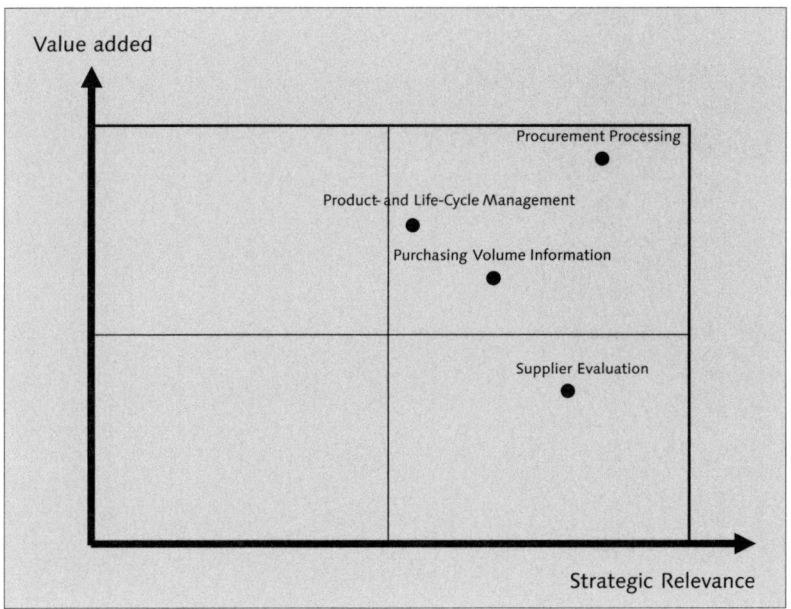

Figure 3.7 Determination of Priorities for Road Map Definition

In the future, supplier evaluations will be used as a tool for improving quality with the supplier.

To further promote supplier collaboration, a common *SAP NetWeaver Business Intelligence* (BI) system is planned for these areas.

This chapter describes the supplier collaboration business processes supported in SAP SNC 5.1. The individual processes and their steps are explained in detail. In addition, you are given an overview of the generic and scenario-specific master data.

4 Business Processes in SAP SNC 5.1

This chapter focuses on the supplier collaboration business processes supported in SAP SNC 5.1. The first section deals with the generic master data. Separate sections are then devoted to each of the different business processes available in SAP SNC 5.1. This chapter not only discusses order-based processes, such as forecast delivery schedule processing, purchase order handling, subcontracting, work order collaboration, the Delivery Control Monitor, and kanban processing; it also looks at demand-based processes, such as Supplier Managed Inventory and dynamic replenishment, as well as the functions that exist independently of business processes, namely, advanced shipping notifications, goods receipt, and invoice processing. For each business process, you are offered an overview of the process flow and business-process-specific master data, as well as a detailed description of the individual process steps, any additions to SAP SNC 5.1, and the required Customizing settings.

4.1 Generic Master Data

Two types of master data are required in SAP SNC: generic master data used in all business scenarios, and business-process-specific master data.

Generic master data

The generic master data in SAP SNC consists of:

- **Location**
  A location describes both a supplier's ship-from location and a customer's production plant. A distinction is made on the basis of the location type.

- **Product**
  Location-specific products are required for the business processes in SAP SNC.

- **Business Partners**
  A basic distinction is made between business partners of type *organization* and *person*. Organization business partners represent a company. A business partner of type organization represents a company and can have several different locations assigned to it, but any given location can only be assigned to one business partner of type organization. A business partner of type person represents a real person who works in the SAP SNC web browser and therefore has user access. By assigning a business partner of type person to one of type organization, a connection between the location and the individual user is established. A business partner of type organization can have several users assigned to it, but a user can only be assigned to one business partner of type organization.

- **External Procurement Relationship and Transportation Lane**
  The supply relationship for the procurement of a product between ship-from location and customer location is mapped by means of the external procurement relationship and transportation lane.

Figure 4.1 shows the basic master data model in SAP SNC.

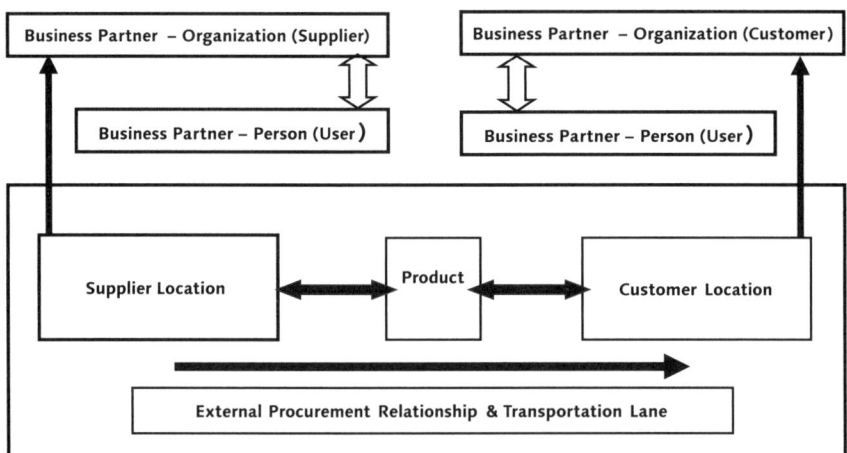

Figure 4.1 Basic Master Data Model in SAP SNC

The generic master data objects, such as product, location, external procurement relationship, and transportation lane, have to be assigned to Active Model 000 and Active Planning Version 000 in SAP SNC.

Model and planning version

The business-process-specific master data is described in separate sections for each business process.

4.2 Supplier Managed Inventory (SMI)

This section first provides an overview of the *Supplier Managed Inventory* business process with SAP SNC 5.1 (see Figure 4.2). It then takes a closer look at the individual process steps and settings in SAP SNC.

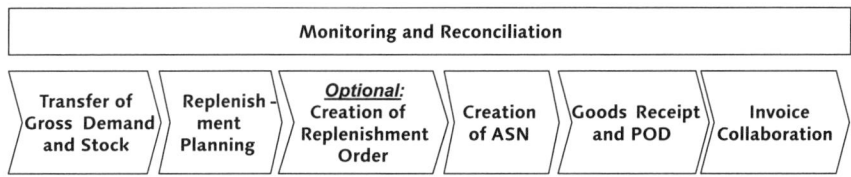

Figure 4.2 Process Flow for Replenishment Planning with SMI

4.2.1 Process Overview

If a customer outsources replenishment planning to a supplier, the supplier determines the quantity that must be delivered in each time bucket in the planning period to cover the customer's requirements in sufficient time. Planning takes place on the basis of the data (gross demand, stock) that the customer sends from the customer SAP ERP system to SAP SNC.

Replenishment planning with SMI

One outcome of planning is calculated receipts. This key figure provides information about the quantity that the supplier intends to deliver to the customer in each time bucket. The supplier must define the planned receipts such that the projected stock always falls between the minimum and maximum stock levels. The projected stock represents the product quantity available to the customer at the end of each time bucket. Current stock on hand as well as requirements and receipts are taken into account when the projected stock is calculated. It is possible to make Customizing settings to define exactly which requirements and receipts are included in the projected stock calculation. The receipts maintained by the supplier are not binding and are only visible in SAP SNC. Following planning, the supplier can opt to create any of the following documents to be sent to the customer's backend system:

Replenishment Order

When a replenishment order is published, a purchase order is created in the customer backend system, and a sales order can optionally be created in the supplier backend system. The replenishment order represents a binding receipt for the customer.

Advanced Shipping Notification (ASN)

Depending on whether a replenishment order has been used, the supplier creates an advanced shipping notification (ASN) either for the replenishment order or directly for the planned receipt.

The goods receipt is posted once the goods have been physically received and put away at the customer's place of business. A proof of delivery message confirms to the supplier the actual quantity received by the customer. Furthermore, reasons for any quantity differences and the confirmation date can be provided.

Invoice collaboration takes place with reference to either the replenishment order or ASN on the basis of conventional invoice processing or self-billing (see Section 4.12 Invoice Collaboration).

Replenishment monitors and alerts to draw attention to any exception situations are used to monitor replenishment planning between the customer and supplier.

Replenishment planning simplifies the procurement process. The material is no longer planned by the customer by means of an MRP run, but rather by the supplier within a lower and upper limit. This leads to a reduction in stock on hand for both customer and supplier, because the supplier gains insight into future requirements. It also allows the supplier to adjust capacities, because operations are facilitated by requirements being communicated in advance.

Alternatives to Replenishment Planning

There are two variations of replenishment planning. In both cases, the supplier maintains the planned receipts in the system.

In the first variant, the ASNs are maintained directly for the planned receipts. A scheduling agreement is assigned as the purchasing document type, which is also referenced when goods are received in the customer's SAP ERP system.

Replenishment variants

The advantage of this variant lies in its lean process. The supplier must carry out precisely two steps: maintain the planned receipts and create the ASNs for these planned receipts. Data does not become visible in the customer's backend system until the ASNs have been created and published. However, because the supplier has overall control of planning and is responsible for ensuring that the material is available within the agreed minimum and maximum stock levels, there should be no need for further information in the backend system.

In the second variant, the supplier maintains not only the planned receipts but also the purchase orders—referred to as replenishment orders—to which the supplier assigns the ASNs.

These replenishment orders are sent to the customer's backend system. This means the supplier's planning becomes visible in this backend system at a relatively early stage and is used mainly to verify whether goods arrive on schedule. As far as the supplier is concerned, this equates to increased maintenance work without any gains, unless the customer system generates a sales order from the replenishment order that is then sent to the supplier's back-end system, thus obviating any need for an order to be created manually there.

The problem with this variant is the extremely high level of effort involved in adapting planned receipts and, in particular, already published replenishment orders to fluctuations in demand. The customer and supplier can alleviate this by agreeing to maintain replenishment orders only within a relatively short time frame because only a small number of demand fluctuations are anticipated in this period.

New to SAP SNC 5.1 are the two separate monitors, depending on whether the supplier works with replenishment orders (*Min/Max Replen-*

ishment Monitor) or ASNs (*SMI Monitor*). If replenishment orders are used, they can now also be taken into account as receipts when calculating projected stock.

The process flows for replenishment planning with SMI are shown in Figures 4.3 and 4.4.

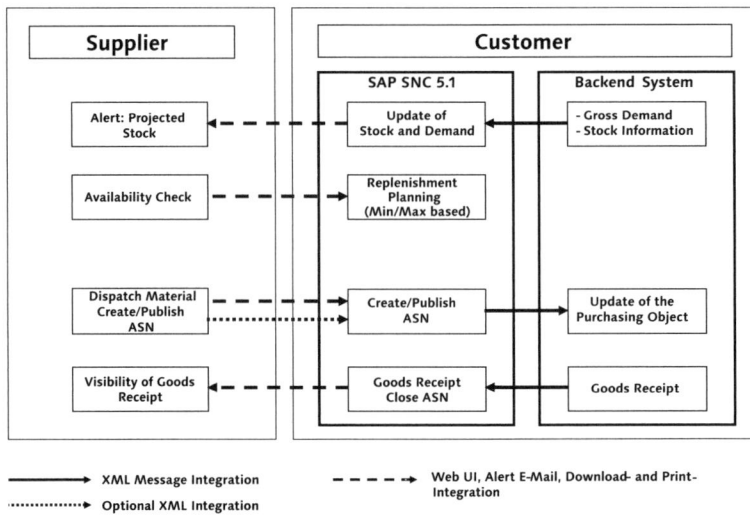

Figure 4.3 Replenishment Variant Without Replenishment Order

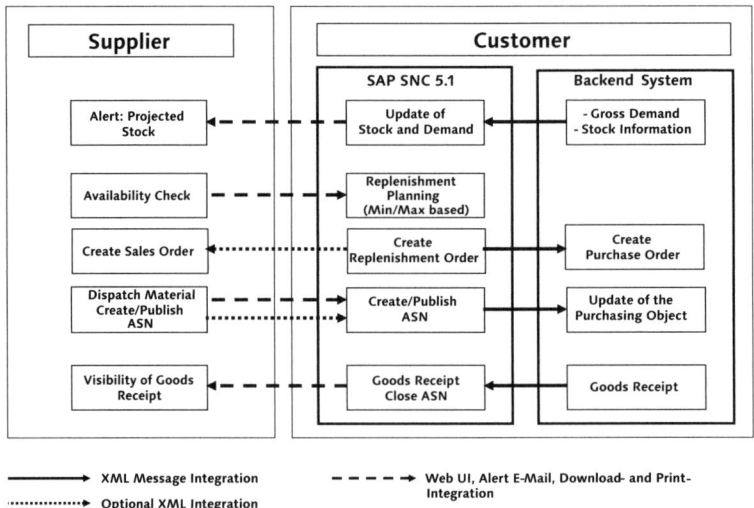

Figure 4.4 Replenishment Variant with Replenishment Order

4.2.2 SMI-Specific Master Data

Beyond the generic master data, the following additional master data is required for the SMI process:

Master data

- For the replenishment variant without replenishment order: purchase scheduling agreement
- For the replenishment variant with replenishment order: purchase contract

4.2.3 Determining and Transferring Gross Demands and Stock Information

For a supplier to view stock/requirements data in SAP SNC, the data must first be sent from the customer backend system. A standard report exists for this purpose in SAP ERP, RSMIPROACT, which generates IDoc type PROACT01 (see Figure 4.5).

Transaction data

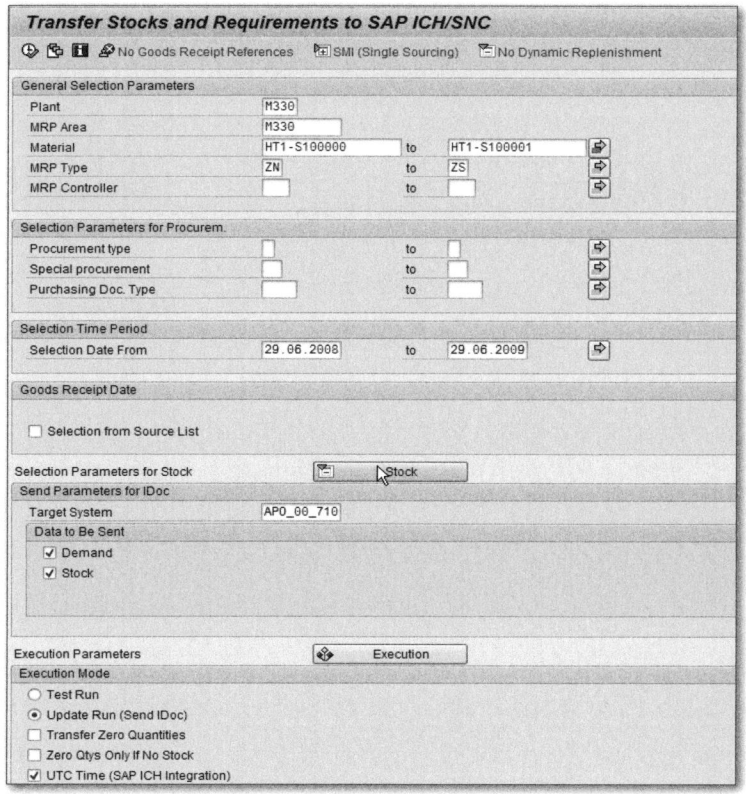

Figure 4.5 Report for Transferring Stock and Requirements

As of SAP ECC 6.0 Enhancement Package 2, report RSMIPROACT2 is provided as an alternative, which can optionally create the ProductActivityNotification XML message type directly.

As a basic principle, the SMI process can also accommodate more than one supplier for each material (*multisourcing*). Please note the following when transferring data:

Multisourcing/ single sourcing

If a report is run for *single sourcing*, a valid entry is required in the source list.

In multisourcing, the system accepts the source in the source list if several sources of supply for the material and one quota for each source of supply have been created. The daily requirement is distributed among the suppliers according to the quotas. The suppliers of stock must be clearly identifiable with batch management or by means of vendor consignment stock.

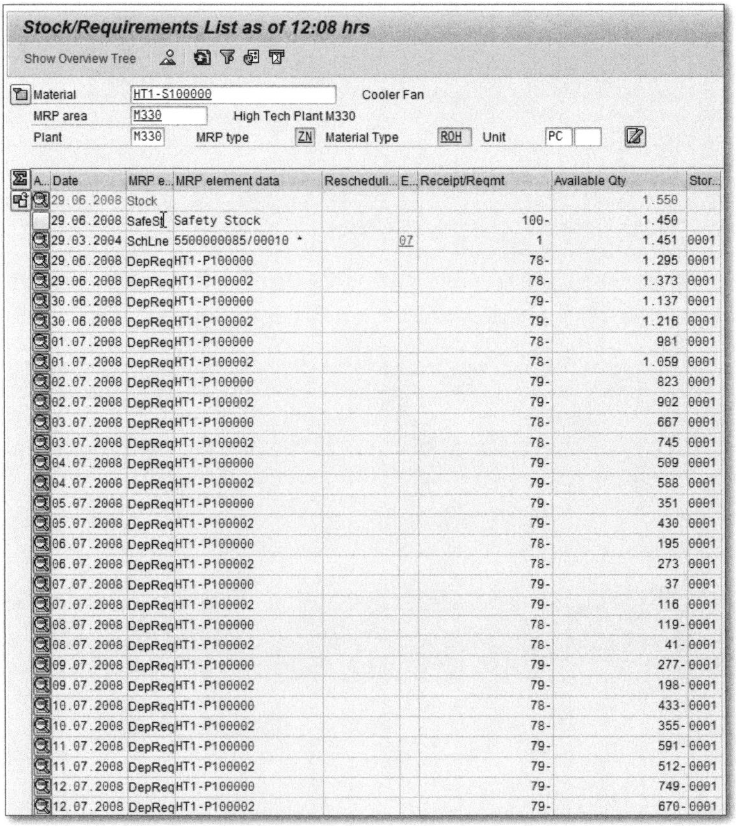

A...	Date	MRP e...	MRP element data	Rescheduli...	E...	Receipt/Reqmt	Available Qty	Stor...
	29.06.2008	Stock					1.550	
	29.06.2008	SafeSt	Safety Stock			100-	1.450	
	29.03.2004	SchLne	5500000085/00010 *		07	1	1.451	0001
	29.06.2008	DepReq	HT1-P100000			78-	1.295	0001
	29.06.2008	DepReq	HT1-P100002			78-	1.373	0001
	30.06.2008	DepReq	HT1-P100000			79-	1.137	0001
	30.06.2008	DepReq	HT1-P100002			79-	1.216	0001
	01.07.2008	DepReq	HT1-P100000			78-	981	0001
	01.07.2008	DepReq	HT1-P100002			78-	1.059	0001
	02.07.2008	DepReq	HT1-P100000			79-	823	0001
	02.07.2008	DepReq	HT1-P100002			79-	902	0001
	03.07.2008	DepReq	HT1-P100000			78-	667	0001
	03.07.2008	DepReq	HT1-P100002			78-	745	0001
	04.07.2008	DepReq	HT1-P100000			79-	509	0001
	04.07.2008	DepReq	HT1-P100002			79-	588	0001
	05.07.2008	DepReq	HT1-P100000			79-	351	0001
	05.07.2008	DepReq	HT1-P100002			79-	430	0001
	06.07.2008	DepReq	HT1-P100000			78-	195	0001
	06.07.2008	DepReq	HT1-P100002			78-	273	0001
	07.07.2008	DepReq	HT1-P100000			79-	37	0001
	07.07.2008	DepReq	HT1-P100002			79-	116	0001
	08.07.2008	DepReq	HT1-P100000			78-	119-	0001
	08.07.2008	DepReq	HT1-P100002			78-	41-	0001
	09.07.2008	DepReq	HT1-P100000			79-	277-	0001
	09.07.2008	DepReq	HT1-P100002			79-	198-	0001
	10.07.2008	DepReq	HT1-P100000			78-	433-	0001
	10.07.2008	DepReq	HT1-P100002			78-	355-	0001
	11.07.2008	DepReq	HT1-P100000			79-	591-	0001
	11.07.2008	DepReq	HT1-P100002			79-	512-	0001
	12.07.2008	DepReq	HT1-P100000			79-	749-	0001
	12.07.2008	DepReq	HT1-P100002			79-	670-	0001

Figure 4.6 Stock/Requirements List

The report takes into account the same demand data as shown in the STOCK/REQUIREMENTS list (Transaction MD04) (see Figure 4.6).

4.2.4 Replenishment Planning Variant 1

If you want to manage replenishment planning with minimum and maximum stock levels but without replenishment orders, you use the SMI Monitor in SAP SNC.

The SMI Monitor can be accessed via menu path REPLENISHMENT • SMI MONITOR • SMI OVERVIEW (see Figure 4.7).

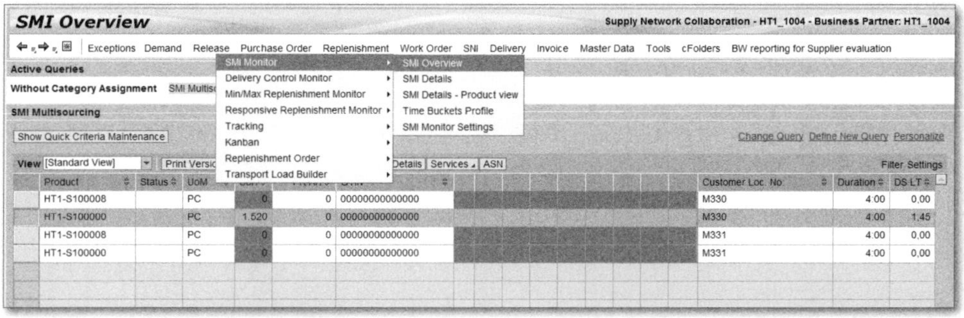

Figure 4.7 SMI Overview Monitor

A new feature in SAP SNC 5.1 is that you can arrange for the system to plan the calculated receipts interactively in the overview monitor. To do so, you have to select the lines containing the location products to be planned and click on the SERVICES button to call the PROPOSE PLANNED RECEIPTS function (see Figure 4.8). This prompts the system to generate the planned receipts for the selected products.

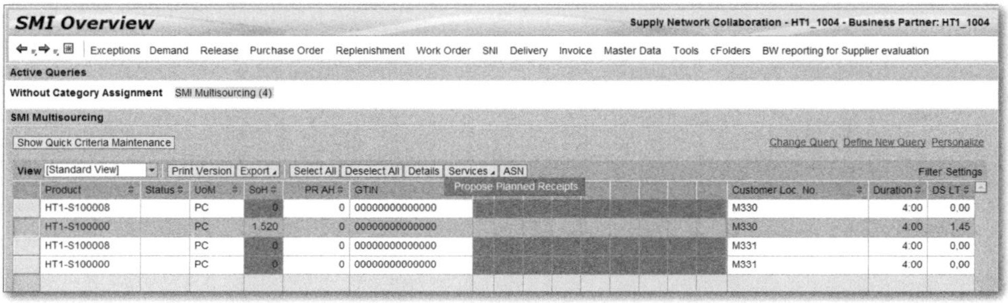

Figure 4.8 Interactive Planning in the SMI Overview Monitor

The supplier can access the details monitor by selecting one or more lines and clicking on the DETAILS button.

The SMI Details Monitor provides the key figures shown in Table 4.1 for each material and customer location (plant).

Data	Description
Demand	The gross demand in a time bucket
Average Demand	SAP SNC averages the actual gross demand and displays this as the calculated average demand. The following two averaging procedures are available in the standard delivery: ▸ Moving average calculation method ▸ Arithmetic mean calculation method The parameters required for the calculation are defined as Customizing settings (see Section 4.2.14).
Net Demand, Raw	The unrounded net demand of the customer in a given time bucket that the supplier must actually cover in this bucket. In contrast to the gross demand, the existing stock and receipts are taken into account here.
Planned Receipts	The total quantity that the supplier intends to deliver to the customer in a time bucket.
In-Transit Quantity	The total quantity in a time bucket that is in transit to the customer, but for which goods receipt has not yet taken place.
Projected Stock	The stock that is expected to be available to the customer at the end of a time bucket (see Section 4.2.12).
Days' Supply	This key figure specifies how long the projected stock of a time bucket will last to cover the demands of subsequent buckets.
Minimum Proposal	The quantity that the supplier has to deliver to the customer in a time bucket so that the projected stock reaches the agreed minimum stock level at the end of the bucket.
Maximum Proposal	The quantity that the supplier has to deliver to the customer in a time bucket so that the projected stock reaches the agreed maximum stock level at the end of the bucket.
Minimum Stock Level	The minimum quantity of stock that must be available in the customer's warehouse.
Maximum Stock Level	The maximum quantity of stock that should be available in the customer's warehouse.

Table 4.1 Key Figures in the SMI Details Monitor

The supplier is now able to maintain the planned receipts manually in the SMI Details Monitor (see Figure 4.9).

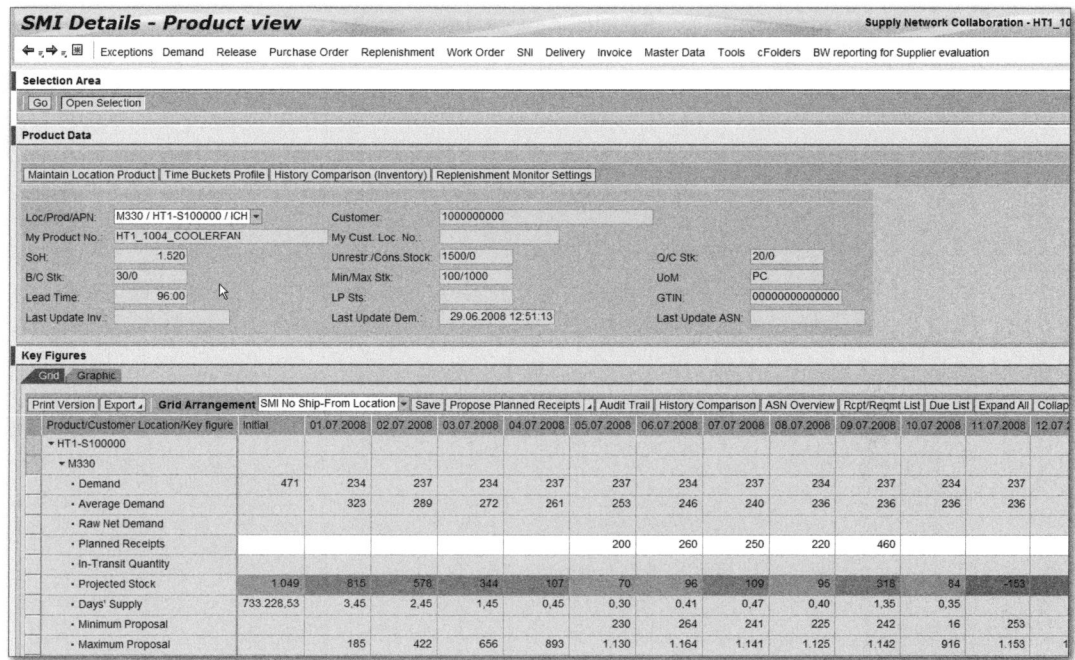

Figure 4.9 SMI Details Monitor with Planned Receipts

If the supplier does not want to maintain the planned receipts manually, the option also exists on the details screen to obtain suggested planned receipts interactively from the planning service. To use this function, the supplier must click on the PROPOSE PLANNED RECEIPTS button (see Figure 4.10). The quantity of the planned receipts depends on the gross demand and stock level, on the one hand, and the calculation of projected stock (see Section 4.2.12 Calculating the Projected Stock in the SAP SNC System) and replenishment method selected in Customizing (see Sections 4.2.13 Maintaining Replenishment Service Profiles and 4.2.14 Assigning the Settings for Replenishment Planning), on the other.

Maintain planned receipts

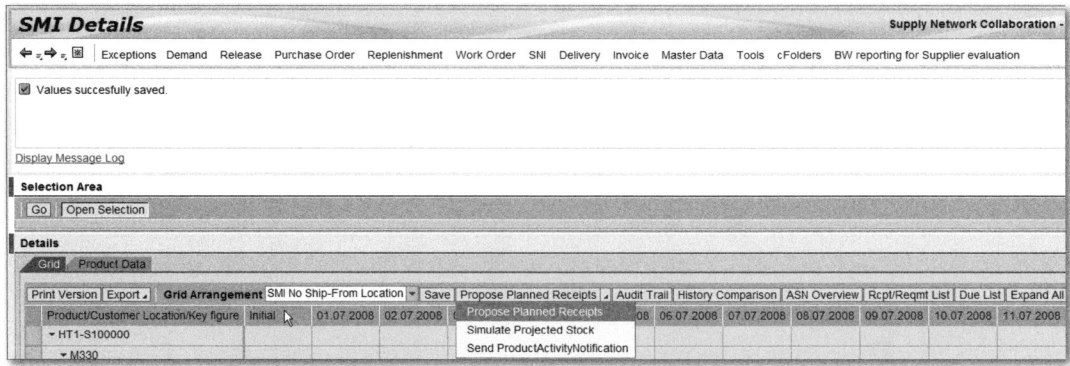

Figure 4.10 Service Call for Interactive Planning in the SMI Details Monitor

4.2.5 Creating the ASN for Replenishment Variant 1

Once the planned receipts have been saved, the deliveries are visible in the DUE LIST FOR PLANNED RECEIPTS (SMI). The due list can either be called up from the SMI Details Monitor directly or via the menu path DELIVERY • RECEIPTS AND REQUIREMENTS • DUE LIST FOR PLANNED RECEIPTS (SMI) (see Figure 4.11).

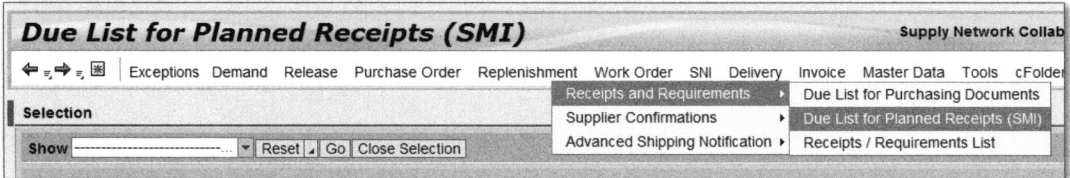

Figure 4.11 Calling the Due List for Planned Receipts (SMI)

The DUE LIST FOR PLANNED RECEIPTS (SMI) contains all of the planned receipts that have been created manually or automatically by the system (see Figure 4.12).

The supplier can now select one or more lines for which an ASN is to be created (see Figure 4.13) and then click on the CREATE ASN button.

4.2 Supplier Managed Inventory (SMI)

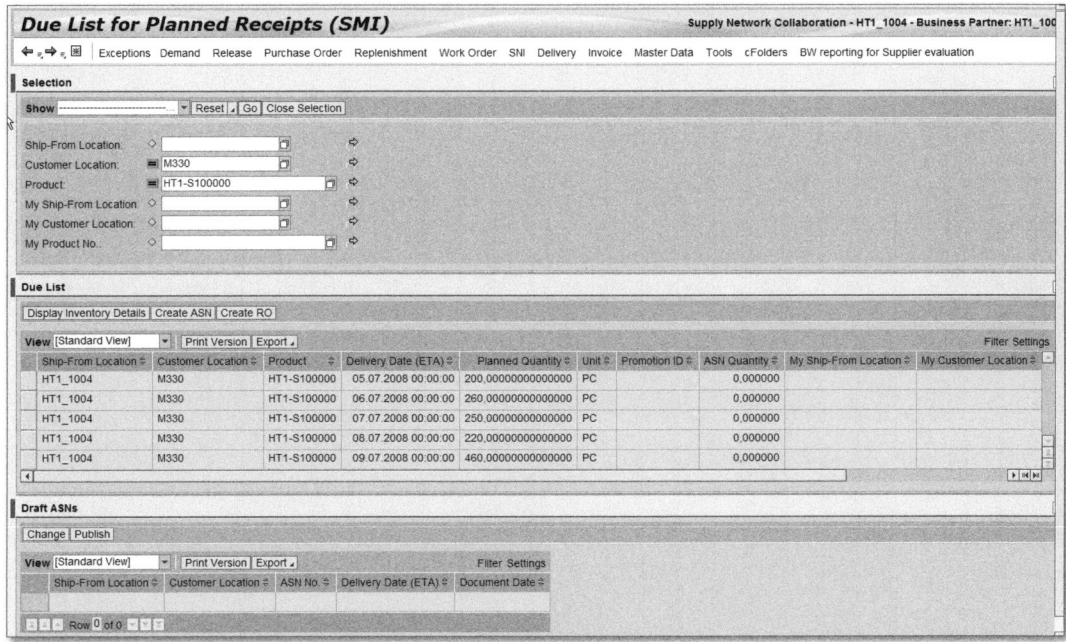

Figure 4.12 Due List with Planned Receipts for Creating an ASN

Figure 4.13 Selecting Multiple Planned Receipts in the Due List

When the ASN is created, all of the relevant data is extracted from the due list but can also be revised (see Figure 4.14). For example, the sup-

Due list

plier can store a different ASN number, change the ASN quantity, and alter the delivery and shipping dates.

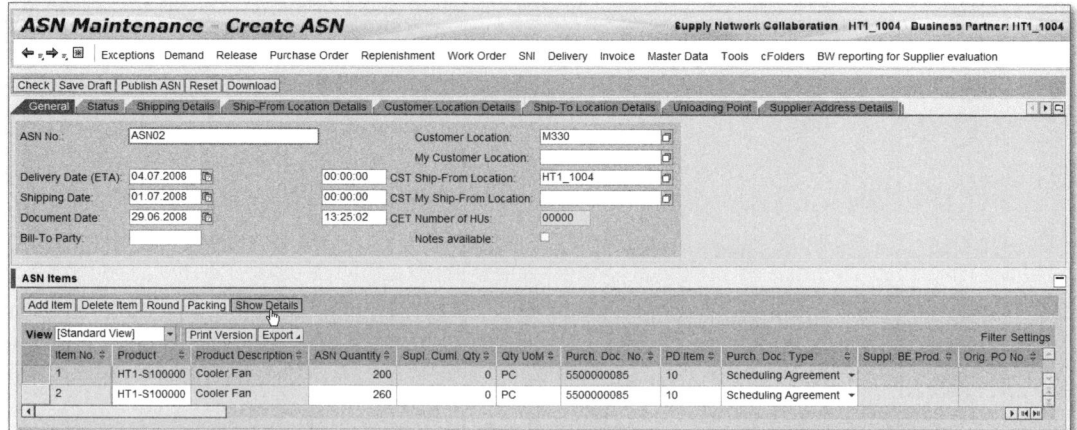

Figure 4.14 Creating an ASN from the Due List for Planned Receipts

If the supplier publishes the ASN, the quantity can also be seen in the SMI Details Monitor as an IN-TRANSIT QUANTITY (see Figure 4.15).

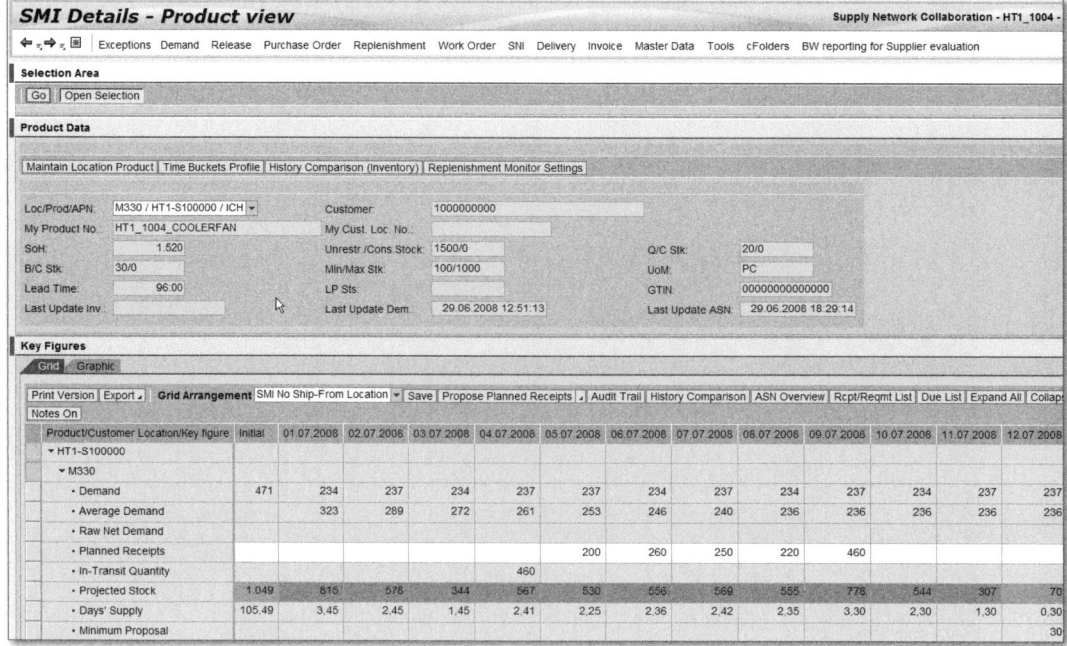

Figure 4.15 Display of the ASN Quantity in the SMI Details Monitor in SAP SNC

Once the ASN has been published, SAP SNC sends an XML message of type *DispatchedDeliveryNotification* (DDN) to SAP NetWeaver Process Integration (PI), which converts the message into the DESADV.DELVRY03 IDoc and sends it to the customer's SAP ERP system.

The ASN then becomes visible in the STOCK/REQUIREMENTS list in the customer's SAP ERP system (see Figure 4.16).

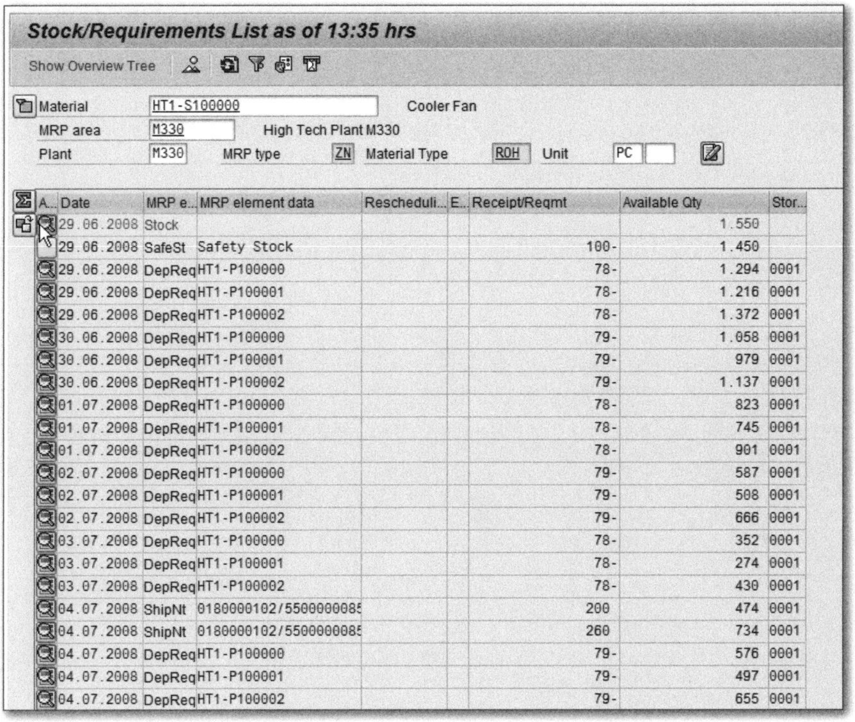

A...	Date	MRP e...	MRP element data	Rescheduli...	E...	Receipt/Reqmt	Available Qty	Stor...
	29.06.2008	Stock					1.550	
	29.06.2008	SafeSt	Safety Stock			100-	1.450	
	29.06.2008	DepReq	HT1-P100000			78-	1.294	0001
	29.06.2008	DepReq	HT1-P100001			78-	1.216	0001
	29.06.2008	DepReq	HT1-P100002			78-	1.372	0001
	30.06.2008	DepReq	HT1-P100000			79-	1.058	0001
	30.06.2008	DepReq	HT1-P100001			79-	979	0001
	30.06.2008	DepReq	HT1-P100002			79-	1.137	0001
	01.07.2008	DepReq	HT1-P100000			78-	823	0001
	01.07.2008	DepReq	HT1-P100001			78-	745	0001
	01.07.2008	DepReq	HT1-P100002			78-	901	0001
	02.07.2008	DepReq	HT1-P100000			79-	587	0001
	02.07.2008	DepReq	HT1-P100001			79-	508	0001
	02.07.2008	DepReq	HT1-P100002			79-	666	0001
	03.07.2008	DepReq	HT1-P100000			78-	352	0001
	03.07.2008	DepReq	HT1-P100001			78-	274	0001
	03.07.2008	DepReq	HT1-P100002			78-	430	0001
	04.07.2008	ShipNt	0180000102/550000008			200	474	0001
	04.07.2008	ShipNt	0180000102/550000008			260	734	0001
	04.07.2008	DepReq	HT1-P100000			79-	576	0001
	04.07.2008	DepReq	HT1-P100001			79-	497	0001
	04.07.2008	DepReq	HT1-P100002			79-	655	0001

Figure 4.16 Display of ASN in Stock/Requirements List in SAP ERP

4.2.6 Goods Receipt

The goods receipt is posted in the customer's SAP ERP system as a reference to the ASN (see Figure 4.17). There are several transactions for goods receipts. In this example, Transaction VL32n has been used because it offers the advantage that the customer's SAP ERP system sends the STPPOD.DELVRY03 IDoc to SAP NetWeaver PI immediately. This IDoc is converted into an XML message of type *ReceivedDeliveryNotification* (RDN) and sent to SAP SNC.

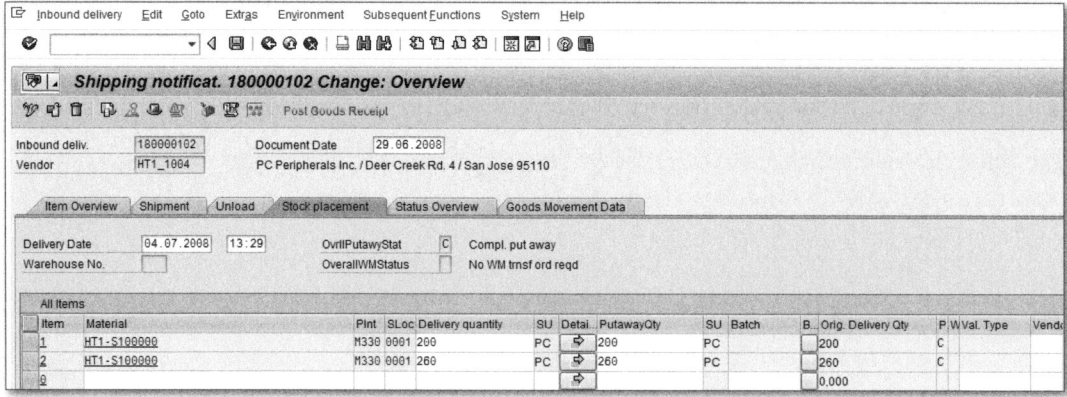

Figure 4.17 Goods Receipt Posting in SAP ERP

Once the goods receipt has been posted, the ASN is updated in SAP SNC (see Figure 4.18).

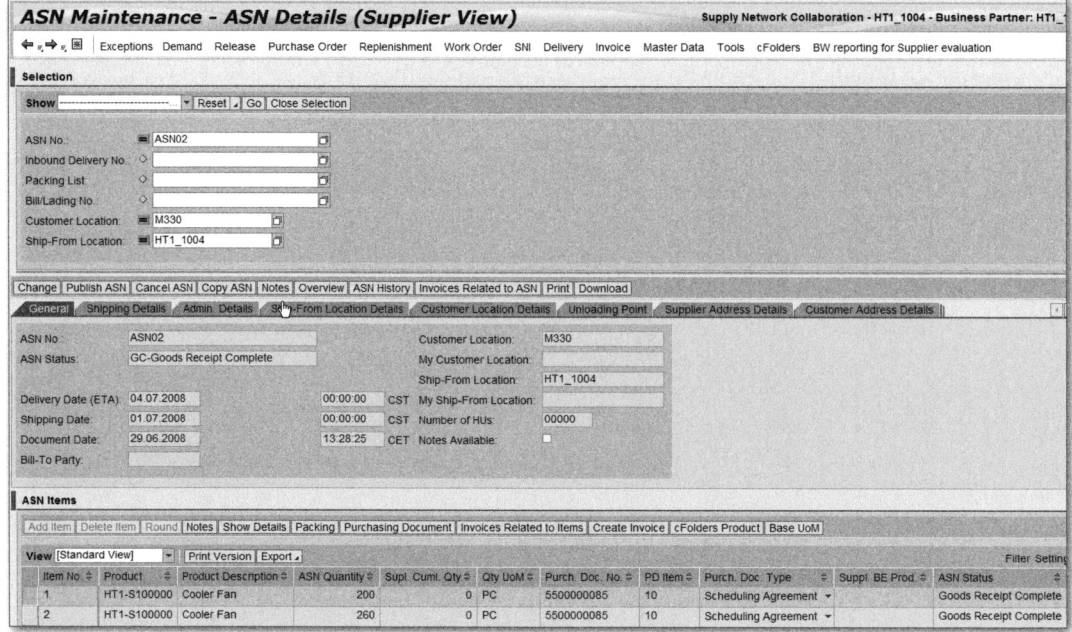

Figure 4.18 Fully Posted Goods Receipt in SAP SNC

4.2.7 Replenishment Planning Variant 2

This variant, like the first one, also makes use of the minimum and maximum stock levels. Unlike the SMI Monitor, the Min/Max Monitor used in the second variant allows replenishment orders to be created for the planned receipts. The ASNs are then set up for the replenishment orders.

Replenishment orders

The supplier accesses the Min/Max Monitor via menu path REPLENISHMENT • MIN/MAX REPLENISHMENT MONITOR • MIN/MAX REPLENISHMENT OVERVIEW (see Figure 4.19).

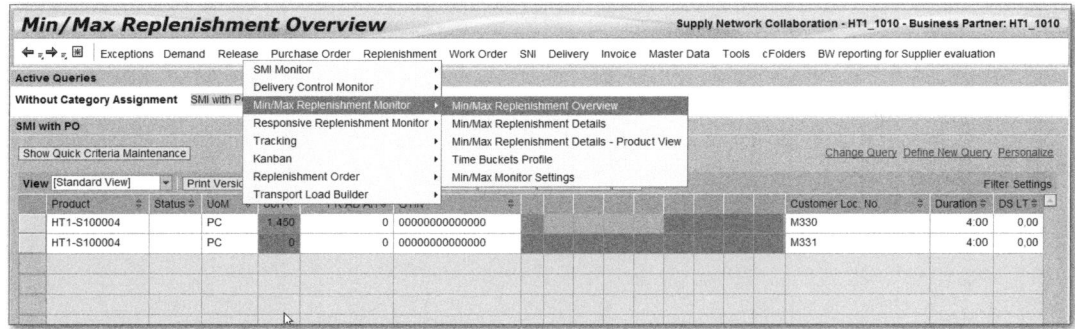

Figure 4.19 Min/Max Overview Monitor

The supplier can also have the system interactively plan planned and firm receipts in the Min/Max Replenishment Overview Monitor. To do so, the supplier has to select the lines containing the location products to be planned and click on the SERVICES button and select PROPOSE PLANNED RECEIPTS or PROPOSE FIRM RECEIPTS (see Figure 4.20).

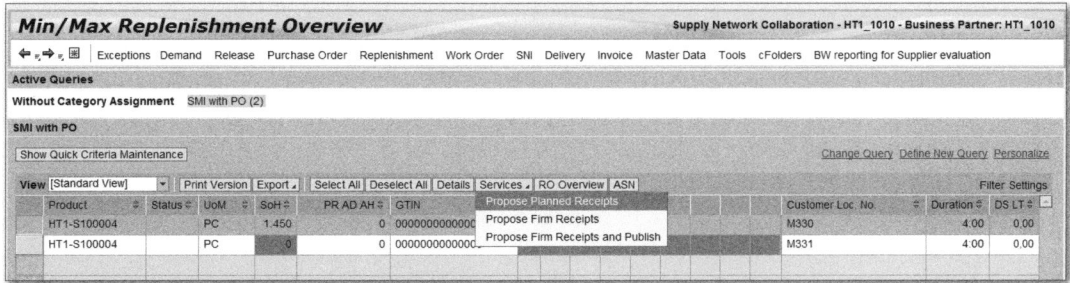

Figure 4.20 Calling Interactive Services in the Min/Max Overview Monitor

After selecting one or more lines, the supplier is taken to the details monitor. The Min/Max Details Monitor provides the key figures shown in Table 4.2 for each material and customer location (plant).

Data	Description
Demand	The gross demand in a time bucket
Average Demand	SAP SNC averages the actual gross demand and displays this as the calculated average demand. The following two averaging procedures are available in the standard delivery: ▶ Moving average calculation method ▶ Arithmetic mean calculation method The parameters required for the calculation are defined as Customizing settings (see Section 4.2.14).
Net Demand, Raw	The unrounded net demand of the customer in a given time bucket that the supplier must actually cover in this bucket. In contrast to the gross demand, the existing stock and receipts are taken into account here.
Planned Receipts	The total quantity that the supplier intends to deliver to the customer in a time bucket.
In-Transit Quantity	The total quantity in a time bucket that is in transit to the customer, but for which goods receipt has not yet taken place.
Firm Receipts (Published – Due)	The total quantity due from published replenishment orders in a time bucket.
Firm Receipts (Not Received)	The total quantity due for a replenishment order for which an ASN has already been created but goods receipt has not yet taken place on the customer's end.
Projected Stock	The stock that is expected to be available to the customer at the end of a time bucket (see Section 4.2.12).
Days' Supply	This key figure specifies how long the projected stock of a time bucket will last to cover the demands of subsequent buckets.
Minimum Proposal	The quantity that the supplier has to deliver to the customer in a time bucket so that the projected stock reaches the agreed minimum stock level at the end of the bucket.
Maximum Proposal	The quantity that the supplier has to deliver to the customer in a time bucket so that the projected stock reaches the agreed maximum stock level at the end of the bucket.
Minimum Stock Level	The minimum quantity of stock that must be available in the customer's warehouse.
Maximum Stock Level	The maximum quantity of stock that should be available in the customer's warehouse.

Table 4.2 Key Figures in the Min/Max Details Monitor

The supplier is now also able to maintain the planned receipts manually in the Min/Max Details Monitor (see Figure 4.21).

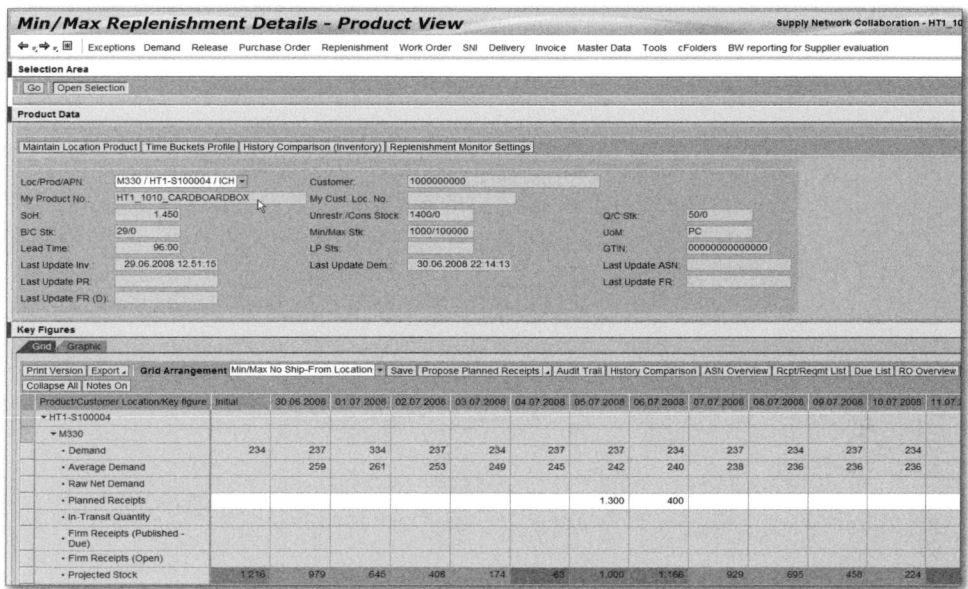

Figure 4.21 Min/Max Details Monitor with Planned Receipts

The supplier can also have the system interactively plan the planned receipts in the details monitor by clicking on the PROPOSE PLANNED RECEIPTS button (see Figure 4.22).

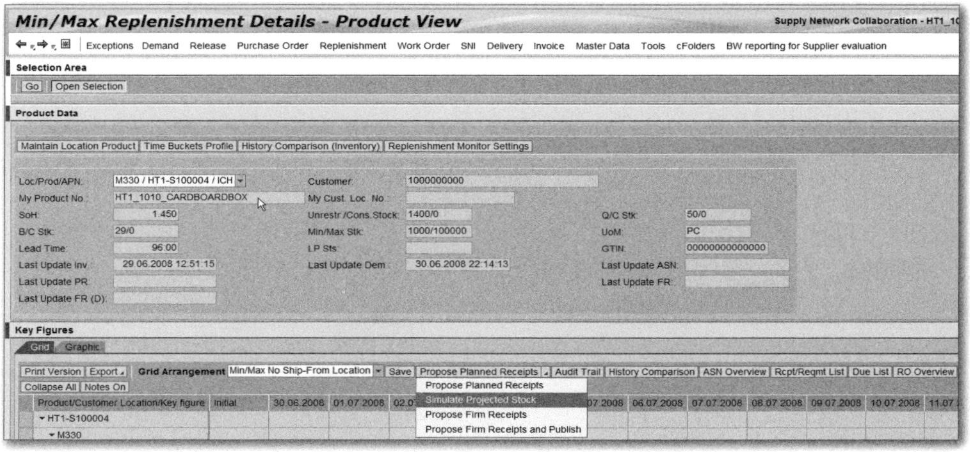

Figure 4.22 Calling the Planning Service in the Min/Max Details Monitor

4.2.8 Creating Firm Receipts for Replenishment Variant 2

Due list
Firm receipts (replenishment orders) can be created by clicking on the PROPOSE PLANNED RECEIPTS or PROPOSE FIRM RECEIPTS buttons or by means of the DUE LIST FOR PLANNED RECEIPTS (SMI) (see Figure 4.23).

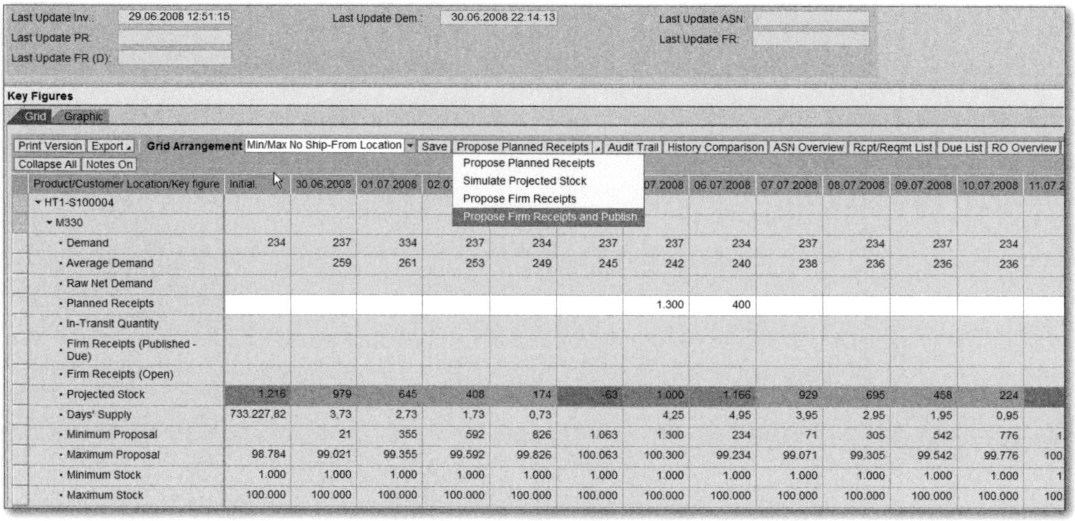

Figure 4.23 Creating Replenishment Orders Using the Min/Max Details Monitor

The due list can either be called up from the Min/Max Details Monitor directly or via the menu path DELIVERY • RECEIPTS AND REQUIREMENTS • DUE LIST FOR PLANNED RECEIPTS (SMI) (see Figure 4.24).

The supplier can now select one or more lines for which a replenishment order is to be created and then click on the CREATE RO button (see Figure 4.25).

4.2 Supplier Managed Inventory (SMI)

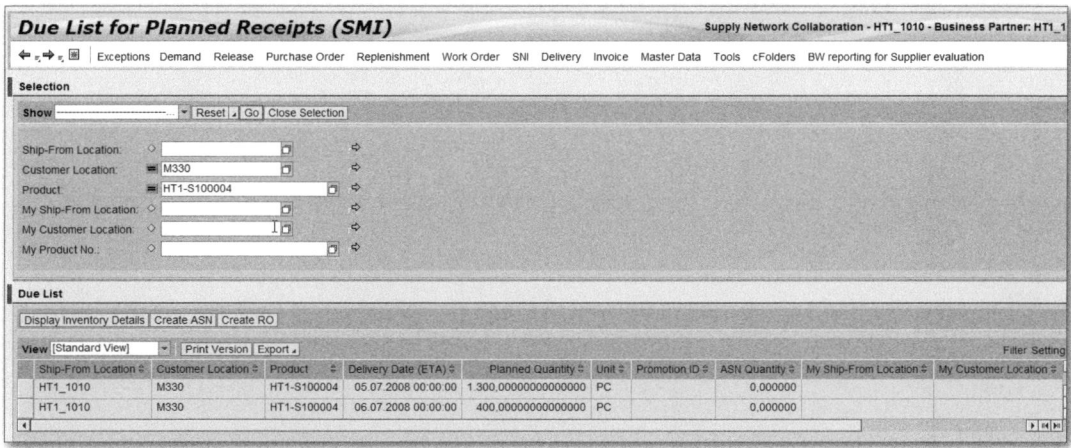

Figure 4.24 Creating Replenishment Orders Using the Due List for Planned Receipts (SMI)

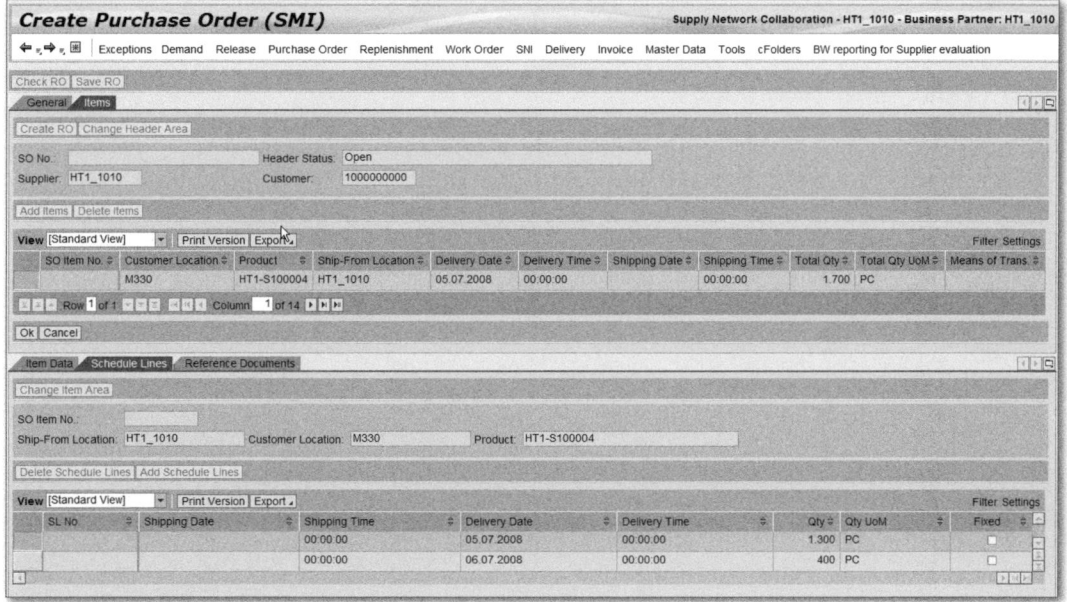

Figure 4.25 Creating a Replenishment Order

Once they have been published, the replenishment orders become visible in the FIRM RECEIPTS (PUBLISHED - DUE) row in the Min/Max Details Monitor and can, depending on Customizing settings, be offset against the planned receipts (see Figure 4.26).

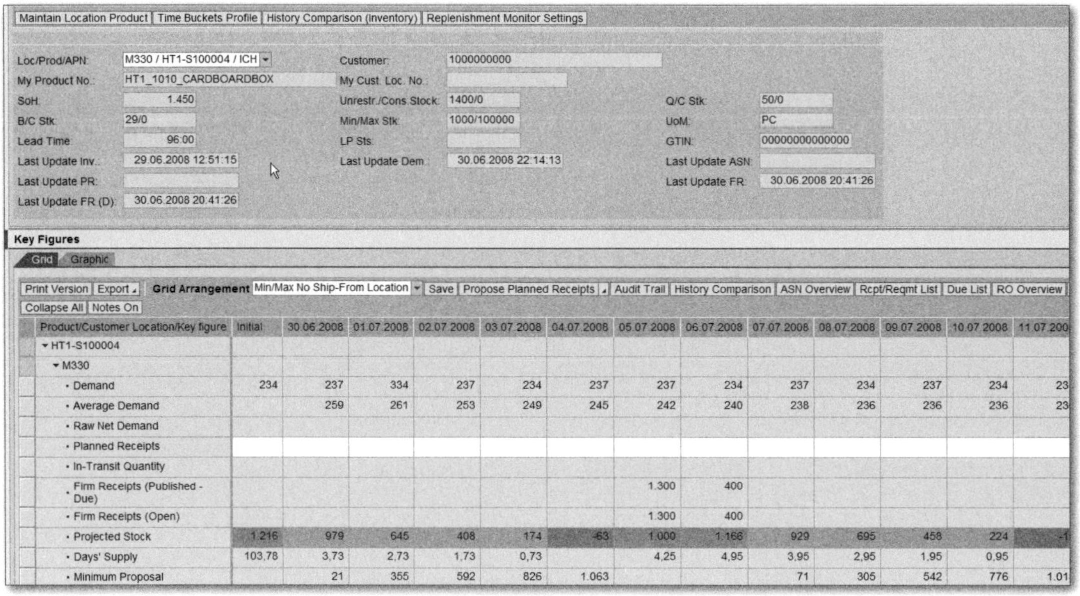

Figure 4.26 Visibility of Published Replenishment Orders in the Min/Max Monitor

4.2.9 Creating the ASN for Replenishment Variant 2

Once the supplier has made a firm commitment in the form of replenishment orders, the deliveries are visible in the DUE LIST FOR PURCHASING DOCUMENTS (see Figure 4.27).

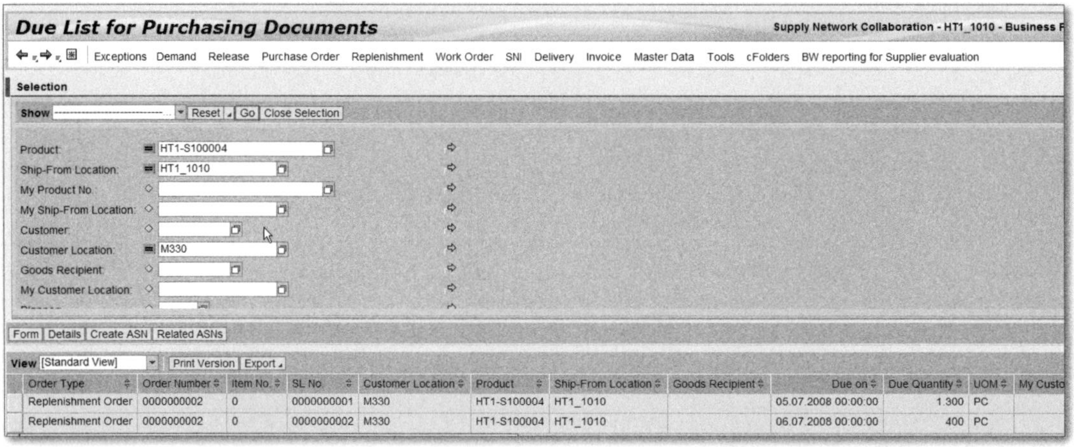

Figure 4.27 Replenishment Orders in the Due List for Purchasing Documents

The supplier now creates an ASN with reference to the replenishment order (see Figure 4.28).

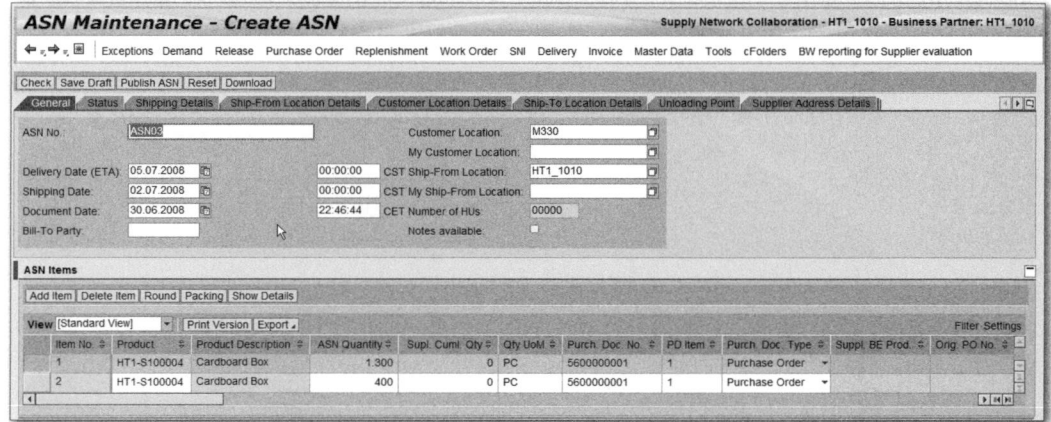

Figure 4.28 Creating an ASN with Reference to a Replenishment Order

The ASN can be seen in the Min/Max Detail Monitor in the IN-TRANSIT QUANTITY row, whereas the replenishment order is shown in the FIRM RECEIPTS (OPEN) row (see Figure 4.29).

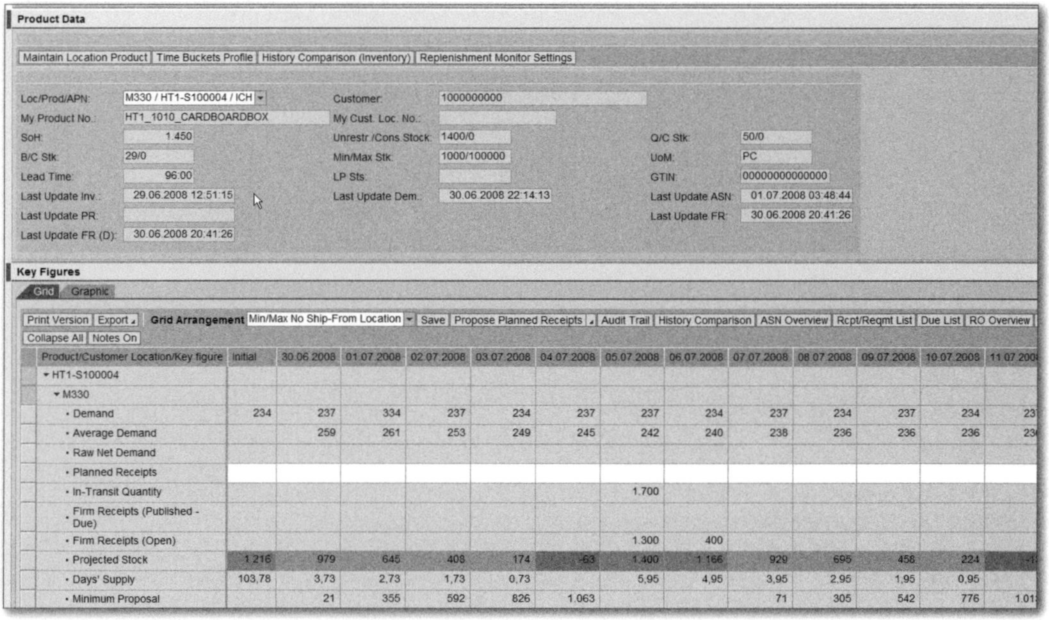

Figure 4.29 Min/Max Monitor with ASN Quantities

4.2.10 Goods Receipt

Goods receipt in the customer's SAP ERP backend system takes place for replenishment variant 2 exactly as described for variant 1 (Section 4.2.6 Goods Receipt).

4.2.11 Monitoring Replenishment Planning with Supplier Managed Inventory (SMI)

Min/Max and SMI Monitors

Both the supplier and the customer can use the Min/Max and SMI Monitors to oversee replenishment planning with the Supplier Managed Inventory (SMI), which in some cases highlight exception situations with different colors. For instance, stockouts are shown in red, projected stock below and above the minimum level are shown in orange and blue, respectively, and projected stock within the min/max levels is shown in green.

In SAP SNC 5.1, the monitors can be configured to meet the preferences and requirements of customers and suppliers through flexible use of self-defined queries and the option to hide key figures without further modifications.

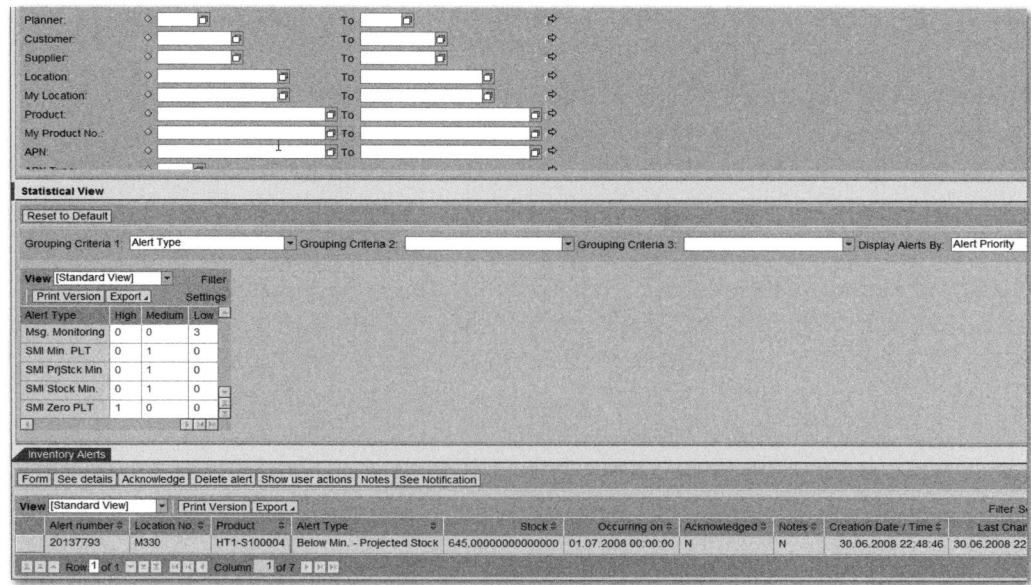

Figure 4.30 Example Alert for Actual Stock on Hand

Another function for monitoring replenishment planning is *alerts*. SAP SNC 5.1 provides a range of alert types that inform the customer or supplier of exception situations in replenishment planning. These alert types are visible to both the customer and the supplier. The Alert Monitor in SAP SNC displays the alerts that belong to a given alert type (see Figure 4.30).

Table 4.3 provides an overview of the alert types included in the standard shipment for replenishment planning with SMI in SAP SNC 5.1, which indicate if there is a critical situation concerning projected stock or actual stock on hand.

Alert Type	Description
Below Min. – Projected Stock	The projected stock is below the minimum stock level.
Above Max. – Projected Stock	The projected stock exceeds the maximum stock level.
Stockout – Projected Stock	The projected stock is zero or below zero.
Below Min. – In the Lead Time	The projected stock falls below the minimum stock level within the lead time.
Above Max. – In the Lead Time	The projected stock exceeds the maximum stock level within the lead time.
Stockout – In the Lead Time	The projected stock falls to zero or below zero within the lead time.
Below Min. – Stock on Hand	The actual stock on hand is below the minimum stock level.
Above Max. – Stock on Hand	The actual stock on hand is above the maximum stock level.
Stockout – Stock on Hand	The actual stock on hand is zero.

Table 4.3 Standard Alert Types in Replenishment Planning for SMI

4.2.12 Calculating the Projected Stock in the SAP SNC System

The projected stock is calculated on the basis of requirements, receipts, and stocks. It represents the stock of a product that is expected to be available at the location at the end of a time bucket.

Stock formula

You can define which requirements, receipts, and stocks are included in the calculation in Customizing (SPRO • SUPPLY NETWORK COLLABORATION • REPLENISHMENT • REPLENISHMENT PLANNING • PROJECTED STOCK • DEFINE PROFILES FOR THE PROJECTED STOCK) (see Figure 4.31).

Depending on the formula used to calculate the projected stock, the PLANNED RECEIPTS key figure is updated when the replenishment order or ASN is published.

Projected Stock Profile	Term	Term Type	Sign
ASN	Unrestricted Stock	Stock Type	Plus
ASN	Demand	Key Figure	Minus
ASN	In Transit	Key Figure	Plus
ASN	Planned Receipts	Key Figure	Plus

Figure 4.31 Example Profile for Calculating Projected Stock

4.2.13 Maintaining Replenishment Service Profiles

A new feature of SAP SNC 5.1 is that you can maintain replenishment service profiles in Customizing under SUPPLY NETWORK COLLABORATION • REPLENISHMENT • REPLENISHMENT PLANNING • PLANNING SERVICES • DEFINE REPLENISHMENT SERVICE PROFILES.

In a replenishment service profile, you make the following settings for supplier collaboration (see Figure 4.32).

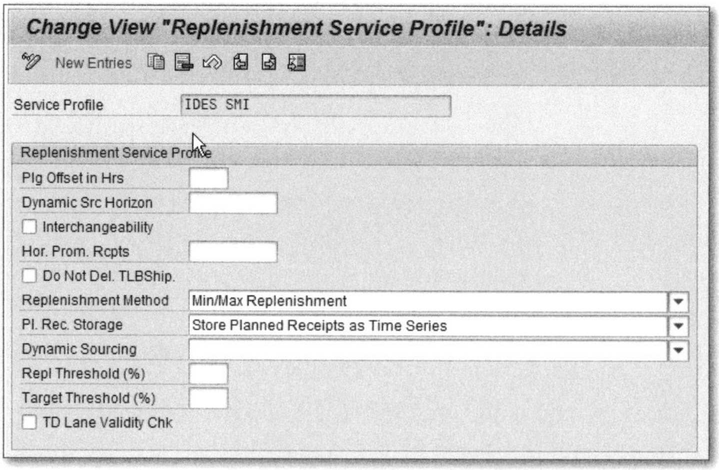

Figure 4.32 Example of a Replenishment Service Profile

Planning Offset in Hours

The value that you enter here determines the start of the replenishment planning horizon. In the standard delivery, the planning horizon starts at the current time.

Replenishment Method

You can select one of the following methods:

- Min/max replenishment
- Net-demand-based replenishment

With the min/max replenishment method, you use minimum and maximum stock levels. The target stock is either the maximum stock level or is calculated on the basis of the minimum and maximum stock levels. If the projected stock is lower than the reorder point, replenishment planning creates a planned receipt to bring the projected stock back up to the target stock level. You can make settings in the following fields for min/max replenishment:

Min/max replenishment

- **Repl Threshold (%)**

    If you choose the min/max replenishment method, you are required to enter a percentage value so that the reorder point can be calculated. To determine the reorder point, use the following formula:

    Reorder point = minimum stock level + percentage replenishment threshold value × (maximum stock level − minimum stock level)/100

    If you do not enter a value for the replenishment threshold, the default value is 0. You only use this formula if you have not defined the reorder point separately in the location product master data.

- **Target Threshold (%)**

    If you choose the min/max replenishment method, you are required to enter a percentage value so that the target stock can be calculated. To determine the target stock, use the following formula:

    Target stock = minimum stock level + target threshold value x (maximum stock level − minimum stock level)/100

    In the SMI scenario, the maximum stock level is taken as the target stock. Therefore, you must enter 100%. If you do not enter a value for the target stock, the default value is 100.

Net-demand-based replenishment
If you use the net-demand-based replenishment method, the safety stock is taken as the reorder point and target stock. If the projected stock is lower than the target stock, replenishment planning creates a planned receipt to bring the projected stock back up to the safety stock level.

Pl. Rec. Storage

You define how you want replenishment planning to save planned receipts in the PL. REC. STORAGE field. They can be saved either as time series or replenishment orders.

TD Lane Validity Chk

Set the TD LANE VALIDITY CHK indicator if you want replenishment planning to check the validity of the transportation lane for each time bucket of the planning horizon. A transportation lane can be used to satisfy demand in a bucket only if the lane is valid for that bucket. If you do not set this indicator, replenishment planning carries out the validity check only for the current moment, not for every time bucket.

4.2.14 Assigning the Settings for Replenishment Planning

The profiles created in this section and the previous one, Section 4.2.13 Maintaining Replenishment Service Profiles, can now be assigned to a supplier, plant, and product.

In addition, you can define here how the average demand in both replenishment monitors (SMI Monitor and Min/Max Monitor) is calculated and how long you want the horizon to be for proposals of planned and firm receipts if these values are planned automatically. You also define here whether you want existing planned receipts to be deleted before new planning commences.

You can make the required settings for this in Customizing under SUPPLY NETWORK COLLABORATION • REPLENISHMENT • REPLENISHMENT PLANNING • ASSIGN SETTINGS • ASSIGN SETTINGS FOR REPLENISHMENT PLANNING AND SNI (see Figure 4.33).

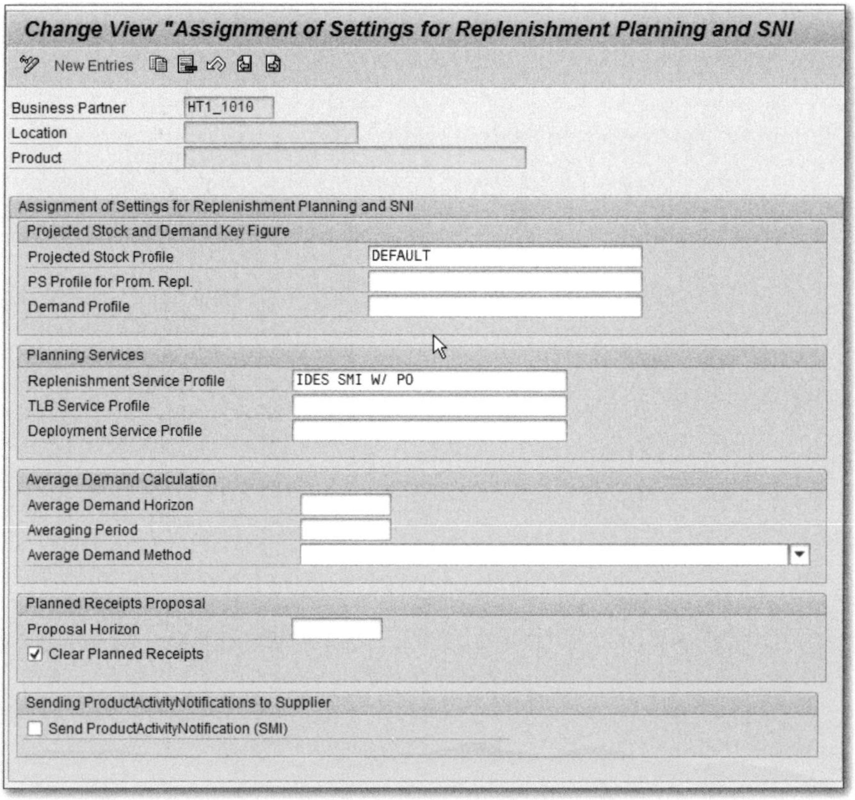

Figure 4.33 Assigning the Settings for Replenishment Planning

4.2.15 Automatic Planning

As of SAP SNC 5.1, a range of replenishment planning activities can be performed automatically using the *Planning Service Manager*. For instance, you can opt to have the system plan the planned receipts or replenishment orders.

Planning Service Manager

To do so, you must carry out the following activities in Customizing under SCM BASIS • PLANNING SERVICE MANAGER:

1. **Define Process Profile**
   Here, you define how the system handles planning profile process blocks. Depending on your settings, the system creates packages of objects that it processes together. You can define the method used for package creation, the maximum and minimum package size, applica-

tion log settings, and whether you want the system to process packages in parallel (see Figure 4.34).

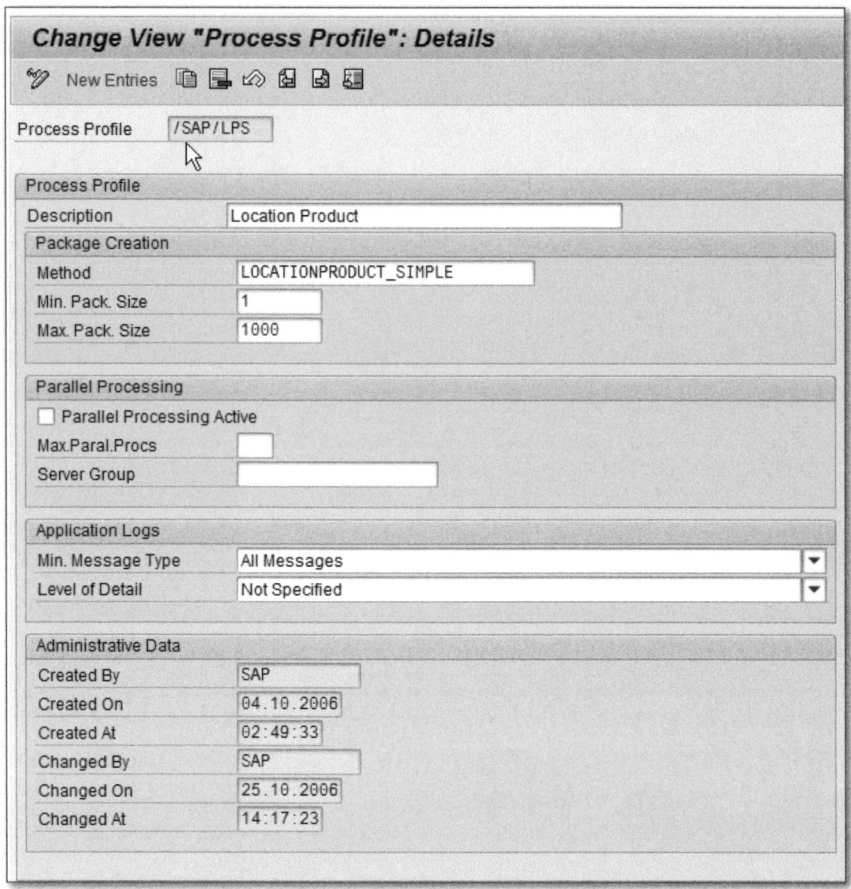

Figure 4.34 Example of a Process Profile

2. **Define Selections**
   You use selections to define the master data (location product, location, transportation lane, and so on) that is to be taken into account in automatic planning (see Figure 4.35).

3. **Define Planning Profile**
   The planning profile contains the definition of the planning services to be called. All of the planning activities listed here are performed when a planning profile is executed and the results saved. You have

to define at least one process profile and one selection profile before you can create a planning profile.

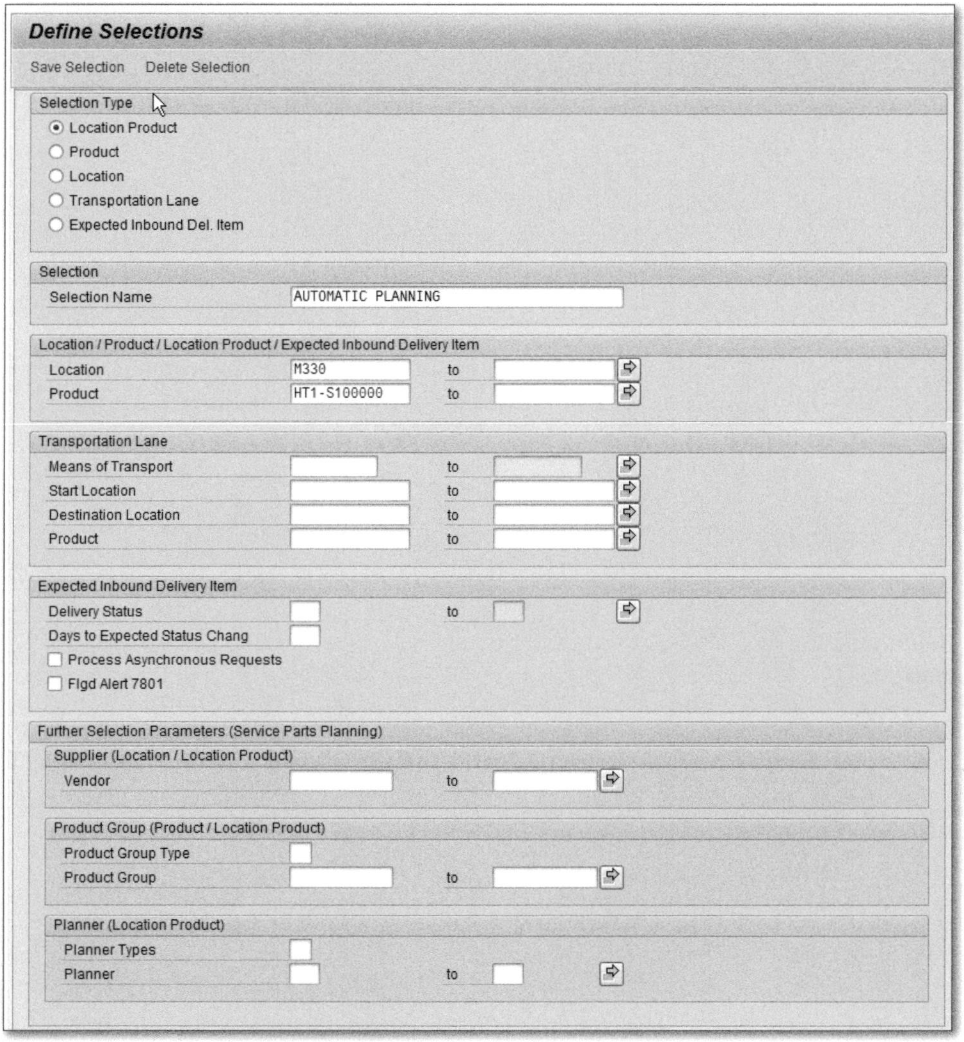

Figure 4.35 Example of a Selection Profile

The planning profile consists of three areas:

- **Header data**
  Here, you enter a name and relationship for the new planning profile (see Figure 4.36).

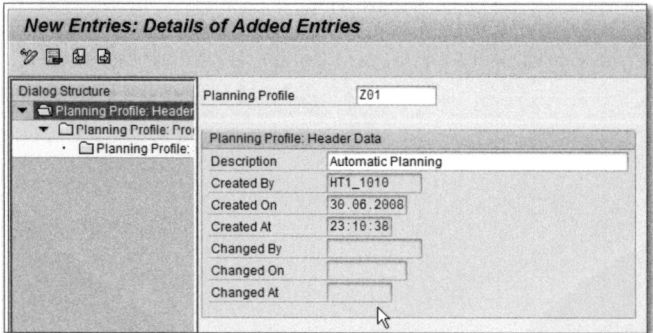

Figure 4.36 Example of a Planning Profile – Header Data

- **Process block**
  In the process block, you store the process profile you created prior to creating the planning profile, as well as a planning version. The process block number determines the sequence if you store several process profiles (see Figure 4.37).

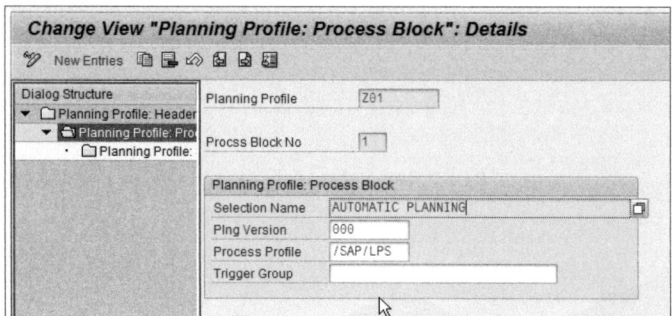

Figure 4.37 Example of a Planning Profile – Defining a Process Block

- **Service List**
  Here, you save the planning service that you want to be called (for example, replenishment service). The planning service is provided by default by the respective application (see Figure 4.38).

- **Executing the planning profile**
  To do this, follow the menu path SCM BASIS • PLANNING SERVICE MANAGER • /SAPAPO/PE_RUN in the SAP Easy Access menu. The planning profile defined in Customizing can be called here and scheduled as a job (see Figure 4.39).

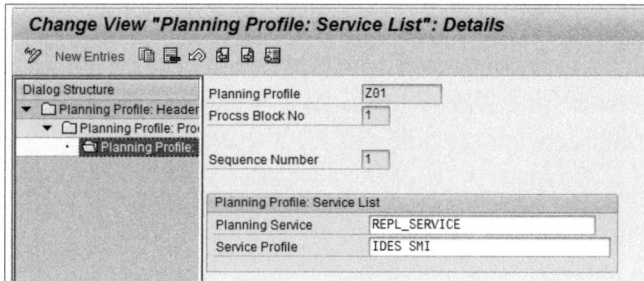

Figure 4.38 Example of a Planning Profile – Defining the Service List

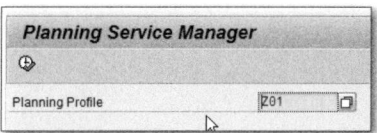

Figure 4.39 Executing the Planning Profile Defined in Customizing

- **Displaying the application log of the Planning Service Manager**
  Once the job has been executed, you can display an application log by following the menu path SCM BASIS • PLANNING SERVICE MANAGER • /SAPAPO/PE_LOG_DISP in the SAP Easy Access menu (see Figure 4.40).

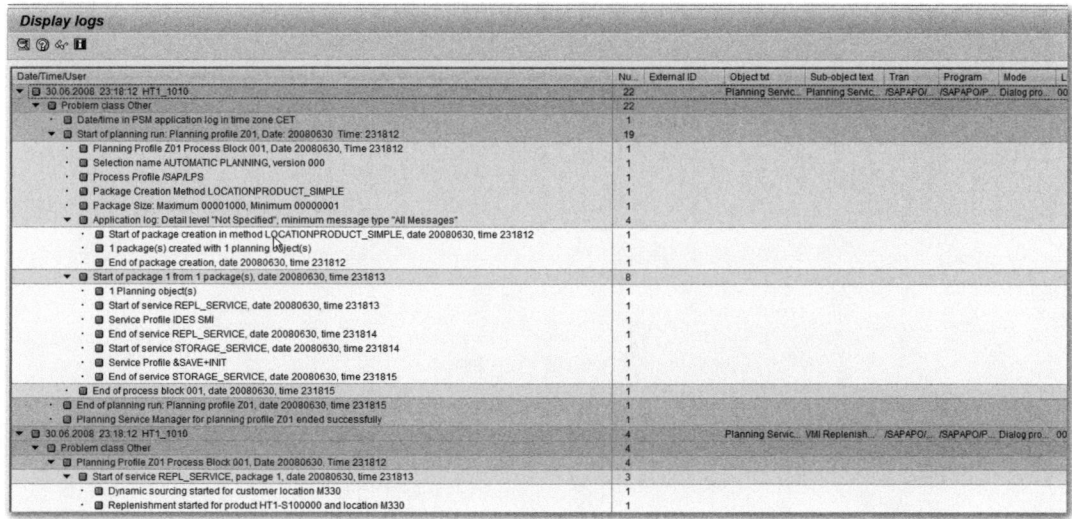

Figure 4.40 Log After Automatic Planning Has Been Executed

4.2.16 Downloading SMI Data

SMI XML In the SMI scenario, gross demands and stocks are sent from the customer's backend system to SAP SNC as an XML message. The supplier maintains the planned receipts on the basis of this data.

As of SAP SNC 5.1, it is also possible to send this data to the supplier's backend system, supplemented with the following time series:

- Published ASNs
- Planned receipts
- Projected stock

The ProductActivityNotification XML message is enhanced to transfer this data.

It makes sense to download an XML message if the supplier is in a position to process this data in his own backend system. There are a number of ways to download the data, and these are described in the following sections.

Automatically

Automatic downloading works as follows: When the *ProductActivityNotification* is received from the customer's backend system, it is forwarded directly with the supplementary data. To use this function, you have to set the SEND PAN indicator under SUPPLY NETWORK COLLABORATION • REPLENISHMENT • ASSIGN SETTINGS • ASSIGN SETTINGS FOR REPLENISHMENT PLANNING AND SNI (see Figure 4.41).

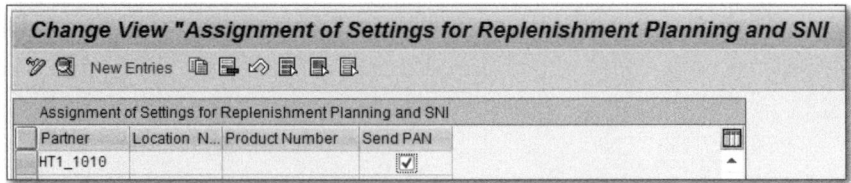

Figure 4.41 Indicator to Automatically Send Enhanced ProductActivityNotification

Manually

You can send SMI data manually in the SAP Easy Access menu under SUPPLY NETWORK COLLABORATION • TOOLS • SEND XML MESSAGES FOR TIME SERIES • /SCA/PRODACT_OUT (see Figure 4.42).

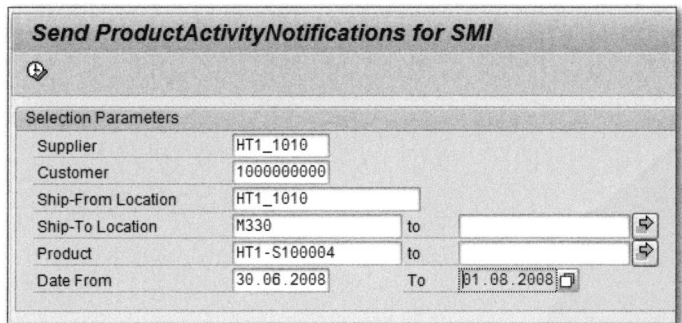

Figure 4.42 Sending Enhanced ProductActivityNotification Manually

The report displays a results log showing the data to be downloaded on the basis of the selection criteria (see Figure 4.43).

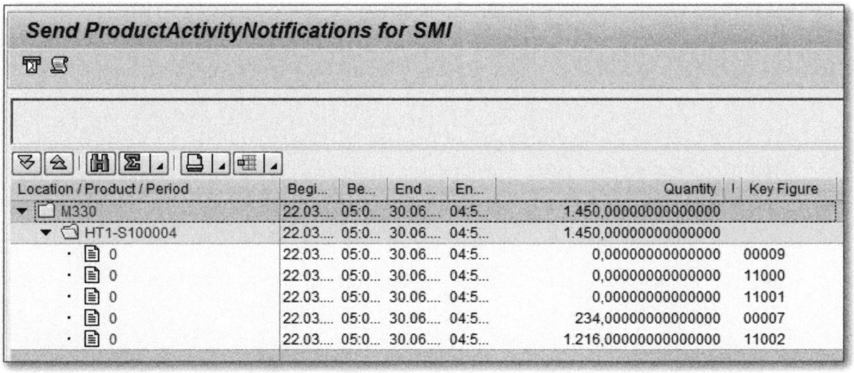

Figure 4.43 Results Log When Enhanced ProductActivityNotification Is Sent Manually

Both customers and suppliers can send data manually in the SMI detailed view by calling the SEND PRODUCTACTIVITYNOTIFICATION function (see Figure 4.44).

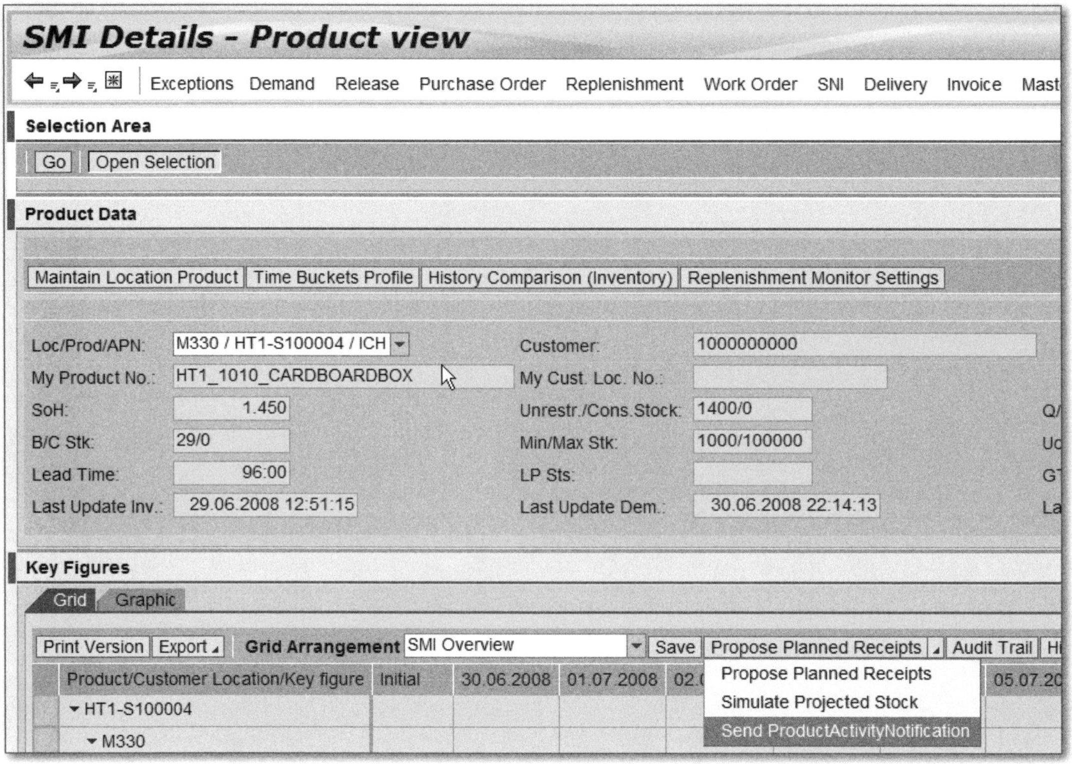

Figure 4.44 Sending Enhanced ProductActivityNotification Manually from the Web Browser

The downloaded XML message can be seen in the monitor for processed SML messages (Transaction SXMB_MONI) (see Figure 4.45). The SENDER INTERFACE is PRODUCTACTIVITYNOTIFICATION_OUT. You can send the XML file to the supplier by means of the connected SAP NetWeaver PI system.

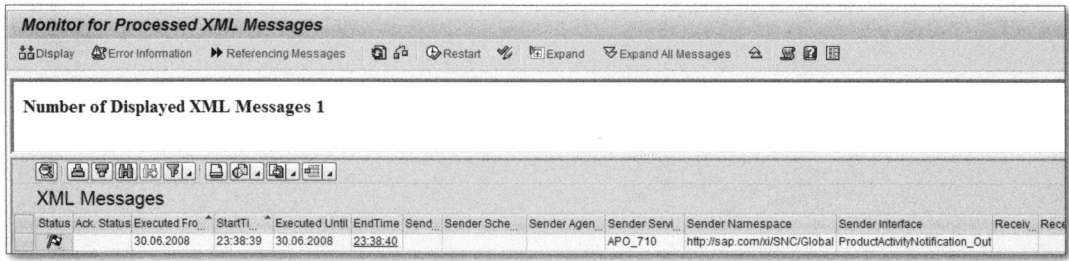

Figure 4.45 Downloaded XML Message

4.3 Forecast Delivery Release Process

This section begins with an overview of the *forecast delivery release process* business process with SAP SNC 5.1 (See Figure 4.46). It then takes a closer look at the individual process steps and settings in SAP SNC.

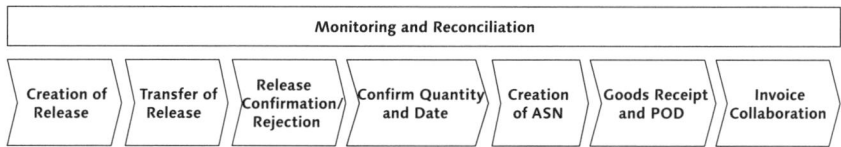

Figure 4.46 Process Flow for Forecast Delivery Release Process

4.3.1 Process Overview

Forecast delivery release process covers all activities, from release creation and planning in the customer's backend system to goods receipt and invoice processing.

A scheduling agreement release is based on a long-term scheduling agreement between a purchasing organization and a supplier, governing the delivery of products at predefined conditions over a certain period. Forecast delivery schedule processing can be carried out with both external suppliers and suppliers within the company (stock transfers).

Delivery schedules inform the supplier of the required quantity of a product and the date/time for its delivery. A distinction is made between forecast delivery schedules and just-in-time (JIT) schedules. A forecast delivery schedule gives the supplier longer-term notice, whereas a JIT schedule lets the supplier know about product quantities and delivery dates/times in the immediate future.

JIT and forecast delivery schedules

The first step is to create a delivery schedule from the results of a planning run in the form of (released) schedule lines with quantities and dates/times. The parameters from a release creation profile are taken into account here. Next, the time and medium for sending the scheduling agreement release to the supplier are determined.

The supplier can confirm or reject the entire forecast delivery schedule, or confirm scheduling agreement delivery schedule lines individually, in which case the supplier can confirm a delivery date/time and quantity that differ from those requested. Supplier confirmations often count as provisional receipt elements created at the supplier's end on the basis of production and capacity planning.

Shortly before physically sending the goods, the supplier can create ASNs to notify the customer of binding delivery quantities and dates/times. An ASN can also contain information about the means of transport, duration of transportation, and type of packaging used. The notified quantities can be offset against the quantities in the scheduling agreement delivery schedule lines.

The goods receipt is posted once the goods have been physically received and put away at the customer's location. A proof of delivery message confirms to the supplier the actual quantity received by the customer. Furthermore, reasons for any quantity differences and the confirmation date can be provided.

Invoice collaboration takes place with reference to the ASN on the basis of conventional invoice processing or self-billing (see Section 4.12 Invoice Collaboration).

Cumulative quantities and alerts to draw attention to any exception situations are used to monitor forecast delivery schedule processing between customer and supplier.

The forecast delivery release process shortens processing times and reduces paper-based activities in procurement processing, because a scheduling agreement delivery schedule line can replace a stack of purchase orders. In addition, by specifying the exact delivery time, JIT deliveries are made possible, which means stock on hand can be kept at a low level. The suppliers can work with shorter lead times because they are not required to provide the total purchase order quantity in a single delivery, but rather—in accordance with the schedule lines—in several deliveries of smaller quantities.

The process flow for forecast delivery release process is shown in Figure 4.47.

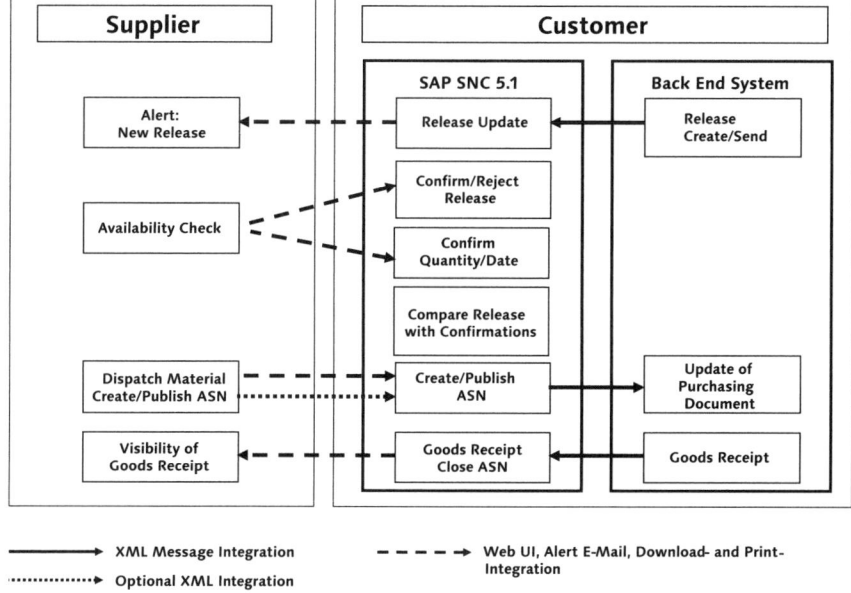

Figure 4.47 Forecast Delivery Release Process with SAP SNC 5.1

4.3.2 Master Data Specific to Forecast Delivery Schedule Processing

In addition to the generic master data (see Section 4.1 Generic Master Data) for the business processes in SAP SNC, purchase scheduling agreements must also be maintained in the customer's backend system for forecast delivery schedule processing.

4.3.3 Creating and Sending the Forecast Delivery Schedule

The scheduling agreement delivery schedule lines, created on the basis of the planning run in SAP ERP, are converted into JIT or forecast schedule lines here. This process may use the following parameters from the release creation profile:

Release creation profile

- Release horizon for JIT and forecast delivery schedules
- Whether a backlog and immediate requirement are determined and included in the release

- Whether a tolerance check is carried out for releases that are created due to changes
- Which event triggers the release creation process (changes to schedule lines and the next transmission date being reached)

Furthermore, the scheduling agreement delivery schedule lines can be grouped together as scheduling agreement release schedule lines by aggregating the quantities and delivery dates/times. Depending on its due date (delivery or shipping date), a scheduling agreement release schedule line is assigned to a level of commitment. This assignment is made on the basis of firm/trade-off zones agreed between customer and supplier. A basic distinction is made between the following time zones:

Firm/Trade-Off Zone 1: Firm and Trade-Off Zone

The scheduling agreement release schedule lines in this time zone count as fixed and therefore binding. If the customer cancels a schedule line that falls in this firm/trade-off zone, the supplier is entitled to invoice the customer for the material and production costs incurred as a result of the cancellation.

Firm/Trade-Off Zone 2: Trade-Off Zone

This zone constitutes the release period for the supplier to procure materials required for production. If the customer cancels a schedule line within this firm/trade-off zone, the supplier is only entitled to charge for material costs. Therefore, schedule lines that fall in this zone have a lower level of commitment than those within the first firm/trade-off zone.

Firm/Trade-Off Zone 3: Planning Zone

All scheduling agreement release schedule lines with a due date after the first two firm/trade-off zones are assigned to the planning zone and are nonbinding.

In the following, *forecast delivery schedule* is used to refer to both JIT delivery schedules and forecast delivery schedules.

Message determination and the partner profile must be configured to enable a forecast delivery schedule to be sent from SAP ERP to SAP SNC. Forecast delivery schedules are then generated from SAP ERP as an IDoc of type DELINS.DELFOR01 (for SAP ERP 2005 DIMP: DELFOR.DELFOR02 or DELJIT.DELFOR02). The IDoc is converted in SAP NetWeaver PI into an XML message of type DeliveryScheduleNotification, which can be processed as an inbound message by SAP SNC.

Once the inbound message has been successfully posted, a new release alert is generated. The supplier can be notified of this automatically, for example, by email, and view the forecast delivery schedule with the Release Details view in the SAP SNC web browser (see Figure 4.48).

Release details

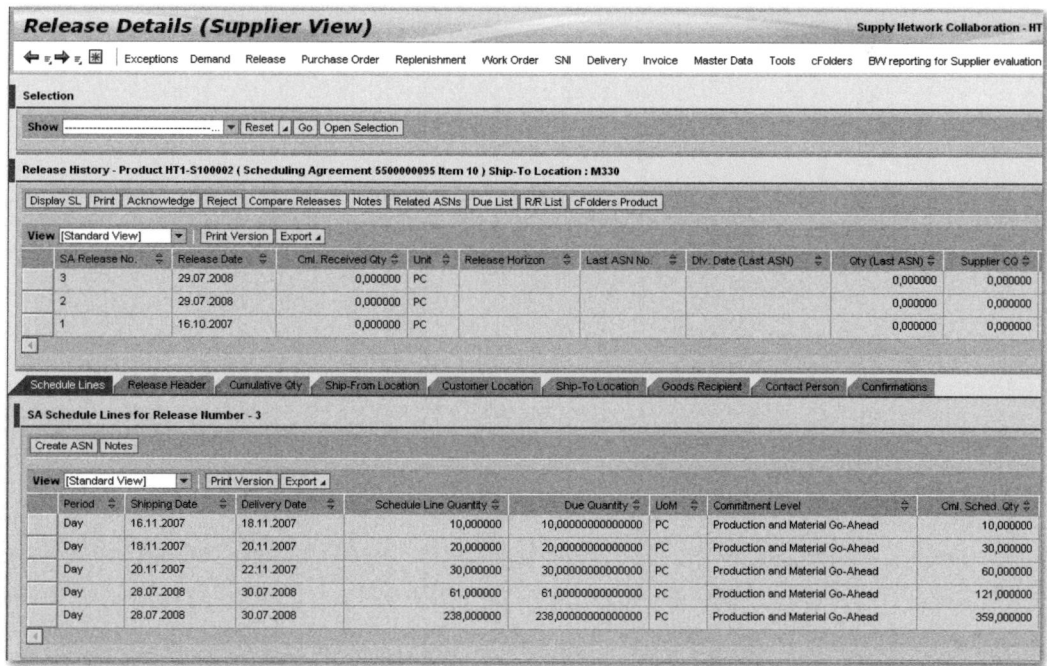

Figure 4.48 Release Details

In the Release Details view, the supplier can obtain information about requested quantities and delivery dates/times, as well as the levels of commitment of the customer's scheduling agreement delivery schedule lines. Furthermore, cumulative quantities and other information relating to the release type, date, and horizon are displayed at the release header

Release header and schedule lines

level. A distinction is made between ship-from location, customer location, ship-to location, and goods recipient. The ship-from location is the supplier location that is to deliver the product. The location that ordered the product is referred to as the customer location. The ship-to location denotes the location to which the supplier delivers the product. Goods recipient is used if the supplier is to deliver the products to a business partner other than the customer.

Comparing Forecast Delivery Schedules

In SAP SNC, all of the forecast delivery schedules for a scheduling agreement item are documented. Two forecast delivery schedules can be compared on the basis of this release history to identify variances at the schedule line level. The quantities, delivery dates/times, and cumulative received quantities are used in this comparison (see Figure 4.49).

Period	Ship Date	Delivery Start Date	Release No.2 Quantity	Release No.2 Cumulative Quantity	Release No.3 Quantity	Release No.3 Cumulative Quantity	Delta Quantity	Delta Cumulative Quantity
Day	16.11.2007	18.11.2007	10,000000	10,000000	10,000000	10,000000	0,000000	0,000000
Day	18.11.2007	20.11.2007	20,000000	30,000000	20,000000	30,000000	0,000000	0,000000
Day	20.11.2007	22.11.2007	30,000000	60,000000	30,000000	60,000000	0,000000	0,000000
Day	28.07.2008	30.07.2008	530,000000	590,000000	538,000000	598,000000	8,000000	8,000000
Day	29.07.2008	31.07.2008	234,000000	824,000000	232,000000	830,000000	2,000000-	6,000000
Day	30.07.2008	01.08.2008	708,000000	1.532,000000	704,000000	1.534,000000	4,000000-	2,000000
Day	02.08.2008	04.08.2008	237,000000	1.769,000000	235,000000	1.769,000000	2,000000-	0,000000
Day	03.08.2008	05.08.2008	234,000000	2.003,000000	233,000000	2.002,000000	1,000000-	1,000000-

Figure 4.49 Release Comparison

4.3.4 Confirming or Rejecting the Forecast Delivery Schedule

The supplier can confirm or reject the entire forecast delivery schedule in SAP SNC. A rejection triggers an alert to the customer, which can help initiate further consultation between the customer and supplier. In addition, it is also possible to trigger an alert to the customer if the supplier fails to confirm the forecast delivery schedule after a certain period. The time at which a forecast delivery schedule is confirmed, rejected, printed, or downloaded is also documented.

4.3.5 Confirming Quantities and Dates/Times

The forecast delivery schedule lines sent to the supplier describe the customer's requested quantities and dates/times. In SAP SNC, the supplier can confirm the customer's requested quantities and delivery dates/times or propose alternatives on the basis of production and capacity planning. This type of supplier confirmation can also be created multiple times with reference to a release schedule line (see Figure 4.50).

Forecast delivery schedule confirmation

Req. Shipping	Req. Delivery	Req. Qty	Conf. Qty	Difference	Cumulated Difference	Conf. Ship Date	Conf. Ship Time	Conf. Delivery Date
28.07.2008 12:00:00	30.07.2008 12:00:00	61,000000	0,000000	61,000000-	350,000000-		00:00:00	
28.07.2008 12:00:00	30.07.2008 12:00:00	238,000000	238,000000	0,000000	350,000000-	28.07.2008	12:00:00	30.07.2008
29.07.2008 12:00:00	31.07.2008 12:00:00	232,000000	0,000000	232,000000-	582,000000-		00:00:00	
30.07.2008 12:00:00	01.08.2008 12:00:00	235,000000	0,000000	235,000000-	817,000000-		00:00:00	
30.07.2008 12:00:00	01.08.2008 12:00:00	236,000000	0,000000	236,000000-	1.053,000000-		00:00:00	
30.07.2008 12:00:00	01.08.2008 12:00:00	233,000000	233,000000	0,000000	1.053,000000-	30.07.2008	12:00:00	01.08.2008
02.08.2008 12:00:00	04.08.2008 12:00:00	235,000000	0,000000	235,000000-	1.288,000000-		00:00:00	
03.08.2008 12:00:00	05.08.2008 12:00:00	233,000000	0,000000	233,000000-	1.521,000000-		00:00:00	

Figure 4.50 Schedule Lines and Confirmations

To manage forecast delivery schedule confirmations, you can define in Customizing for SAP SNC 5.1 (in Transaction SPRO, follow the menu path SUPPLY NETWORK COLLABORATION • DELIVERY • CONFIRMATION CONTROL • SET CONFIRMATION CONTROL) whether forecast delivery schedule confirmations are mandatory, optional, or not allowed for forecast delivery schedule lines (see Figure 4.51). You make this definition against a combination of attributes, namely, customer, supplier, customer location, ship-from location, and product.

Settings for forecast delivery schedule confirmation

In addition, if you have selected optional or mandatory confirmation control for the customer, supplier, and product attributes, you can specify whether you want SAP SNC to create a confirmation request automatically for each forecast delivery schedule line (in Transaction SPRO, follow the menu path SUPPLY NETWORK COLLABORATION • DELIVERY • EXTENDED CONFIRMATION MANAGEMENT (ECM) AND LOCATION PRODUCT CONFIRMATIONS • SET CREATION OF CONFIRMATION REQUESTS). A confirmation request represents an explicit request from the customer to the

Confirmation request

supplier to confirm particular forecast delivery schedule lines. If a confirmation request has been set up, the corresponding forecast delivery schedule line is highlighted in the SAP SNC web browser for the supplier (see Figure 4.52).

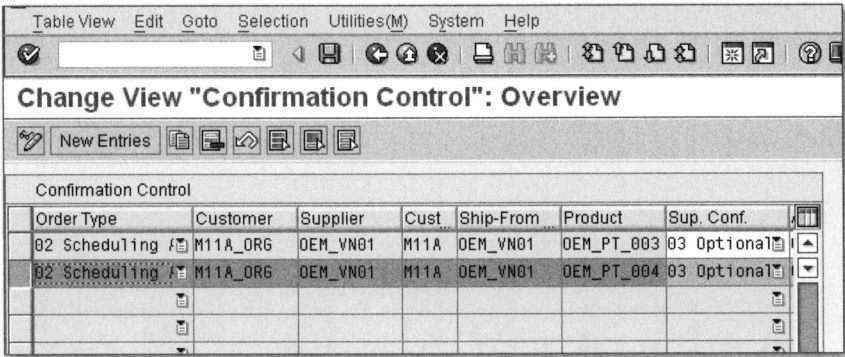

Figure 4.51 Confirmation Control

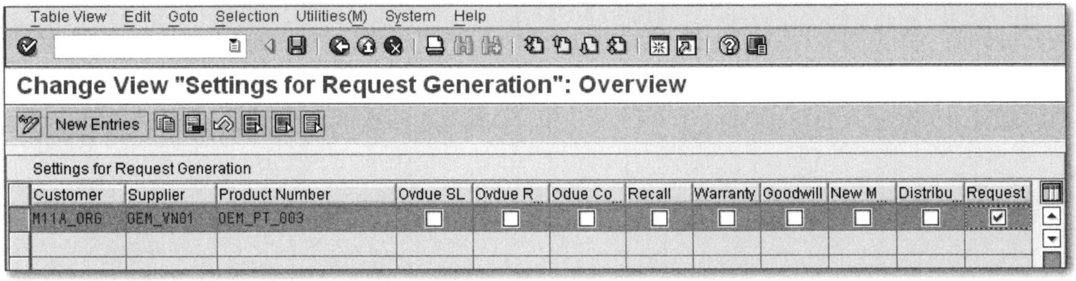

Figure 4.52 Managing Confirmation Requests

For example, you can set up the system so that confirmation requests are only created for forecast delivery schedule lines for which no confirmation requests have been created and whose shipping dates have passed.

In addition to the option to maintain differing quantities and dates/times, the supplier can also enter notes about a confirmation in SAP SNC and thereby communicate messages to the customer. Furthermore, the supplier can use a *note-only confirmation*, which has a quantity of zero, to inform the customer of anything preventing a delivery from taking place.

The customer can view the quantities and dates and times confirmed by the supplier in SAP SNC and compare these against the originally requested quantities and dates/times (see Figure 4.53).

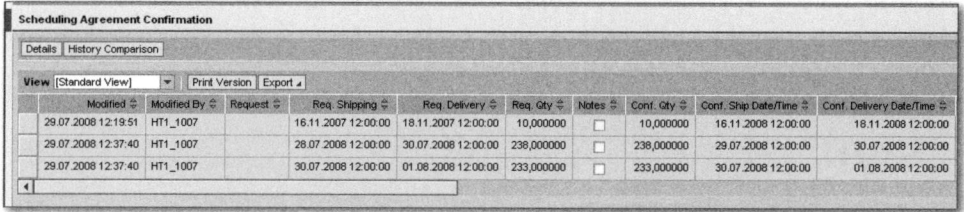

Figure 4.53 Customer View – Comparison of Requested and Confirmed Data

4.3.6 Creating and Publishing an ASN

The supplier can use an ASN to inform the customer of an upcoming delivery for a forecast delivery schedule. The ASN can be created manually in the SAP SNC web browser or sent from the supplier's backend system to SAP SNC. When the ASN is published in SAP SNC, it is sent to the customer's backend system. To achieve this, an XML message of type *DispatchDeliveryNotification* is created in SAP SNC and converted into an IDoc of type DESADV.DELVRY03 in SAP NetWeaver PI. In SAP ERP, an inbound delivery is created on the basis of the ASN.

In SAP SNC, it is possible to define whether ASNs are mandatory, optional, or not allowed for a forecast delivery schedule (in Transaction SPRO, follow the menu path SUPPLY NETWORK COLLABORATION • DELIVERY • CONFIRMATION CONTROL • SET CONFIRMATION CONTROL). This definition is made against a combination of attributes, namely customer, supplier, customer location, ship-from location, and product. If NOT ALLOWED is selected, the supplier cannot create ASNs in the SAP SNC web browser.

Settings for ASN processing

The MANDATORY and OPTIONAL settings allow the supplier to create ASNs for forecast delivery schedule lines in SAP SNC directly from the Release Details view or from the due list for purchasing documents.

Within forecast delivery schedule processing, the DUE LIST FOR PURCHASING DOCUMENTS shows the forecast delivery schedule lines that are due (see Figure 4.54).

Due list for purchasing documents

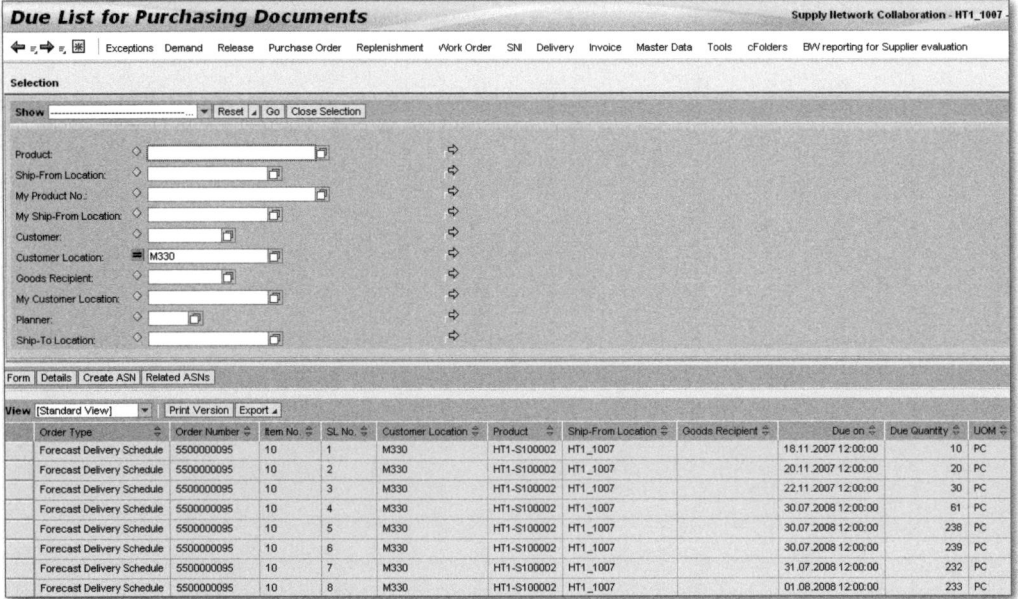

Figure 4.54 Due List for Purchasing Documents

A forecast delivery schedule line counts as due when two conditions are met:

First, the forecast delivery schedule line's level of commitment type must be flagged as relevant for the determination of due schedule lines in Customizing for the SAP SNC system (in Transaction SPRO, follow the menu path SUPPLY NETWORK COLLABORATION • DELIVERY • DUE QUANTITY CALCULATION • DETERMINE DUE SCHEDULE LINE QUANTITIES). This setting can be made against the customer, supplier, customer location, ship-from location, and product attributes (see Figure 4.55). Either the shipping date/time or delivery date/time can be set as the due date/time.

Second, the forecast delivery schedule line quantity must not be covered completely by an ASN quantity. SAP SNC assigns the ASN quantities of release-relevant ASNs to the forecast delivery schedule lines here.

Sections 4.8.4 and 4.9.4 Creating an ASN explore more functions for creating ASNs in SAP SNC.

When an ASN is created and published for a forecast delivery schedule, the due quantity is reduced by the ASN quantity, and an XML message of type *DispatchedDeliveryNotification* is generated. The XML message is converted into an IDoc of type DESADV.DELVRY03 in SAP NetWeaver PI and sent to SAP ERP. When the IDoc is posted in SAP ERP, an inbound delivery is created and offset against the scheduling agreement item and forecast delivery schedule on a quantity basis.

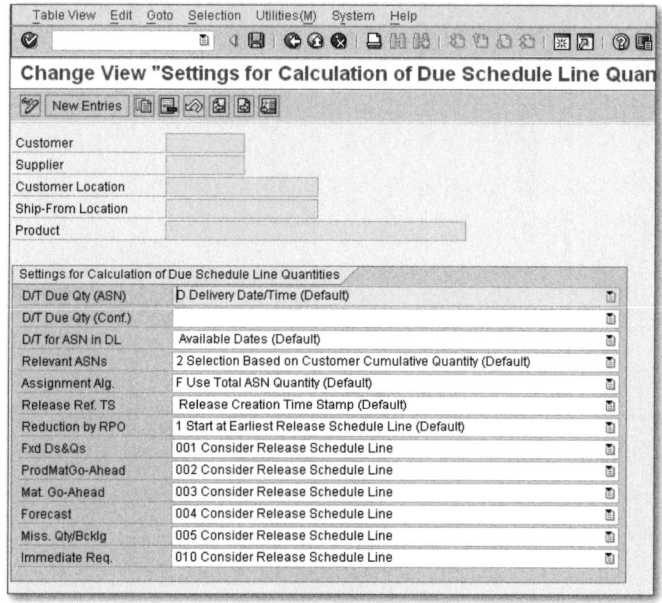

Figure 4.55 Determining Due Schedule Line Quantities

4.3.7 Goods Receipt and Proof of Delivery

Goods receipt takes place in SAP ERP with reference to the inbound delivery created on the basis of the ASN. Once the customer has entered the quantity actually received and posted the goods receipt, a proof of delivery can be generated from the SAP ERP system in the form of an IDoc of type STPPOD.DELVRY03. The IDoc is converted into an XML message of type ReceivedDeliveryNotification in SAP NetWeaver PI and sent to SAP SNC.

A proof of delivery allows the supplier to establish whether the goods arrived at the customer in full or only in part. To this end, the status of the ASN is set to GOODS RECEIPT COMPLETE or GOODS RECEIPT PARTIAL in SAP SNC, and the actual quantity received is shown in the ASN.

Proof of delivery

4.3.8 Monitoring Forecast Delivery Release Process

Cumulative quantities and *alerts* are used in SAP SNC to monitor delivery progress and identify exception situations in forecast delivery release process.

Cumulative quantities

Cumulative quantities are provided by the customer (or supplier) to inform the supplier (or customer) of planned or delivered quantities. The following section describes the most important cumulative quantities.

A *cumulative scheduled quantity* represents the total quantity delivered so far of a (forecast delivery) schedule line quantity delivery. It is displayed in SAP SNC under release details (see Figure 4.48 in Section 4.3.3 Creating and Sending the Forecast Delivery Schedule).

The *customer cumulative quantity* represents the total quantity for a scheduling agreement item that the customer regards as received or in transit. A setting in SAP ERP at the scheduling agreement item level defines whether the customer cumulative quantity is calculated on the basis of inbound deliveries or goods receipts (*cumulative received quantity*). The customer cumulative quantity can be sent from SAP ERP to SAP SNC with the forecast delivery schedule and made visible to the supplier at the header level of the forecast delivery schedule.

The *supplier cumulative quantity* represents the quantities already sent from the supplier's perspective. The supplier communicates it with the ASN or enters it in the SAP SNC web browser when creating the ASN.

If the customer and supplier cumulative quantities differ (for example, in the event of an overdelivery or underdelivery), the customer and supplier must reach an agreement and synchronize the two cumulative quantities by maintaining an *agreed cumulative quantity* and a reconciliation date at the item level in the forecast delivery schedule.

Alerts in forecast delivery schedule processing

Alerts are another function used to monitor forecast delivery schedule processing. SAP SNC 5.1 provides a range of alert types that inform the customer or supplier of exception situations in forecast delivery schedule processing. Some alert types are only visible for the customer or the supplier. The Alert Monitor in SAP SNC displays the alerts that belong to a given alert type to the respective partner.

Table 4.4 provides an overview of the alert types included in the standard shipment for the forecast delivery release process in SAP SNC 5.1.

Alert Type	Addressee	Description
New forecast delivery schedule	Supplier	A new forecast delivery schedule has been created in SAP SNC with the inbound interface.
Unconfirmed forecast delivery schedule	Supplier, customer	The supplier has not yet confirmed the forecast delivery schedule. The alert is created by report /SCA/RELUNACKNALERTWRITE.
Unloading point has changed	Supplier	The unloading point of the current forecast delivery schedule differs from the unloading point of the predecessor forecast delivery schedule.
Cumulative received quantity is smaller	Supplier	The cumulative received quantity of the current forecast delivery schedule is less than the cumulative received quantity of the predecessor forecast delivery schedule.
Fiscal year has changed	Supplier	The fiscal year of the current forecast delivery schedule differs from the fiscal year of the predecessor forecast delivery schedule.
Scheduling agreement release with a demand that cannot be covered	Supplier, customer	The forecast delivery schedule contains schedule lines that the supplier cannot cover within the lead time. This also takes into account deliveries already sent by the supplier to the customer.
Forecast delivery schedule overdue	Supplier, customer	The forecast delivery schedule contains schedule lines with a due date/time in the past.
Forecast delivery schedule due within the lead time	Supplier, customer	The forecast delivery schedule contains schedule lines in the future that lie within the lead time and have due quantities.
New note for forecast delivery schedule	Supplier, customer	The customer or supplier has entered a note in SAP SNC about a forecast delivery schedule or a confirmation.
Forecast delivery schedule rejected	Customer	The supplier has rejected the forecast delivery schedule in the SAP SNC web browser.
Exception during validation of forecast delivery schedule	Supplier, customer	The system's validation of the forecast delivery schedule identified missing, invalid, or different data.

Table 4.4 Alerts in Forecast Delivery Release Process

Receipts and Requirements List

Receipts and Requirements List

The RECEIPTS AND REQUIREMENTS LIST in SAP SNC offers customers and suppliers an overview of receipt and requirements elements. Published ASNs and delivery confirmations are regarded as receipt elements in forecast delivery schedule processing. Schedule lines of the current forecast delivery schedule are depicted as requirements elements. The receipts and requirements list displays the elements in chronological order as standard (see Figure 4.56).

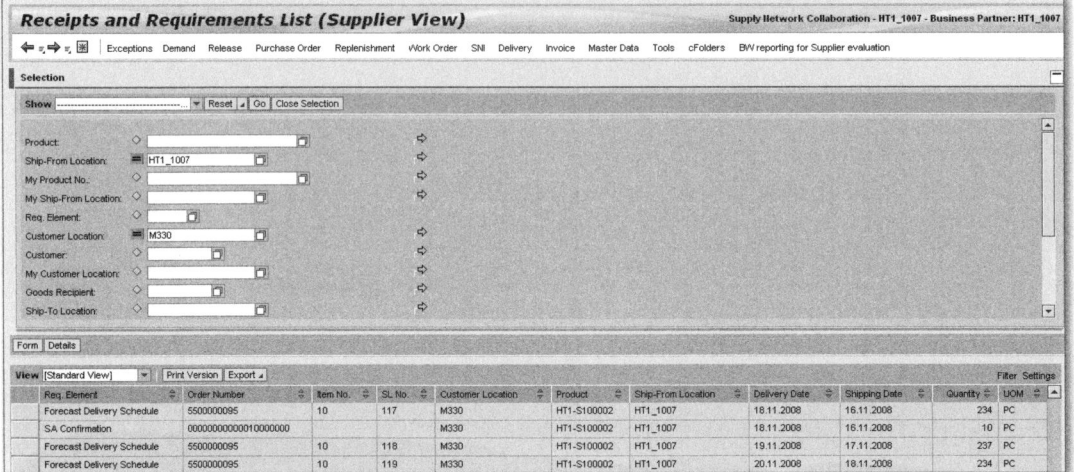

Figure 4.56 Receipts and Requirements List

4.4 Purchase Order Process

This section begins with an overview of the *purchase order process* business process with SAP SNC 5.1. It then takes a closer look at the individual process steps and settings in SAP SNC.

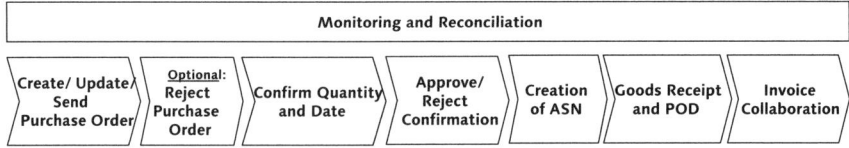

Figure 4.57 Process Flow for Purchase Order Process

4.4.1 Process Overview

The purchase order process is composed of all of the steps from creating a purchase order in the customer's backend system to goods receipt and invoice processing (see Figure 4.57).

Purchase orders can be used both for one-time procurement transactions and for contract release orders based on long-term outline agreements (contracts) with suppliers.

Structure of a purchase order

One of the functions of a purchase order is to inform the supplier of the customer's requested delivery quantities and dates/times for one or more products. For this purpose, the purchase order has a three-level structure: header, item, and schedule line. The purchase order header contains information that is not product specific, but rather applies to the entire purchase order. A purchase order item groups together product-related purchase order information. A schedule line is assigned to a purchase order item and allows the purchase order quantity to be distributed over more than one delivery date/time.

The supplier can reject the entire purchase order or individual purchase order items, or confirm a single purchase order schedule line, in which case the supplier can confirm a delivery date/time and quantity that differ from those requested. If the supplier chooses to confirm different quantities and dates/times for a purchase order schedule line, these can be made subject to an approval process and, if approved, transferred to the purchase order.

The supplier can use an ASN to provide the customer with a binding notification of the delivery quantities that will actually be shipped for one or more products. Information from the ASN is included in the purchase order, and the ASN quantity is offset against the original purchase order quantity.

The goods receipt is posted once the goods have been physically received and put away at the customer's location. A proof of delivery message confirms to the supplier the actual quantity received by the customer. Furthermore, reasons for any quantity differences and the confirmation date can be provided.

Invoice collaboration takes place with reference to either the purchase order or ASN on the basis of conventional invoice processing or self-billing (see Section 4.12 Invoice Collaboration).

Alerts and notes that are visible to the other partner are used to monitor purchase order handling between the customer and supplier.

A new feature of SAP SNC 5.1 is the option to process purchase order confirmations with ease in a worklist view (see Figure 4.58). This function allows the supplier to confirm multiple purchase order schedule lines in one step rather than having to navigate to the Purchase Order Details view for each purchase order.

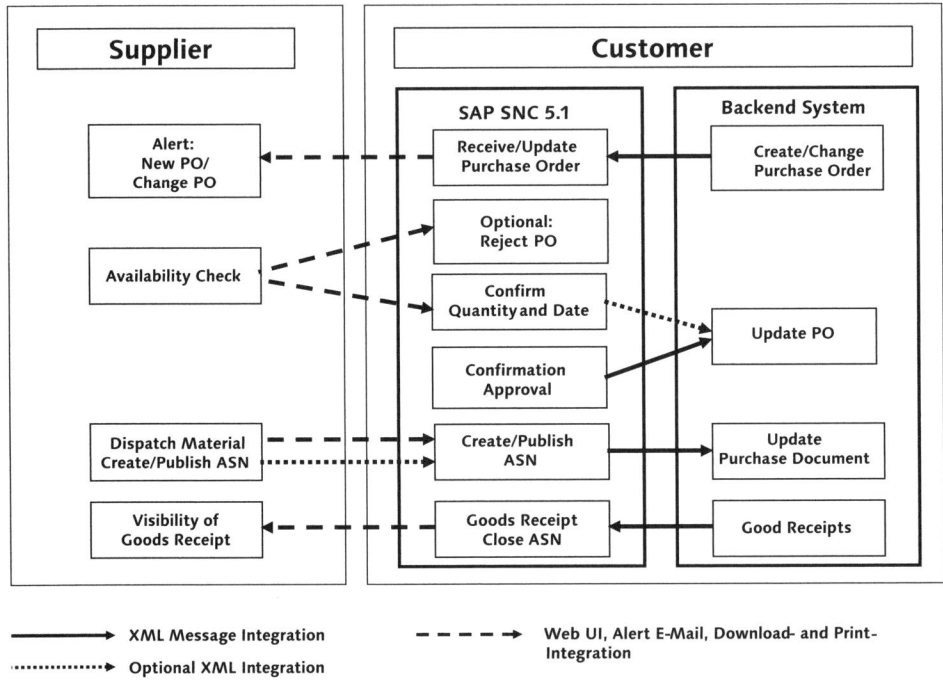

Figure 4.58 Purchase Order Process with SAP SNC 5.1

4.4.2 Master Data Specific to Purchase Order Process

In addition to the generic master data (see Section 4.1 Generic Master Data) for the business processes in SAP SNC, purchase scheduling agreements and contracts should also be maintained in the customer's backend system for the purchase order handling process.

4.4.3 Creating and Sending a Purchase Order

Purchase orders are created from the MRP run or manually in the customer's backend system on the basis of net demands. In SAP systems, differing procurement types are distinguished with purchase order item categories. The following section looks at purchase orders of procurement type normal. Section 4.5 Subcontracting deals with processing purchase orders of procurement type subcontracting in SAP SNC. Message determination and the partner profile must be configured to enable a purchase order to be sent from SAP ERP to SAP SNC.

Purchase order in SAP ERP

A new or modified purchase order is generated from SAP ERP in the form of an IDoc of type ORDERS.ORDERS05 or ORDCHG.ORDERS05 (as of SAP ECC 6.0, also IDoc type PORDCR1.PORDCR102). The IDoc is converted in SAP NetWeaver PI into an XML message of type *Replenishment OrderNotification*, which can be processed as an inbound message by SAP SNC. Once the inbound message has been successfully posted, a new purchase order item alert or changed purchase order item alert is generated. The supplier can be notified of this automatically, for example, by email.

In the SAP SNC web browser, the supplier can navigate from the generated purchase order alert or the purchase order overview to the Purchase Order – Details view. The purchase order overview displays a list of purchase orders that can be selected according to particular selection criteria. The supplier is able to view and, if required, edit purchase order data in the Purchase Order – Details view (see Figure 4.59). Echoing the structure of the purchase order, the Purchase Order – Details view is subdivided into header, item, and schedule line areas.

Purchase order details

Attributes displayed in the header area include payment and delivery conditions, contact data, and status information describing which stage has been reached in purchase order handling. A distinction is made between the header status and distribution status. The header status displays which editing processes have been performed on the purchase order. The system determines the header status as an aggregated status based on the purchase order items (see item status, below).

4 | Business Processes in SAP SNC 5.1

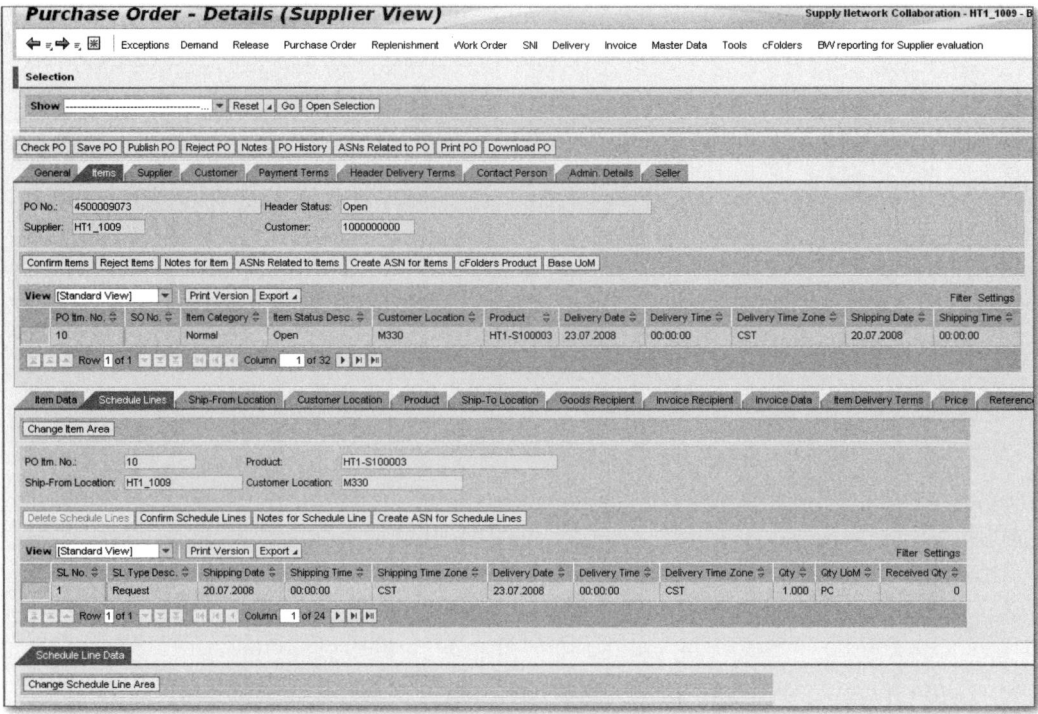

Figure 4.59 Purchase Order Details

Distribution status

The distribution status indicates who last made binding changes to the purchase order and which changes may still be made. The distribution status can have the following values:

- **Updated by customer**
  A purchase order acquires this status if it is created or changed in the customer's backend system and sent to SAP SNC. The supplier can process the purchase order.

- **Published by supplier**
  The supplier has published the purchase order in SAP SNC. The supplier can no longer change the purchase order.

- **Updated by supplier**
  A purchase order acquires this status when the purchase order confirmation is sent from the supplier's backend system to SAP SNC. However, SAP SNC has not yet forwarded the purchase order to the customer backend system. The supplier can publish the purchase order.

4.4 Purchase Order Process

Additional status information provided at the header level is presented with the relevant process steps in purchase order handling (see Figure 4.60).

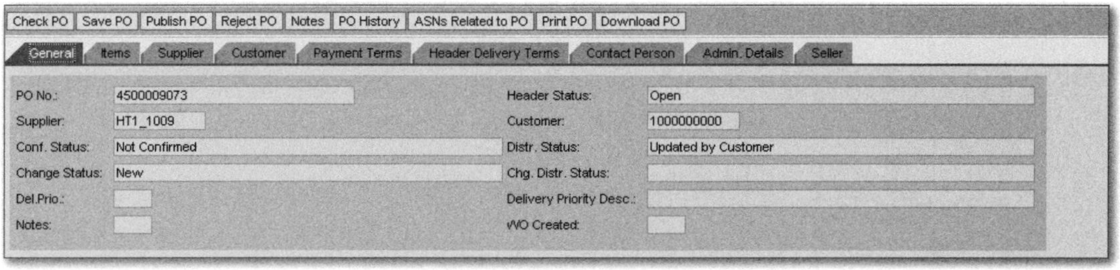

Figure 4.60 Status Information at the Header Level in a Purchase Order

The item area of the Purchase Order Details view provides not only product-related quantities and dates/times, but also tolerance limits for underdeliveries and overdeliveries, price data, billing information, goods and invoice recipients, and the item status. The item status shows which editing processes have been performed on a purchase order item. It can have the following values:

Item status

- **Open**
  A purchase order has been sent from the customer's backend system to SAP SNC, but no further editing steps have been performed on the purchase order item.

- **Partially delivered**
  The supplier has delivered part of the ordered quantity.

- **Delivery completed**
  The supplier has delivered the ordered quantity. If the delivered quantity is below the underdelivery tolerance, the purchase order item acquires this status.

- **Rejected**
  The supplier has rejected the purchase order item.

- **Canceled**
  The purchase order item has been deleted in the customer's backend system.

- **Closed**
  The customer has closed the purchase order in SAP SNC using report /SCA/PO_SET_CLOSED.

- **Blocked**
  The purchase order item has been blocked in the customer's backend system.

The schedule line area in the Purchase Order Details view contains information about the request and confirmation schedule lines in a purchase order item.

4.4.4 Rejecting a Purchase Order

Rejecting a purchase order

If a purchase order is for items that cannot be supplied, the supplier can choose to reject individual purchase order items or the entire purchase order. If the entire purchase order is rejected, SAP SNC sets the purchase order header status to REJECTED and generates a PURCHASE ORDER REJECTED alert to inform the customer of this outcome. All purchase order items acquire the item status REJECTED. If the supplier rejects just one purchase order item, a PURCHASE ORDER ITEM REJECTED alert is created.

The customer can view rejected purchase order items in the purchase order worklist in the SAP SNC web browser. Rejections of purchase orders or purchase order items are not sent to the customer's backend system in SAP SNC 5.1.

4.4.5 Purchase Order Confirmation

Settings for purchase order confirmations

The supplier can confirm the requested quantities and dates/times in the purchase order schedule lines or propose alternatives in SAP SNC. To manage purchase order confirmations, you can define in Customizing for SAP SNC 5.1 (in Transaction SPRO, follow the menu path SUPPLY NETWORK COLLABORATION • DELIVERY • CONFIRMATION CONTROL • SET CONFIRMATION CONTROL) whether purchase order confirmations are mandatory, optional, or not allowed for purchase order schedule lines. You make this definition against a combination of attributes, namely, customer, supplier, customer location, ship-from location, and product.

Purchase order worklist

In the SAP SNC web browser, the supplier can enter purchase order confirmations in the PURCHASE ORDER DETAILS view or the PURCHASE ORDER WORKLIST view (see Figure 4.61). In the PURCHASE ORDER WORKLIST, the supplier can see lists (queries) that group purchase order data according to different criteria. The standard shipment of SAP SNC differentiates between the following groups:

- TO BE CONFIRMED
- TO BE PUBLISHED
- CANCELED/BLOCKED ITEMS

TO BE CONFIRMED displays schedule lines whose requested quantity is not yet completely covered by confirmations. The quantity that is still to be confirmed is displayed in the DUE QTY field.

Figure 4.61 Purchase Order Worklist

As shown in Figure 4.61, the supplier can confirm one or more schedule lines. Confirmations of different quantities can be entered in the CONF. QTY field. To confirm the entire requested quantity, the supplier sets the CCQ (confirm complete quantity) indicator. The supplier can also confirm either the delivery or shipping dates/times. The dates/times that the supplier can confirm depend on the settings made in Customizing for the SAP SNC system (in Transaction SPRO, follow the menu path SUPPLY NETWORK COLLABORATION • DELIVERY • DUE QUANTITY CALCULATION • DETERMINE DUE SCHEDULE LINE QUANTITIES).

After entering the confirmed quantity and/or confirmed date/time, the supplier clicks on the CONFIRM button. The system then creates a confirmation schedule line in the purchase order.

TO BE PUBLISHED shows a list of purchase orders with purchase order items for which the supplier has created confirmation schedule lines but not yet published the purchase orders. Provided an approval process has not been set up, when the supplier publishes the purchase order, an

XML message of type *ReplenishmentOrderConfirmation* is sent from SAP SNC to the customer's backend system. This XML message is converted in SAP NetWeaver PI into an IDoc of type ORDRSP.ORDERS05, which can be processed by SAP ERP.

CANCELED/BLOCKED ITEMS shows a list of purchase order items that have been canceled or blocked in the customer's backend system.

It is possible to define and apply further user-specific queries in the PURCHASE ORDER WORKLIST.

4.4.6 Approving the Purchase Order Confirmation

Approval process

The confirmation schedule lines that the supplier enters for a purchase order item may differ from the request schedule lines in terms of quantities and dates/times. Deviating confirmation schedule lines can be accepted automatically in SAP SNC. Alternatively, an approval process can be set up so that the customer is required to verify and approve deviating confirmation quantities manually in the SNC Web browser. The standard shipment of SAP SNC 5.1 does not have an approval process set up.

The following two types of approval process are distinguished:

- Approval process without tolerances
- Approval process based on consensus finding

Approval Process Without Tolerances

In this approval process, you define how you want SAP SNC to react to deviating confirmation schedule lines. If the confirmation schedule line does not deviate from the request schedule line, the system sets the approval status of the confirmation schedule line to ACCEPTED. Against a combination of attributes—customer, supplier, and product—the system can control whether the approval status is set to ACCEPTED or MANUAL APPROVAL REQUIRED.

Settings for the approval process

To this end, an approval profile is assigned to the combination of attributes customer, supplier, and product in SAP SNC (in Transaction SPRO, follow the menu path SUPPLY NETWORK COLLABORATION • PURCHASE ORDER • APPROVAL PROCESS • APPROVAL PROCESS WITHOUT TOLERANCES •

ASSIGN APPROVAL PROFILES). In the approval profile (in Transaction SPRO, follow the menu path SUPPLY NETWORK COLLABORATION • PURCHASE ORDER • APPROVAL PROCESS • APPROVAL PROCESS WITHOUT TOLERANCES • CREATE APPROVAL PROCESSES), you define whether deviating confirmation schedule lines are approved automatically or require manual approval (see Figure 4.62).

If the approval status has been set to MANUAL APPROVAL REQUIRED, the customer can verify and accept or reject the confirmation schedule line as appropriate in the SAP SNC web browser. If the customer accepts the confirmation schedule line, the system can transfer the approved confirmation data to the purchase order as request data. The customer can publish the purchase order to send the updated request data it contains to the customer's backend system. If the customer rejects the confirmation schedule line, the approval status is set to REJECTED at confirmation schedule line level and purchase order item level, and a CONFIRMATION REJECTED alert is created for the supplier.

Approval status

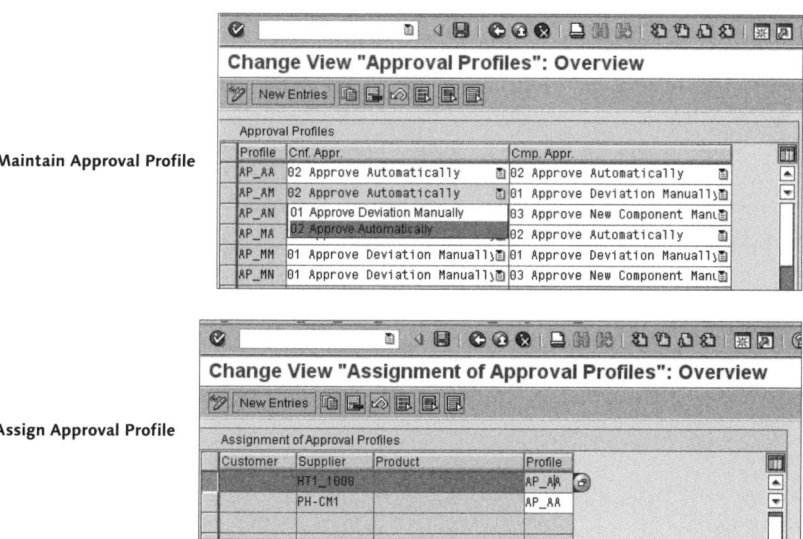

Maintain Approval Profile

Assign Approval Profile

Figure 4.62 Approval Process Without Tolerances

Approval Process Based on Consensus Finding

In this approval process, SAP SNC takes the deviation analysis from *consensus finding* and *condition technique* as the basis for the decision as to

Consensus finding and condition technique

whether quantity and date/time deviations in the confirmation schedule line are accepted automatically or require manual approval (in Transaction SPRO, follow the menu path SUPPLY NETWORK COLLABORATION • BASIC SETTINGS • CONSENSUS FINDING). Quantity tolerances and date/time tolerances are taken into account. If available, underdelivery and overdelivery tolerances in the purchase order item are taken as the quantity tolerances. If the purchase order item does not have underdelivery and overdelivery tolerances, a corresponding QUANTITY PROFILE can be taken into account in consensus finding. Date/time tolerances are mapped in consensus finding using a time profile (in Transaction SPRO, follow the menu path SUPPLY NETWORK COLLABORATION • BASIC SETTINGS • CONSENSUS FINDING • CONSENSUS PROFILES).

In condition technique for consensus finding, determination procedures can be assigned to quantity and time profiles on a customer-specific and supplier-specific basis (in Transaction SPRO, follow the menu path SUPPLY NETWORK COLLABORATION • BASIC SETTINGS • CONSENSUS FINDING • CONDITION TECHNIQUE FOR CONSENSUS FINDING).

SAP SNC approves confirmation schedule lines within the tolerances automatically and sets the approval status to ACCEPTED. Confirmation schedule lines with deviations outside the tolerances acquire approval status MANUAL APPROVAL REQUIRED.

The approval process can be used with a customer backend system with SAP ERP 6.0 or higher. Special IDocs are required for receiving and sending purchase orders (PORDCH.PORDCH02, and PORDCR1. PORDCR102).

4.4.7 Creating and Publishing an ASN

The supplier can use an ASN to inform the customer of an upcoming delivery for a purchase order item. The ASN can be created manually in the SAP SNC web browser or sent from the supplier's backend system to SAP SNC. When the ASN is published in SAP SNC, a new purchase order schedule line of type ASN-Confirmed is created, and the ASN is sent to the customer's backend system. To achieve this, an XML message of type *DispatchDeliveryNotification* is created in SAP SNC and converted into an

IDoc of type DESADV.DELVRY03 in SAP NetWeaver PI. In SAP ERP, an inbound delivery is created on the basis of the ASN.

In SAP SNC, it is possible to define whether ASNs are mandatory, optional, or not allowed for a purchase order item (in Transaction SPRO, follow the menu path SUPPLY NETWORK COLLABORATION • DELIVERY • CONFIRMATION CONTROL • SET CONFIRMATION CONTROL). This definition is made against a combination of attributes, namely, customer, supplier, customer location, ship-from location, and product.

Furthermore, in SAP SNC 5.1, it is not possible to create ASNs for purchase order items with item status REJECTED, CANCELED, CLOSED, or BLOCKED.

In the SAP SNC web browser, the supplier can create ASNs for a purchase order item directly from the PURCHASE ORDER DETAILS view or from the due list for purchasing documents.

Within PURCHASE ORDER HANDLING, the due list for purchasing documents shows the ASN-based due purchase order schedule lines. A purchase order schedule line counts as due when the schedule line quantity is not completely covered by ASNs. To determine due purchase order schedule lines, the system assigns purchase order schedule lines with ASNs that relate to the purchase order item. Only ASNs with status PUBLISHED, GOODS RECEIPT COMPLETE, or GOODS RECEIPT PARTIAL are taken into account.

4.4.8 Goods Receipt and Proof of Delivery

Goods receipt in SAP ERP can take place with reference to the inbound delivery or the purchase order item. Once the customer has entered the quantity actually received and posted the goods receipt, a proof of delivery can be generated from SAP ERP in the form of an IDoc of type STPPOD.DELVRY03. The IDoc is converted into an XML message of type *ReceivedDeliveryNotification* in SAP NetWeaver PI and sent to SAP SNC.

A proof of delivery allows the supplier to establish whether the goods arrived at the customer in full or only in part. To this end, the status of the ASN is set to GOODS RECEIPT COMPLETE or GOODS RECEIPT PARTIAL in

SAP SNC, and the actual quantity received is shown in the ASN. This also prompts the item status of the purchase order item—taking into account delivery tolerances—to be set to PARTIALLY DELIVERED or DELIVERY COMPLETED as appropriate.

4.4.9 Monitoring Purchase Order Process

Purchase order history

The *purchase order history* in SAP SNC provides a way to document all changes made to a purchase order by the customer or supplier. In the SAP SNC web browser, different versions of a purchase order can be viewed and compared in the purchase order history. This makes it possible to track changes in the status of a purchase order or purchase order item, for example.

In addition, the customer and supplier are each able to enter notes that the other can see at the header, item, and schedule line levels in a purchase order.

Moreover, the standard shipment of SAP SNC comes with a range of alerts that are generated and addressed to the customer and supplier if predefined situations arise in the course of purchase order handling (see Table 4.5).

Alert Type	Addressee	Description
New purchase order item	Supplier	A purchase order containing a new purchase order item has been sent from the customer's backend system to SAP SNC.
Changed purchase order item	Supplier	A purchase order containing a changed purchase order item has been sent from the customer's backend system to SAP SNC.
Partially confirmed purchase order item	Customer	The total confirmed quantity for a purchase order item is less than the total requested quantity of the purchase order item minus the underdelivery tolerance.

Table 4.5 Alerts in Purchase Order Process

Alert Type	Addressee	Description
Late confirmation of purchase order item	Customer, supplier	The confirmed delivery date/time of at least one confirmation schedule line is after the customer's requested delivery date/time.
Manual approval of confirmation required	Customer	The customer's manual approval of the purchase order confirmation is required as part of the approval process.
Confirmation rejected	Supplier	The customer has manually rejected the purchase order confirmation in the approval process.
Purchase order rejected	Customer	The supplier has rejected the purchase order manually.
Purchase order item rejected	Customer	The supplier has rejected the purchase order item manually.
Overdelivery tolerance exceeded	Customer, supplier	The quantity of the purchase order item confirmed by the supplier is greater than the total requested quantity of the purchase order item plus the overdelivery tolerance.
Underdelivery tolerance not reached	Customer, supplier	The quantity of the purchase order item confirmed by the supplier is less than the total requested quantity of the purchase order item minus the underdelivery tolerance.
New note for purchase order	Customer, supplier	The customer or supplier has created a new note for a purchase order or purchase order confirmation.
Purchase order overdue	Customer, supplier	The purchase order contains due schedule lines in the past.
Purchase order due within lead time	Customer, supplier	The purchase order contains schedule lines that lie within the lead time and have due quantities.
Exception during validation of purchase order	Customer	The validation check performed on the purchase order in SAP SNC identified a problem.

Table 4.5 Alerts in Purchase Order Process (Cont.)

4.5 Subcontracting

This section opens with an overview of the *subcontracting* business process with SAP SNC 5.1. It then takes a closer look at the individual process steps and settings in SAP SNC.

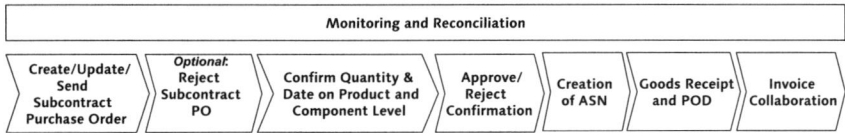

Figure 4.63 Process Flow for Subcontracting

4.5.1 Process Overview

In the subcontracting process, the supplier (subcontractor) is provided with components (subcontracting components) required to produce the product ordered. The subcontracting components may be provided to the subcontractor directly by the customer or by a third-party supplier.

Subcontract order

In SAP SNC 5.1, subcontracting is a variant of purchase order handling. It covers all of the steps in the process, from creation of the subcontract order in the customer's backend system and confirmation of component consumption by the subcontractor to goods receipt and invoice processing at the customer (see Figure 4.63).

In addition to information about the ordered product, a subcontract order also contains details of the components and quantities to be provided. Once the subcontract order has been sent, the customer can deliver the components directly to the subcontractor or arrange for delivery from a third-party supplier. Just like in the purchase order handling process, the subcontractor is able to reject the entire purchase order or individual purchase order items. Purchase order schedule lines can be confirmed with different quantities and dates/times. Furthermore, the subcontractor can confirm the actual component requirements for a confirmation schedule line, which may differ from the customer's expectations.

The subcontractor's confirmations at the product and component level can be made subject to an approval process. If approved, the confirmation data is transferred to the purchase order as request data.

The other subcontracting subprocesses, such as ASN creation, goods receipt processing, and invoice processing, are covered to a large extent by the purchase order handling subprocesses and are therefore not examined in closer detail here (see Section 4.4 Purchase Order Handling).

Figure 4.64 provides a diagram of the information flow that takes place in subcontracting with SAP SNC 5.1.

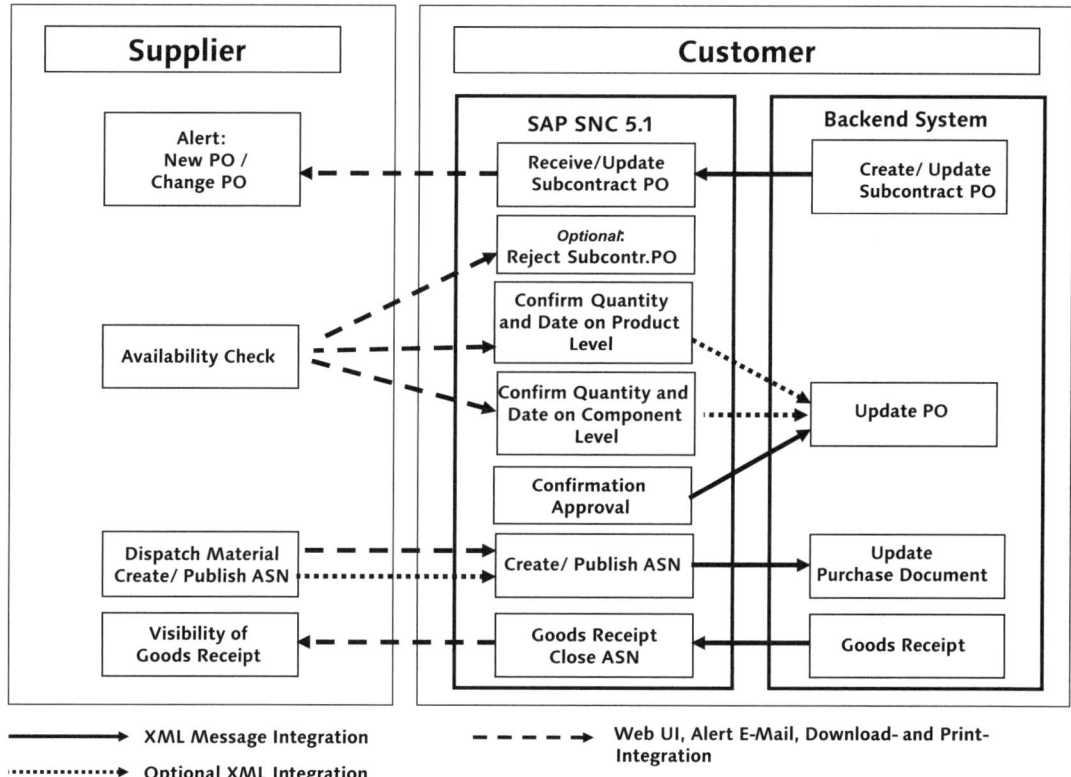

Figure 4.64 Subcontracting with SAP SNC 5.1

4.5.2 Master Data Specific to Subcontracting

In addition to the generic master data (see Section 4.1 Generic Master Data) for the business processes in SAP SNC, subcontracting purchasing info records and contracts with subcontracting items and bills of material should also be maintained in the customer's backend system for the subcontracting process.

4 | Business Processes in SAP SNC 5.1

4.5.3 Creating and Sending a Subcontract Order

Subcontract order in SAP ERP

Subcontract orders are created in the customer's backend system on the basis of net demands from the MRP run or manually. In an SAP ERP system, subcontract order items are assigned to item type L. The components that the supplier needs to manufacture the ordered product are specified in the purchase order. This is achieved by referencing the components stored in the bill of material for the ordered product when the order is created. Message determination and the partner profile must be configured to enable a contract order to be sent from SAP ERP to SAP SNC. Subcontract orders are sent as IDocs of type PORDCR1. PORDCR102 (as of SAP ECC 6.0), converted into XML messages of type *ReplenishmentOrderNotification* in SAP NetWeaver PI, and sent on to SAP SNC.

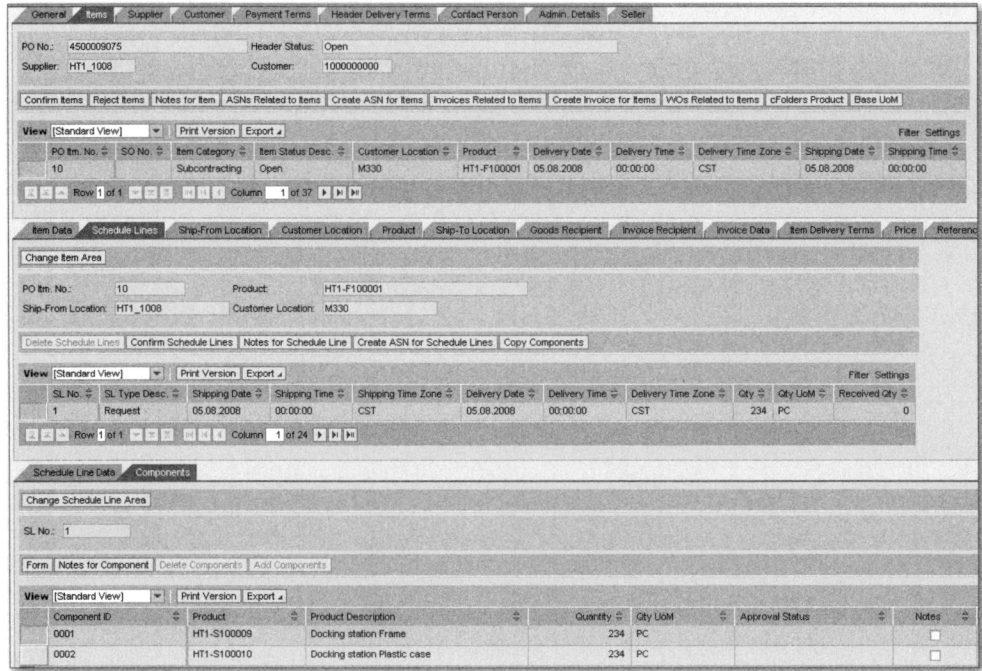

Figure 4.65 Purchase Order Details with Subcontracting Components

Similar to the purchase order handling process, the subcontractor can navigate to the Purchase Order Details view in the SAP SNC web browser from order alerts or the purchase order overview. In addition to purchase order data about the product, the details view shows the customer's expected component requirements for the purchase order schedule line (see Figure 4.65).

The components provided to the subcontractor are managed in the customer's backend system in the *stock of material provided to vendor*. These stocks of material can be monitored in SAP ERP in Transaction ME2O. The following information is displayed for subcontracting components:

Stock of material provided to vendor

- Current stock situation
- Planned receipts
- Planned issues

Furthermore, it is also possible to provide components to the subcontractor for existing orders here. This can be done by posting a goods receipt directly or by creating a delivery. The advantage of delivering subcontracting components to the subcontractor by means of shipping is that the customer then has shipping documents and delivery notes.

4.5.4 Rejecting a Subcontract Order

The supplier can reject a single subcontract order item or the entire subcontract order (see also Section 4.4.4 Rejecting a Purchase Order).

4.5.5 Purchase Order Confirmation

As in purchase order handling, the subcontractor can confirm a purchase order schedule line or propose different delivery quantities and delivery dates/times. The subcontracting process also allows the supplier to confirm component requirements with differences in the SNC web browser; the subcontractor can add further components that were not included in the component requirements communicated by the customer.

The actual component requirements are entered with reference to the confirmation schedule line (see Figure 4.66). First, the component requirements from the request schedule line are copied to the confirmation schedule line (see Figure 4.67). Next, the CHANGE SCHEDULE LINE AREA function can be used to make changes to component quantities or

Actual component requirement

enter new components. The contractor can send messages to the customer for each component using the note function.

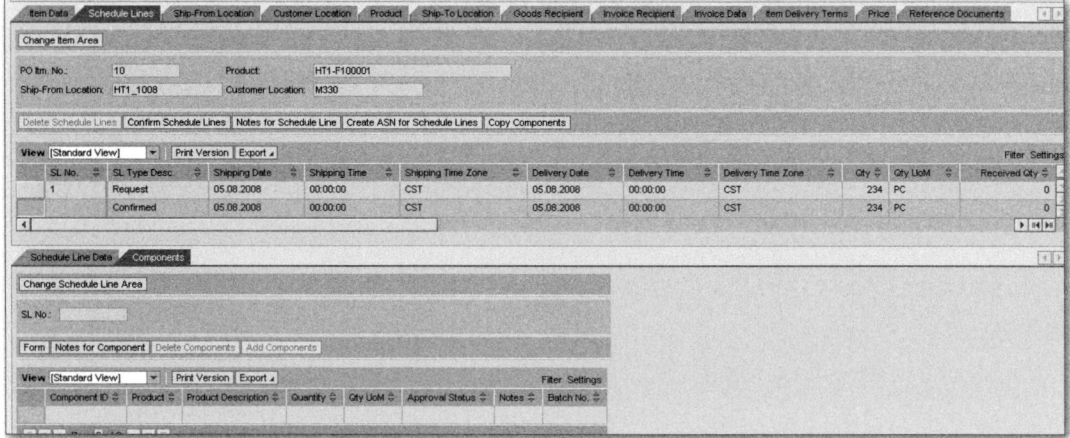

Figure 4.66 Confirmation Schedule Line Without Components

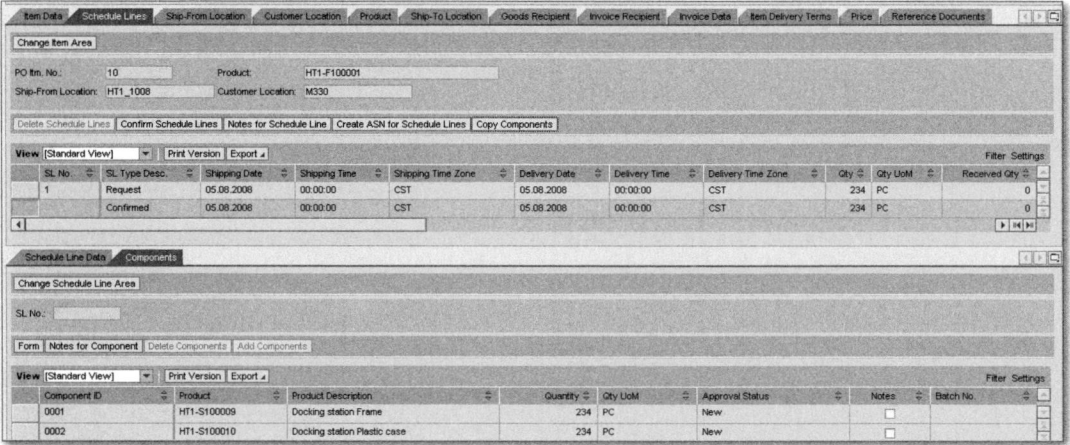

Figure 4.67 Confirmation Schedule Line with Components

When the subcontractor publishes a subcontract order, an XML message of type *ReplenishmentOrderConfirmation* is sent from SAP SNC to the customer's backend system, provided an approval process has not been implemented. This XML message is converted in SAP NetWeaver PI into an IDoc of type PORDCH.PORDCH02 (as of SAP ECC 6.0), which can be processed by SAP ERP.

4.5.6 Approving the Purchase Order Confirmation

Confirmation schedule lines and component confirmations for a subcontract order can be made subject to an approval process in SAP SNC 5.1. The approval process for confirmation schedule lines is described in this section.

In SAP SNC, using a combination of attributes—customer, supplier, and product—it is possible to define the way in which component confirmations are approved. The attribute combination is assigned to an approval profile. One of the following three options can be selected in the approval profile:

Approval of component confirmations

- **Approve deviations manually**
  If the component consumption confirmed by the subcontractor deviates from the customer's expectation or if the subcontractor has added new components, the system sets the component confirmation approval status to MANUAL APPROVAL REQUIRED. The customer is required to approve the component confirmation in the SAP SNC web browser.
- **Approve automatically**
  If this option is selected, the system approves the component confirmations automatically.
- **Approve new components manually**
  Component confirmations for components added by the subcontractor acquire approval status MANUAL APPROVAL REQUIRED.

4.5.7 Monitoring Subcontract Order Processing

The same functions as can be used to monitor purchase order handling can also be used for subcontract order processing. Additionally, SAP SNC has alerts that are particular to subcontracting. These are described in Table 4.6.

Alert Type	Addressee	Description
Manual approval of component requirement required	Customer	The component requirement confirmed by the supplier must be approved manually by the customer in SAP SNC.
Component requirement rejected	Supplier	The component requirement confirmed by the supplier has been rejected by the customer in SAP SNC.

Table 4.6 Subcontracting Alerts

4.6 Supply Network Inventory

This section begins with an overview of the *Supply Network Inventory* business process with SAP SNC 5.1 (see Figure 4.68). It then takes a closer look at the individual process steps and settings in SAP SNC.

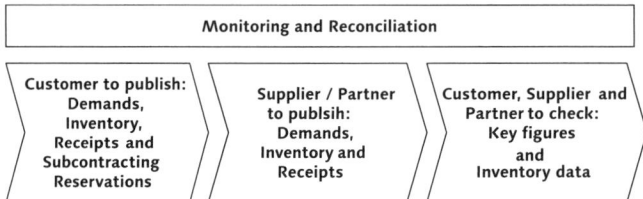

Figure 4.68 Process Flow for Supply Network Inventory

4.6.1 Process Overview

The aim of the Supply Network Inventory (SNI) business scenario in SAP SNC 5.1 is to support customers, subcontractors, suppliers of the first level and up (suppliers of the supplier), and other partners (for example, third-party logistics providers) in monitoring the stock and requirements situation of products at selected locations in the supply chain.

For selected products, the following data is extracted from the customer's backend system and sent to SAP SNC: current stock, subcontracting reservations, receipts, and requirements in a particular period. In addition, in SAP SNC 5.1, it is possible to receive and process up-to-date stock, requirements, and receipts data from the backend systems of the associated suppliers and partners.

In the *SNI Monitor* in the SAP SNC web browser, data is prepared and displayed in a view based on time buckets and time series. The projected stock is calculated for each time bucket.

The projected stock and actual stock on hand are compared with the minimum and maximum stock levels agreed upon by customer and supplier for a location product. If the threshold values are not reached or are exceeded, alerts are generated.

Supply Network Inventory offers improved visibility of stock at different stages in the supply chain. In the subcontracting process, the SNI Monitor offers both the customer and the supplier a single view of the stock situation for the most important components, which means they can quickly obtain an overview of critical stock situations. Furthermore, the customer can simulate the effects that changes to receipts would have on the projected stock for components.

Improved visibility

Figure 4.69 shows the process flow for the Supply Network Inventory.

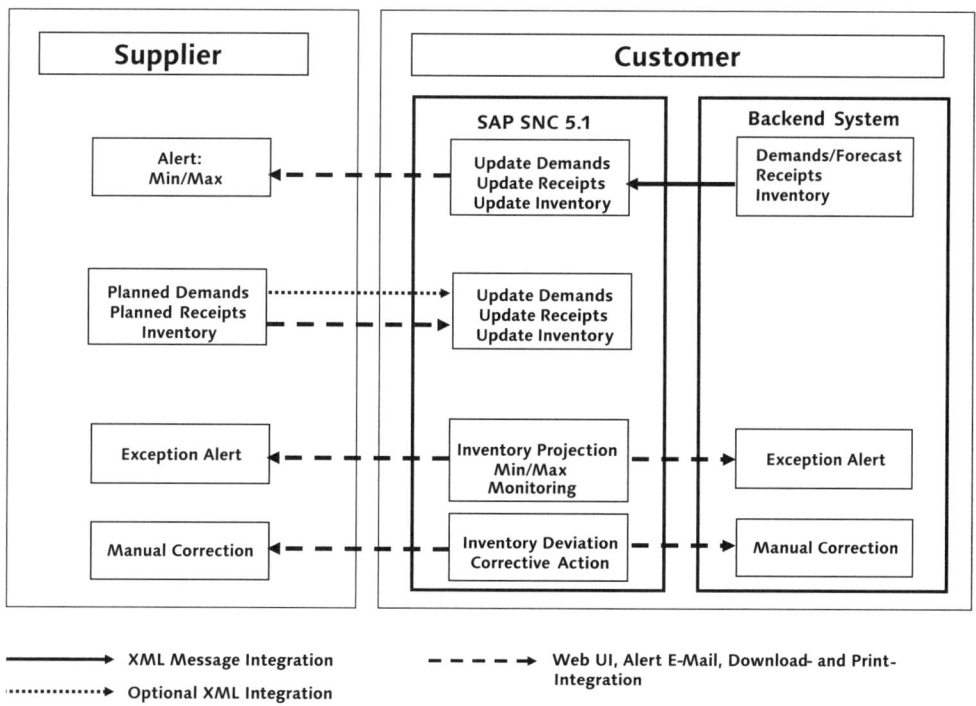

Figure 4.69 Supply Network Inventory with SAP SNC 5.1

4.6.2 Master Data Specific to SNI

SNI-specific master data has a particular bearing on location products and their visibility in the SNI Monitor.

Location Product

Location product master data

To show stock and requirements for a product in the different locations along the supply chain, the following master data is required:

- Location product at the customer's location
- Location product at the supplier's location
- Location product at the third-party logistics provider's location

In addition, the following planning parameters should be stored in the location product master to help identify critical stock situations (in the SAP menu, follow the menu path SUPPLY NETWORK COLLABORATION • MASTER DATA • PRODUCT • PRODUCT; Lot Size tab page):

- Minimum and maximum stock levels as static stock limit values
- Minimum and maximum days' supply for dynamic calculation of the minimum and maximum stock levels (see Figure 4.70)

Scenario control in the location product master can be used to define whether the location product is displayed in the SNI Monitor.

Visibility Concept

Visibility control

A visibility concept based on profiles and parameters is used in SAP SNC to control the visibility of stock data and key figures for location products in the SNI Monitor for the different business partners and users. For this purpose, selection mode *TSDM_INV_C* has been configured in the standard shipment of the SAP SNC system, which enables profile-based visibility control in the SNI Monitor (see Figure 4.71 and Transaction SPRO (follow the menu path SUPPLY NETWORK COLLABORATION • BASIC SETTINGS • VISIBILITY • DISPLAY SAP DEFAULT SELECTION MODES OF APPLICATION).

Supply Network Inventory | 4.6

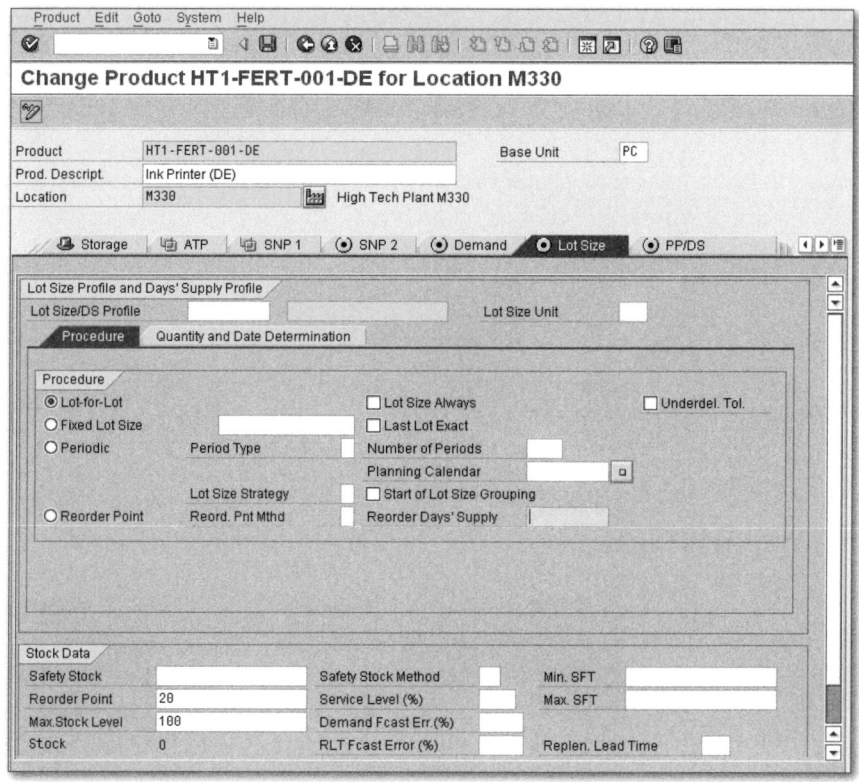

Figure 4.70 Location Product Master

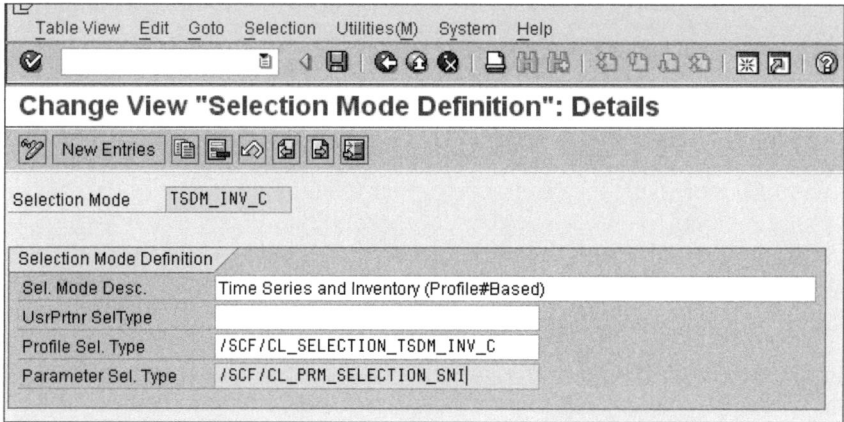

Figure 4.71 SNI Selection Mode

125

On the basis of the default selection mode, one or more visibility control profiles can be assigned to a user or business partner.

In a visibility control profile, visibility can be restricted by selecting location products and other parameters (in the SAP menu, follow the menu path SUPPLY NETWORK COLLABORATION • MASTER DATA • VISIBILITY • MAINTAIN AND ASSIGN VISIBILITY CONTROL PROFILES). For instance, you can restrict the location product selection by location, product, supplier, and ship-from location. In addition, the following parameters can be used to make stock data and key figures visible for data that belongs to stock owners, data-providing partners, assigned partners, and assigned locations:

- **Stock owner**
  The stock owner is the business partner to whom the stock belongs.

- **Data-providing partner**
  This is the business partner that provided stock data and key figures by sending an XML message from his backend system to SAP SNC.

- **Assigned partner, assigned location**
  This is the customer location or business partner to whose supply chain the data displayed belongs. This parameter is only relevant if SAP SNC is used with multiple customers and a supplier is able to deliver to multiple customers or customer locations. The assigned partner is the customer to whom the stock data and key figures relate. This makes it possible to differentiate between the data of several customers, even if they keep different customers' products in the same location (for example, in the third-party logistics location) (see Figure 4.72).

User assignment — Visibility control profiles can be assigned to a user or business partner in SAP SNC for a particular period of time (see Figure 4.73). In addition, it is also possible to specify when making the assignment whether the visibility control profiles should be restricted to particular SNI applications. SNI applications such as the SNI Monitor, SNI Audit Trail, or change history, represent SNI functions in the SAP SNC web browser.

Supply Network Inventory | 4.6

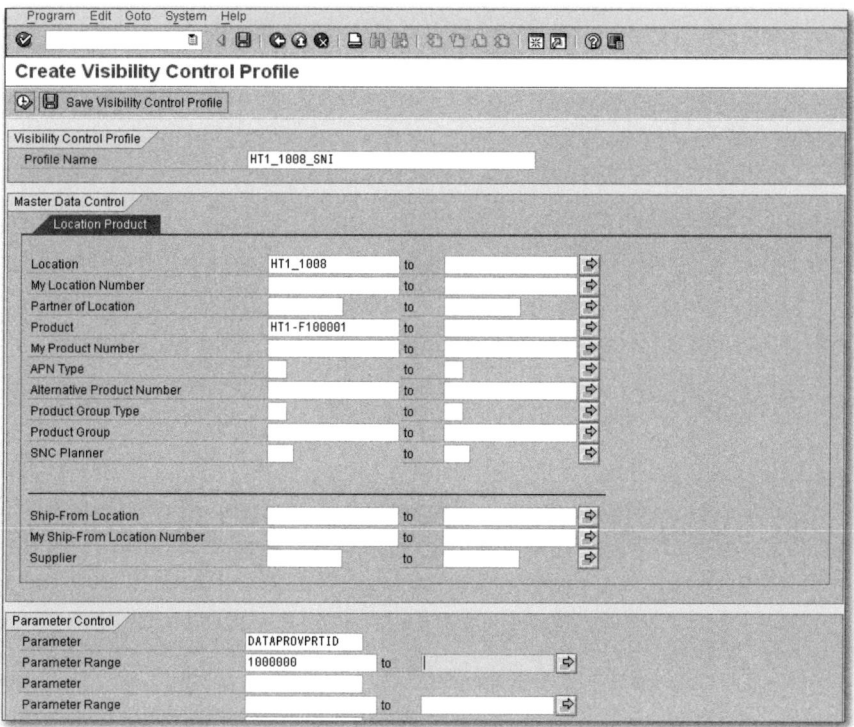

Figure 4.72 Creating a Visibility Profile

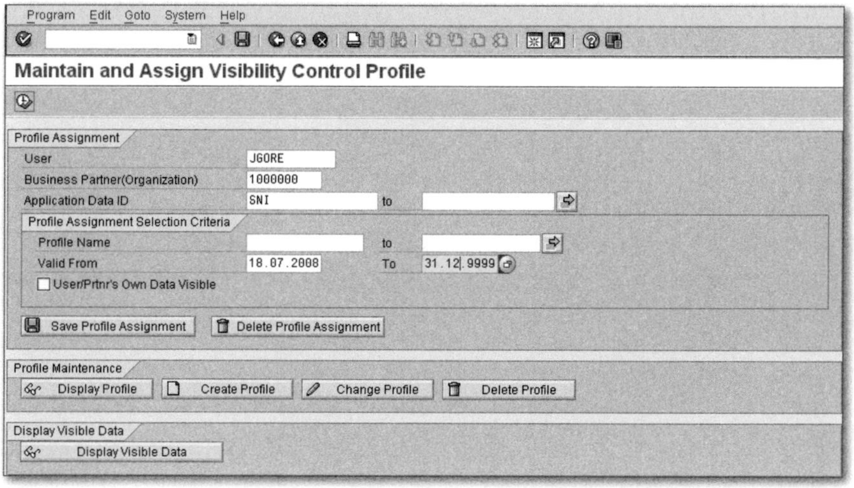

Figure 4.73 Assigning Visibility Profiles

It is possible to create an overview of data visible to a user or business partner in SAP SNC (in the SAP menu, follow the menu path SUPPLY NETWORK COLLABORATION • MASTER DATA • VISIBILITY • DISPLAY DATA VISIBILITY).

4.6.3 Integrating Customer Data

Data must be sent from the customer's backend system to SAP SNC to enable stock data and key figures to be prepared and displayed. The standard SAP ERP shipment provides reports for extracting data.

Up to SAP ECC 6.0, you can use the ROEMPROACT and RCMPROACT reports. As of SAP ECC 6.0 Enhancement Package 2, three new reports are provided, namely, ROEMPROACT2, RCMPROACT2, and RPRTPROACT. These new reports allow for a more detailed breakdown of requirements and make it possible to extract *consignment stock* and the *in-transit* key figure. In addition, data extracted with the new reports is generated from SAP ERP as an XML message of type *ProductActivityNotification* and sent to SAP SNC.

The following section describes the data that can be extracted from SAP ERP using the new reports.

Report ROEMPROACT2 is used to extract and send data for customer-specific products in customer-specific plants for a particular period. Figure 4.74 shows the relevant master data selection parameters.

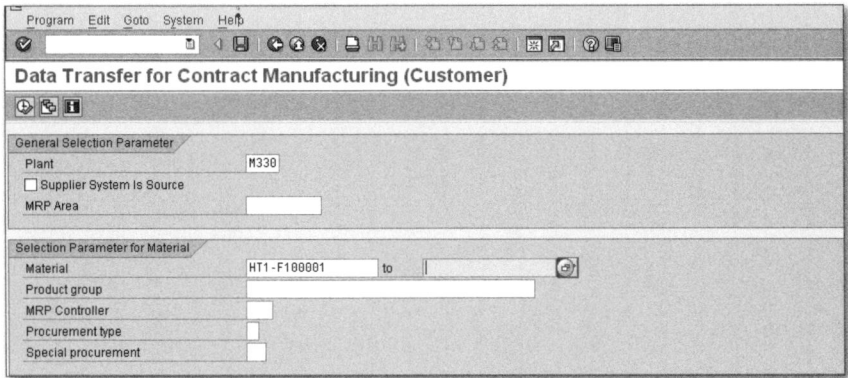

Figure 4.74 *Master Data Selection Parameters (ROEMPROACT2)*

In terms of stock data, you can extract data about your own stock, consignment stock of types UNRESTRICTED-USE STOCK and BLOCKED STOCK, and STOCK IN QUALITY INSPECTION (see Figure 4.75).

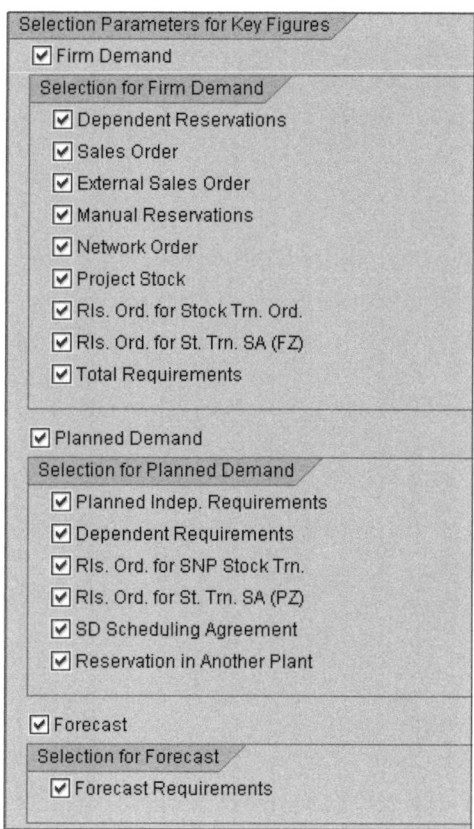

Figure 4.75 Selection Parameters for Stock Data (ROEMPROACT2)

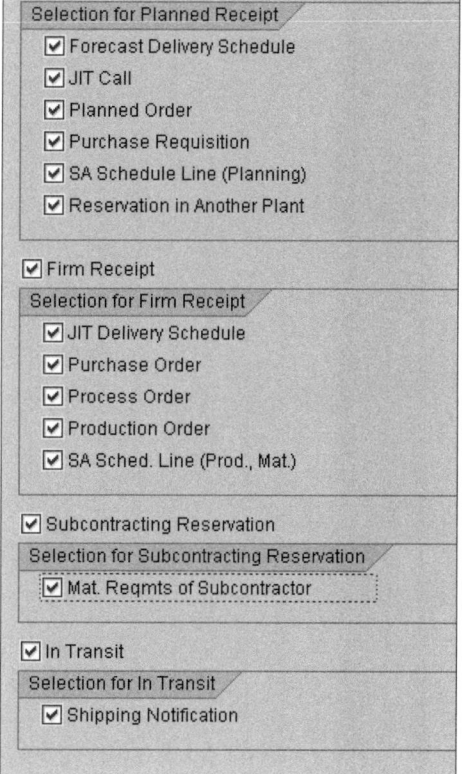

Figure 4.76 Selection Parameters for Key Figures (ROEMPROACT2)

Furthermore, you can define which MRP elements are used to determine key figures for demand and receipts. Figure 4.76 lists the MRP elements that are available for selection. The MRP elements you select are grouped together in accordance with the SAP SNC web browser display, namely, in the following categories: FIRM DEMAND, PLANNED DEMAND, FIRM RECEIPT, PLANNED RECEIPT, IN TRANSIT, FORECAST, and SUBCONTRACTING RESERVATION. In addition, you can restrict your key figure selection to a specific period.

Report RCMPROACT2

Report RCMPROACT2 is used to extract and send data for products in the supplier's plants from the customer's own SAP ERP system for a particular period. Figure 4.77 shows the relevant selection parameters in terms of master data. This report allows you to restrict your selection not only to the PLANT, but also to an MRP AREA and VENDOR.

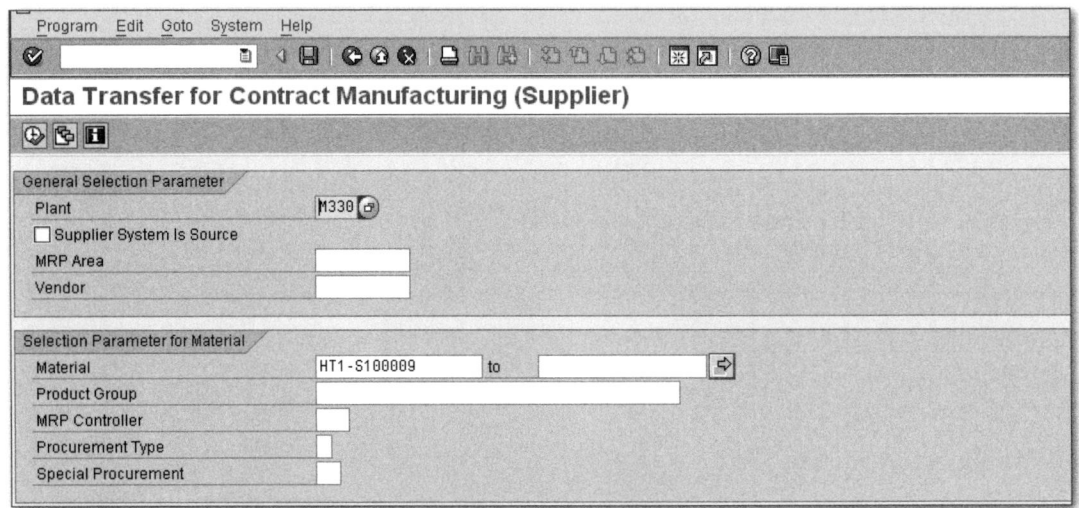

Figure 4.77 Master Data Selection Parameters (RCMPROACT2)

In addition, you can define which MRP elements are taken into account when determining stock data and key figures (see Figure 4.78). For instance, with RCMPROACT2 it is possible to determine the stock of components provided to the supplier as part of subcontract order processing and send this data to SAP SNC.

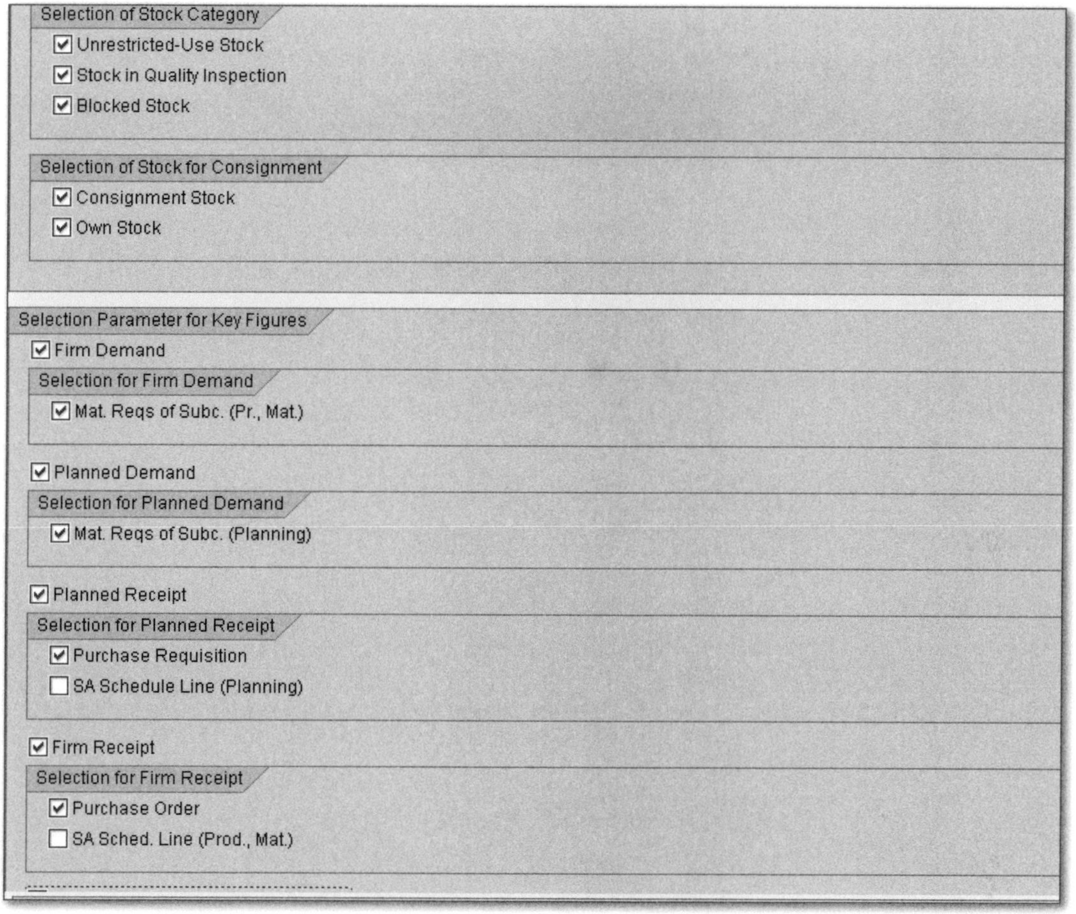

Figure 4.78 Selection Parameters for Stock and Key Figures (RCMPROACT2)

Report RPRTPROACT can be used when stockholding plants that physically belong to another partner in the supply chain (for example, a third-party logistics provider) are modeled in the customer's own SAP ERP system. Using this report, stock data and key figures about products in the aforementioned plants can be extracted and sent to SAP SNC. Figure 4.79 shows the selection parameters for RPRTPROACT.

Report RPRTPROACT

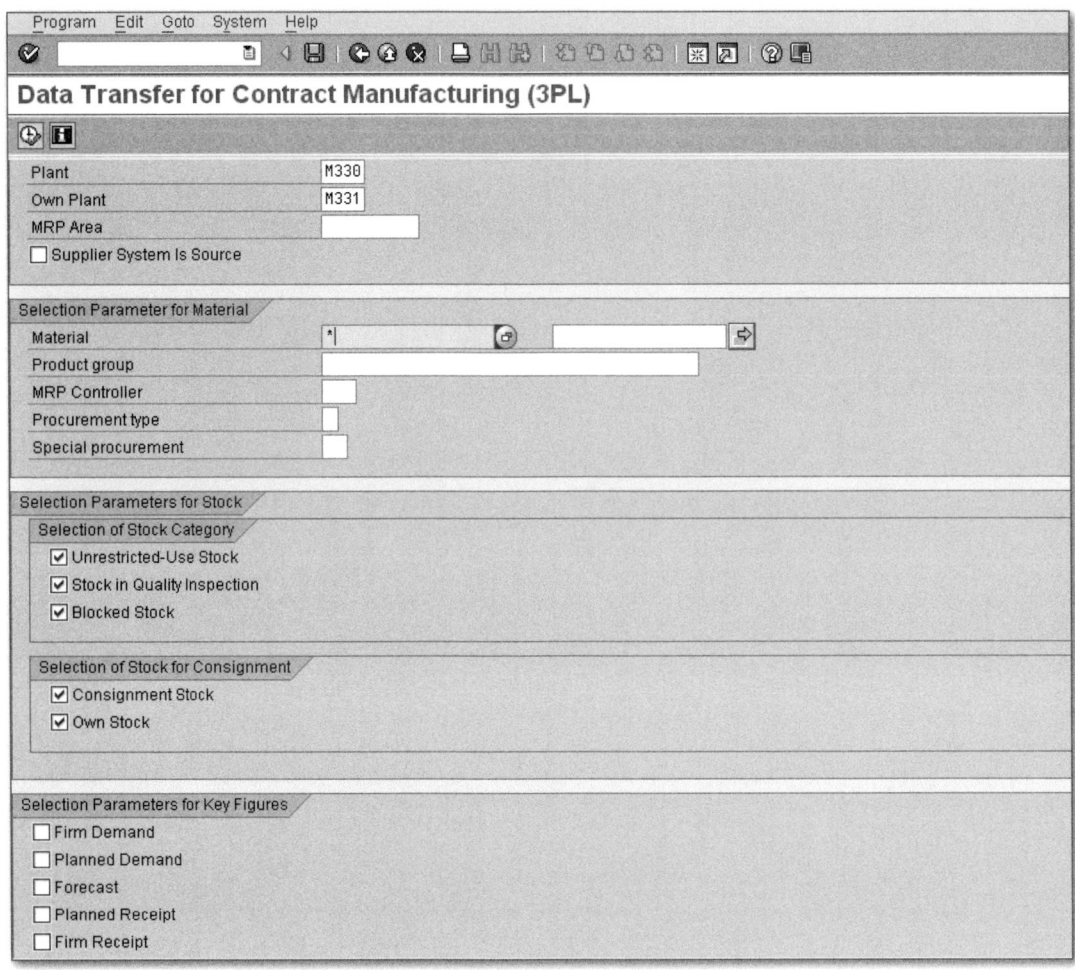

Figure 4.79 Selection Parameters (RPRTPROACT)

4.6.4 Integrating Supplier and Partner Data

Supplier and partner data integration

Suppliers and other partners in the supply chain (for example, third-party logistics providers) can send stock data and key figures from their backend systems to SAP SNC. In the standard SAP SNC shipment, XML messages of type *ProductActivityNotification* can be processed by the inbound interface for this purpose.

Suppliers and partners that have an SAP ERP system with SAP ECC 6.0 Enhancement Package 2 can use reports ROEMPROACT2, RCMPRO-ACT2, and RPRTPROACT to determine and send data to SAP SNC.

In this case, the SUPPLIER SYSTEM IS SOURCE indicator must be set in the general selection parameters for the reports (see Figures 4.74, 4.77, and 4.79). Once this indicator has been set, the business partner numbers of the message sender (supplier), recipient (customer), and supplier can be specified in SAP SNC so that data can be assigned correctly.

Using report ROEMPROACT2, suppliers can determine and send stock data and key figures relating to their own products and plants. Similarly, reports RCMPROACT2 and RPRTPROACT enable suppliers to extract stock data and key figures of their own suppliers (suppliers of the supplier) and partners stored in their SAP ERP system.

In addition to the option of sending stock data and key figures from the backend systems of the supplier and partner, it is also possible to edit requirements and receipts manually under SNI DETAILS or SNI DETAILS – PRODUCT VIEW in the SAP SNC web browser.

4.6.5 Verifying Key Figures and Stock

The SNI Monitor in the SAP SNC system prepares stock data and key figures for location products and displays these in different views. Customers, suppliers, and partners can view this data in the SAP SNC web browser and make changes if necessary.

A time buckets profile is needed at the level of location or product location to display stock data and key figures in the SNI Monitor. The entire planning period and its period division in the SNI Monitor are defined in the TIME BUCKETS PROFILE (SNI) (see Figure 4.80). Here, either a positive or negative number of days can be entered as the OFFSET by which the start of the planning period is either postponed or moved into the past. Furthermore, it is also possible to define which time buckets in the planning period are shown in days, weeks, months, and years in the SNI Monitor.

SNI time buckets profile

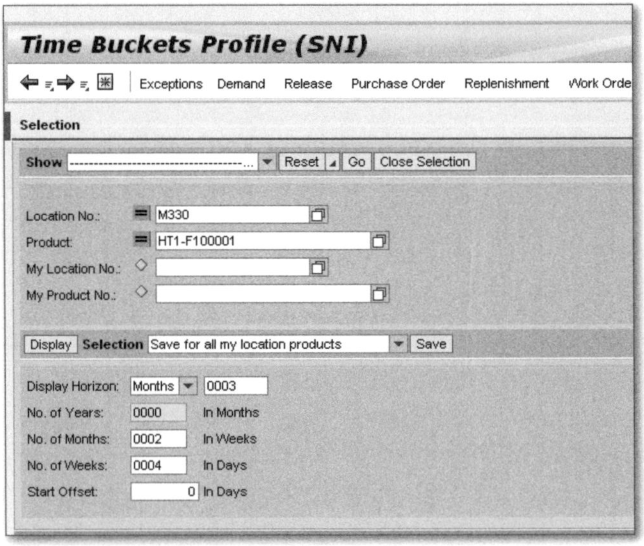

4 | Business Processes in SAP SNC 5.1

Figure 4.80 SNI Time Buckets Profile

SNI Monitor Stock data and key figures received from the backend systems of the customer, supplier, or partner are displayed in the SNI Monitor. In addition, the following key figures are calculated by SAP SNC for each time bucket:

- **Demand**
  Demand is calculated as an aggregation of the planned demand, firm demand, and the forecast.

- **Projected stock**
  The projected stock reveals the stock of a location product that will be available at the location at the end of a time bucket. The projected stock offers you an insight into the development of the stock situation for a given location product over time, allowing you to identify critical situations earlier. You can define how you want the system to calculate the projected stock in Customizing for the SAP SNC system (in Transaction SPRO, follow the menu path SUPPLY NETWORK COLLABORATION • SUPPLY NETWORK INVENTORY • DEFINE PROFILES FOR THE PROJECTED STOCK).

- **Minimum and maximum stock levels**
  The minimum and maximum stock levels represent the stock limits

agreed upon by the customer and supplier that the projected stock must not fall below or exceed. They can either be predefined independently of demand or calculated dynamically for each time bucket on the basis of a fixed minimum days' supply and maximum days' supply.

- **Minimum and maximum proposals**
  The minimum and maximum proposals represent the location product quantities required in a given time bucket to ensure that the projected stock hits the minimum or maximum stock levels.

- **Days' supply**
  The days' supply indicates how long the projected stock for a location product in a time bucket would last to cover demand in subsequent time buckets if there were no receipts in those buckets.

Stock data and key figures are shown in the different views of the SNI Monitor.

The SNI Overview enables you to quickly get an overview of the stock on hand for several location products and the stock status in the time buckets in the planning period. Buckets with critical projected stock values are highlighted in this view (see Figure 4.81).

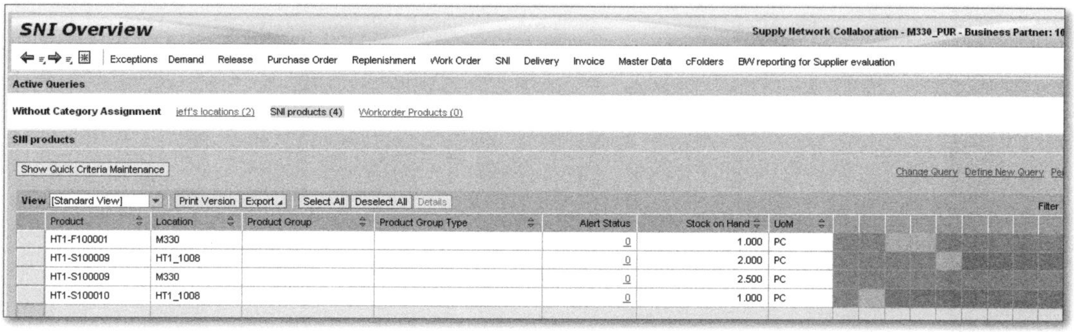

Figure 4.81 SNI Overview

In the SNI Details view, you can select different views of requirements, receipts, and stock for one or more location products (see Figure 4.82). You can group and sort the data displayed by key figure, product, location, or business partner. For instance, you can view the data grouped together at the product level instead of at the location product level.

4 | Business Processes in SAP SNC 5.1

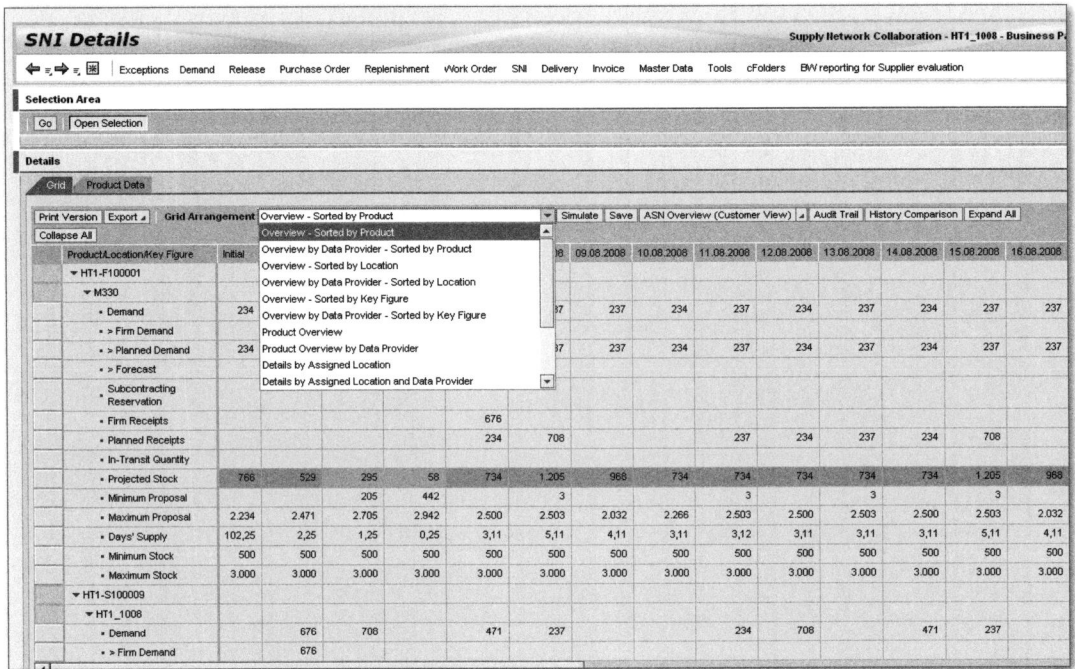

Figure 4.82 SNI Details

The SNI DETAILS – PRODUCT VIEW provides you with a detailed view of stock data and key figures pertaining to a location product (see Figure 4.83). In addition to the table showing stock data and key figures, a curve view is also provided here depicting the development of projected stock over time (see Figure 4.84). Furthermore, the most recent updates to stock data and key figures from the backend systems are logged.

In the SNI DETAILS – PRODUCT VIEW, you can edit key figures manually and create simulations.

The graphical depiction of the projected stock for a location product charts the development of the projected stock against the maximum and minimum stock levels.

Supply Network Inventory | **4.6**

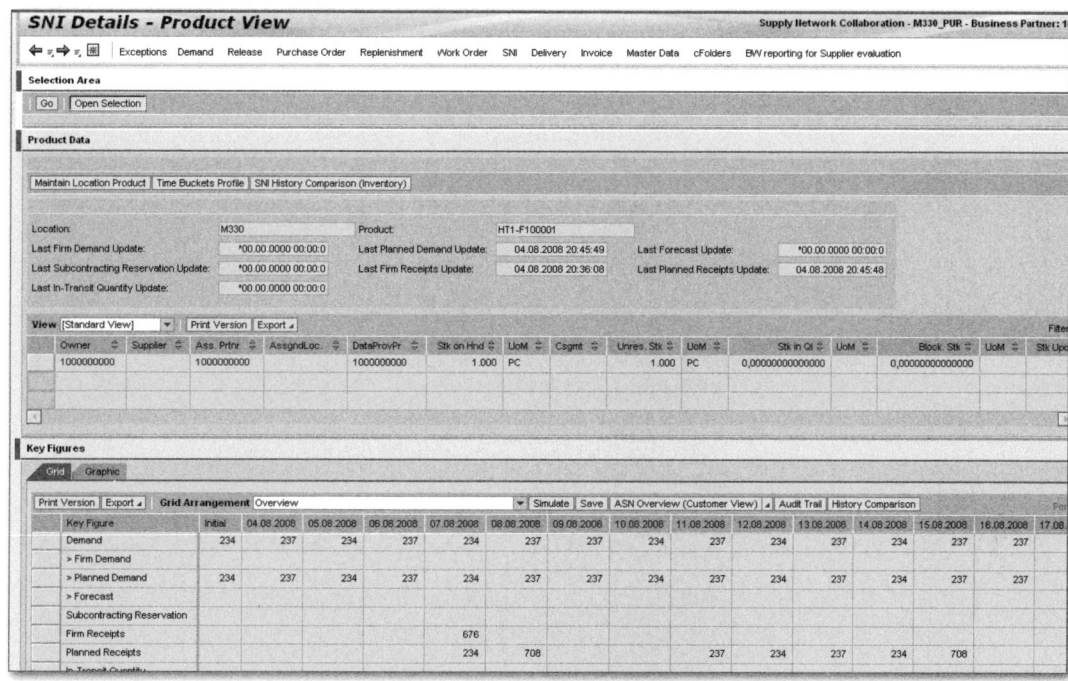

Figure 4.83 SNI Details – Product View

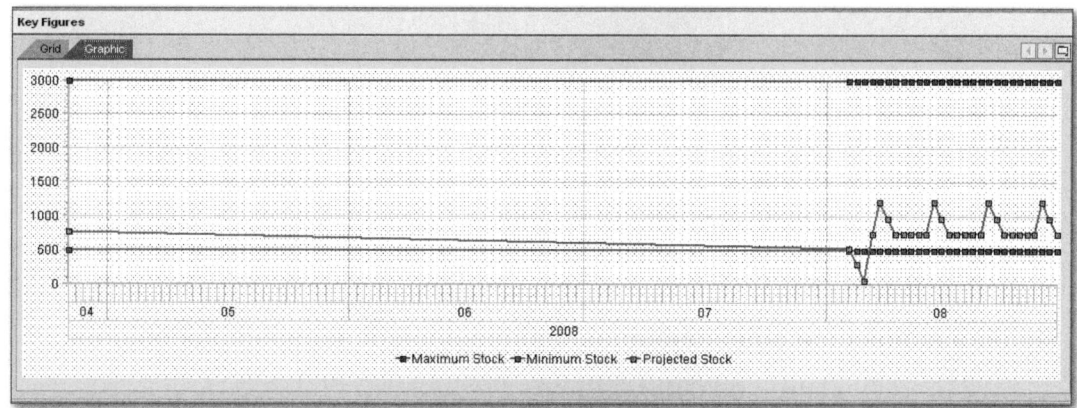

Figure 4.84 SNI Details – Graphical Display in the Product View

4.6.6 Monitoring and Making Adjustments

You can use alerts, history comparisons of key figures and stock, and audit trail functions to monitor your collaboration activities with the Supply Network Inventory.

137

Table 4.7 provides an overview of the alert types for SNI included in the standard shipment of SAP SNC 5.1.

Alert Type	Addressee	Description
Below min. – projected stock (SNI)	Customer, supplier, partner	Projected stock falls short of minimum stock level.
Above max. – projected stock (SNI)	Customer, supplier, partner	Projected stock exceeds maximum stock level.
Stockout – projected stock (SNI)	Customer, supplier, partner	Projected stock is less than or equal to zero.
Below min. stock on hand (SNI)	Customer, supplier, partner	The actual stock on hand is below the minimum stock level.
Above max. stock on hand (SNI)	Customer, supplier, partner	The actual stock on hand is above the maximum stock level.
Stockout – stock on hand (SNI)	Customer, supplier, partner	The actual stock on hand is zero.
SNI Alert	Customer	Can be set up for a location product with conditions configured on a customer-specific basis.

Table 4.7 Supply Network Inventory Alerts

You can generate the alerts relevant to SNI in SAP SNC using Transaction SCA/SNIALERTSWRITE.

SNI Alert Rules

You can define customer-specific SNI alerts in the SAP SNC web browser (see Figure 4.85). The alert is generated if the conditions defined in the alert rule for DEMAND, STOCK, TIME, and DAYS' SUPPLY, which can be restricted to certain locations, products, or planners, are met.

The CREATE ALERT button in the SAP SNC web browser allows you to trigger the generation of alerts for an SNI alert rule. Alternatively, the alerts of an SNI alert rule can be generated in SAP SNC in Transaction SCA/SNIALERTSWRITE.

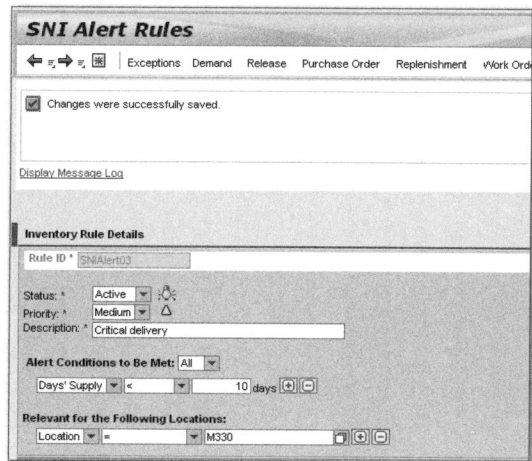

Figure 4.85 Defining SNI Alert Rules

SNI History Comparison

The history comparison enables you to compare stock or key figures from two different points in time.

SNI Audit Trail

The audit trail function makes it possible to log changes to stock data or key figures. The time of the change, processor, and value are documented.

4.7 Work Order Collaboration

This section begins with an overview of the *work order collaboration* business process with SAP SNC 5.1 (Figure 4.86). It then takes a closer look at the individual process steps and settings in SAP SNC.

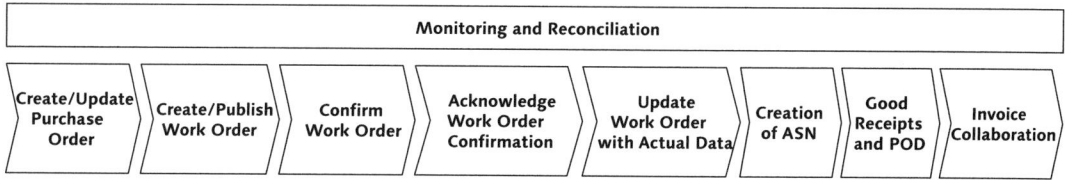

Figure 4.86 Process Flow for Work Order Collaboration

4.7.1 Process Overview

The work order collaboration business process in SAP SNC 5.1 is aimed at improving collaboration with outsourced production areas. It makes order progress more transparent for those involved, allowing them to identify bottlenecks early on and make adjustments in time to remove them.

Work order collaboration covers all steps, from creating a purchase order in the customer's backend system and generating a corresponding work order to the supplier in SAP SNC to delivery and invoice processing.

The process flow for work order collaboration is shown in Figure 4.87.

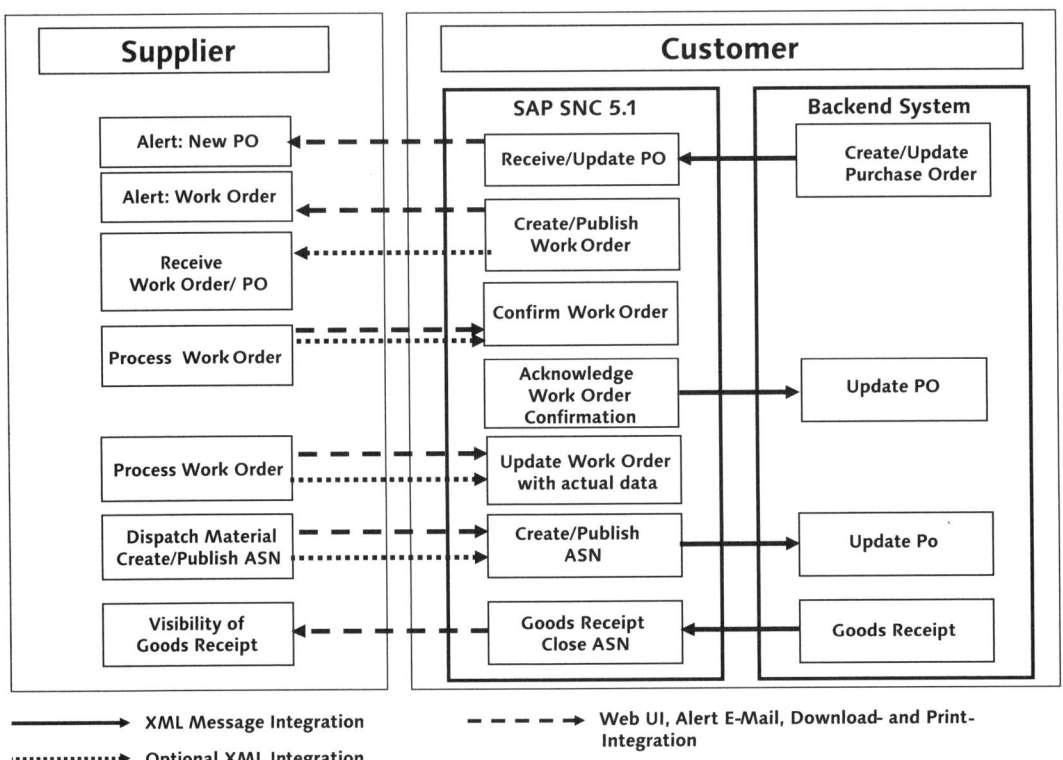

Figure 4.87 Work Order Collaboration with SAP SNC

Work order on the basis of a purchase order

The customer creates a (subcontract) order in his backend system and sends it to SAP SNC. A work order is generated to the supplier on the basis of the purchase order item or schedule line. The work order informs the supplier of the planned manufacturing levels (phases) and the requested quantities and dates/times. The supplier can confirm the work order with deviating quantities and dates/times if necessary. In the event of such deviations, the customer and supplier can negotiate and agree upon quantities and dates/times. During production, the supplier can update the work order with actual data about the individual phases. Based on the actual data, the system calculates the delivery quantities and dates/times expected and displays them in the work order. At a later point in time, the supplier can include the delivery in the work order as actual data or create and publish an ASN indirectly for the purchase order item. Goods receipt and invoice processing then take place with reference to the purchase order or ASN.

4.7.2 Master Data Specific to Work Orders

In addition to the master data required for the subcontract order (bill of material and so on) in the customer's backend system, further master data specific to work orders must be maintained in SAP SNC. Basically, this is the *master data for the phases* and the *confirmation of the generation of work orders* to the supplier.

Master data

Master Data for the Phases

In essence, a *phase* represents a manufacturing level in the production process that is relevant for work order collaboration. You should only map manufacturing levels whose progress you and your suppliers want to monitor as phases.

Manufacturing levels mapped as phases

To determine the required phases when generating a work order, you can use the *phase structure*, the *production process model* (PPM), or the *product data structure* (PDS) (in the SAP menu, follow the menu path SUPPLY NETWORK COLLABORATION • MASTER DATA • APPLICATION-SPECIFIC MASTER DATA • WORK ORDER • WORK ORDER COLLABORATION).

Phase Structure

A phase structure maps a product's relevant manufacturing levels that the supplier performs in a particular order when manufacturing the

Phase structure

product. A phase structure may contain one or more phases (see Figure 4.88). Input and output components are assigned to each phase. Input components are consumed at the beginning of a phase, whereas the output components are provided at the end. For each phase structure, the system automatically creates a *transportation phase* for the transportation between the ship-from and customer location.

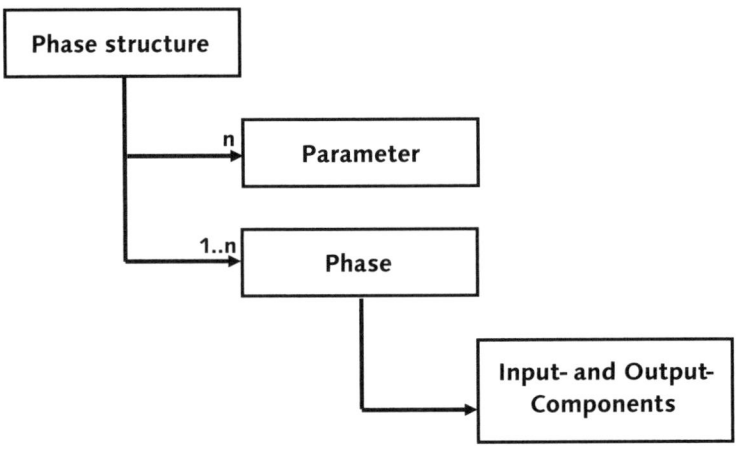

Figure 4.88 Phase Structure

Parameters that are shown in the work order can be assigned to a phase structure. These parameters allow for special information about the manufacturing process to be passed on to the supplier in the work order and additional documents to be attached for each phase in a phase structure. The attachments are included in the work order and displayed to the supplier in the SAP SNC web browser.

Production Process Model (PPM)/Product Data Structure (PDS)

Production process model/product data structure

The production process models or product data structures used in *SAP Advanced Planning & Optimization* (APO) for *Supply Network Planning* (SNP) can be used here to determine the phases of a work order. When a work order is generated, source determination in SAP APO identifies a PPM or PDS. A phase with corresponding input and output components is created in the work order for each activity in the PPM or PDS.

Configuring the Generation of Work Orders

To ensure that the right master data is determined when a work order is generated, *component assignment rules* must first be defined. In a component assignment rule, components—for instance from subcontracting, the PPM, or PDS—are assigned to the phases of a phase structure.

Next, a phase structure, component assignment rule, and validity period are selected for a combination of customer, supplier, ship-from location, customer location, and product. Alternatively, you can assign a PPM or PDS in the Master Data Assignment Details (see Figure 4.89).

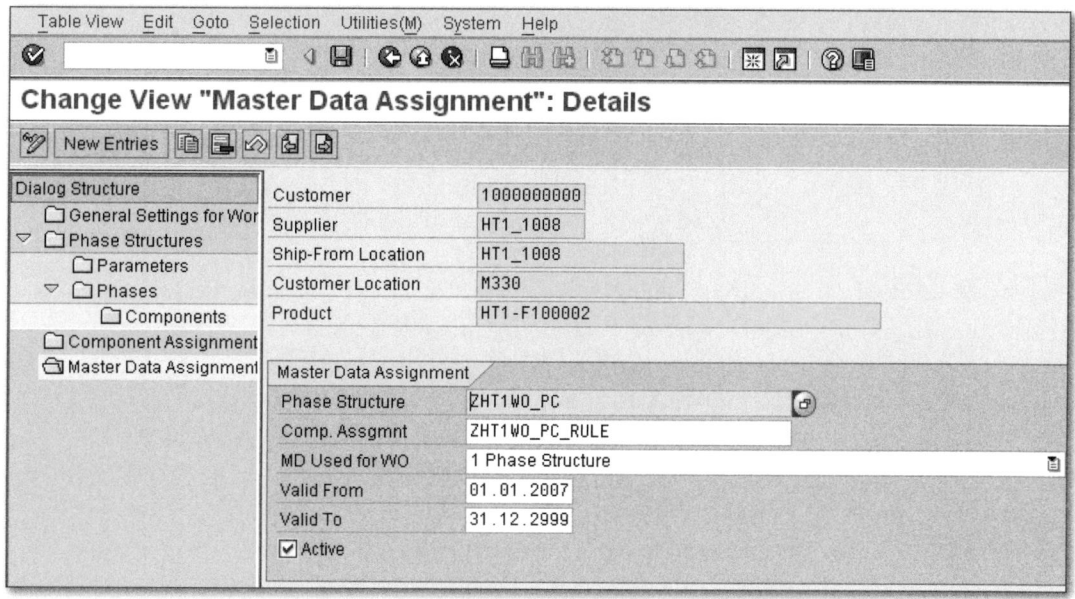

Figure 4.89 Assigning Master Data

To control the way that work orders are generated for a combination of customer, supplier, ship-from location, customer location, and product, you can define the following (see Figure 4.90):

Controlling work order generation

- Whether a work order is generated for each purchase order item or purchase order schedule line
- Whether a work order is generated as soon as a purchase order is received or by a report at a later time

- Whether the work order is published immediately after being generated or after it has been updated due to a change in the purchase order

- The type of work order. You can define different work order types in Customizing for the SAP SNC system (in Transaction SPRO, follow the menu path SUPPLY NETWORK COLLABORATION • WORK ORDER • CODES • DEFINE CODES AND DESCRIPTIONS FOR WORK ORDER TYPES)

- Whether *binning* is used, in which case the supplier assigns the product to be delivered to a bin (depending on the test result)

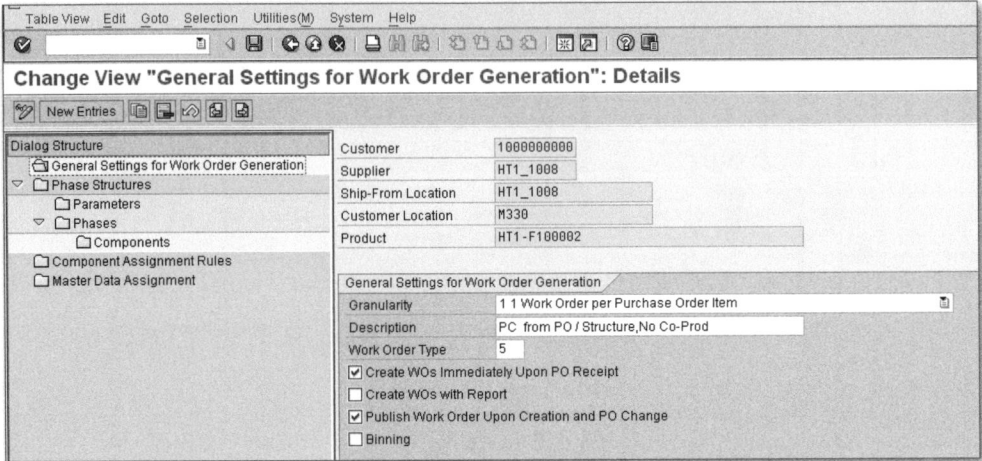

Figure 4.90 Settings for Work Order Generation

4.7.3 Creating and Sending a Purchase Order

Purchase orders are created from the MRP run or manually in the customer's backend system on the basis of net demands. Purchase orders in the *normal* or *subcontracting* item categories represent the starting point for further work order collaboration in an SAP ERP system. A new or modified purchase order is sent from an SAP ERP system in the form of an IDoc of type ORDERS.ORDERS05 or ORDCHG.ORDERS05 (as of SAP ECC 6.0, also IDoc type PORDCR1.PORDCR102). Message determination and the partner profile must be configured to enable this to take place. The IDoc message is converted in SAP NetWeaver PI into an XML message of type *ReplenishmentOrderNotification* and sent to SAP SNC. Once the inbound message has been successfully posted, a new purchase order item alert or changed purchase order item alert is generated. The supplier can be notified of this automatically, for example, by email.

4.7.4 Generating and Publishing a Work Order

Depending on the system settings made for work order generation (see Figure 4.90), a work order can either be generated automatically when the purchase order inbound message is received or triggered by a special report at a later point in time (in the SAP menu, follow the menu path SUPPLY NETWORK COLLABORATION • WORK ORDER • CREATE WORK ORDERS).

Generating a work order

As shown in Figure 4.91, the report can be used to generate the corresponding work orders for an individual purchase order or for several purchase orders.

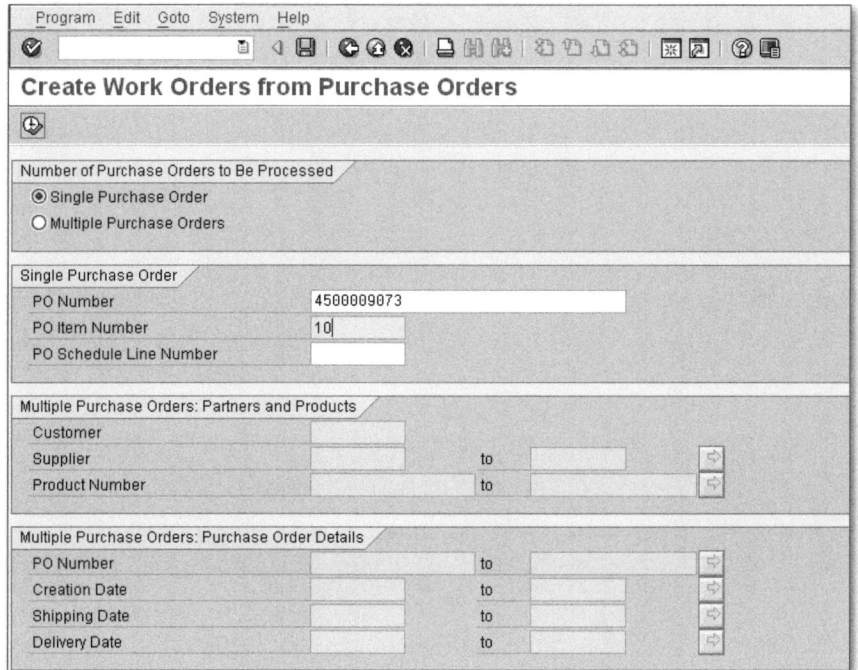

Figure 4.91 Creating Work Orders

The phases in the production process are mapped in the resulting work order according to the settings made in the master data (see Section 4.2.2 SMI-Specific Master Data).

4 Business Processes in SAP SNC 5.1

Publishing a work order

A work order must first be published by the customer to enable the supplier to react to it. Publishing can take place automatically when the work order is created or at a later point in time, either manually in the SAP SNC web browser or by means of a special report (see Figure 4.90). You can call up the report, as shown in Figure 4.92, in the SAP menu by following the menu path SUPPLY NETWORK COLLABORATION • WORK ORDER • PUBLISH WORK ORDERS.

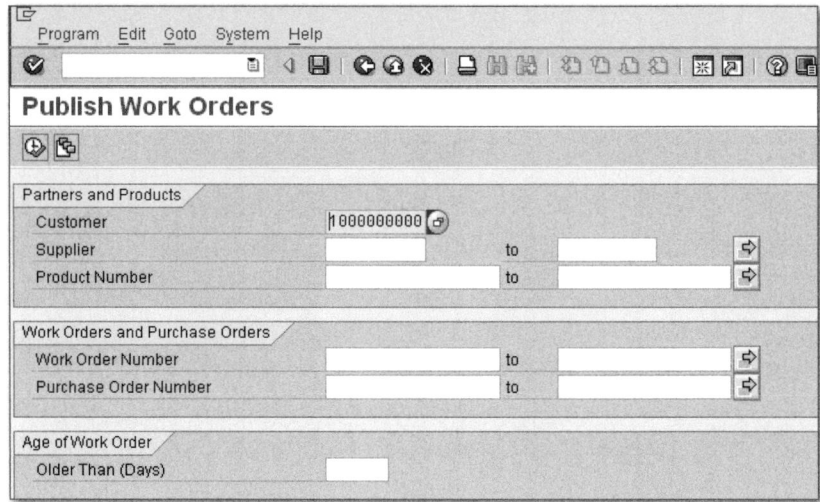

Figure 4.92 Publishing Work Orders

As soon as the work order has been published, the supplier is informed by a work order proposal alert. Moreover, the work order can be sent from SAP SNC to the supplier's backend system. To achieve this, an XML message of type *ManufacturingWorkOrderRequest* is created.

Work order details

In the SAP SNC web browser, the supplier can navigate from the generated alert or from the WORK ORDER OVERVIEW to the WORK ORDER DETAILS view (see Figure 4.93). The WORK ORDER OVERVIEW displays a list of work orders that can be selected according to particular selection criteria. In the WORK ORDER DETAILS view, the supplier (and the customer) can view the work order data and make any necessary changes.

Work order header

As shown in Figure 4.94, among other things, the header area of the WORK ORDER DETAILS view contains data pertaining to the work order number, purchase order number, product, phase sequence, and negotiation status. The first time the work order is published, its negotiation status is CINE (contents in negotiation).

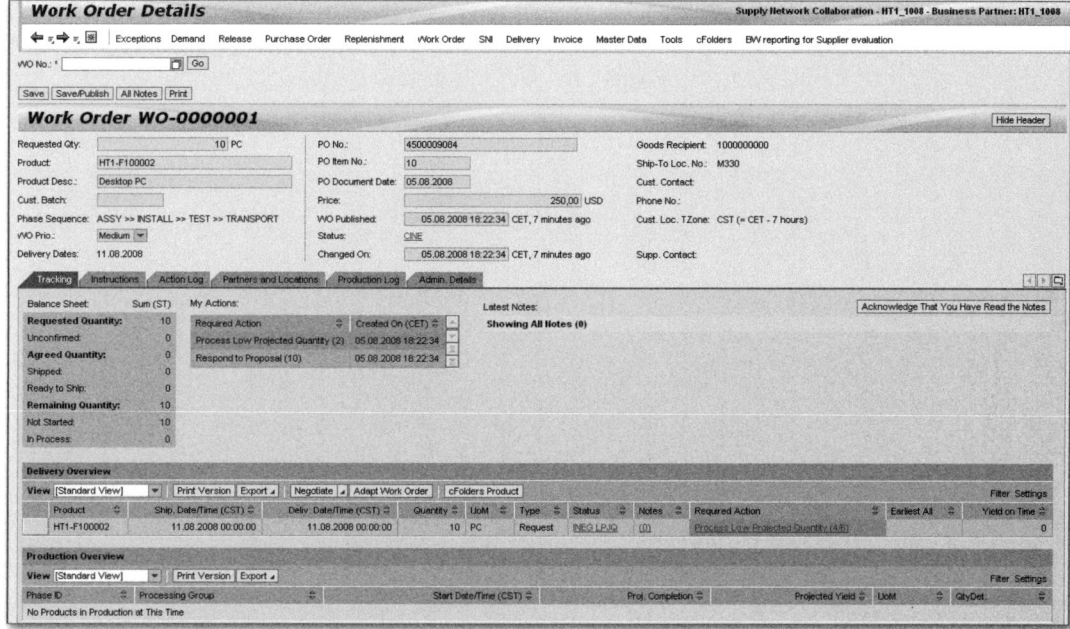

Figure 4.93 Work Order Details

Figure 4.94 Work Order Header Data

Extensive information about the processing status of the work order is provided to the supplier and the customer on a range of tab pages in the WORK ORDER DETAILS view.

The TRACKING tab page (see Figure 4.95) shows the following information:

- The customer's requested quantities
- Quantities agreed in negotiations

- Remaining quantities
- Required actions
- Production status with regard to delivery quantities and dates/times in the delivery overview
- Production status in the individual phases in the production overview

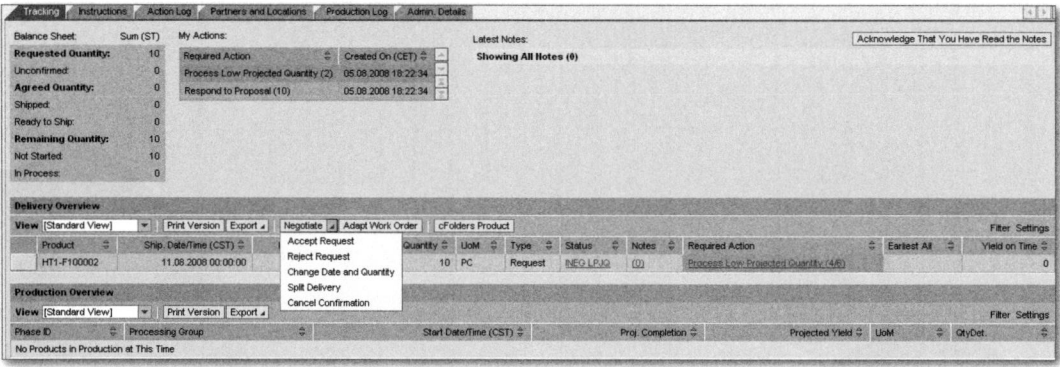

Figure 4.95 Work Order Details – Tracking

The INSTRUCTIONS tab page (see Figure 4.96) displays all of the phases of the work order, their input and output components, and their negotiation status. After the customer has published the work order for the first time, the negotiation status is CINE. In addition, the customer and supplier can save attachments and notes on this tab page.

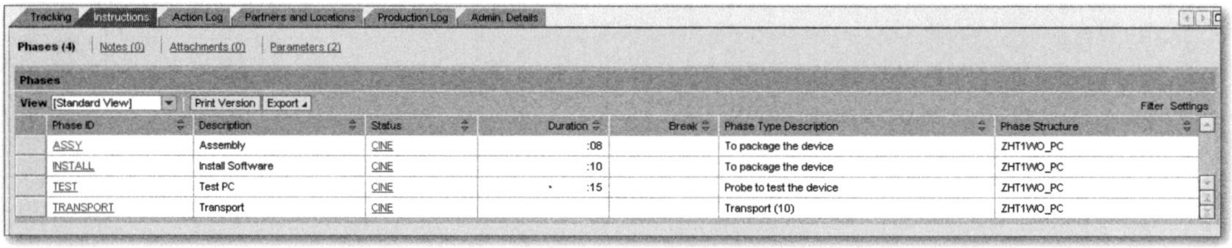

Figure 4.96 Work Order Details – Instructions

The PRODUCTION LOG tab page (see Figure 4.97) documents order progress for each of the phases. The supplier can enter the actual data about the phases here.

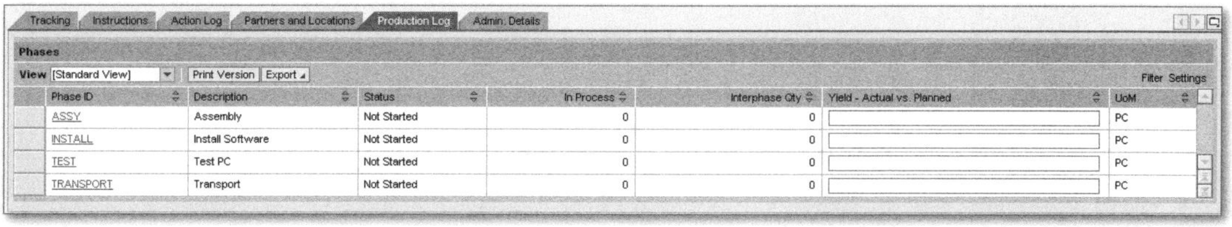

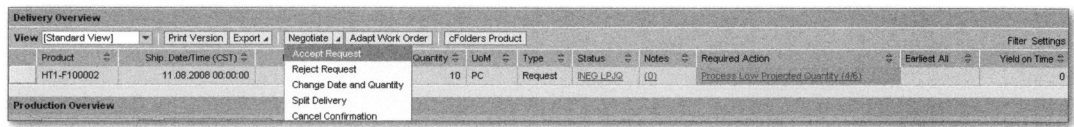

Figure 4.97 Work Order Details – Production Log

4.7.5 Confirming a Work Order

The supplier can react to the work order published by the customer in the WORK ORDER DETAILS view. In the delivery overview on the TRACKING tab page, the supplier clicks on the NEGOTIATE button and then has the option of accepting or rejecting requested quantities and dates/times or replying with different ones. The supplier can also cancel confirmations.

Confirming quantities and dates/times

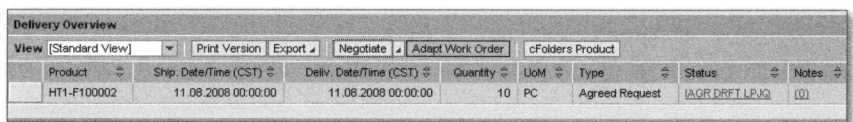

Figure 4.98 Negotiating a Work Order

After confirming a work order with differences in the delivery overview, the supplier can click on the ADAPT WORK ORDER button to adapt all phases of the work order to the confirmed quantities and dates/times (see Figure 4.99).

Figure 4.99 Adapting a Work Order

Alternatively, the supplier can enter a confirmation for the individual input and output components in a phase on the INSTRUCTIONS tab page (see Figure 4.100).

4 | Business Processes in SAP SNC 5.1

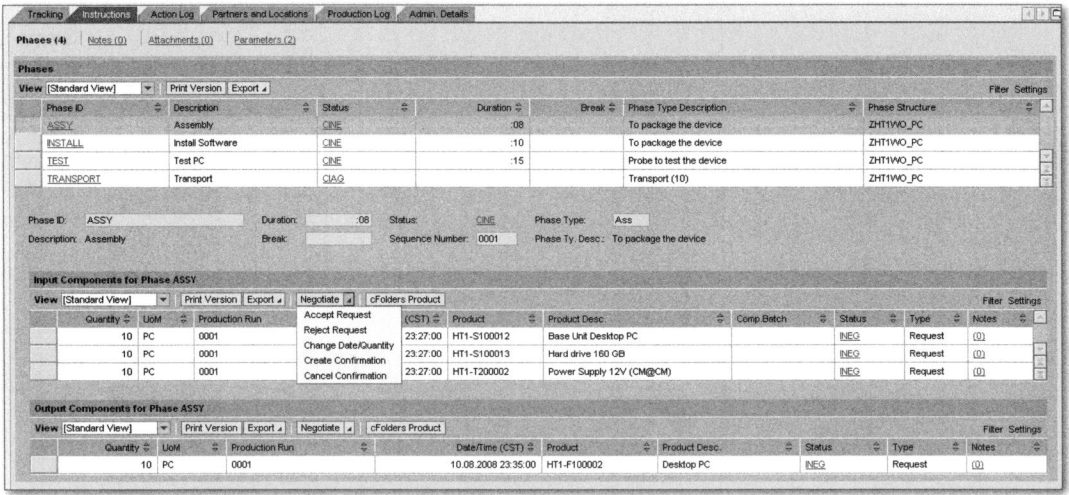

Figure 4.100 Negotiating Phases

Updating the negotiation status

Once the supplier has confirmed the delivery quantities and dates/times as well as the individual phases in the production process, the negotiation status changes at the phase and work order levels. The following status values are possible:

- IN NEGOTIATION
- IN AGREEMENT
- CANCELED
- REJECTED

After making all of the required confirmations, the supplier publishes the work order.

Confirmations can be sent from the supplier's backend system to SAP SNC. SAP SNC can process the supplier confirmations in the form of XML messages of type *ManufacturingWorkOrderConfirmation*.

The customer can view, accept, reject, or make a counterproposal to the supplier's confirmations in the WORK ORDER DETAILS view. The customer then publishes the work order, and the supplier can react to any changes.

The negotiation process can continue in this way until the customer and supplier reach an agreement. When the customer publishes the agreed upon work order, the purchase order from the confirmation data of the work order is updated. The system creates a confirmation schedule line in the purchase order and sends an XML message of type *Replenishment OrderConfirmation* to SAP NetWeaver PI. There, the XML message is converted into an IDoc of type ORDRSP.ORDER05 and sent to the customer's backend system.

If the work order was generated on the basis of a subcontract order, the component consumption reported by the supplier is copied from the work order to the confirmation schedule line in the purchase order.

4.7.6 Approving a Work Order Confirmation

The system compares the confirmations created by the supplier for a work order with the customer's requested data. Using the deviation analysis from the consensus finding and condition technique, the system decides whether quantity and date/time deviations are accepted automatically or whether manual actions are required (in Transaction SPRO, follow the menu path SUPPLY NETWORK COLLABORATION • BASIC SETTINGS • CONSENSUS FINDING). Quantity and time profiles should be maintained for this purpose. Consensus rules are required for every combination of quantity and time profile. To ensure that the system uses the quantity and time profiles for a combination of customer, supplier, product, phase type, phase ID, phase structure, phase output, and phase input, corresponding condition records must be maintained (in Transaction SPRO, follow the menu path SUPPLY NETWORK COLLABORATION • BASIC SETTINGS • CONSENSUS FINDING • CONDITION TECHNIQUE FOR CONSENSUS FINDING).

Approval process

4.7.7 Updating a Work Order with Actual Data

From the moment production begins, the supplier can confirm actual data to the customer about the phases commenced. Data can be sent from the supplier's backend system to SAP SNC. To this end, SAP SNC expects to receive an XML message of type *ManufacturingWorkOrder-WorkInProcessNotification*. The supplier can enter actual data on the PRO-

Maintaining actual data

duction Log tab page in the Work Order Details view (see Figure 4.101).

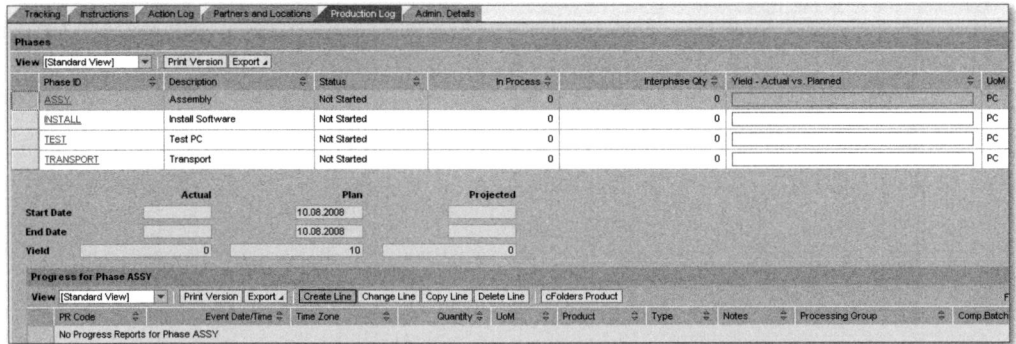

Figure 4.101 Production Log in Work Order Details

Actual data is entered for each phase for the input and output components. Specifically, the supplier confirms which input components have been consumed and when, and which output components have been generated and when. The supplier first selects a phase in the Production Log and then clicks on the Create Line button (see Figure 4.101).

Figure 4.102 shows the screen in the SAP SNC web browser on which the supplier enters confirmations for input and output components.

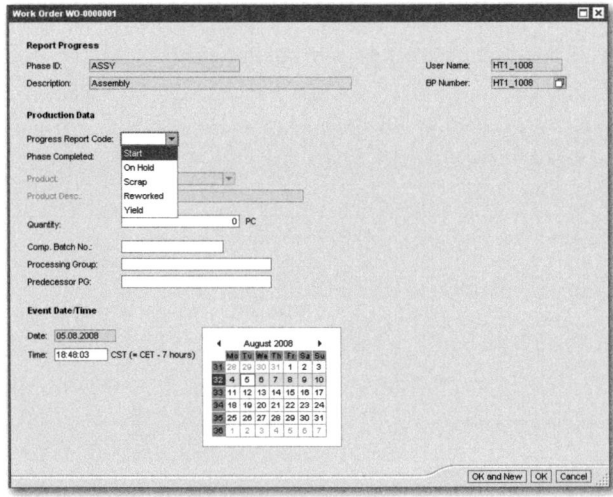

Figure 4.102 Reporting Progress

The confirmed quantities are classified with a progress report code. Table 4.8 shows the progress report codes provided in the standard shipment and whether they are used for input or output components.

Progress report code

Progress Report Code	Input/Output	Description
Start	Input	Input component quantity consumed in a phase.
Scrap	Output	Output component quantity is scrap.
Yield	Output	Output component quantity meets quality requirements.
On hold	Output	The supplier leaves it to the customer to decide whether the output component quantity is yield or scrap or should be reworked by the supplier.
Reworked	Output	Output component quantity that was previously put on hold before being reworked by the supplier.
Scrapped	Output	Output component quantity that was previously put on hold before being scrapped at the instruction of the customer.
Shipped	Input of the transportation phase	Input component quantity of the transportation phase that was shipped to the customer.
Delivered	Output of the transportation phase	Output component quantity of the transportation phase that was delivered to the customer.

Table 4.8 Description of Progress Report Codes

The confirmed quantities and dates/times for the components are documented for each phase in the production log (see Figure 4.103).

4 | Business Processes in SAP SNC 5.1

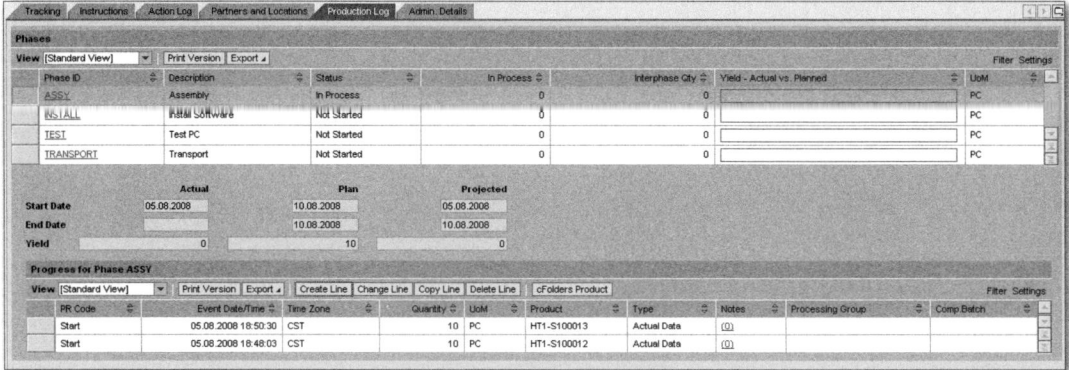

Figure 4.103 Status After Confirmation

The quantity data is updated on the TRACKING tab page in the WORK ORDER DETAILS view (see Figure 4.104).

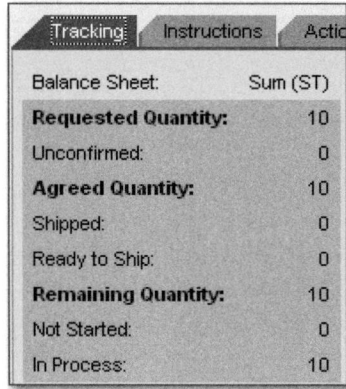

Figure 4.104 Quantity Data

Phase and work order

In addition, the confirmation of the component quantities changes the status at the phase and work order level.

The following phase status values are possible:

▶ NOT STARTED

▶ IN PROCESS

▶ COMPLETED

The work order status can have the following values during the execution phase:

▶ **In execution**
The supplier has confirmed the first component for a production phase.

▶ **In execution & production completed**
All production phases have reached completed status.

▶ **In execution & production completed & shipped**
All production phases have reached completed status, and the last input component for the transportation phase has been confirmed (see Figure 4.105).

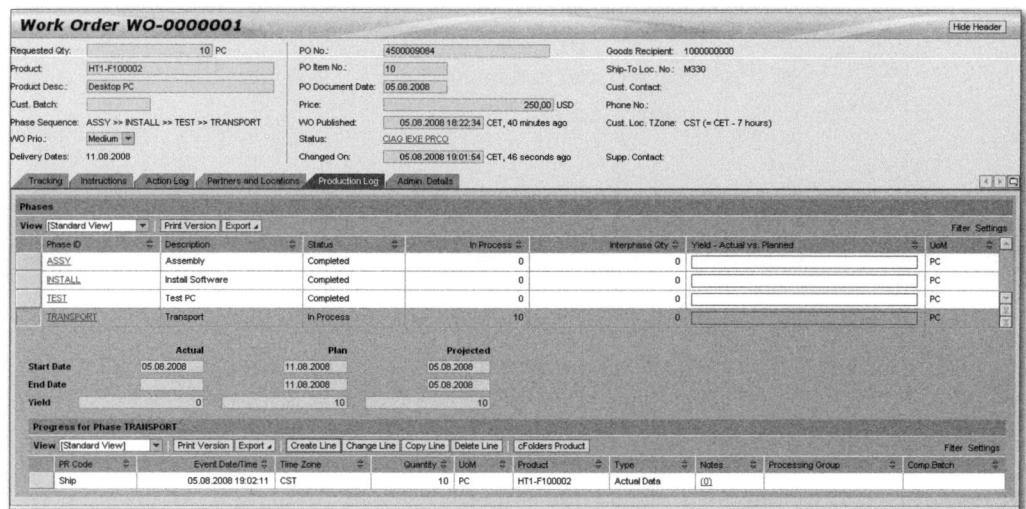

Figure 4.105 Production Phases Completed and Transportation Phase in Process

Upon receiving the delivery, the customer can confirm the output of the transportation phase on the PRODUCTION LOG tab page.

4.7.8 ASN and Goods Receipt

As an alternative to entering actual data about the transportation phase directly, the supplier has the option of maintaining and publishing one or more ASNs for each purchase order item. The ASN can be created manually in the SAP SNC web browser or sent from the supplier's backend system to SAP SNC. When the ASN is published in SAP SNC, a new purchase order schedule line of type ASN-Confirmed is created, and the ASN is sent to the customer's backend system. To achieve this, an XML message of type *DispatchDeliveryNotification* is created in SAP SNC and converted into an IDoc of type DESADV.DELVRY03 in SAP NetWeaver PI. In SAP ERP, an inbound delivery is created on the basis of the ASN. The system uses the ASN data to create actual data for the input components of the transportation phase. In addition, the phase status and work order status are both updated accordingly.

When goods receipt is entered in the customer's backend system for the inbound delivery and the proof of delivery message is sent to SAP SNC, the ASN is updated in SAP SNC with the received quantities (see Section 4.4.8 Goods Receipt and Proof of Delivery). On the basis of the received quantities, the system updates the ASN-confirmed schedule line for the purchase order item and the actual data for the output components of the transportation phase.

4.7.9 Monitoring and Making Adjustments

Required actions

To monitor work order collaboration during the negotiation and execution phases, a number of alert types exist. These alerts expose situations that require action from the customer and supplier. A required action is displayed for each alert. The customer or supplier must perform this action to eliminate the exception situation. The required actions are shown on the TRACKING tab page in the WORK ORDER DETAILS view (see Figure 4.106).

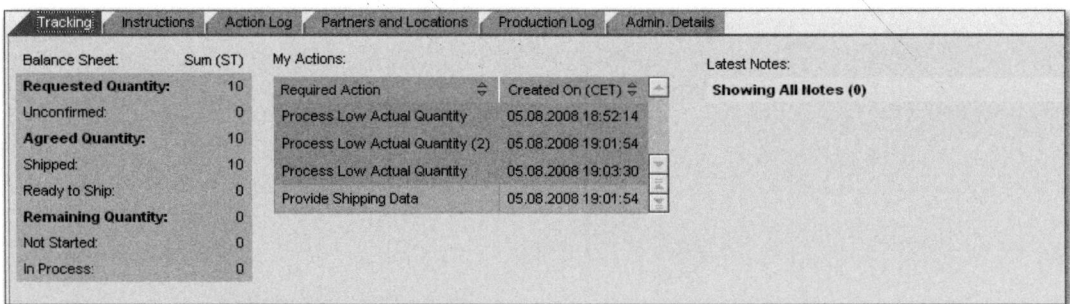

Figure 4.106 Required Action

Table 4.9 provides a list of the alert types that are relevant for work order collaboration.

Alert Type	Addressee	Description
Publish Changes	Customer, supplier	Changes in the work order have not yet been published.
Respond to Proposal	Customer, supplier	A response to the proposals of the other business partner is required.
Respond to Rejection	Customer, supplier	A response to the rejection of the other business partner is required.
Provide Actual Data	Supplier	The supplier can confirm the actual data for the production phases.
Provide Shipping Data	Supplier	The supplier can confirm the actual data for the transportation phase.
Provide Delivery Data	Customer	The customer can confirm the actual data for the transportation phase.
Actual Data out of Tolerance	Customer, supplier	Quantity or date/time deviations between planning and actual data are outside the permitted tolerance. The customer and supplier must respond to this, for instance, by agreeing on different quantities or dates/times.
Projected Data out of Tolerance	Customer, supplier	Quantity or date/time deviations between planning data and projected delivery data are outside the permitted tolerance. The customer and supplier must respond to this, for instance, by agreeing on different quantities or dates/times.
Acknowledge Cancellation	Customer, supplier	A response to the cancellation request of the other business partner is required.
Decide Status of On-Hold Components	Customer	The supplier has reported actual data with "on hold" as the progress report code. The customer must now make a decision.
Process On-Hold Components According to Decision	Supplier	The supplier must process the quantity in accordance with the customer's decision (rework, scrap, or continue).
Acknowledge Note	Customer, supplier	The business partner must confirm that the note has been read.

Table 4.9 Alerts in Work Order Collaboration

In addition, the WORK ORDER HISTORY documents the previous versions of a work order and can therefore be used to track changes (see Figure 4.107).

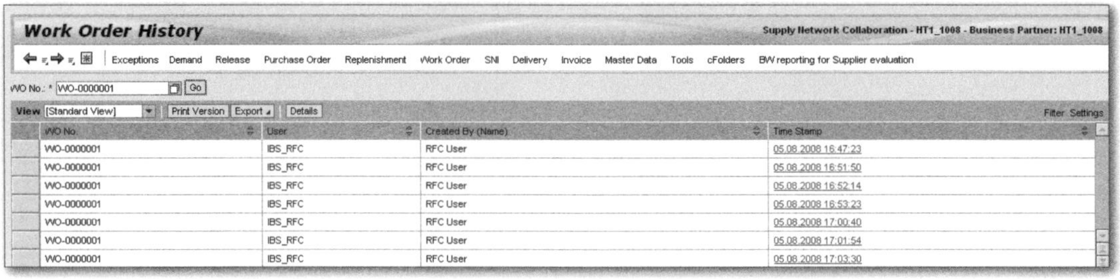

Figure 4.107 Work Order History

4.8 Kanban

This section begins with an overview of the *kanban* business process with SAP SNC 5.1 (see Figure 4.108). It then takes a closer look at the individual process steps and settings in SAP SNC.

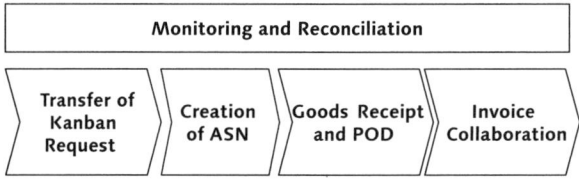

Figure 4.108 Kanban Process Flow

4.8.1 Process Overview

Kanban request

If a particular quantity of a given product is to be procured from a supplier with whom a kanban processing agreement is in place, the customer sends a kanban request from his backend system to SAP SNC in the form of an XML message. This kanban request corresponds to the kanban card of an empty kanban container.

Both the customer and supplier can monitor kanbans on the web user interface of the SAP SNC system. An overview provides information about all of the kanbans in a kanban control cycle, the kanban status, and the quantities. The supplier can deliver to empty kanbans.

To do so, the supplier creates an ASN, publishes it, and sends it to the customer's backend system. On the basis of this ASN, SAP SNC automatically updates the kanban status to IN TRANSIT. If the customer posts a goods receipt for this ASN, this information is sent to SAP SNC, and the kanban status is changed to FULL.

In this way, the kanban determines to some extent the lot size produced by the supplier at one time. The complete production quantity is made up of the number of kanbans sent to the supplier in a particular period of time. The replenishment frequency is guided by actual consumption. In other words, if more of a material is required, the kanbans circulate between the supplier and customer more quickly; if the material requirement is lower, the kanbans circulate at a slower rate. If a material is not required for a particular period, all of the kanbans with that material are kept at the customer's location so that the material is immediately available there. There is never more material in circulation than the number of kanbans defined with the control cycle.

Goods receipt is posted once the goods have been physically received and put away at the customer's location. A proof of delivery message confirms to the supplier the actual quantity received by the customer. Invoice collaboration takes place with reference to the ASN on the basis of conventional invoice processing or self-billing (see Section 4.12 Invoice Collaboration).

The Kanban Monitor and alerts are used to monitor kanban processing between the customer and supplier.

If the customer wants to provide a supplier with advanced notification of required quantities, it is possible to send a kanban forecast delivery schedule from the customer's backend system to SAP SNC. These kanban forecast delivery schedules are for information purposes only; it is not possible to create ASNs for them.

The kanban process achieves an optimum procurement logistics process because only the quantity that is actually needed is replenished. SAP SNC offers the further option of printing kanban cards at any time.

A new feature of SAP SNC 5.1 is the option to configure one-time kanbans. If a one-time kanban is used, the FULL status does not exist; rather, the status is set directly to CLOSED after goods receipt. A one-time kanban card with the CLOSED status can be reused in a different one-time kanban control cycle, and the automatic packing function for ASNs for kanbans can be used.

The process flow for kanban planning is shown in Figure 4.109.

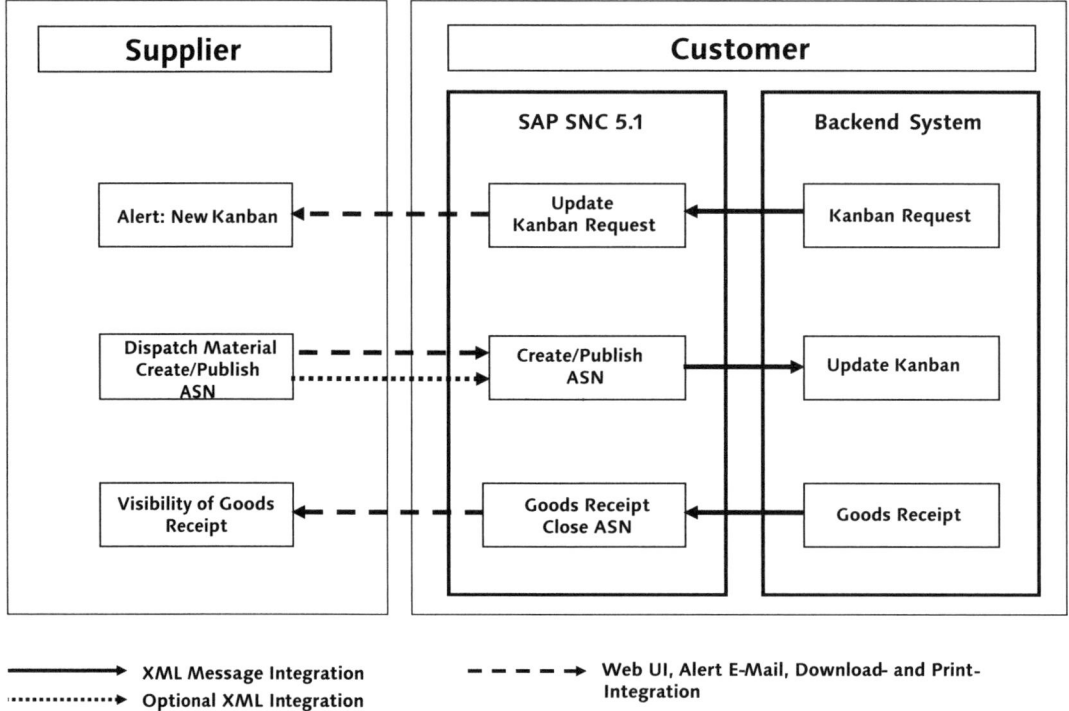

Figure 4.109 Kanban Process Flow

4.8.2 Master Data Specific to Kanban

Master data

In addition to the generic master data (see Section 4.1 Generic Master Data), the following master data is also required for the kanban process:

- Production supply area
- Replenishment strategy
- Control cycle

The following section describes how this master data must be maintained in the customer's SAP ERP system.

Production Supply Area

In preparation for the kanban process, you have to set up a production supply area in SAP ERP (Transaction PK05) (see Figure 4.110).

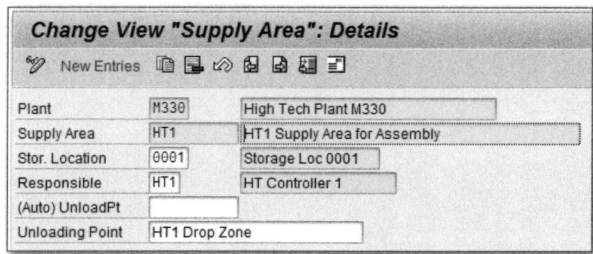

Figure 4.110 Maintaining the Production Supply Area

The *production supply area* (PSA) functions as an interim storage facility in production so that materials for production can be provided directly to the production line or work center.

The PSA is assigned to the following objects:

- Plant
- Storage location
- Person responsible

Replenishment Strategy

The replenishment strategy for external procurement used in the control cycle must be defined in Customizing in the customer's backend system (see Figure 4.111).

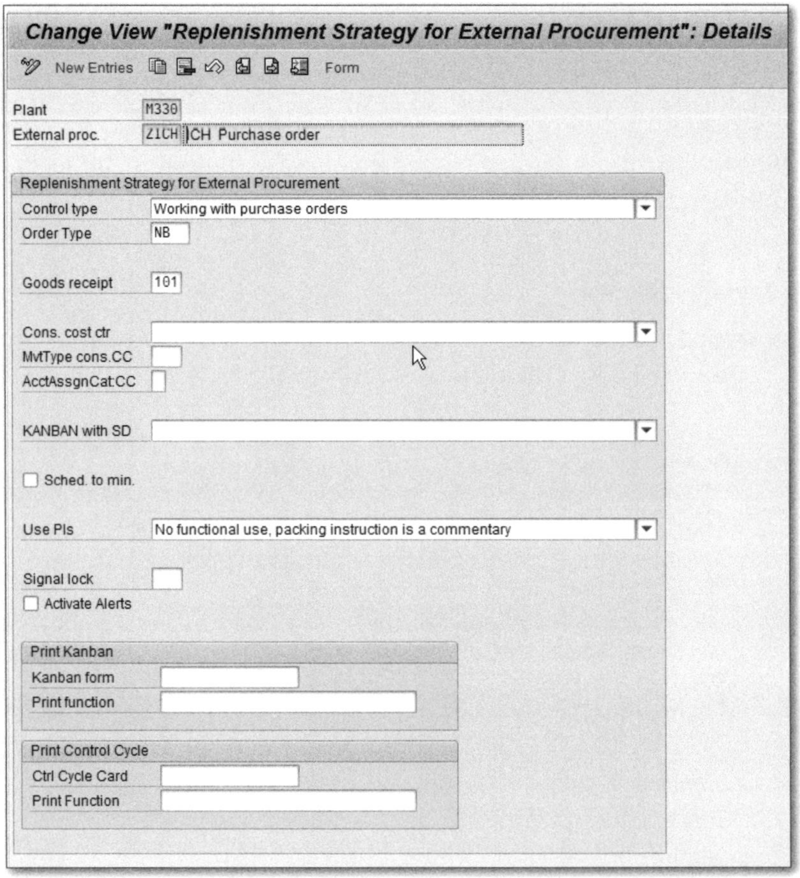

Figure 4.111　Maintaining the Replenishment Strategy for External Procurement

Control Cycle

A control cycle must also be defined (Transaction PKMC) (see Figure 4.112).

The demand source is defined in the control cycle by means of the following data:

- Material number
- Plant
- Production supply area of the demand source

4.8 Kanban

You also store the replenishment strategy between the demand source and supplier that you have maintained in Customizing.

The following data must be maintained for the kanban circulation:

- The number of kanbans in circulation between the supplier and demand source
- The material quantity for each kanban

The supplier is specified using the following data:

- Purchasing organization
- Supplier
- Contract/scheduling agreement

The kanban process with SAP SNC and SAP ERP Core only works with contracts and, therefore, purchase orders.

SAP kanban processes require purchase orders

SAP ERP DIMP is required to execute the process with scheduling agreements.

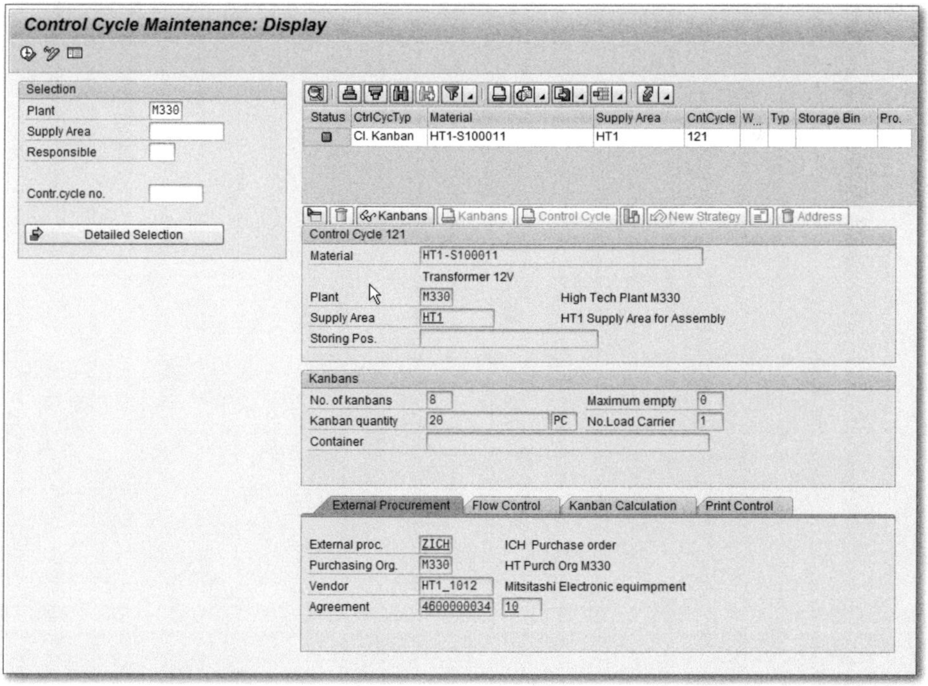

Figure 4.112 Maintaining Control Cycles

Sending the Production Supply Area and Control Cycle

You can send data from the production supply area and the control cycle to SAP SNC using report KANBAN_MD_TRANSMIT in the SAP ERP system (see Figure 4.113). By using this report, you can avoid having to maintain this master data again.

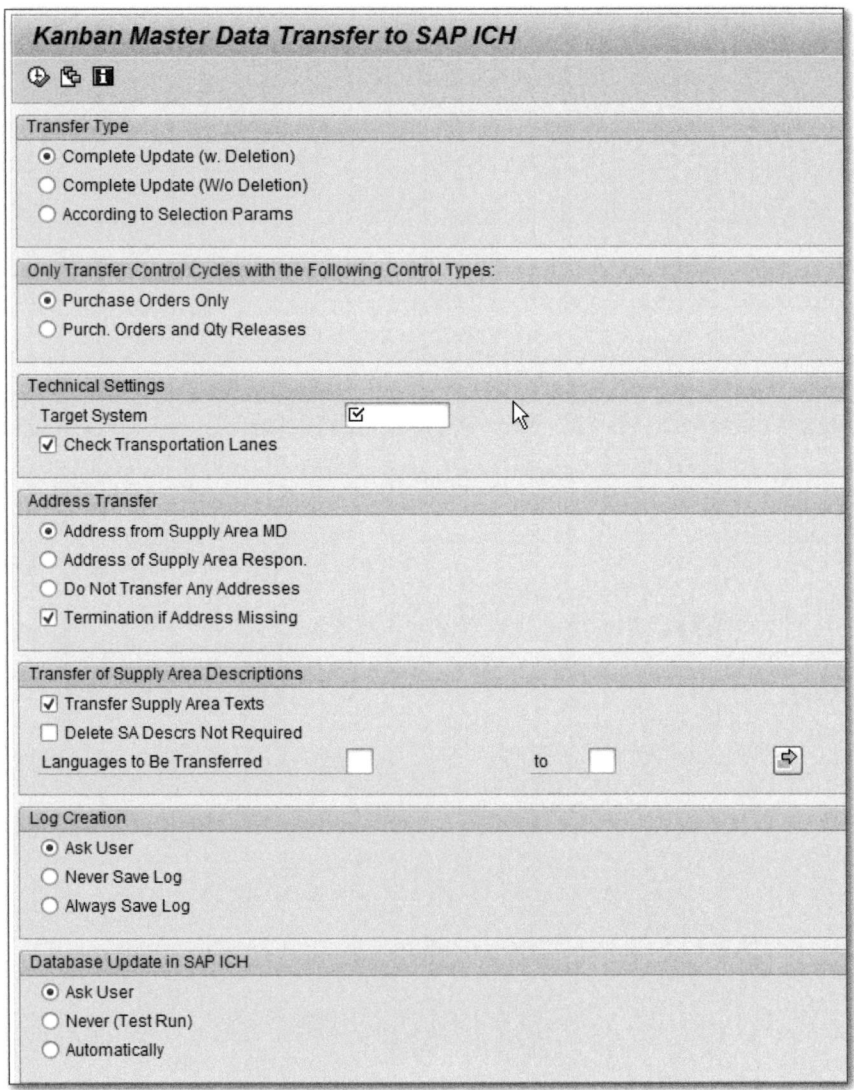

Figure 4.113 Sending Kanban Master Data to SAP SNC

The master data you have sent can then be seen in SAP Easy Access under SUPPLY NETWORK COLLABORATION • MASTER DATA • APPLICATION-SPECIFIC MASTER DATA • KANBAN (see Figure 4.114).

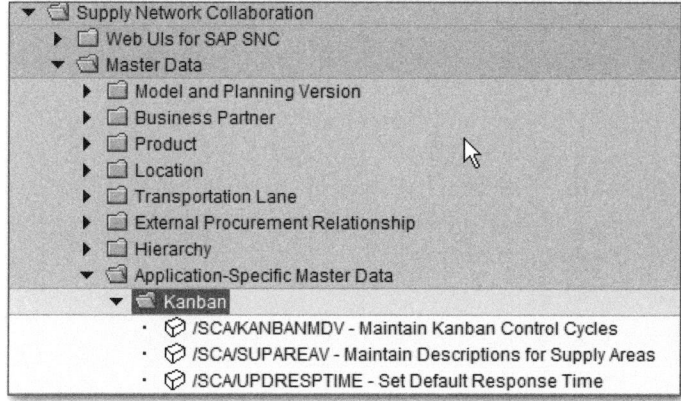

Figure 4.114 Maintaining Kanban Master Data in SAP SNC

4.8.3 Sending a Kanban Request

The kanban board (Transaction PK13n) in the customer's backend system provides an overview of all the kanbans at a particular time (see Figure 4.115).

Each kanban has its own status, and the status values are color-coded.

- A newly created kanban has status WAITING (INITIAL) and is shown in magenta.
- An empty kanban is shown in red.
- Green indicates a full kanban.
- Yellow denotes kanbans that are in transit.

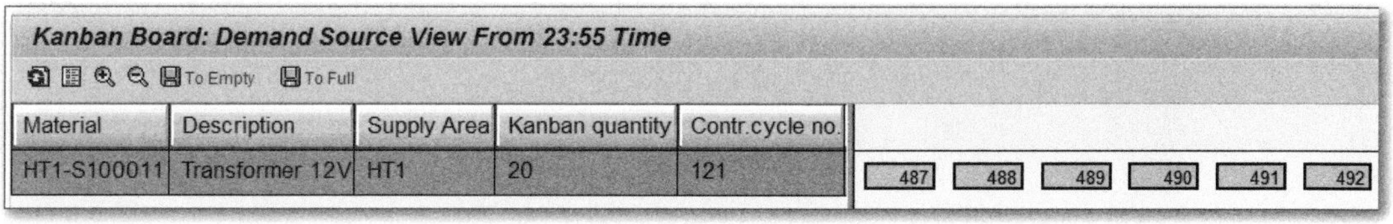

Figure 4.115 Kanban Board with Several Initial Kanbans

If you select a new or full kanban and set it TO EMPTY, its color changes as well (see Figure 4.116).

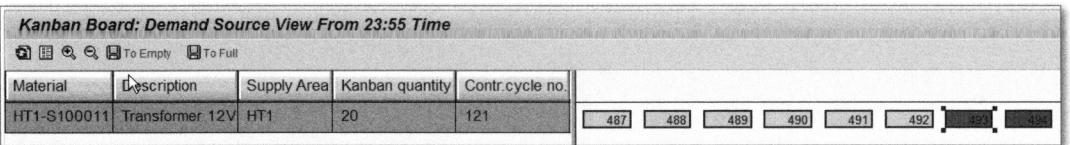

Figure 4.116 A Kanban That Has Been Set to Empty in the Back-End System

When you set the kanban card to empty and thereby create a kanban request, you also prompt an IDoc message to be created automatically. The IDoc ORDERS.ORDERS03 is sent to the customer's SAP NetWeaver PI system, where it is converted into an XML message of type *ReplenishmentOrderNotification* (RON) and sent on to SAP SNC.

4.8.4 Creating an ASN

Kanban monitor

The ASN is created using the Kanban Monitor, which you access in SAP SNC by selecting REPLENISHMENT • KANBAN (see Figure 4.117).

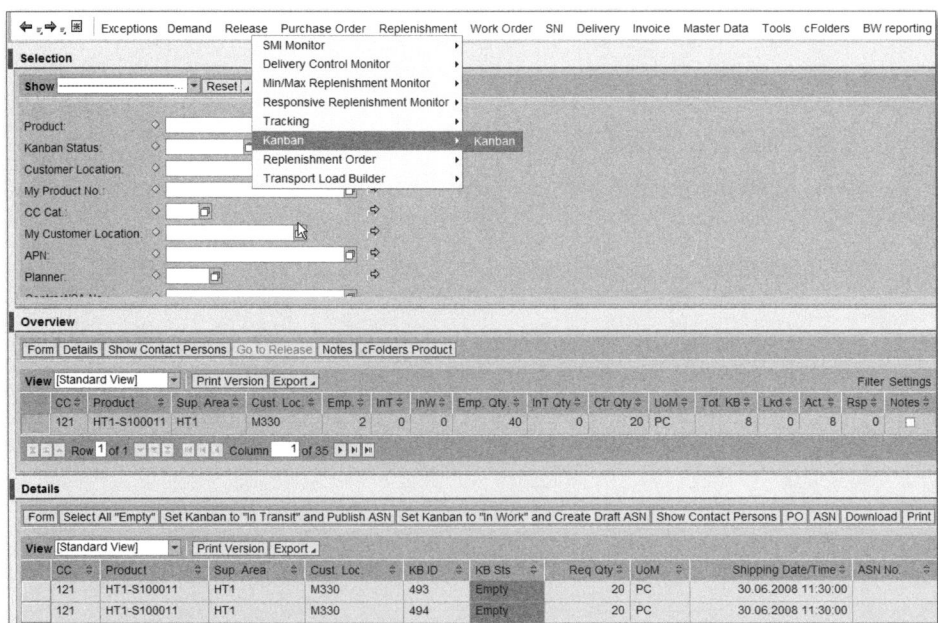

Figure 4.117 Kanban Monitor in the SAP SNC Menu Path

The supplier can view relevant kanban cards by choosing from a range of selection criteria.

Unlike in SAP ERP, only kanbans with status EMPTY, FULL, or IN TRANSIT are displayed (see Figure 4.118).

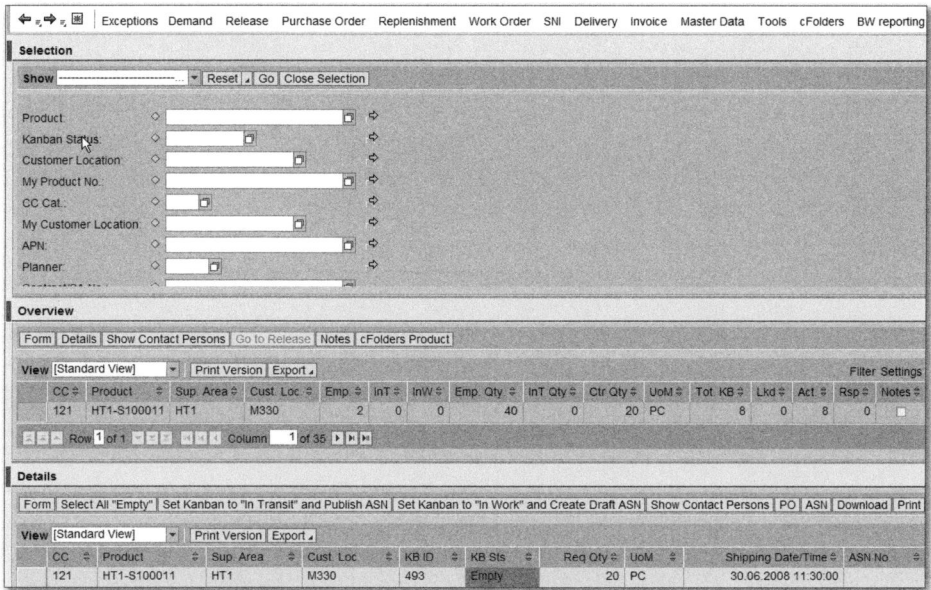

Figure 4.118 Supplier View of the Kanban Monitor in SAP SNC

Initial kanbans that have been newly created in the customer's backend system cannot be seen in SAP SNC.

The supplier can now change the status from EMPTY to IN TRANSIT by creating an ASN for the kanban.

To do so, the supplier must select one or more empty kanbans and click on the SET KANBAN TO "IN TRANSIT" AND PUBLISH ASN button (see Figure 4.119).

In the ASN work area, the supplier is still able to change the quantity of the kanban and have the material packed automatically using a packaging specification.

Once the ASN has been published, SAP SNC sends an XML message of type *DispatchedDeliveryNotification* (DDN) to the SAP NetWeaver PI system, which converts the message into the DESADV.DELVRY03 IDoc and sends it to the customer's SAP ERP system.

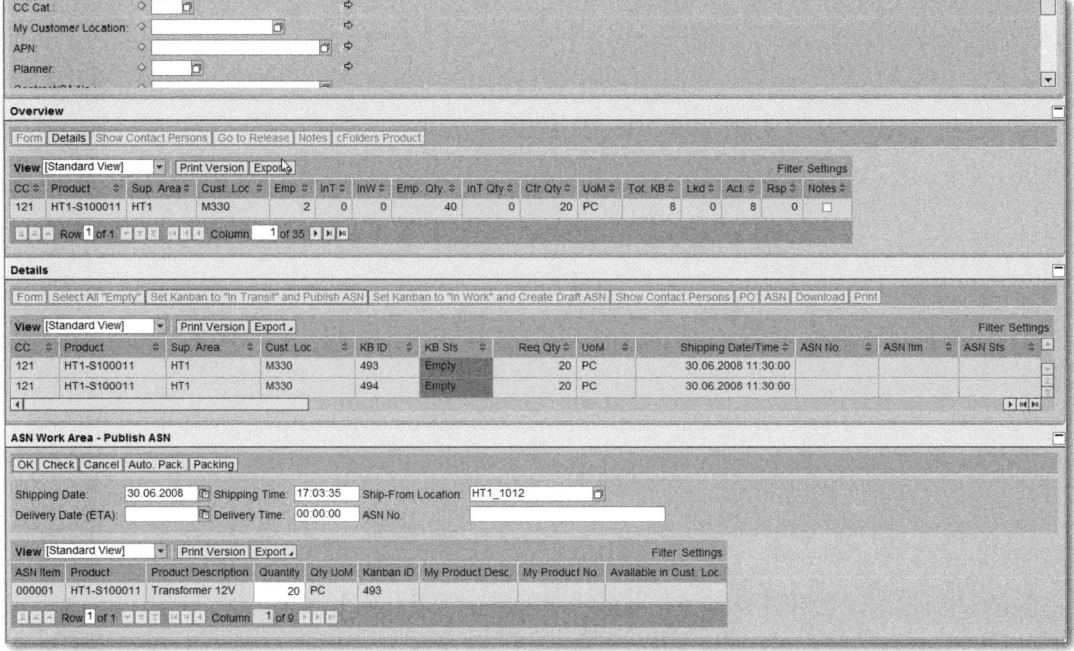

Figure 4.119 Creating an ASN in the Kanban Monitor

The kanban status changes from EMPTY to IN TRANSIT in SAP SNC (see Figure 4.120).

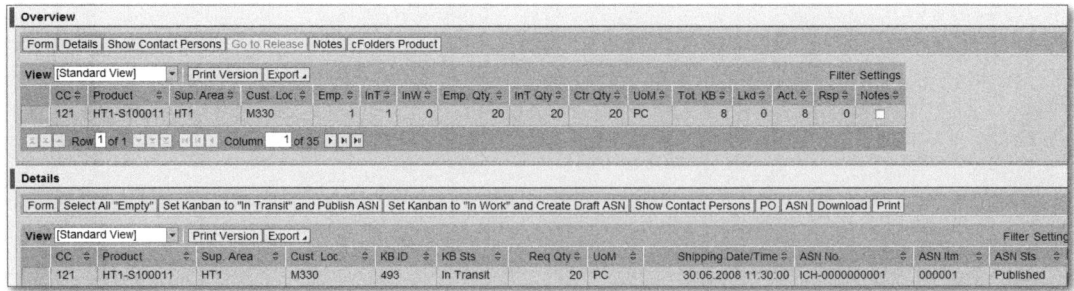

Figure 4.120 Changed Kanban Status After the ASN Has Been Published

Similarly, the status in the kanban board in the customer's SAP ERP backend system also changes from EMPTY to IN TRANSIT when the ASN is received (see Figure 4.121).

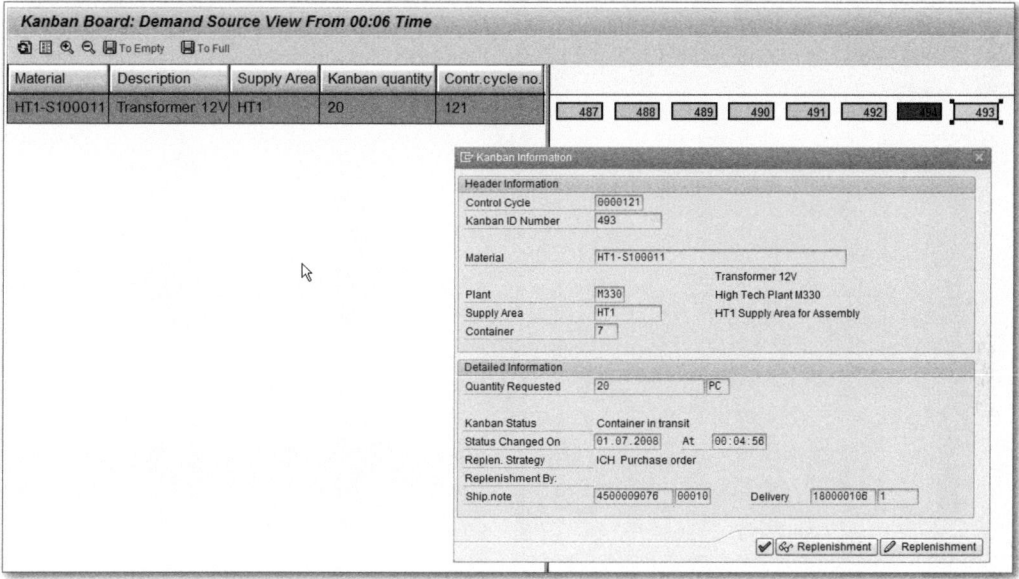

Figure 4.121 Kanban Board in the Customer's SAP ERP Backend System

The ASN also appears in the STOCK/REQUIREMENTS LIST (Transaction MD04) in SAP ERP (see Figure 4.122).

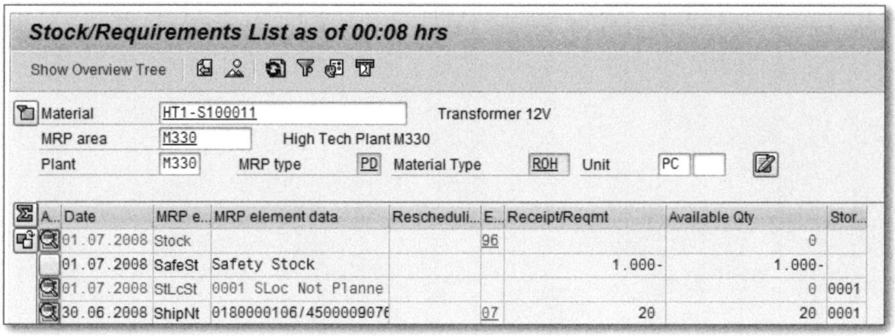

Figure 4.122 ASN Visible in the Stock/Requirements List

You can open the ASN by double-clicking on it in the STOCK/REQUIREMENTS LIST (see Figure 4.123).

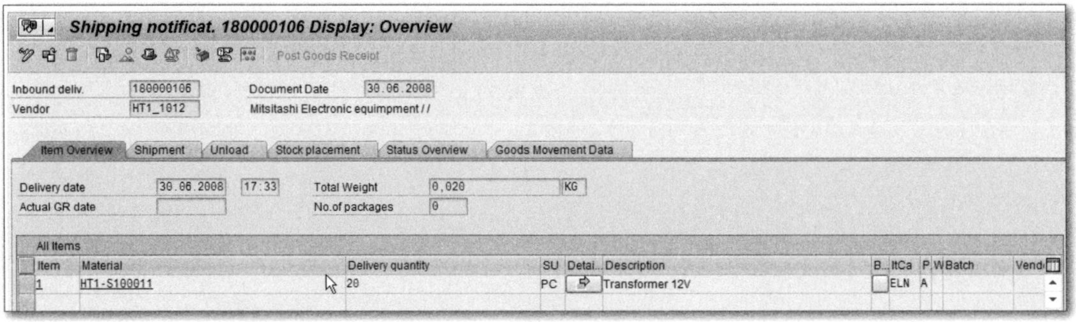

4 | Business Processes in SAP SNC 5.1

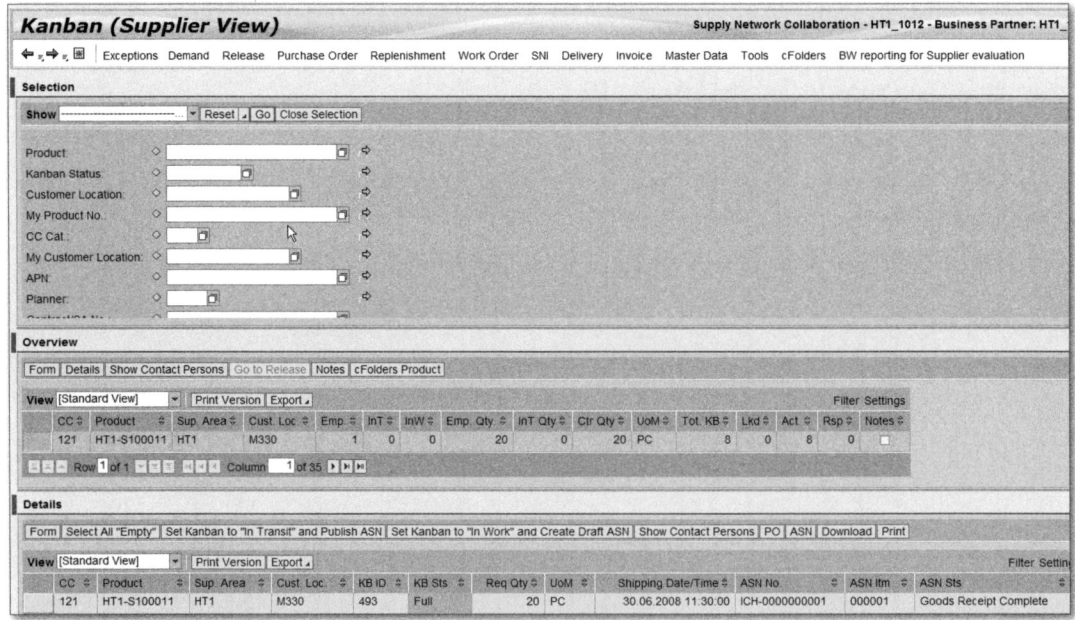

Figure 4.123 Displaying the ASN

4.8.5 Posting Goods Receipt

The customer sets the kanban with status IN TRANSIT to FULL in the kanban board in the SAP ECC 6.0 backend. The status change also prompts a change of color from yellow to green. Goods receipt is posted automatically for the ASN. The customer's SAP ERP system sends the IDoc STPPOD. DELVRY03 to SAP NetWeaver PI, where it is converted to an XML message of type *ReceivedDeliveryNotification* (RDN) and sent on to SAP SNC.

Figure 4.124 Updated Status in SAP SNC After Goods Receipt

Once the goods receipt information has been sent to SAP SNC, the status of the kanban card is also changed here from IN TRANSIT to GOODS RECEIPT COMPLETE, and the color changes from yellow to green (see Figure 4.124).

4.8.6 Monitoring the Kanban Process

For the purpose of monitoring the kanban process, both the supplier and the customer can use the Kanban Monitor, which displays the status of the kanbans.

Alerts are another function used to monitor the kanban process. SAP SNC 5.1 provides alert types that are visible to the customer and the supplier. The ALERT MONITOR in SAP SNC displays the alerts that belong to a given alert type (see Figure 4.125).

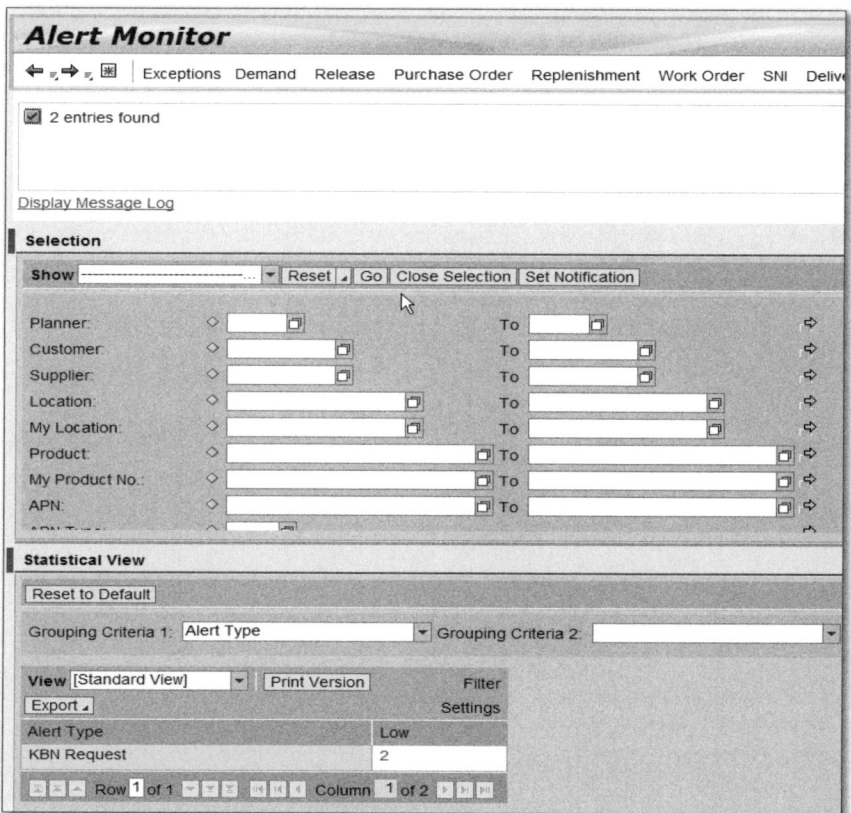

Figure 4.125 Alert – Kanban Request

You can view the alert in more detail by clicking on the row containing the alert type (see Figure 4.126).

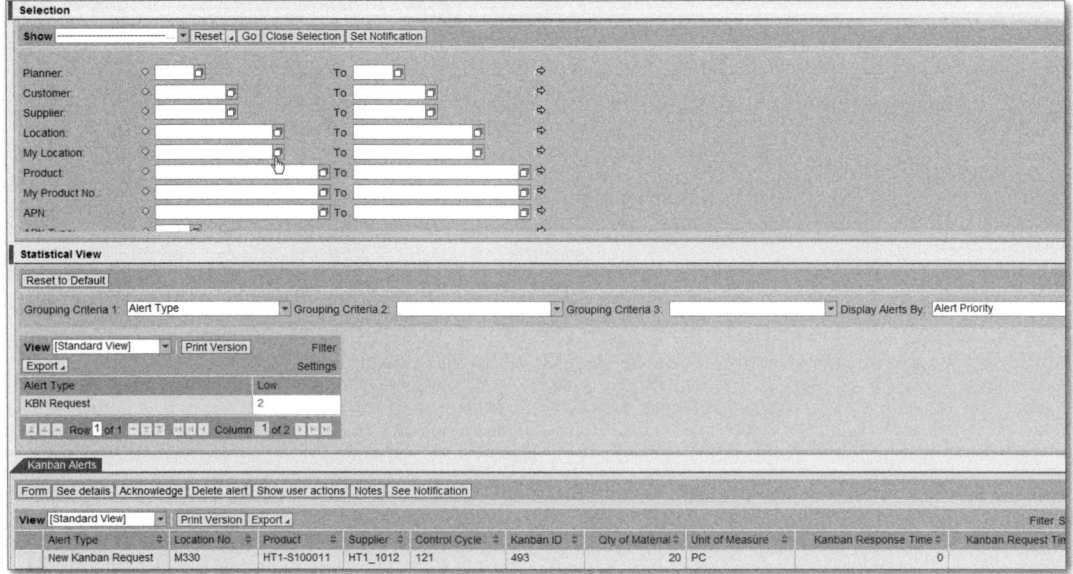

Figure 4.126 Detailed View of the New Kanban Request Alert

By selecting the alert and clicking on the SEE DETAILS button, you are taken directly to the Kanban Monitor.

Table 4.10 provides an overview of the alert types included in the standard shipment for the kanban process in SAP SNC 5.1.

Alert Type	Description
New kanban request	SAP SNC generates this alert automatically when a new kanban request is received.
Late kanban response	This alert is generated when a response time is exceeded.

Table 4.10 Standard Alert Types in the Kanban Process

Late Kanban Response

The customer expects the supplier to respond to an empty kanban and create an ASN within a particular time frame. You can define a default response time in SAP Easy Access under SUPPLY NETWORK COLLABORATION • MASTER DATA • APPLICATION-SPECIFIC MASTER DATA • KANBAN • / SCA/UPDRESPTIME (see Figure 4.127).

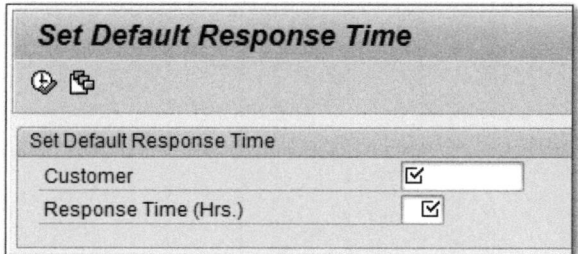

Figure 4.127 Setting the Default Response Time

To monitor the response time, the customer can execute report SCA/DM_KNBN_ALRT_LATERESP at regular intervals in SAP SNC. This report checks whether the response time has been exceeded for empty kanbans. If so, an alert is generated (see Figure 4.128).

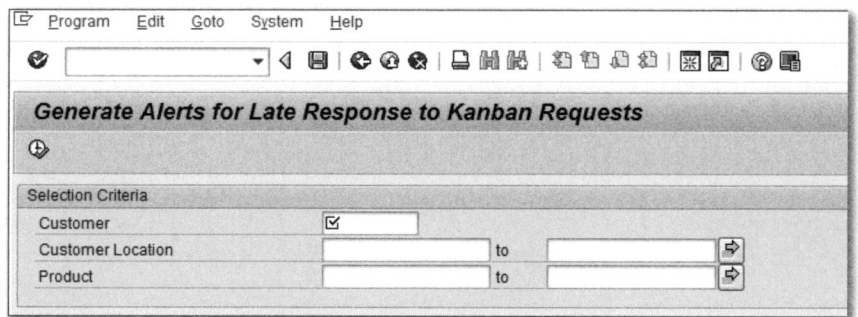

Figure 4.128 Report SCA/DM_KNBN_ALRT_LATERESP

4.9 Delivery Control Monitor

This section first provides an overview of the replenishment process using the *Delivery Control Monitor* (DCM) with SAP SNC 5.1 (see Figure 4.129). It then takes a closer look at the individual process steps and settings in SAP SNC.

Sub-daily replenishment

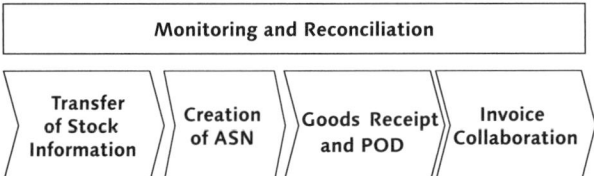

Figure 4.129 Process Flow for Replenishment Planning with the Delivery Control Monitor

4.9.1 Process Overview

The supplier uses the Delivery Control Monitor up to several times a day to monitor the current stock on hand at the customer's location. As in the SMI scenario, the supplier is obliged to adhere to the stock limits (minimum and maximum stock levels). If stock falls below a reorder point between the minimum and maximum stock levels, the system generates an alert. At this point, the supplier should replenish the stock at the customer's location without delay to eliminate the risk of a stock shortage occurring. To do so, the supplier creates an ASN.

Goods receipt is posted once the goods have been physically received and put away at the customer's location. A proof of delivery message confirms to the supplier the actual quantity received by the customer. Furthermore, reasons for any quantity differences and the confirmation date can be provided.

Invoice collaboration takes place with reference to the ASN on the basis of conventional invoice processing or self-billing (see Section 4.12).

The Delivery Control Monitor and a range of alerts to draw attention to any exception situations are used to monitor replenishment planning between customer and supplier.

The DCM is a practical tool to use if the customer is in a position to react quickly to the current stock on hand. In concrete terms, the transportation duration must not be overly long, and the product must be in stock at the supplier's location.

In contrast to the SMI scenario, the DCM does not result in requirements being sent from the customer to the supplier. The DCM is not intended for planning because it does not contain any information about the future development of the customer's stock situation.

For the DCM to display a situation that is as up to date as possible, which enables the supplier to respond in an appropriate way, stock data must be transferred regularly and in a timely fashion from the customer's backend system to SAP SNC.

The process flow for replenishment planning with the DCM is shown in Figure 4.130.

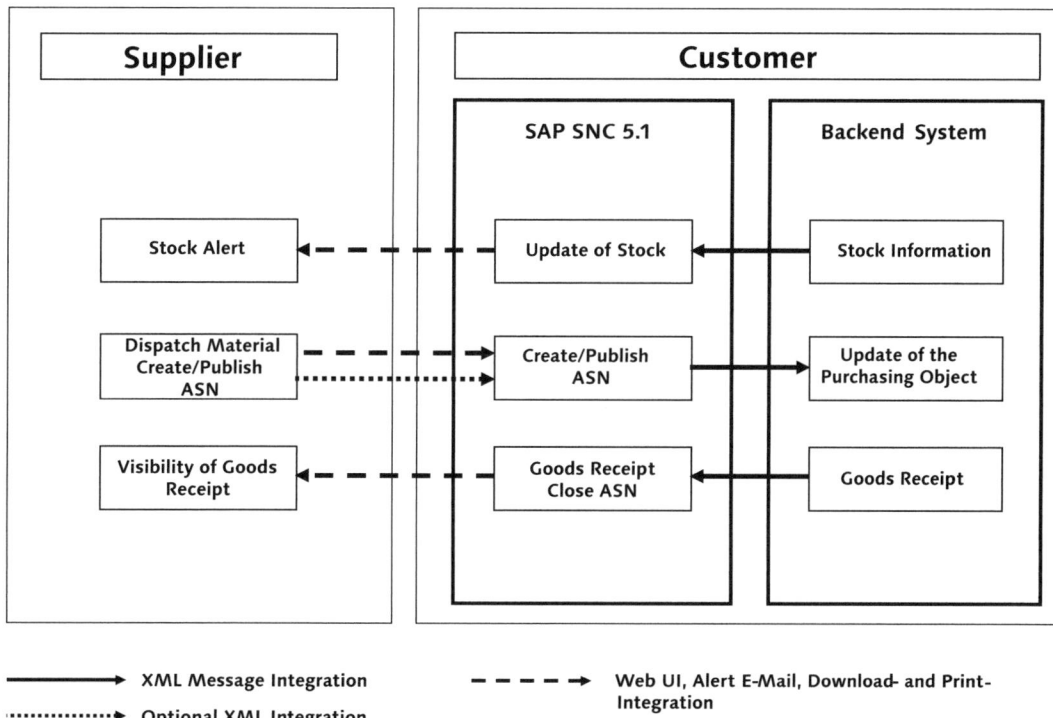

Figure 4.130 Process Flow for Replenishment Planning with the Delivery Control Monitor

4.9.2 Master Data Specific to the DCM

In addition to the generic master data (see Section 4.1 Generic Master Data), purchase scheduling agreements are also required as master data for the replenishment planning process with the DCM.

Master data

4.9.3 Determining and Sending Stock Information

For a supplier to view stock data in SAP SNC, the data must first be sent from the customer's backend system. This is achieved with the same report as described in Section 4.2.3 Determining and Transferring Gross Demands and Stock Information. In this case, however, requirements are not communicated (see Figure 4.131).

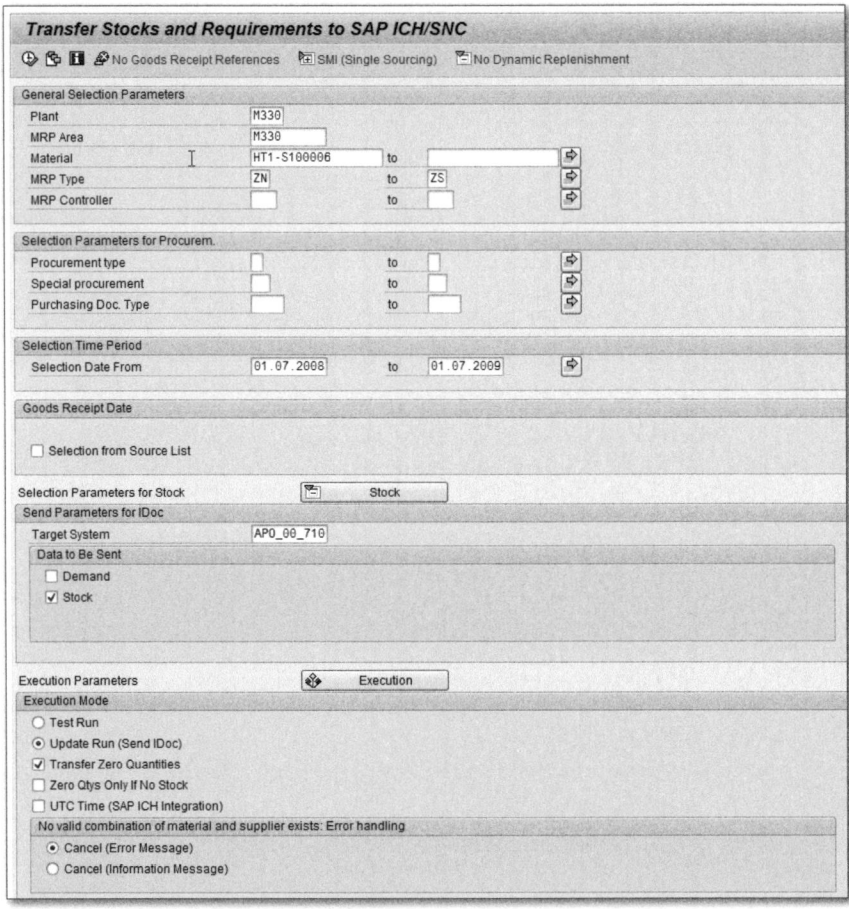

Figure 4.131 Report for Sending Stock Data

The stock data to be sent is the same as the data provided in the STOCK OVERVIEW (Transaction MMBE) in the customer's SAP ERP system (see Figure 4.132).

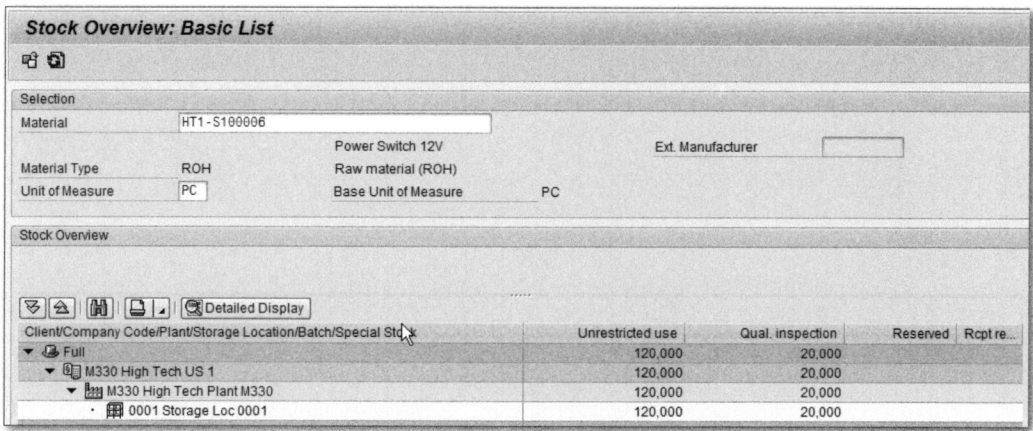

Figure 4.132 Stock Data Display in the Customer's Backend System

4.9.4 Creating an ASN

You use the Delivery Control Monitor to create the ASN. You can find the Kanban Monitor in SAP SNC under REPLENISHMENT • DELIVERY CONTROL MONITOR • DCM (see Figure 4.133).

Delivery Control Monitor

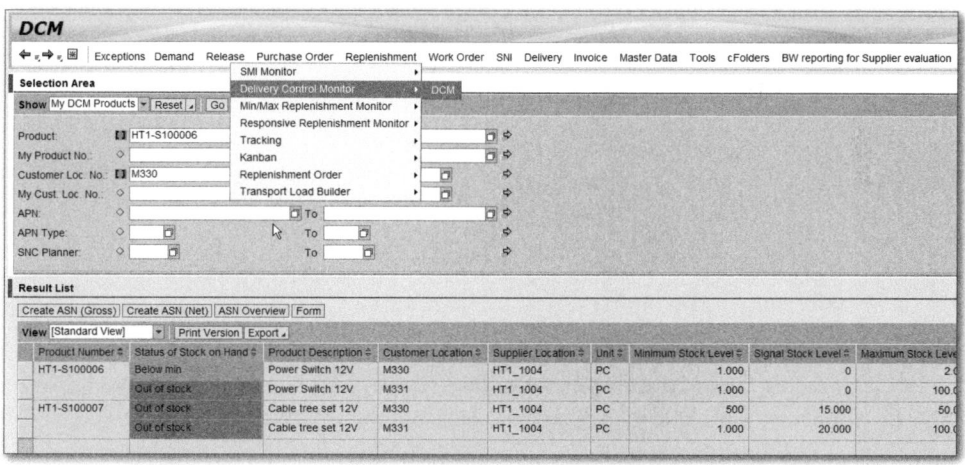

Figure 4.133 Delivery Control Monitor in the SAP SNC Menu Path

The supplier can view relevant materials by choosing from a range of selection criteria.

The system displays the data shown in Table 4.11 for each material and customer location (plant).

Data	Description
Status of stock on hand	The status of the stock on hand is compared with the reorder point and minimum and maximum stock levels.
Minimum stock level	The stock on hand should not fall below this threshold value.
Reorder point	At this threshold value, the supplier should initiate delivery.
Maximum stock level	The stock on hand should not exceed this threshold value.
Gross delivery quantity	The quantity proposed by the system that the supplier is to deliver to the customer to replenish stock to the maximum stock level. Stock in transit is not taken into account.
Net delivery quantity	The quantity proposed by the system that the supplier is to deliver to the customer to replenish stock to the maximum stock level. Stock in transit is taken into account.
Stock on hand	The stock on hand is composed of the following stock types: unrestricted-use, blocked, quality inspection, and consignment stock.
	If you want to calculate the stock on hand on a different basis, this can be achieved with the profile for calculating projected stock (see Section 4.2.12).
In-transit quantity	The total open delivery quantity of all ASNs with PUBLISHED status.
In-transit quantity of today	The total open delivery quantity of ASNs with PUBLISHED status whose delivery date is the current date.
Overdue in-transit quantity	The total open delivery quantity of published ASNs whose delivery date is in the past.

Table 4.11 Key Figures in the Delivery Control Monitor

Calculating the delivery quantity

The supplier can now change the status by creating an ASN. To do so, the supplier selects one or more lines and clicks on the CREATE ASN (GROSS) or CREATE ASN (NET) button. The system calculates the gross or net delivery quantity as follows:

Gross delivery quantity = maximum stock level − stock on hand
Net delivery quantity = maximum stock level − stock on hand − stock in transit

If you were to click on the CREATE ASN (GROSS) button for the second line in the following example (see Figure 4.134), the system would create an ASN for 99,790 pieces. If you were to click on CREATE ASN (NET), the system would not create an ASN because an ASN for the same amount already exists.

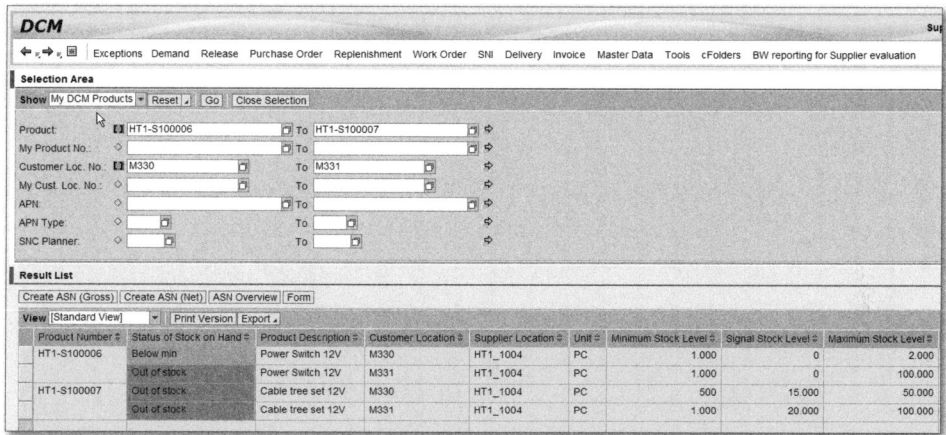

Figure 4.134 Sample Data in the Delivery Control Monitor

This would not make any difference in the case of the example in the first line because the system has not found a published ASN; therefore, it would create an ASN for 99,859 pieces in both gross and net calculations.

In this example, an ASN has been created and published for the first line (see Figure 4.135).

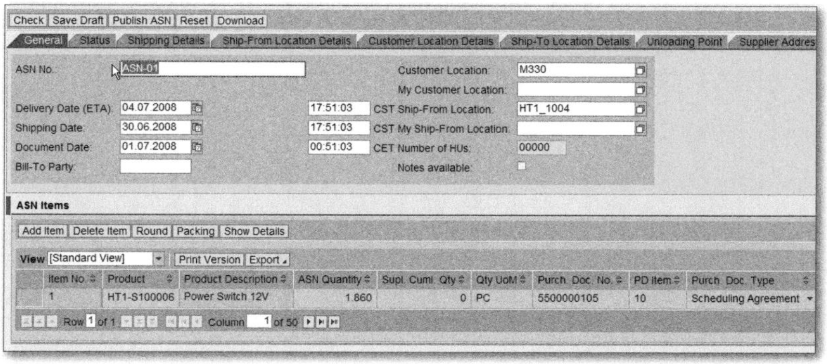

Figure 4.135 Creating an ASN

The data in the DCM changes to reflect the fact that the net delivery quantity is zero and the stock in transit has been increased by the quantity entered in the ASN (see Figure 4.136).

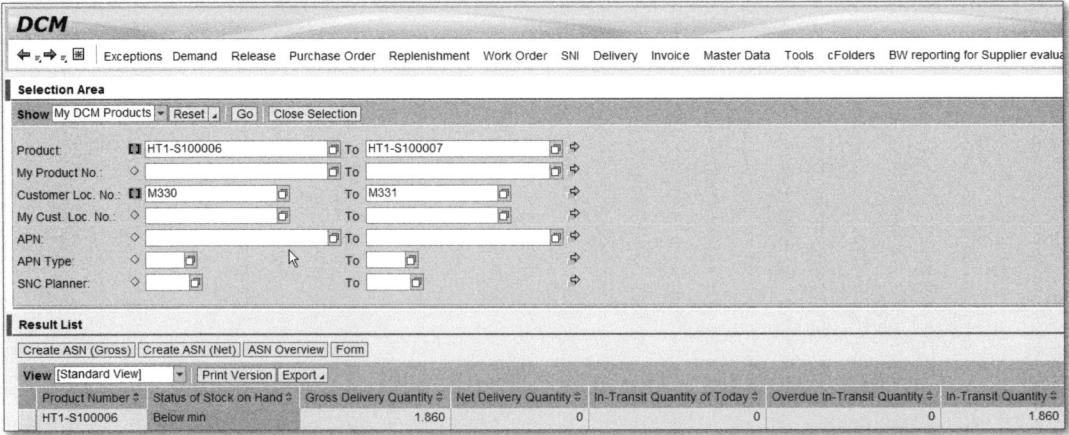

Figure 4.136 Changed Data in the DCM After an ASN Has Been Created

Once the ASN has been published, SAP SNC sends an XML message of type *DispatchedDeliveryNotification* (DDN) to the SAP NetWeaver PI system, which converts the message into the DESADV.DELVRY03 IDoc and sends it on to the customer's SAP ERP system.

The ASN also appears in the stock/requirements list (Transaction MD04) in SAP ERP (see Figure 4.137).

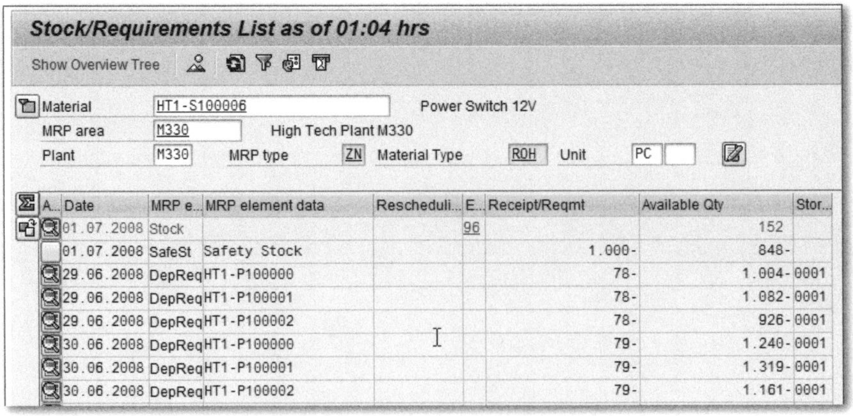

Figure 4.137 ASN Visible in the Stock/Requirements List

4.9.5 Posting Goods Receipt

Goods receipt is posted in the customer's SAP ERP system as a reference to the ASN. There are several transactions for goods receipt. In this example, Transaction VL32n has been used because it offers the advantage that the customer's SAP ERP system immediately sends the STPPOD.DELVRY03 IDoc to SAP NetWeaver PI. This IDoc is converted into an XML message of type *ReceivedDeliveryNotification* (RDN) and sent to SAP SNC.

Once the goods receipt has been posted, the status of the ASN is changed in SAP SNC and the Delivery Control Monitor is updated (see Figure 4.138).

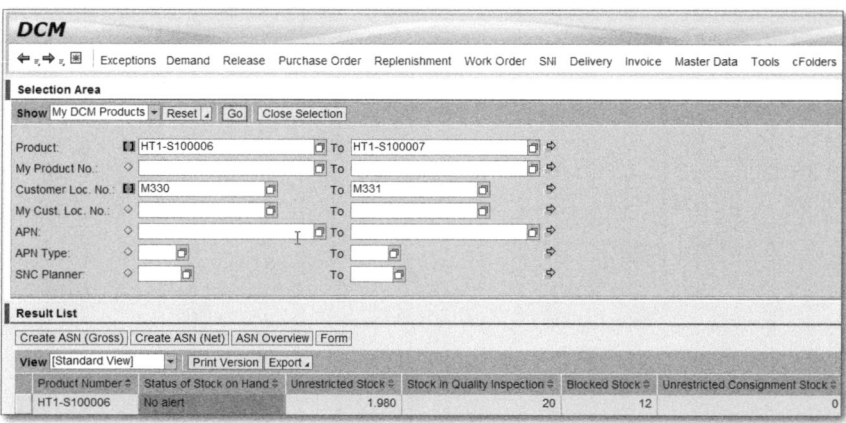

Figure 4.138 Updated DCM After Goods Receipt

4.9.6 Monitoring Replenishment Planning with the Delivery Control Monitor

Both the supplier and the customer can use the Delivery Control Monitor for their monitoring activities. Exception situations are shown in a range of colors. For instance, stockouts are shown in red, stock below the minimum limit in orange, stock between the reorder point and minimum stock level in yellow and above the maximum stock level in blue, and stock within the maximum limit and reorder point in green.

Alerts are another function used to monitor replenishment planning with the DCM. SAP SNC 5.1 provides a range of alert types that inform the customer or supplier of exception situations in replenishment planning with the Delivery Control Monitor. These alert types are visible to both customer and supplier. The ALERT MONITOR in SAP SNC displays the alerts that belong to a given alert type (see Figure 4.139).

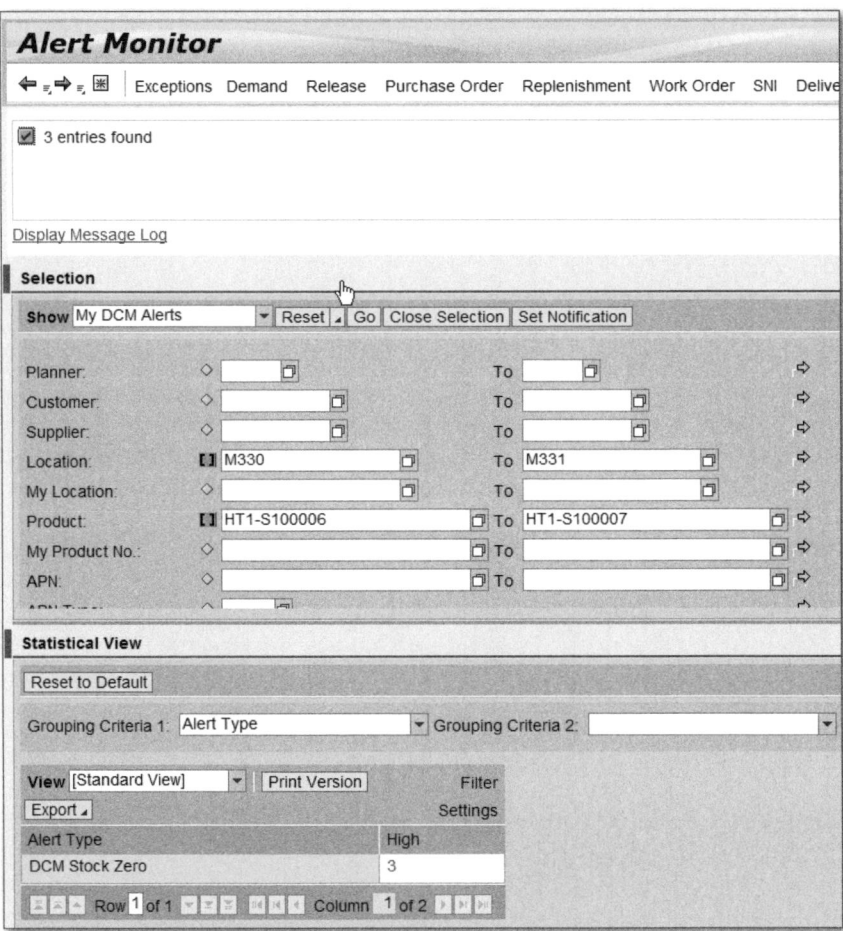

Figure 4.139 DCM Alert – Stock Below Minimum Level

You can view the alert in more detail by clicking on the row containing the alert type (see Figure 4.140).

Table 4.12 provides an overview of the alert types included in the standard shipment for replenishment planning with the DCM in SAP SNC 5.1 to indicate if there is a critical stock situation.

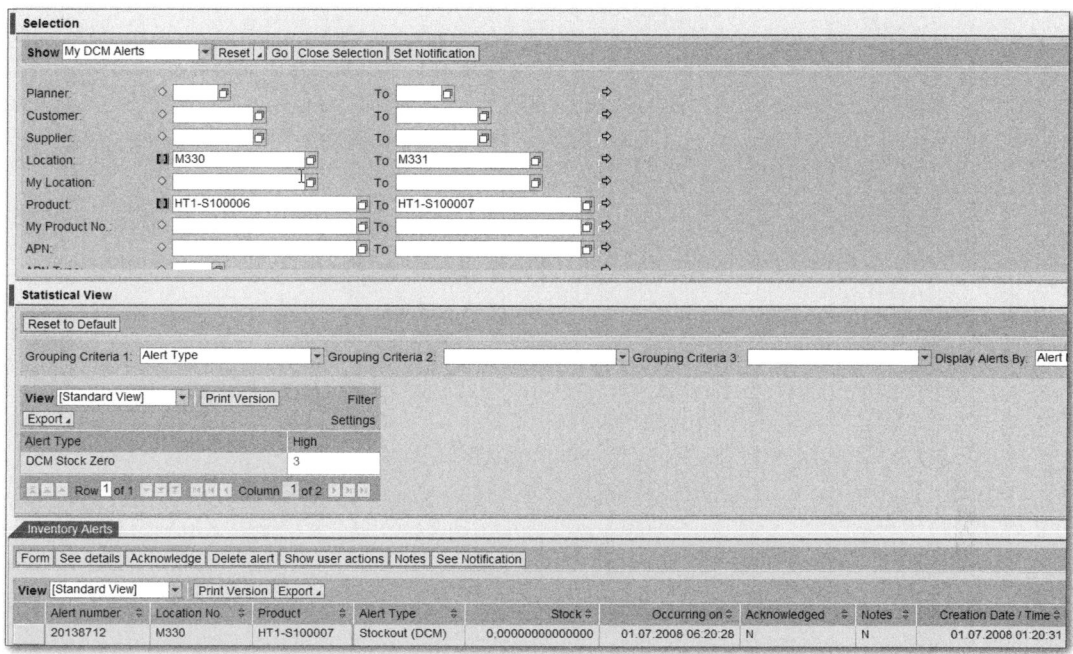

Figure 4.140 Detailed Alert View

Alert Type	Description
Stock Below Minimum (DCM)	The stock on hand is below the minimum stock level.
Stock Above Maximum (DCM)	The stock on hand is above the maximum stock level.
Stockout (DCM)	The stock on hand is zero.
Reorder Point Reached (DCM)	The stock on hand is equal to or has fallen below the reorder point.

Table 4.12 Standard Alert Types in the Delivery Control Monitor

4.10 Dynamic Replenishment

This section begins with an overview of the *dynamic replenishment* business process with SAP SNC 5.1. It then takes a closer look at the individual process steps and settings in SAP SNC (see Figure 4.141).

4 Business Processes in SAP SNC 5.1

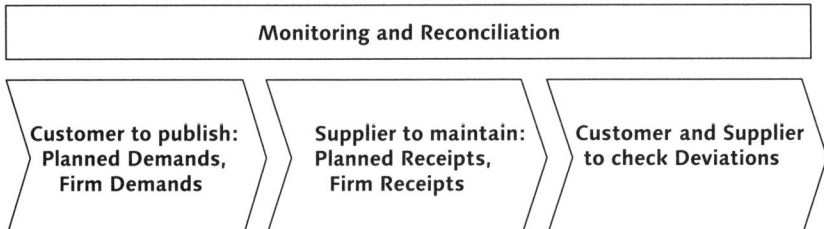

Figure 4.141 Process Flow for Dynamic Replenishment

4.10.1 Process Overview

Dynamic replenishment allows a comparison of the customer's net demands and supplier receipts over a chosen period of time. Deviations are calculated automatically and made visible to the customer and the supplier. The customer transfers planned and firm demands from his backend system to SAP SNC. The supplier can either send planned and firm receipts from his backend system to SAP SNC or maintain them manually in the SAP SNC web browser (see Figure 4.142). The system automatically calculates the absolute and percentage differences between the customer demands and supplier receipts. It also compares the differences with the predefined tolerance limits and threshold values and color-codes the time buckets. Both the customer and the supplier quickly obtain an overview of critical situations, allowing them to adapt planning and delivery capacity.

Dynamic replenishment is used as a tactical tool to agree on customer and supplier planning. Actual operational processing is achieved with the purchase order processing and forecast delivery schedule processing business processes.

New as of SAP SNC 5.1 A new feature of SAP SNC 5.1 is the option to set the tolerance limits and threshold values for the calculation of deviations in Customizing for consensus finding. Deviations can be calculated using the Planning Service Manager (PSM). In addition, the tool previously known as the Demand Monitor has been renamed the *Order Forecast Monitor* (OFM).

Dynamic Replenishment | 4.10

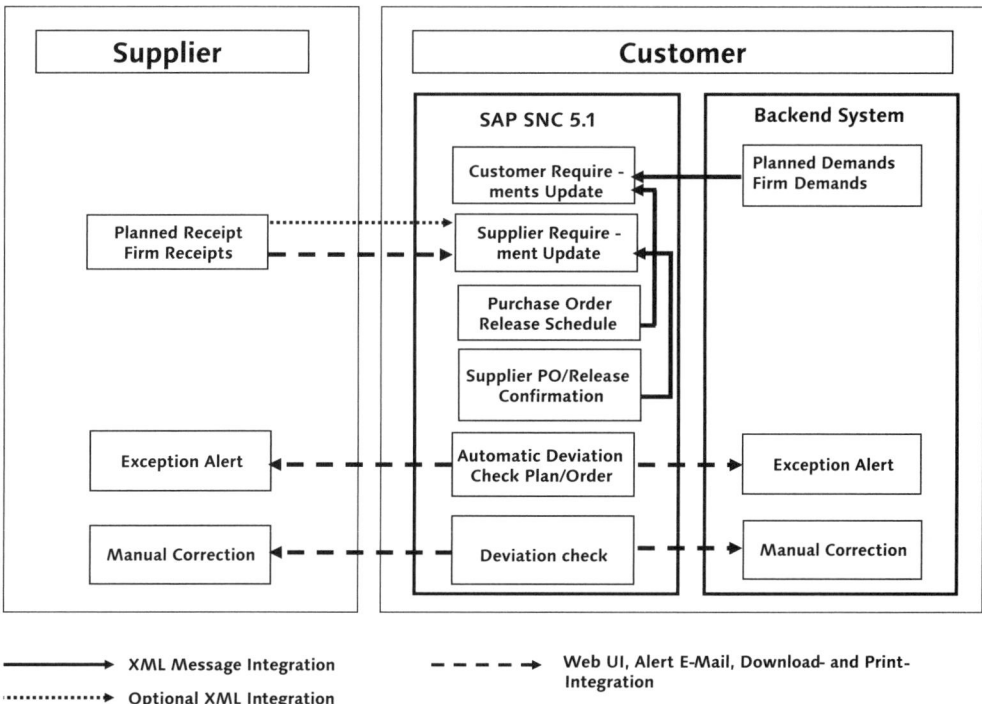

Figure 4.142 Dynamic Replenishment with SAP SNC 5.1

4.10.2 Master Data for Dynamic Replenishment

Dynamic replenishment is generally used in combination with forecast delivery schedule processing or purchase order processing (see Sections 4.3 Forecast Delivery Schedule Processing and 4.4 Purchase Order Handling). Purchase orders and firm forecast delivery schedules are treated as customer firm demands, whereas forecast delivery schedule confirmations and purchase order confirmations from the supplier are treated as supplier firm receipts.

The result is that it is possible to establish dynamic replenishment on the basis of the master data stored for purchase order processing or forecast delivery schedule processing.

To prepare and display customer demands, supplier receipts, and the calculated differences in the Order Forecast Monitor, you should create a time buckets profile at location and location product levels (menu path DEMAND • ORDER FORECAST MONITOR • TIME BUCKETS PROFILES).

Time buckets profile for the OFM

185

The entire planning period and its period division in the Order Forecast Monitor are defined in the time buckets profile (see Figure 4.143). Here, either a positive or negative number of days can be entered as the OFFSET by which the start of the planning period is either postponed or moved into the past. It is also possible to define which time buckets in the planning period are shown in days, weeks, months, and years in the Order Forecast Monitor.

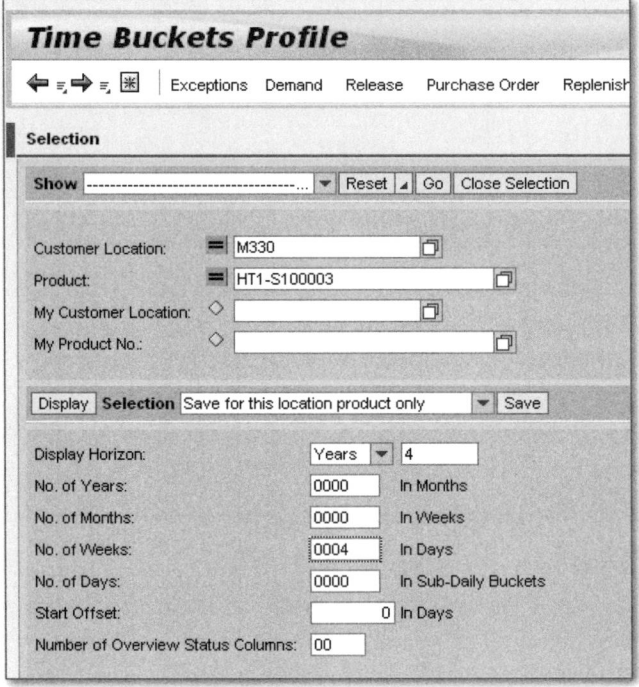

Figure 4.143 Time Buckets Profile for the Order Forecast Monitor

4.10.3 Transferring Customer Demands

Customer planned and firm demands
The customer planned and firm demands are extracted from the customer's backend system and sent to SAP SNC. In an SAP ERP system (as of Release 4.6C), report RSMIPROACT is used to extract the customer demands (see Figure 4.144). In the selection parameters area for master data, you can select the products and restrict the demand time period using a range of parameters. You can then define the demand elements

you would like to be transferred. The following demand elements can be selected:

- Independent demands
- Purchase requisitions
- Purchase orders
- Dependent demands from planned orders
- Scheduling agreement delivery schedule lines

Purchase orders and scheduling agreement delivery schedule lines in the first firm/trade-off zone are treated as firm demands. Purchase requisitions, dependent demands from planned orders, scheduling agreement delivery schedule lines as of the second firm/trade-off zone, and independent demands are transferred as planned demands.

The extracted data is sent to SAP NetWeaver PI as an IDoc of type PROACT.PROACT01, where it is mapped to an XML message of type *Product ActivityNotification* and sent on to SAP SNC.

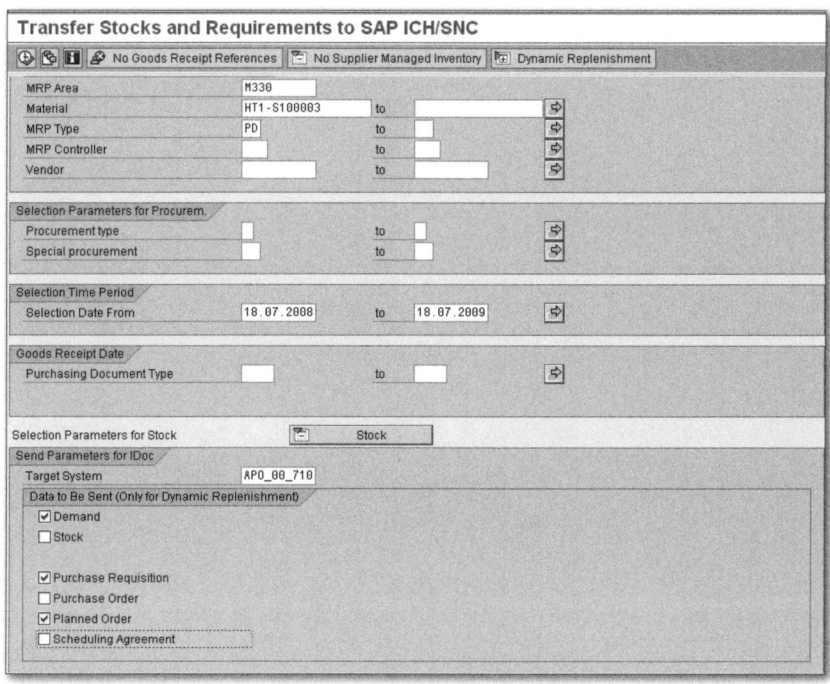

Figure 4.144 Extracting Customer Demands (RSMIPROACT)

4 | Business Processes in SAP SNC 5.1

4.10.4 Maintaining Supplier Receipts

Supplier planned and firm demands

The supplier can transfer planned and firm receipts from his backend system to SAP SNC. The supplier planned receipts can be sent as messages of type *ProductForecastNotification* or *ProductForecastRevisionNotification*. Supplier firm receipts are sent to SAP SNC with an XML message of type *ReplenishmentOrderConfirmation*.

Alternatively, the supplier can maintain planned receipts manually in the SAP SNC web browser (see Figure 4.145) by selecting ORDER FORECAST DETAILS – PRODUCT VIEW (menu path DEMAND • ORDER FORECAST MONITOR • ORDER FORECAST DETAILS – PRODUCT VIEW) and then selecting the OVERVIEW • IN TRANSIT INFORMATION • MULTI SOURCING MODE grid arrangement. The supplier can enter or change the planned receipt quantity for each time bucket.

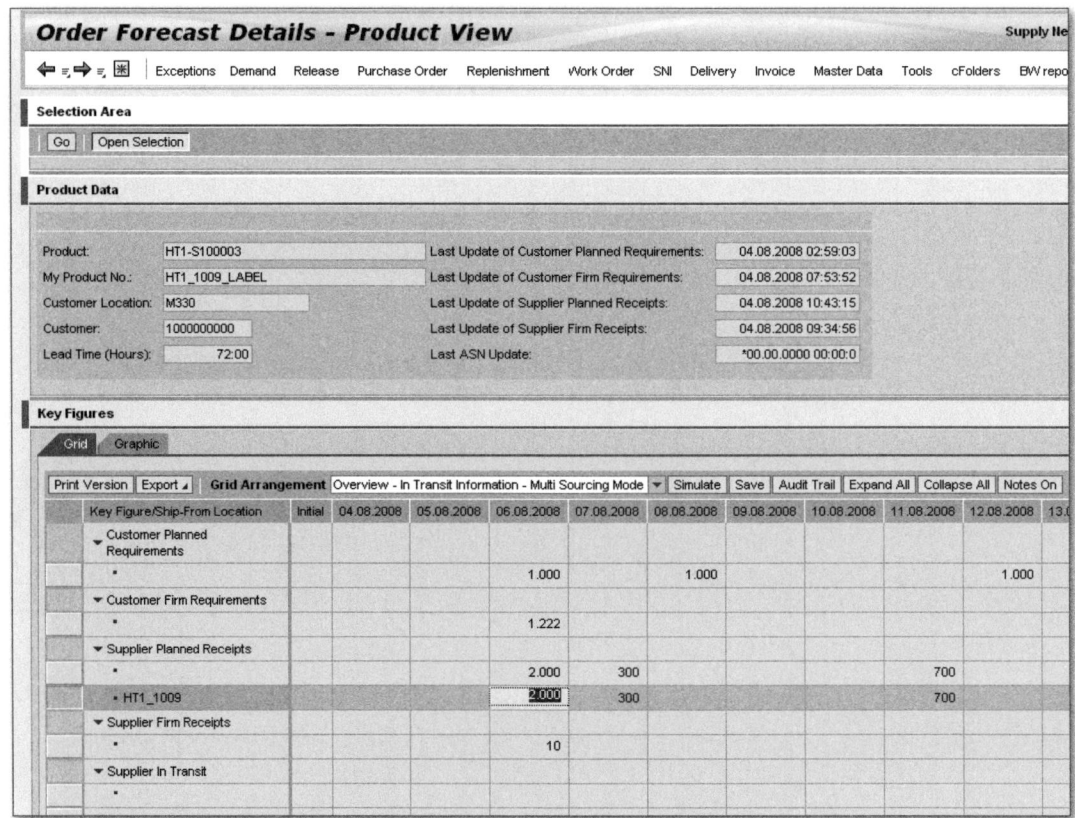

Figure 4.145 Maintaining Supplier Planned Receipts

The supplier can enter firm receipts indirectly in the SAP SNC web browser by means of forecast delivery schedule confirmations or purchase order confirmations (see Sections 4.3.5 Confirming Quantities and Dates/Times and 4.4.5 Purchase Order Confirmation).

The stock in transit represents the sum of quantities that are on their way to the customer. It is determined from the quantities in the ASNs. The supplier can send ASNs from his backend system to SAP SNC using an XML message of type *DispatchedDeliveryNotification* or create and publish them manually in the SAP SNC web browser.

Stock in transit

4.10.5 Calculating and Checking Deviations

SAP SNC compares customer requirements and supplier receipts and determines the absolute and percentage differences for each time bucket. Table 4.13 provides a list of the calculated key figures shown in the Order Forecast Monitor.

Key Figure	Calculation
Difference Planned Receipts/Planned Requirements (%)	100 × (supplier planned receipts – customer planned demands)/customer planned demands
Difference Planned Receipts/Planned Requirements	Supplier planned receipts – customer planned demands
Difference Firm Receipts/Firm Requirements (%)	100 × (supplier firm receipts – customer firm demands)/customer firm demands
Difference Firm Receipts/Firm Requirements	Supplier firm receipts – customer firm demands

Table 4.13 Calculated Key Figures in the Order Forecast Monitor

The key figures calculated by the system are compared with tolerance values. If these tolerance values are breached, the respective time bucket is color-coded in the Order Forecast Monitor.

Consensus finding and condition technique

You can override the default tolerance settings with your own settings and define specific tolerance values in Customizing for consensus finding and the condition technique (in Transaction SPRO, follow the menu path SUPPLY NETWORK COLLABORATION • BASIC SETTINGS • CONSENSUS FINDing). Quantity profiles are defined to establish occurrences of overdeliveries and underdeliveries. In addition, the condition technique can be used with consensus rules to determine tolerance values for a combination of supplier, product, and ship-to location.

Furthermore, you can execute the Order Forecast Monitor calculation in the Planning Service Manager. To do so, you have to define a service profile (see Figure 4.146) in Customizing (in Transaction SPRO, follow the menu path SUPPLY NETWORK COLLABORATION • DEMAND • ORDER FORECAST MONITOR • DEFINE SERVICE PROFILES FOR ORDER FORECAST MONITOR).

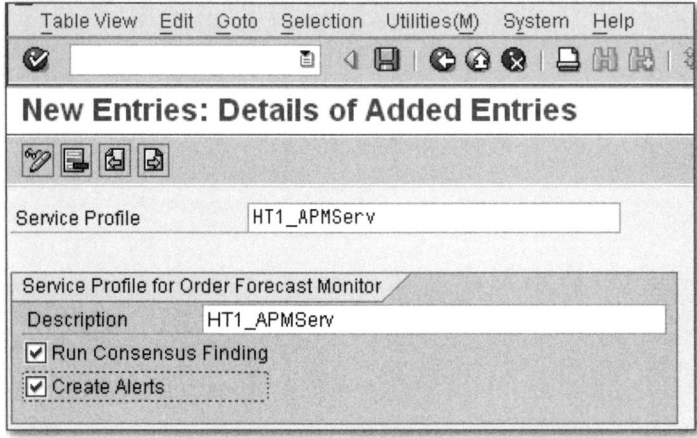

Figure 4.146 Service Profile for the Order Forecast Monitor

Alert profile for the OFM

To enable alerts to be generated if the tolerance limits are not reached or exceeded, an alert profile (see Figure 4.147) for the Order Forecast Monitor is required (in Transaction SPRO, follow the menu path SUPPLY NETWORK COLLABORATION • DEMAND • ORDER FORECAST MONITOR • DEFINE ALERT PROFILES FOR CSF AND OFM). In the alert profile, you can define alert priorities for differences between planned and firm key figures.

Color profile for the OFM

The color profile allows the status of tolerance deviations for a time bucket to be highlighted in color in the Order Forecast Monitor (see Figure 4.148). You can override the default setting with your own color profile (in Transaction SPRO, follow the menu path SUPPLY NETWORK COLLABORATION • DEMAND • DEFINE COLOR PROFILES FOR CSF AND OFM).

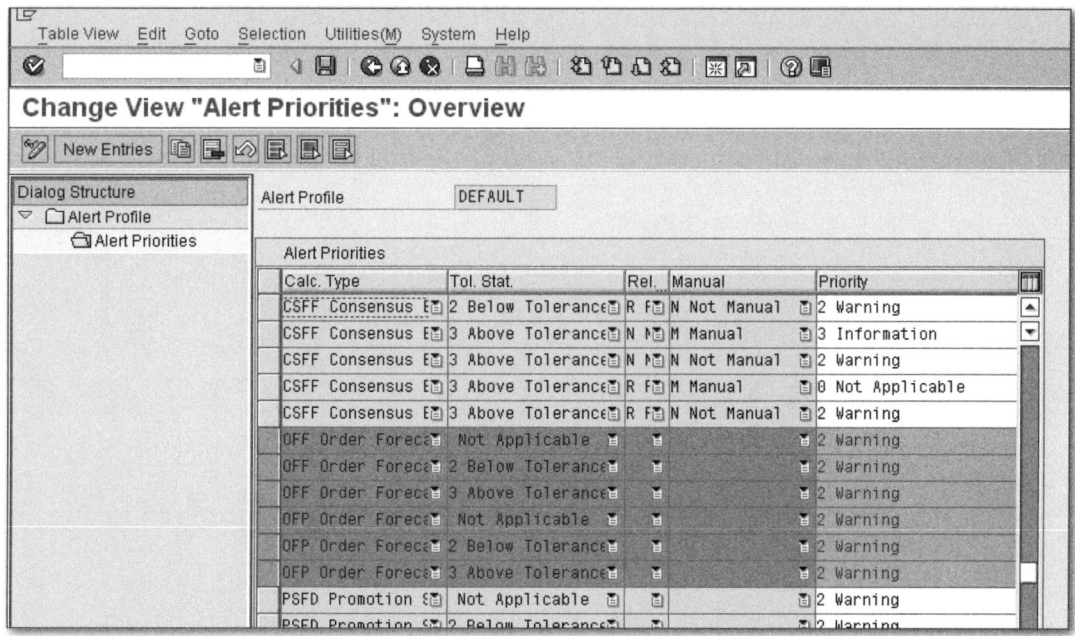

Figure 4.147 Alert Profile for the Order Forecast Monitor

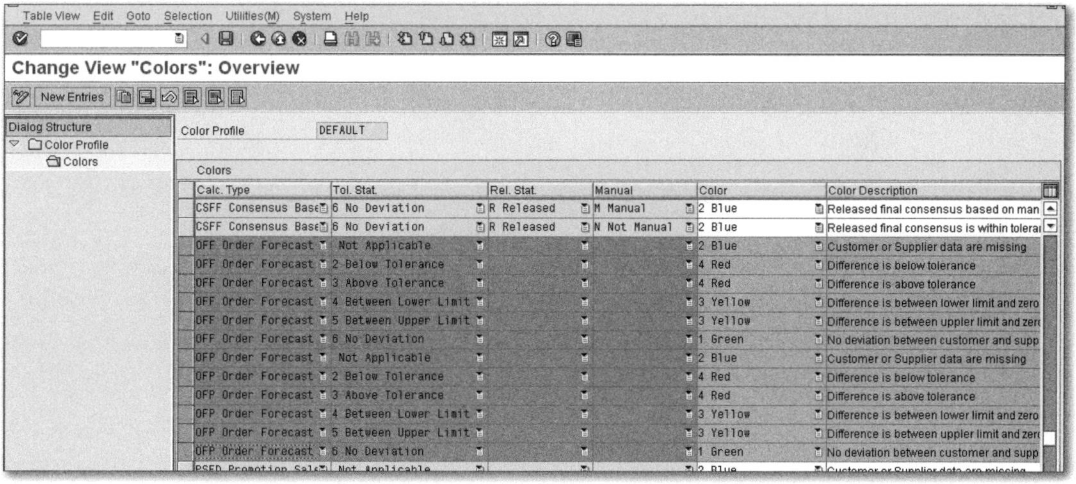

Figure 4.148 Color Profiles for the Order Forecast Monitor

On the basis of the customer requirements transferred, supplier receipts, calculated differences, and tolerance deviations, key figures and status values are displayed in the Order Forecast Monitor. In the ORDER

FORECAST DETAILS – PRODUCT VIEW, the customer and supplier can view the prepared key figures and status information for each time bucket for a location product (see Figure 4.149). In addition, the last updates to customer requirements and supplier receipts are logged.

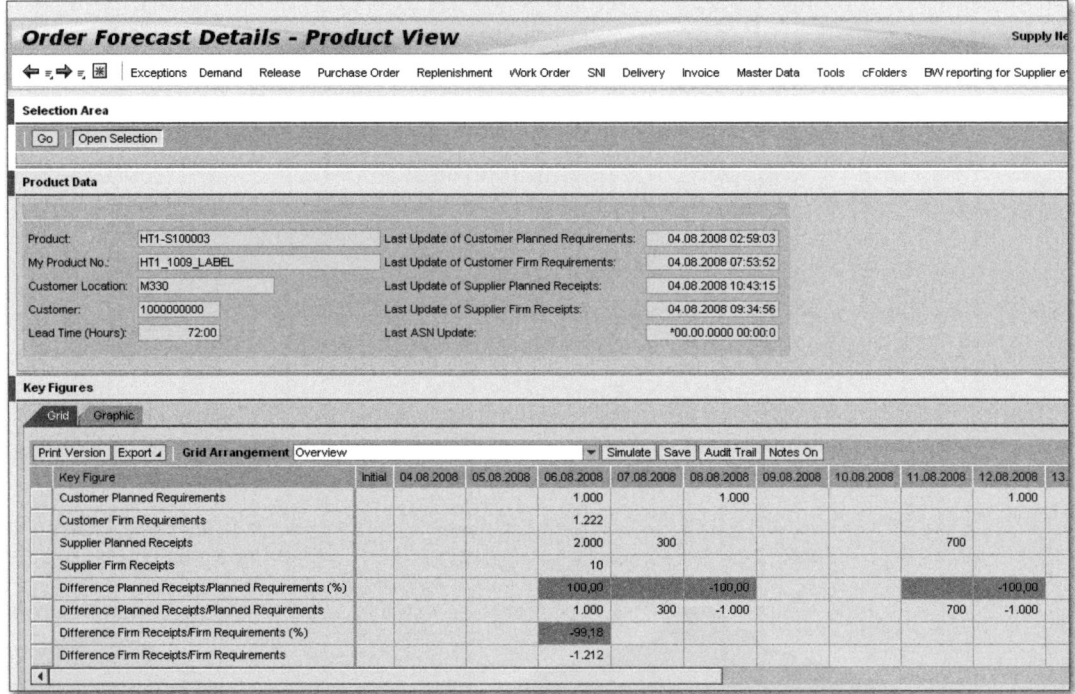

Figure 4.149 Order Forecast Details – Product View

Confirmation quantities for purchase orders or forecast delivery schedules that are entered by the supplier in the SAP SNC web browser or sent from the supplier's backend system are automatically displayed as firm receipts in the Order Forecast Monitor.

Furthermore, quantities in the ASNs published by the supplier are shown in ORDER FORECAST DETAILS – PRODUCT VIEW as SUPPLIER – IN TRANSIT. This can be seen by selecting the OVERVIEW – IN TRANSIT INFORMATION grid arrangement.

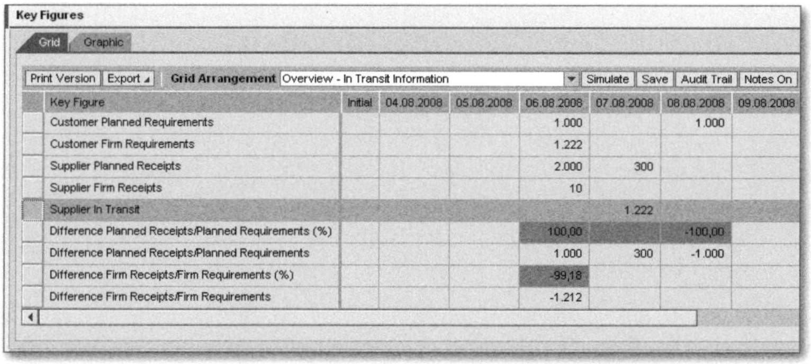

Figure 4.150 Order Forecast Monitor – In Transit Information

When entering planned receipts manually, the supplier can click on the SIMULATE button in the ORDER FORECAST DETAILS – PRODUCT VIEW to see the impact on the difference key figure and the tolerance status (see Figure 4.145).

4.10.6 Monitoring and Making Adjustments

The alerts defined in the alert profile are used to monitor dynamic replenishment. You can edit the alerts in the Alert Monitor in the SAP SNC system.

In addition, you can save notes in the Order Forecast Monitor that are visible to the other business partner.

The audit trail function enables you to track changes made to customer planned demands and supplier planned receipts.

4.11 ASN Processing

This section first describes *ASN processing* with SAP SNC 5.1. It then presents the process of *updating the ASN* using goods receipt.

4.11.1 ASN Processing

ASN processing is a key process step in supplier collaboration. The supplier uses the ASN to inform the customer of the products and quantities in transit and the expected arrival date/time of the delivery, among other things. Once an ASN has been published in SAP SNC, the system generates an XML message of type *DispatchedDeliveryNotification* and sends it via SAP NetWeaver PI to the customer's backend system. If the customer's backend system is an SAP ERP system, SAP NetWeaver PI converts the XML message into an IDoc of type DESADV.DELVRY03 (or as of SAP ECC 6.0, to type DESADV.DELVRY05).

The ASN can be created in the supplier's backend system and sent to SAP SNC or entered manually in the SAP SNC web browser.

ASNs from the supplier's backend system can be sent to SAP SNC with an XML message of type *DispatchedDeliveryNotification*. Once the inbound message has been validated successfully, SAP SNC forwards it to the customer's backend system. ASNs with errors are given RECEIVED status in SAP SNC and can be corrected by the supplier.

ASNs can be created with reference to planned receipts, replenishment orders (see Section 4.2 Supplier Managed Inventory (SMI)), forecast delivery schedules (see Section 4.3 Forecast Delivery Schedule Processing), or purchase order items (see Section 4.4 Purchase Order Handling). In the SAP SNC web browser, on the basis of the due lists, the supplier can set up ASNs with reference to the aforementioned objects, copy existing ASNs, or create new ones directly. No matter the starting point, all ASNs are processed in the ASN MAINTENANCE view (see Figure 4.151).

In the ASN MAINTENANCE view, the supplier can edit the ASN header and item data.

The ASN header is composed of general information, for example, ASN number, ASN status, shipping and delivery date, ship-to and ship-from location, and shipping details.

An ASN item describes product-related ASN data, for instance, quantity, purchasing document (scheduling agreement or purchase order), and weight/volume information.

The supplier has access to a range of functions in ASN Maintenance. The rounding function can be used to round up the item quantity to a whole-number multiple of the rounding value (in the product master).

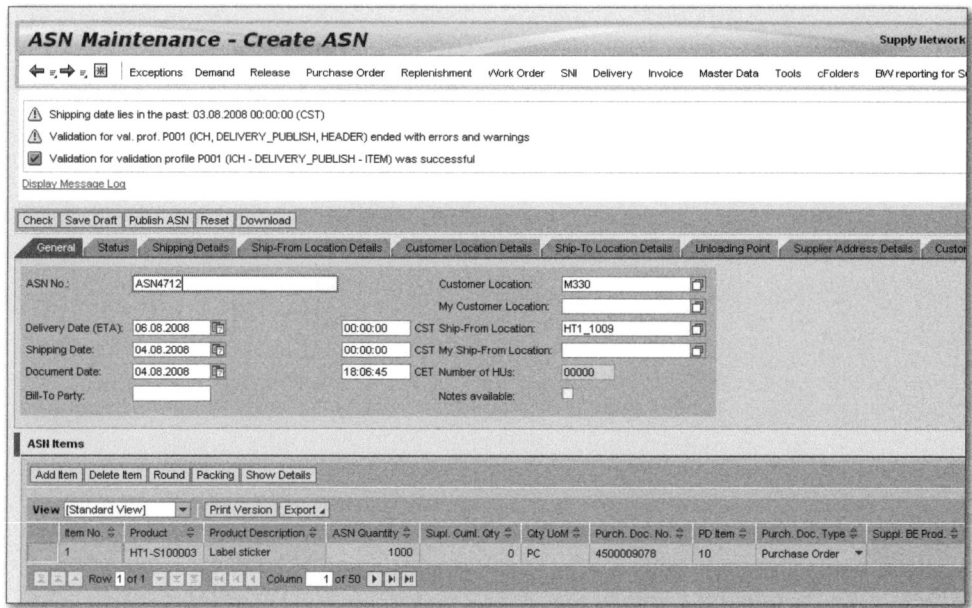

Figure 4.151 ASN Maintenance

The check function can be used to validate the ASN entered. The system checks that the data entered is complete and correct.

If you want to work on the ASN at a later time, you can click on the SAVE DRAFT button to retain the ASN with DRAFT status.

The PUBLISH ASN function enables the supplier to publish the ASN and trigger sending of the ASN to the customer's backend system. In the standard shipment, the supplier cannot change a published ASN.

Publishing ASNs

The supplier can cancel ASNs with DRAFT or PUBLISHED status with the CANCEL ASN function (see Figure 4.152). This is only possible if the ASN does not yet have status GOODS RECEIPT, GOODS RECEIPT PARTIAL, or CLOSED.

Canceling ASNs

Before publishing an ASN, the supplier can pack the products it contains in *handling units*. To do so, the supplier chooses the packing function at the ASN item level (see Figure 4.151). Handling units (HU) consist of products and packaging materials used to pack the products. In addition, handling units can also be nested with each other.

Packing ASNs

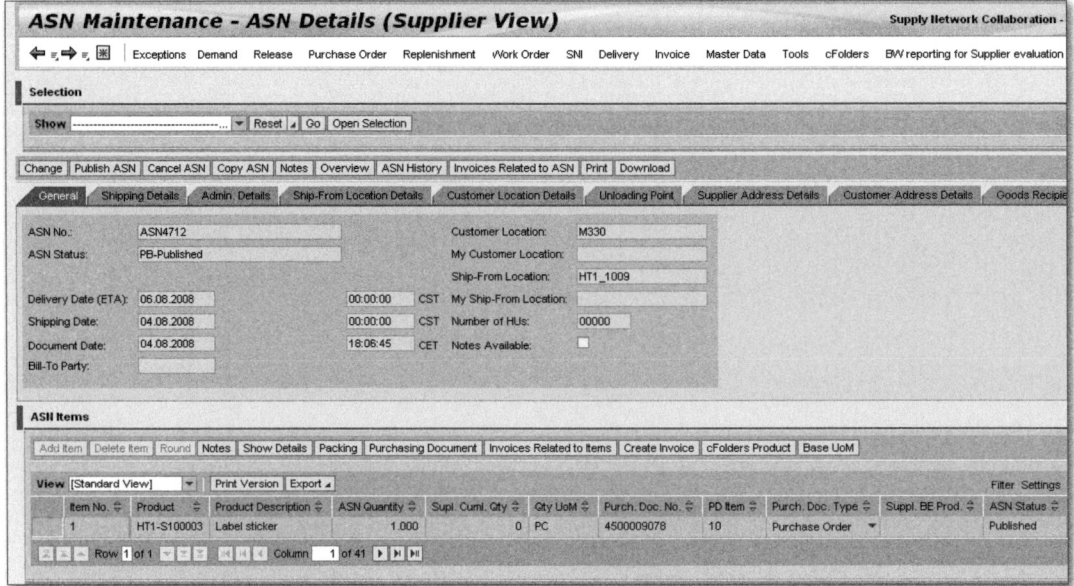

Figure 4.152 ASN Maintenance – Other Functions

Example
One hundred screws are packed in a plastic bag. In turn, 10 plastic bags are packed into a box, and four boxes—held in place with steel fasteners—are loaded onto a palette.

Packaging materials and auxiliary packaging materials must be available as production masters.

As a basic principle, the products in the ASN can be packed manually or automatically.

To pack the products manually, the supplier first creates the required number of handling units. Next, each handling unit can be assigned to a partial quantity of the product. Handling units that have been packed already can be packed in higher-level handling units.

Automatic packing is possible when packaging specifications exist and have been assigned to the products.

Serial numbers
In some business scenarios, a serial number is required in addition to the product number so that a single piece can be distinguished from all other pieces. The supplier can maintain the serial numbers during ASN processing in SAP SNC at the ASN item level (see Figure 4.153).

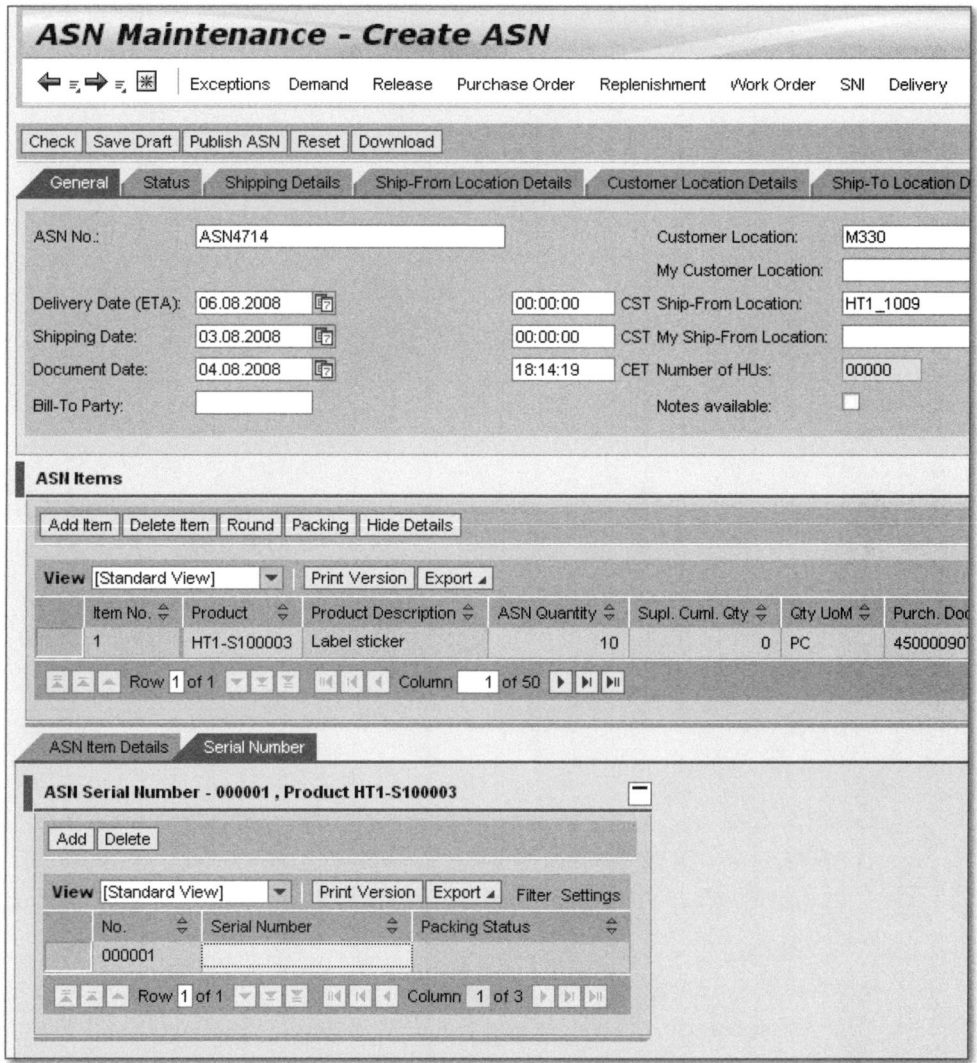

Figure 4.153 Maintaining Serial Numbers

The audit trail function logs all changes made to an ASN. The ASN history in the SAP SNC system relies on this functionality. The customer and supplier can view previous versions of the ASN.

ASN history

Exception situations that concern ASNs are shown using special alerts. Table 4.14 shows the alert types available in ASN processing.

Alerts in ASN processing

Alert Type	Addressee	Description
ASN is overdue	Customer, supplier	All ASN items have not yet been fully delivered, and the delivery date/time falls on a user-defined date at the latest.
Goods receipt quantity differs from ASN quantity	Customer, supplier	The goods receipt quantity for an ASN item differs from the requested item quantity.
Exception during validation of ASN	Supplier, customer	The validation has identified incorrect or missing data in the ASN.

Table 4.14 Alerts in ASN Processing

4.11.2 Updating the ASN from Goods Receipt

On the basis of the ASN data sent from SAP SNC to the customer's backend system, an inbound delivery is created in the customer's backend system.

If this system is an SAP ERP system, the following options are available.

Goods Receipt with Reference to Inbound Delivery

In SAP ERP, goods receipt can take place with reference to the inbound delivery (Transaction VL32n).

A message must be sent to SAP SNC to ensure that the ASN can be updated there on the basis of the goods receipt posted for the inbound delivery. To make it possible for a proof of delivery message to be generated automatically when goods receipt takes place, message determination must be configured accordingly. The proof of delivery message is sent to SAP SNC via SAP NetWeaver PI as a *ReceivedDeliveryNotification*.

If the full ASN quantity is posted when goods receipt takes place, the ASN acquires GOODS RECEIPT COMPLETE status in SAP SNC (see Figure 4.154). If, on the other hand, only part of the ASN quantity is posted, the ASN is given GOODS RECEIPT PARTIAL status in SAP SNC.

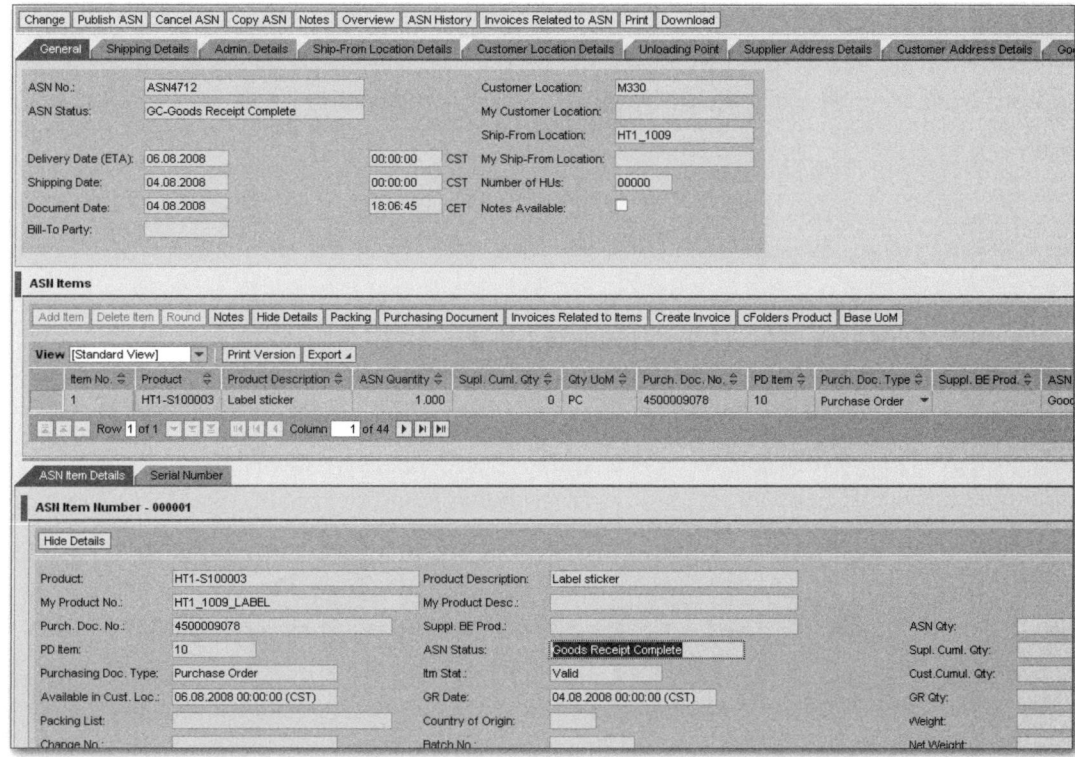

Figure 4.154 ASN Status After Goods Receipt

You must make the respective Customizing setting to ensure that SAP SNC processes partial goods receipts (in Transaction SPRO, follow the menu path SUPPLY NETWORK COLLABORATION • DELIVERY • ASN • GOODS RECEIPT • ALLOW PARTIAL GOODS RECEIPT FOR ASN ITEMS).

The ASN status is also visible to the supplier. This means the supplier is informed of the actual quantity delivered.

If you have configured the SAP ERP system such that a proof of delivery message is not created when goods receipt takes place, you have the option to send goods receipt data to SAP SNC using report RSMPROACT or RSMIPROACT2. In doing so, you can choose between sending data as a *ReceivedDeliveryNotification* or a *ProductActivityNotification*. Because a *ProductActivityNotification* does not transfer quantities at the item level, you can only map complete goods receipts in SAP SNC.

Goods Receipt Without Reference to Inbound Delivery

In this case, you post goods receipt in SAP ERP with Transaction MIGO. The delivery note number, which matches the ASN number, must be entered manually. To update the ASN in SAP SNC, you send a *ReceivedDeliveryNotification* or a *ProductActivityNotification* (report RSMIPROACT or RSMIPROACT2). The ASN status in SAP SNC can only be updated as GOODS RECEIPT COMPLETE.

Using a *ReceivedDeliveryNotification* in this case results in the transfer of the ASN number, product number, and goods receipt quantity for the product, but no item number. Therefore, SAP SNC updates all ASN items with this product.

With a *ProductActivityNotification*, you only transfer the ASN number and the product number; product quantities are not transferred. For this reason, SAP SNC updates all ASN items with this product.

Forecast Delivery Schedule Processing Without Inbound Delivery

If you want to use forecast delivery schedule processing without inbound delivery, you can update the ASN item in SAP SNC on the basis of the cumulative received quantity that is transferred with the forecast delivery schedule (in Transaction SPRO, follow the menu path SUPPLY NETWORK COLLABORATION • DELIVERY • ASN • GOODS RECEIPT • DEFINE SETTINGS FOR RELEASE PROCESSING).

4.12 Invoice Collaboration

This section first provides an overview of the *invoice collaboration* business process with SAP SNC 5.1 (see Figure 4.155). It then takes a closer look at the individual process steps and settings in SAP SNC.

4.12.1 Process Overview

Invoice collaboration enables a supplier or customer to create invoices or credit memos for goods that the supplier has delivered to the customer.

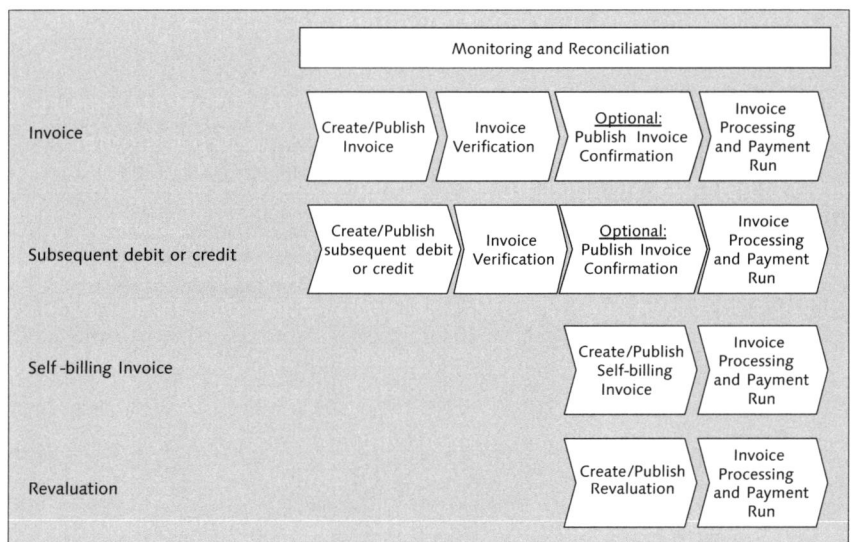

Figure 4.155 Process Flow for Invoice Collaboration

The following new processes are supported by invoice collaboration as of SAP SNC 5.1.

Invoice Processing

The supplier creates an invoice manually in SAP SNC and publishes it. This invoice is sent to the customer's SAP ERP backend system, where it is verified by comparing data in that system with data from the invoice. The customer has the option of sending an invoice confirmation from the backend system to SAP SNC, which prompts the acceptance status of the invoice to be updated. If the invoice contains errors or deviations, it must be edited further until it can be posted. Once the data on the invoice has been accepted, a payment run is triggered, and the payment status is updated in SAP SNC.

Create invoices

The supplier can create invoices for the following:

- Purchase orders
- Replenishment orders
- ASNs

Scheduling agreements and work orders can be billed indirectly using ASNs.

The process flow for invoice processing is shown in Figure 4.156.

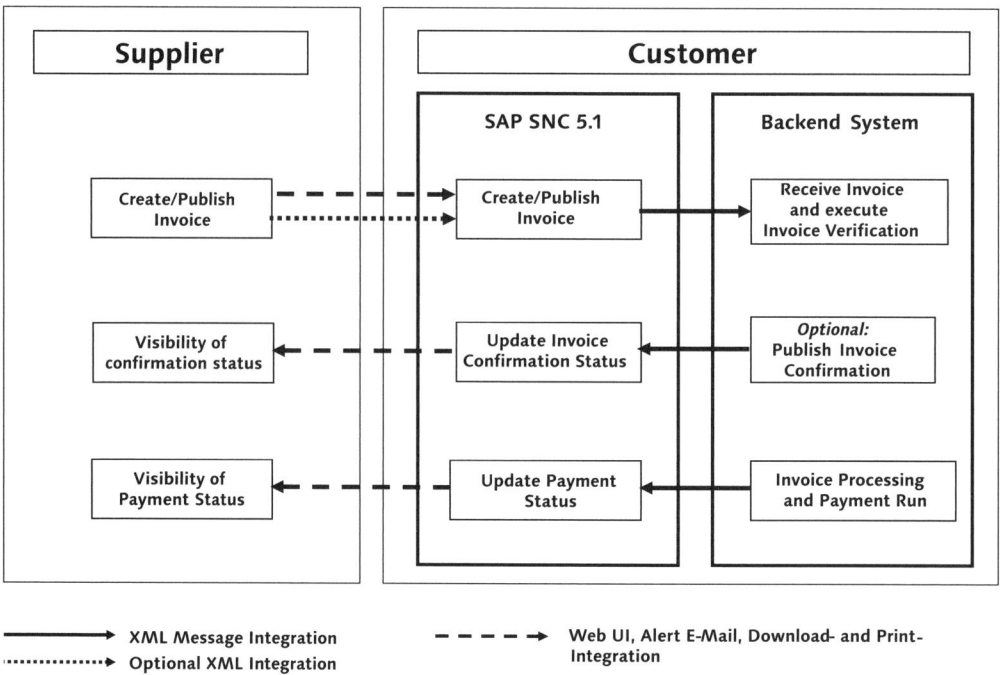

Figure 4.156 Process Flow for Invoice Processing

Subsequent Debit or Credit

The supplier can create a subsequent debit or credit for an invoice that has already been published. A subsequent debit results when a transaction has already been settled and a further invoice is then subsequently received. It is important to note the following: When a subsequent debit is posted, the system only updates the ordering transaction in respect to value, not quantity. The calculated quantity does not change, but the total calculated value does. If a subsequent debit is created, only a price check is performed in the SAP ERP backend system; a quantity check does not take place. The customer has the option of sending a subsequent debit confirmation from the backend system to SAP SNC, which prompts the acceptance status of the subsequent debit to be updated.

Once the data in the subsequent debit has been accepted, a payment run is triggered, and the payment status is updated in SAP SNC.

The process flow for subsequent debit or credit is shown in Figure 4.157.

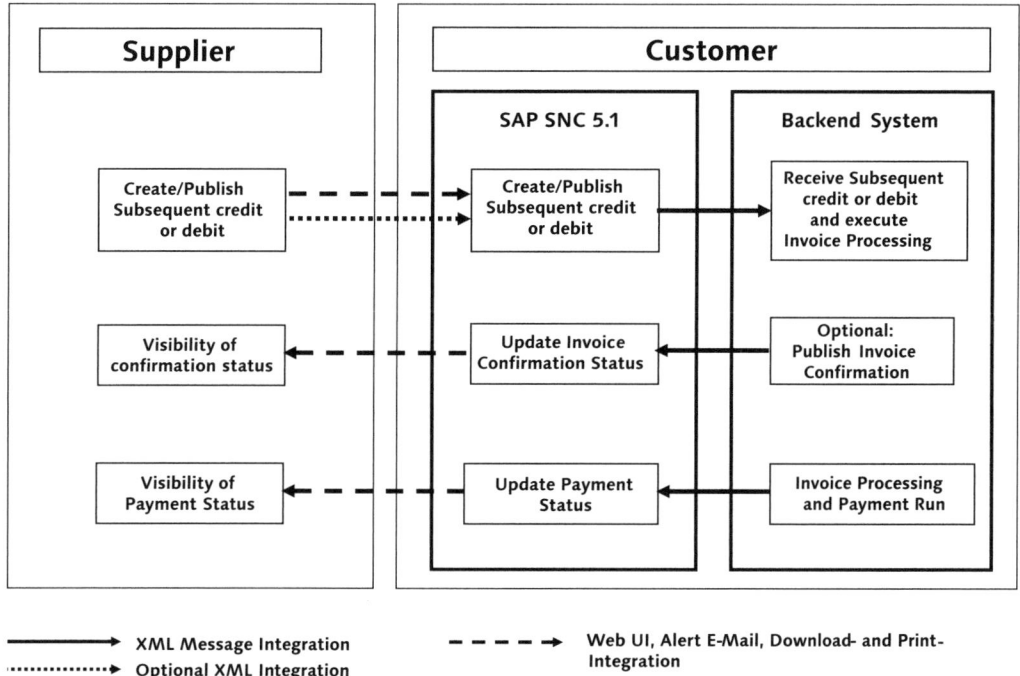

Figure 4.157 Process Flow for Subsequent Debit or Credit

Credit Memo Processing

In credit memo processing, an evaluated receipt settlement (ERS) is created in the customer's SAP ERP backend system. In addition, the supplier agrees not to create invoices. Instead, the customer automatically posts an invoice document based on data from purchase orders or ASNs and goods receipts. This eliminates the potential for invoice deviations and removes any need for an invoice verification step. Evaluated receipt settlement is a good solution when conditions have been clearly agreed upon with the supplier and the purchase orders in the system are always up to date. The evaluated receipt settlement document is sent to SAP SNC by means of an XML message.

Creating a credit memo

Evaluated receipt settlement is particularly well suited to cases in which settlement documents are created periodically, offering the following benefits:

- Ordering transactions are completed with greater speed
- Transmission errors are avoided
- Quantity and price deviations in invoice verification do not occur

The process flow for credit memo processing is shown in Figure 4.158.

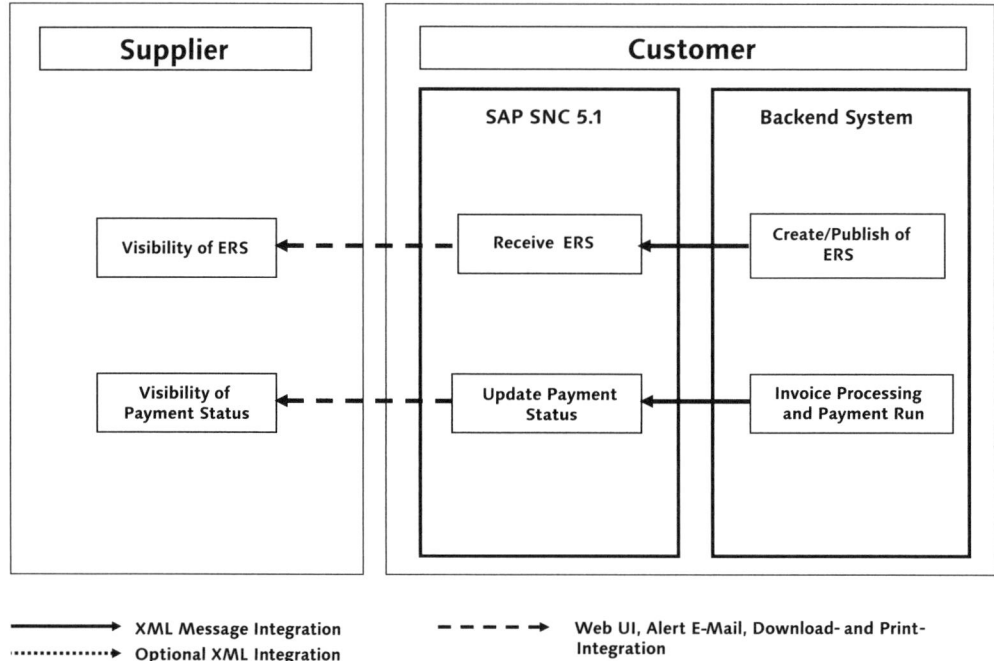

Figure 4.158 Process Flow for Evaluated Receipt Settlement (ERS)

Revaluation

The customer revaluates a purchase order or an ASN if the price of a product changes and the price change is effective retroactively. A revaluation determines the difference in value for items that have already been invoiced. Revaluation is only possible for documents that are permitted for evaluated receipt settlement. The revaluation document is sent to SAP SNC by via XML message.

The process flow for revaluation is shown in Figure 4.159.

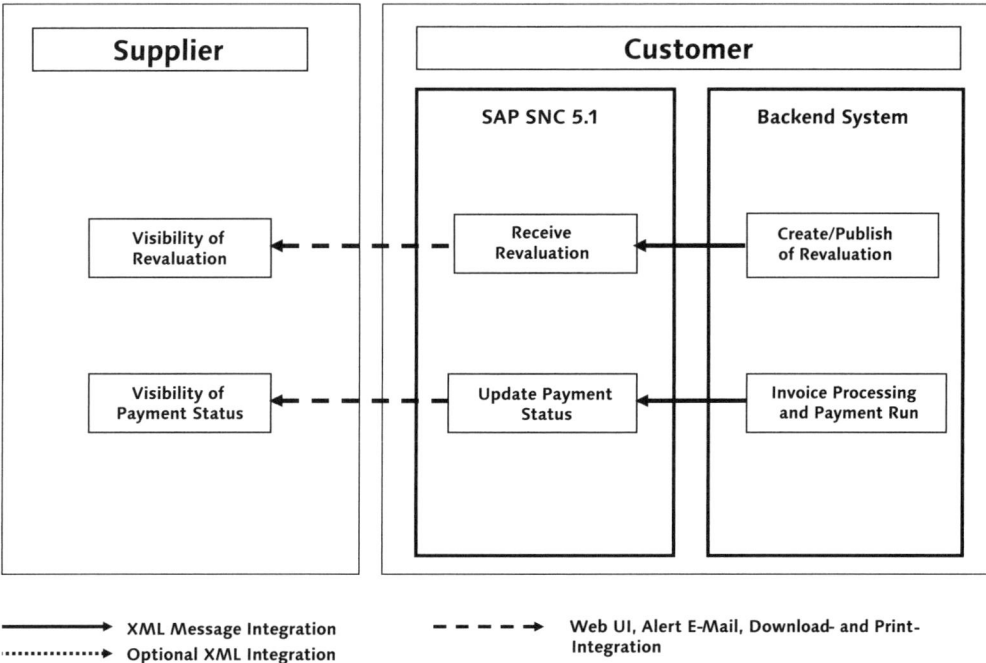

Figure 4.159 Process Flow for Revaluation

4.12.2 Master Data Specific to Invoice Collaboration

In addition to the generic master data (see Section 4.1 Generic Master Data), the following master data is also required in SAP SNC for invoice collaboration:

- Tax code
- Incoterms

The following section describes how this master data must be maintained in the customer's SAP ERP system.

Tax Code

To send calculated tax data between SAP SNC and the customer's backend system, the tax codes maintained in both SAP SNC and SAP ERP must match. This is necessary because SAP ERP uses the tax code to calculate the gross amount.

Tax codes are managed in SAP Easy Access under SUPPLY NETWORK COLLABORATION • INVOICE • CURRENT SETTINGS • MAINTAIN TAX CODES FOR INVOICES (see Figure 4.160).

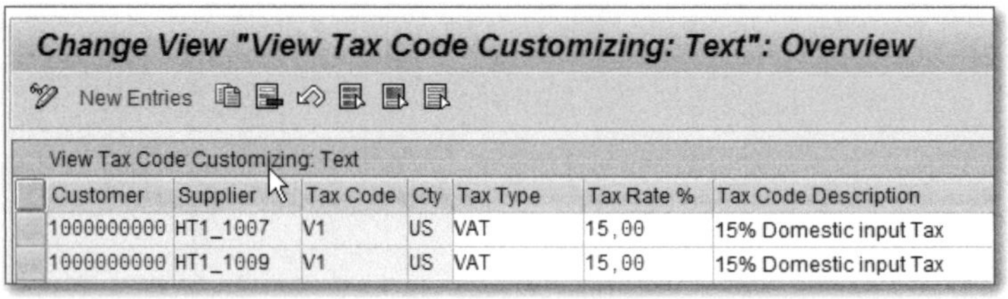
Change View "View Tax Code Customizing: Text": Overview

New Entries

View Tax Code Customizing: Text

Customer	Supplier	Tax Code	Cty	Tax Type	Tax Rate %	Tax Code Description
1000000000	HT1_1007	V1	US	VAT	15,00	15% Domestic input Tax
1000000000	HT1_1009	V1	US	VAT	15,00	15% Domestic input Tax

Figure 4.160 Maintaining Tax Codes in SAP SNC

Incoterms

When you create an invoice, the system transfers the Incoterm and Incoterm location from the reference document to the invoice.

The master data for Incoterms in the customer's backend system, however, is not transferred to SAP SNC. Therefore, you are required to maintain the master data for Incoterms manually in SAP SNC so that it corresponds with the Incoterms in the customer's backend system. You do this in Customizing under SCM BASIS • MASTER DATA • DEFINE INCOTERMS (see Figure 4.161).

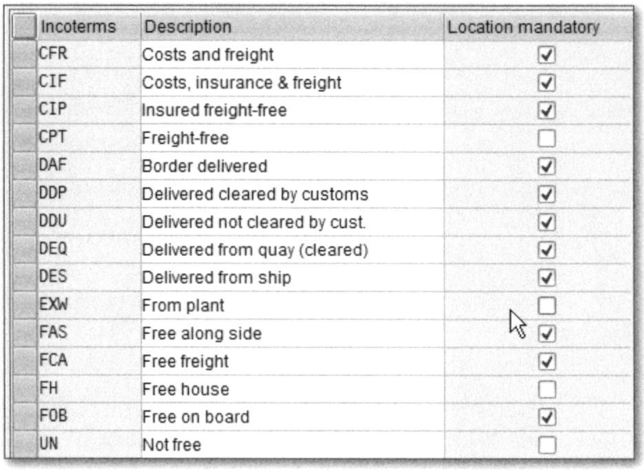

Incoterms	Description	Location mandatory
CFR	Costs and freight	☑
CIF	Costs, insurance & freight	☑
CIP	Insured freight-free	☑
CPT	Freight-free	☐
DAF	Border delivered	☑
DDP	Delivered cleared by customs	☑
DDU	Delivered not cleared by cust.	☑
DEQ	Delivered from quay (cleared)	☑
DES	Delivered from ship	☑
EXW	From plant	☐
FAS	Free along side	☑
FCA	Free freight	☑
FH	Free house	☐
FOB	Free on board	☑
UN	Not free	☐

Figure 4.161 Maintaining Incoterms in SAP SNC

4.12.3 Creating and Publishing an Invoice

You create an invoice in SAP SNC by following the menu path INVOICE • DOCUMENTS REQUIRING INVOICES (see Figure 4.162).

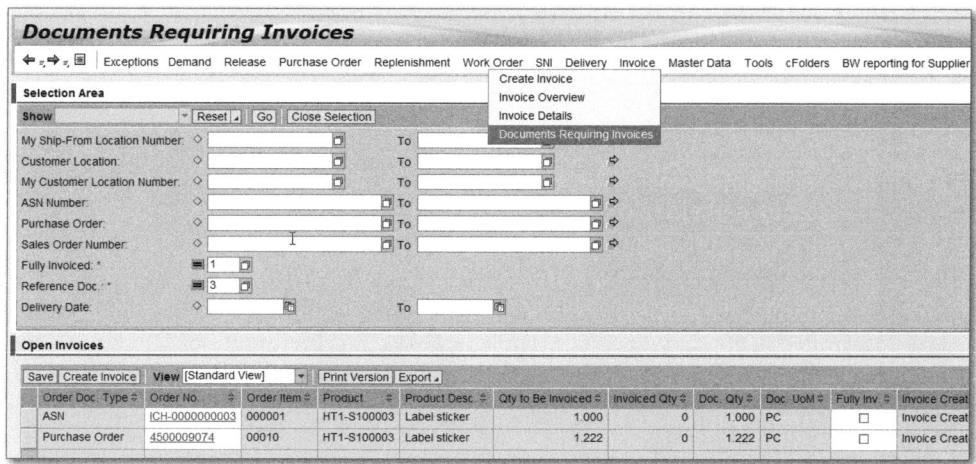

Figure 4.162 Monitor to Display Documents Requiring Invoices

The supplier uses a range of selection criteria to display the relevant order document types for which he can create an invoice. The order document type to be referenced can be a purchase order, replenishment order, or ASN.

The invoice creation type in the purchase order (INVOICE DATA tab page) determines whether an invoice can be created for a purchase order, replenishment order, or ASN (see Figure 4.163).

Invoice data

An invoice can only be created for a purchase order or replenishment order if the GR-BASED INVOICE VERIFICATION indicator was *not* set when the purchase order was issued. An invoice can be created for an ASN if the GR-BASED INVOICE VERIFICATION indicator was set when the purchase order was issued.

The supplier can select one or more lines in the monitor for displaying documents that require invoices and click on the CREATE INVOICE button. The system transfers all of the relevant data from the ASN or purchase order, but this data can also be reworked if necessary (see Figure 4.164).

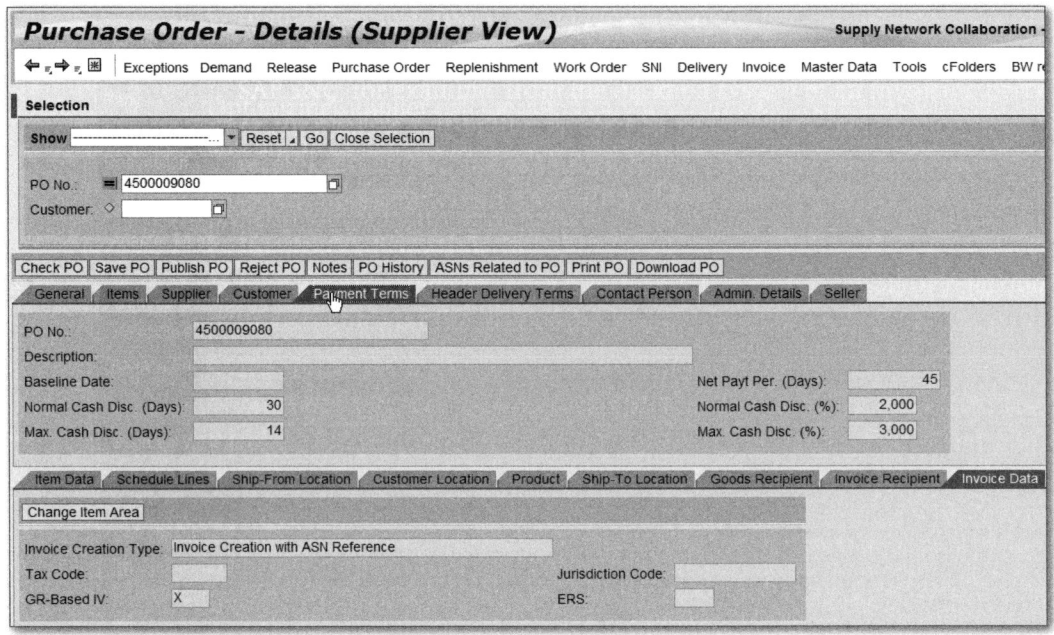

Figure 4.163 Displaying the Invoice Creation Type in the Purchase Order

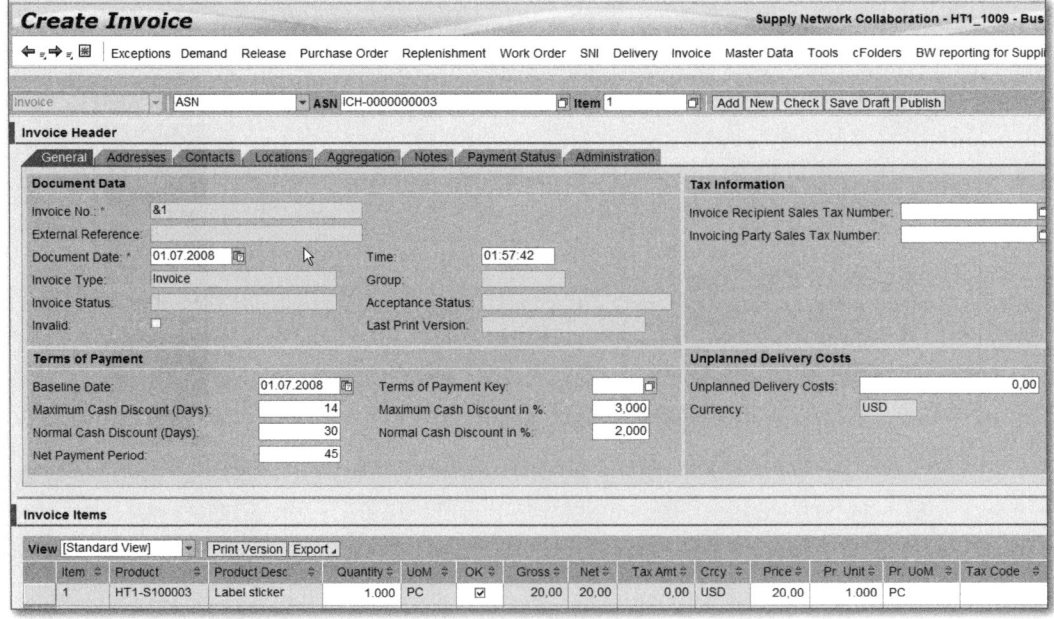

Figure 4.164 Creating an Invoice in SAP SNC

The supplier then publishes the invoice. An XML message of type *Invoice Request* is sent to the SAP NetWeaver PI system, which converts the message into IDoc INVOIC.INVOIC01 and sends it on to the customer's SAP ERP system.

4.12.4 Invoice Verification

The customer verifies the invoice and releases it for payment (Transaction MRBR) (see Figure 4.165).

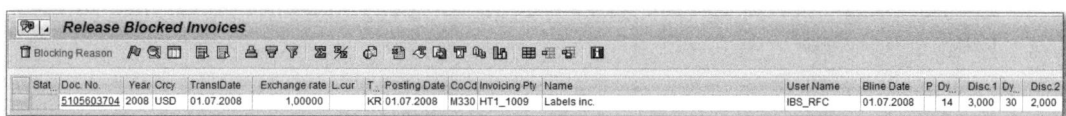

Figure 4.165 Releasing the Supplier's Invoice in the Customer's Backend System

4.12.5 Optional: Publishing an Invoice Confirmation

By confirming an invoice in the backend system, the customer sends an invoice confirmation to SAP SNC by means of an XML message of type *InvoiceConfirmation*. This prompts the invoice's acceptance status to be updated in SAP SNC.

Confirming an invoice

The following values are possible:

- **Pending**
  The customer has not yet accepted or rejected the invoice
- **Accepted**
  The customer has accepted the invoice in the backend system
- **Rejected**
  The customer has rejected the invoice in the backend system

4.12.6 Invoice Processing and the Payment Run

By accepting the invoice, the customer triggers the payment run in the backend system (Transaction F110) (see Figure 4.166).

Payment

After the automatic payment run has taken place, the system creates a log, which is shown in Figure 4.167.

4 | Business Processes in SAP SNC 5.1

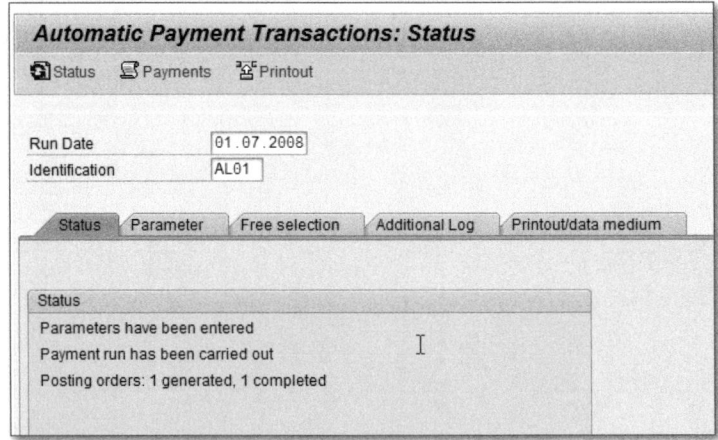

Figure 4.166 Creating an Automatic Payment Run in the Customer's Backend System

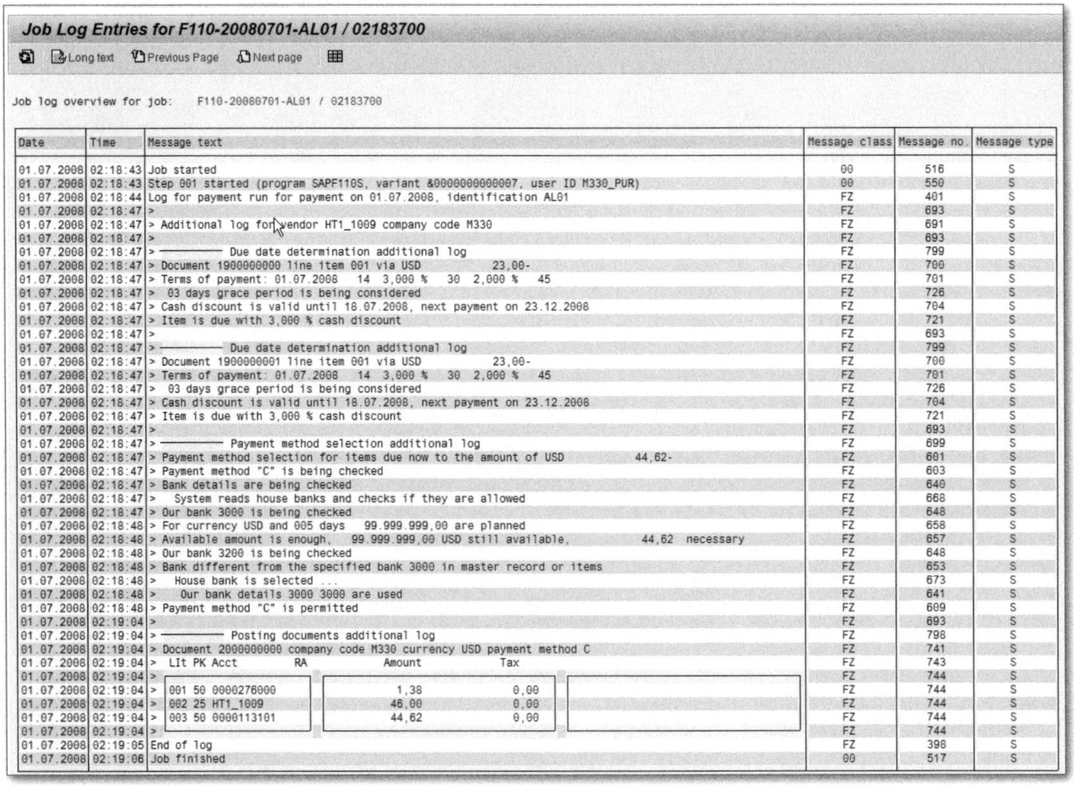

Figure 4.167 Job Log After Completion of the Automatic Payment Run

Once the invoice has been paid in the customer's backend system, an IDoc of type REMADV.PEXR2002 is generated and sent to the SAP NetWeaver PI system, which converts the message into an XML message of type *PaymentAdviceNotification* and sends it on to SAP SNC.

When SAP SNC receives the payment notification, it changes the payment status to PAID (see Figure 4.168).

Payment status

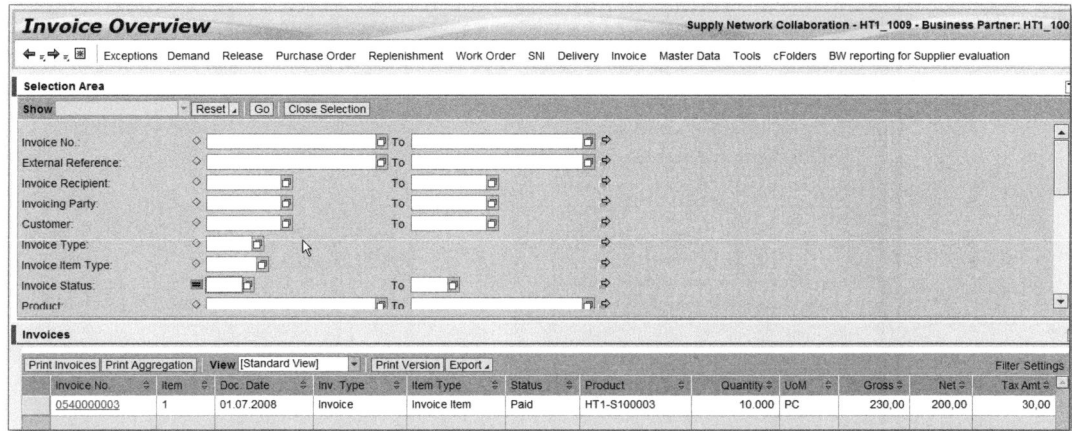

Figure 4.168 Payment Status of the Invoice

The payment advice on the PAYMENT STATUS tab page is updated (see Figure 4.169).

Payment advice

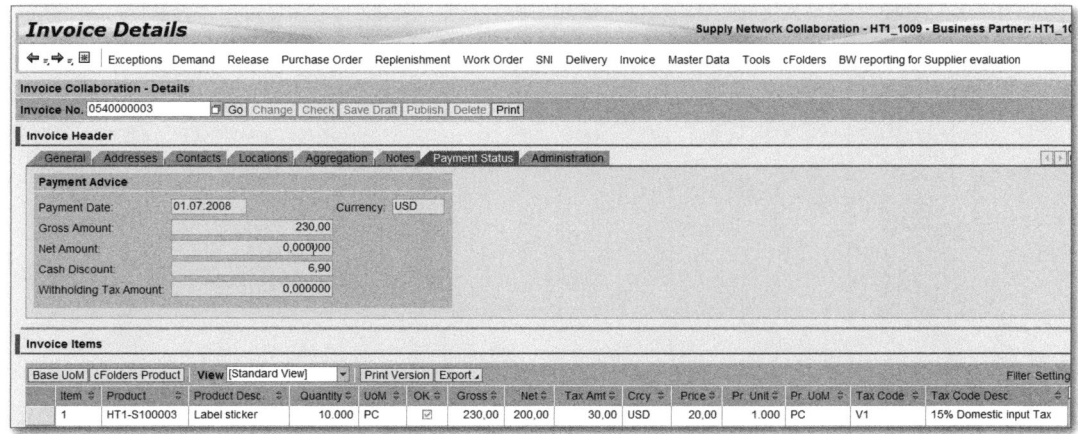

Figure 4.169 Updated Payment Advice in the Invoice

4.12.7 Creating and Publishing a Subsequent Debit or Credit

The supplier can create a subsequent debit or credit for a document for which an invoice already exists by following the menu path INVOICE • CREATE INVOICE (see Figure 4.170).

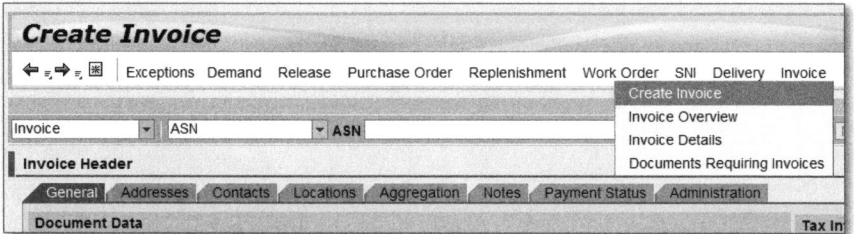

Figure 4.170 Creating a Debit or Credit

Delivery costs In this view, the supplier can select the document for which a debit or credit is to be created and enter the subsequent costs. In the following example, a supplier enters unplanned delivery costs (see Figure 4.171).

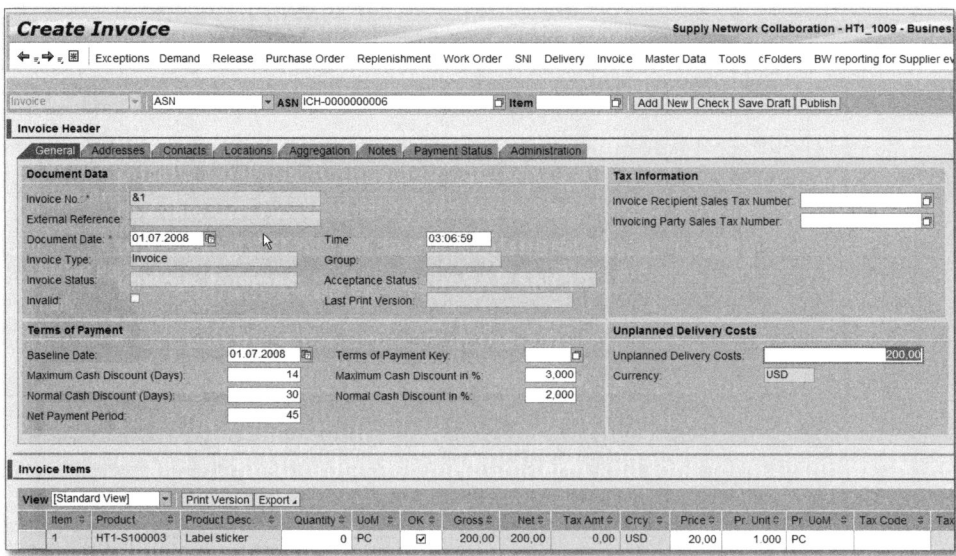

Figure 4.171 Entering Unplanned Delivery Costs as a Subsequent Debit

Once the debit or credit has been published, an XML message of type *InvoiceRequest* is sent to the SAP NetWeaver PI system, which converts the message into IDoc INVOIC.INVOIC01 and sends it on to the customer's SAP ERP system.

4.12.8 Creating and Publishing a Credit Memo

For the customer to carry out an evaluated receipt settlement after goods receipt has taken place, the following conditions must be met:

Evaluated receipt settlement

- Evaluated receipt settlement must be selected in the purchase order item
- The supplier must be selected as ERS-enabled in the supplier master record
- Goods-receipt-based invoice verification must be activated for the purchase order item
- A tax code must be maintained in the purchase order item
- The purchase order price of the materials used must not be an estimated price

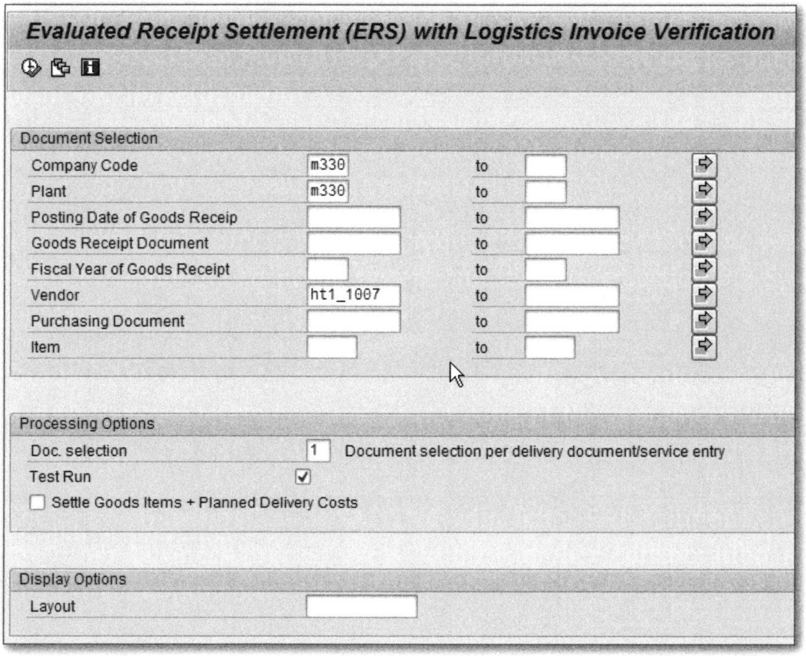

Figure 4.172 Selection for an Evaluated Receipt Settlement in the Customer's Backend System

The customer defines the transactions to be processed in the evaluated receipt settlement in the backend system (Transaction MRRL) (see Figure 4.172).

A log is created showing the invoices that have been settled and those that have not been settled (see Figure 4.173).

Figure 4.173 Log of Documents to Be Settled

Once evaluated receipt settlement has taken place in the customer's backend system, an IDoc of type GSVERF.GSVERF03 is generated and sent to the SAP NetWeaver PI system, which converts the message into an XML message of type *InvoiceRequest* and sends it on to SAP SNC.

The invoice is displayed in SAP SNC with invoice type SELF-BILLING INVOICE and invoice item type SUBSEQUENT DEBIT.

Once the payment run has taken place in the backend system (Section 4.12.6 Invoice Processing and the Payment Run), the payment status for this invoice will be updated in SAP SNC.

4.12.9 Creating and Publishing a Revaluation

After purchasing negotiations have been concluded, changes that are effective retroactively can be made to prices and conditions. The goods receipt is valuated with the purchasing conditions and forms the basis for settlement.

In the case of deliveries and services that have already been settled, this leads to prices that are different from those determined when settlement was carried out. Therefore, the following actions must be carried out:

- Difference values must be determined
- Settlement documents—in the form of invoices or credit memos— must be posted to the supplier's account

- Settlement documents must be sent to the supplier

The customer defines the transactions to be processed in the revaluation in his SAP backend system (Transaction MRNB) (see Figure 4.174).

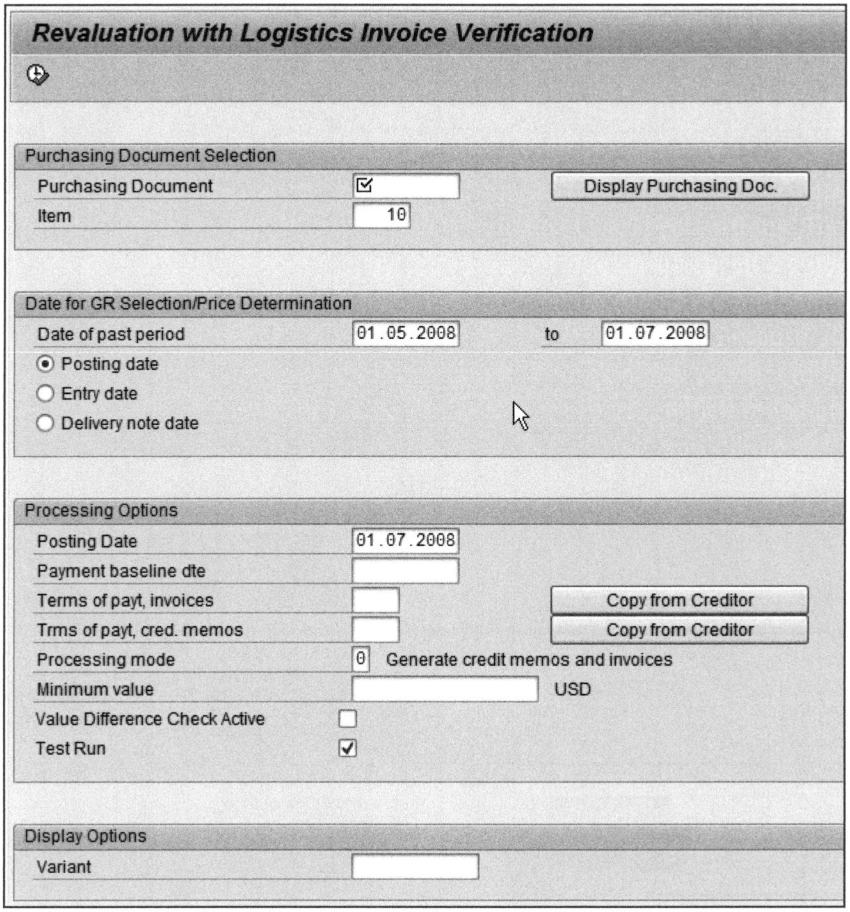

Figure 4.174 Selection for a Revaluation in the Customer's Backend System

Once the revaluation has taken place in the customer's backend system, an IDoc of type GSVERF.GSVERF03 is generated and sent to the SAP NetWeaver PI system, which converts the message into an XML message of type *InvoiceRequest* and sends it on to SAP SNC.

The invoice is displayed in SAP SNC with invoice type SELF-BILLING INVOICE and invoice item type REVALUATION DEBIT or REVALUATION CREDIT.

4.12.10 Monitoring Invoice Collaboration

Both the supplier and the customer can used the various invoice monitors in SAP SNC to monitor invoices and credit memos. The wide range of selection options in the monitors allows users to narrow down the selection of invoices and credit memos according to invoice status and payment status.

This chapter describes the architectural aspects that you should take into account when setting up and integrating an SAP SNC system. It also provides an overview of the basic services that are enabled by supplier collaboration based on SAP SNC.

5 SAP SNC – Architecture

This chapter looks at the components required to achieve supplier collaboration based on SAP SNC from a technical perspective. We begin by classifying SAP SNC itself and then present SAP SNC's system landscape and basic services. Section 5.4 Enterprise SOA Concepts describes the concepts of the *service-oriented architecture* (SOA) underlying SAP SNC.

5.1 Setting Up an SAP SNC System

SAP SNC 5.1 is part of SAP SCM 2007, which is composed of the following components (see Figure 5.1):

SAP SCM 2007

- **SAP Advanced Planning & Optimization (SAP APO)**
  For planning logistics and production processes
- **SAP Supply Network Collaboration (SAP SNC)**
  For collaboration with customers and suppliers
- **SAP Event Management (SAP EM)**
  For coordinating logistical events
- **SAP Extended Warehouse Management (SAP EWM)**
  For processing goods movement and managing stock in a warehouse complex

5 SAP SNC – Architecture

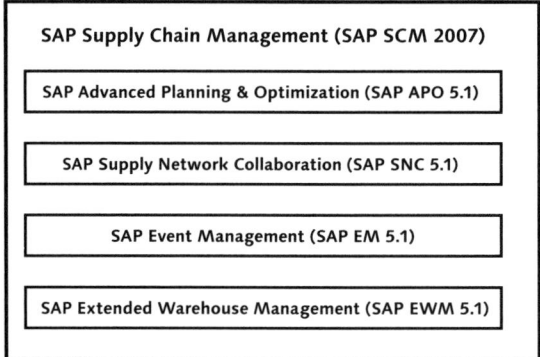

Figure 5.1 SAP SCM 2007

As of Release SAP SCM 2007, SAP SNC can be installed and operated as part of an SCM 5.1 full version with the SAP APO, SAP EM, and SAP EWM components or in the form of a lean SNC 5.1 version that only contains functions relevant for SNC. Figure 5.2 shows the two alternatives.

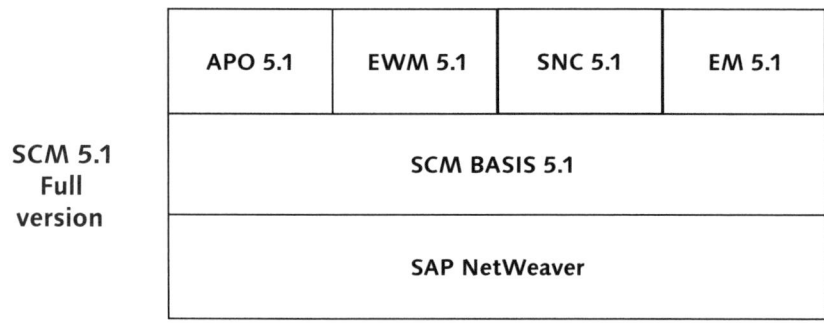

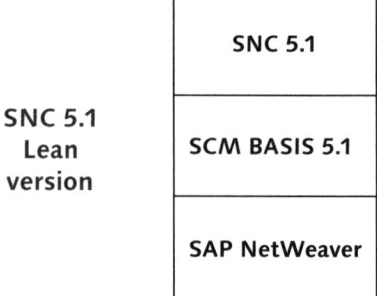

Figure 5.2 Setting Up an SAP SNC System

An SCM 5.1 full version is suited to customers who already use SAP APO, SAP EM, or SAP EWM or plan to do so in the future. In particular, this is the case if an upgrade from SAP SCM 5.0 (or 4.1) to SAP SCM 5.1 is in the pipeline.

SCM 5.1 full version

A lean SNC 5.1 version is suited to customers who do not want to operate any more SCM components on the same server. This version helps lower dependencies in terms of release and support package cycles. It is not possible to upgrade from SAP SCM 5.0 to a lean SNC 5.1 version.

Lean SNC 5.1 version

SAP SNC integration with SAP ERP 6.0 is supported with both alternatives. Table 6.1 presents a comparison of the two alternatives.

	SCM 5.1 Full Version	Lean SNC 5.1 Version
Business Process	It is possible to use PPM and PDS from SAP APO for work order collaboration.	It is necessary to maintain phase structures in SAP SNC.
Implementation	Better integration of the SCM components can be achieved.	No release dependencies with existing SCM components need be taken into account.
Performance	Greater hardware capacity may be required if several SCM components are used.	Improved performance thanks to smaller amounts of master data and transaction data.
Security	Heightened security measures may be necessary to safeguard the systems in use on this SCM platform.	External access to other components on the SCM platform is eliminated.

Table 5.1　Comparison of SAP SNC Alternatives

Note that it is not currently possible to switch from a lean SNC 5.1 version to an SCM 5.1 full version. This necessitates a new installation and implementation.

5.2 System Landscape

Integration with SAP ERP

SAP SNC functions as a platform for collaboration between different business units within a company and different suppliers. The standard shipment can be integrated with the customer's SAP ERP system (release level 4.6C or higher) or SAP APO system. This integration not only allows the master data required for SAP SNC to be copied from the SAP ERP system, but also enables up-to-date transaction data to be exchanged using SAP NetWeaver Process Integration (PI).

Similarly, if a supplier operates an SAP ERP system or other non-SAP systems, these can be integrated into the system landscape. Figure 5.3 shows a sample system landscape for supplier collaboration based on SAP SNC.

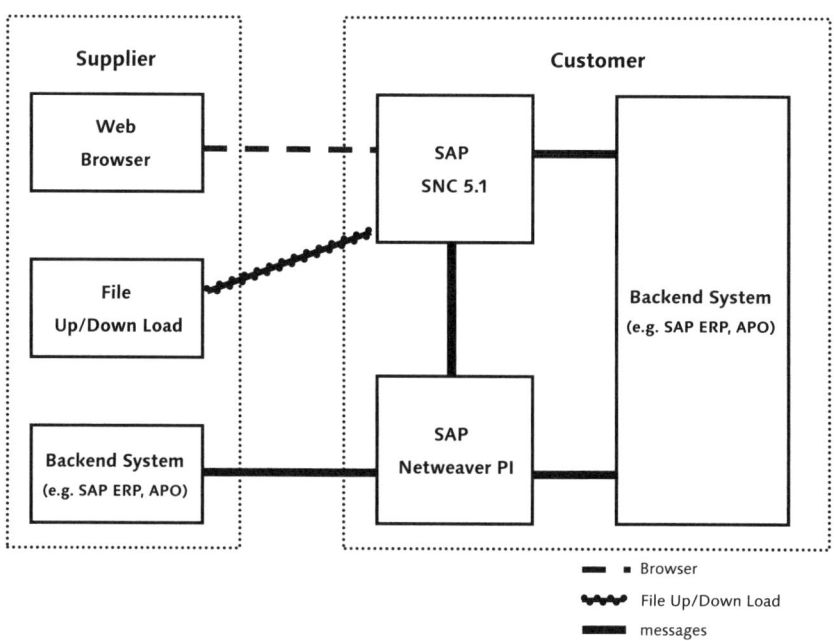

Figure 5.3 System Landscape Incorporating the Supplier's Backend System

If the customer's backend is not an SAP system, one of the first aims of the project must be to establish what data has to be maintained in the customer's backend system to enable integration with SAP SNC and how this integration of the two systems is to be achieved. For this purpose, SAP SNC provides standard interfaces for transferring master data (for example, using BAPIs). SAP NetWeaver PI can be used to load transaction data into SAP SNC from an external customer backend system and vice versa. The *Adapter Engine*, which enables external systems to be connected to SAP NetWeaver PI, is provided in SAP NetWeaver PI for this reason. The Adapter Engine consists of a number of adapters provided by both SAP and third parties (*http://service.sap.com/xi*, SAP XI in Detail, Connectivity).

Suppliers can access SAP SNC using web browsers and, depending on their role in the business process, enter confirmations for planning or execution of the replenishment process. Furthermore, suppliers can, on the one hand, download selected data supplied in SAP SNC to process it in their own systems as required and, on the other hand, upload data to SAP SNC to make it visible to the customer.

Supplier integration using web browsers

It is beneficial to integrate the supplier's backend system if the supplier is in a position to generate transaction data from that system and make it available in electronic form. For instance, ASNs can be created in the supplier's backend system and sent via SAP NetWeaver PI to SAP SNC, from where they can then be forwarded to the customer's backend system.

We would, however, advise against transferring master data from the supplier system, because this should be reserved for the customer for reasons of consistency. Transaction data is integrated from the supplier's backend system to SAP SNC on a project basis. However, if the supplier uses SAP ERP, the effort involved is lower than for a non-SAP backend system.

As Figure 5.4 shows, master data is mainly transferred from SAP ERP using the Core Interface (CIF). The Core Interface is a real-time interface that filters the considerable amount of master data in SAP ERP to locate just the data to be transferred to SAP SNC. To this end, integration models are generated in SAP ERP. These models make it possible to select the master data objects to be transferred, such as selected plants, products, suppliers, and so on. When an integration model is activated, the data objects selected are transferred to SAP SNC (initial transfer).

Integrating master data and transaction data

5 | SAP SNC – Architecture

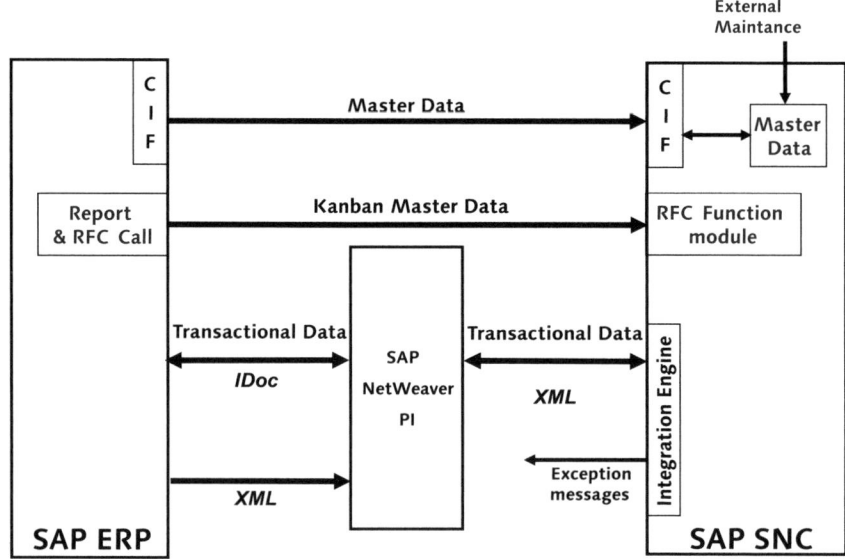

Figure 5.4 Integration of SAP SNC with SAP ERP

If changes are made to master data objects that have already been included in an active integration model, SAP ERP records them with change pointers. Change transfers are used to forward changes to master data objects to SAP SNC. Depending on system settings, change transfers can be made immediately after changes have been made or at regular intervals.

In addition, some master data, such as packaging specifications or control cycles and production supply areas in the kanban scenario, can be created manually in SAP SNC or extracted from SAP ERP using special reports and transferred to SAP SNC with RFC calls.

Integrating transaction data

Transaction data is exchanged between the SAP SNC system and an SAP ERP system by means of SAP NetWeaver PI. SAP SNC receives or sends data in XML format. In SAP ERP, the messages are generally prepared as IDocs. As of SAP ERP 6.0 Enhancement Package 2, data extraction reports that generate XML messages are provided for the SMI and SNI business processes. The different formats are mapped to each other using *interface mapping* in SAP NetWeaver PI. SAP provides default interface mappings that can be enhanced on a project-specific basis.

Master data integration for SAP SNC with SAP APO relies on the relevant master data, for example, plants, suppliers, products, and external procurement relationships, being transferred to both systems from one or more SAP ERP systems by means of the Core Interface. If you use an SAP SCM full version in which SAP APO and SAP SNC run on the same system, both applications can make use of this master data.

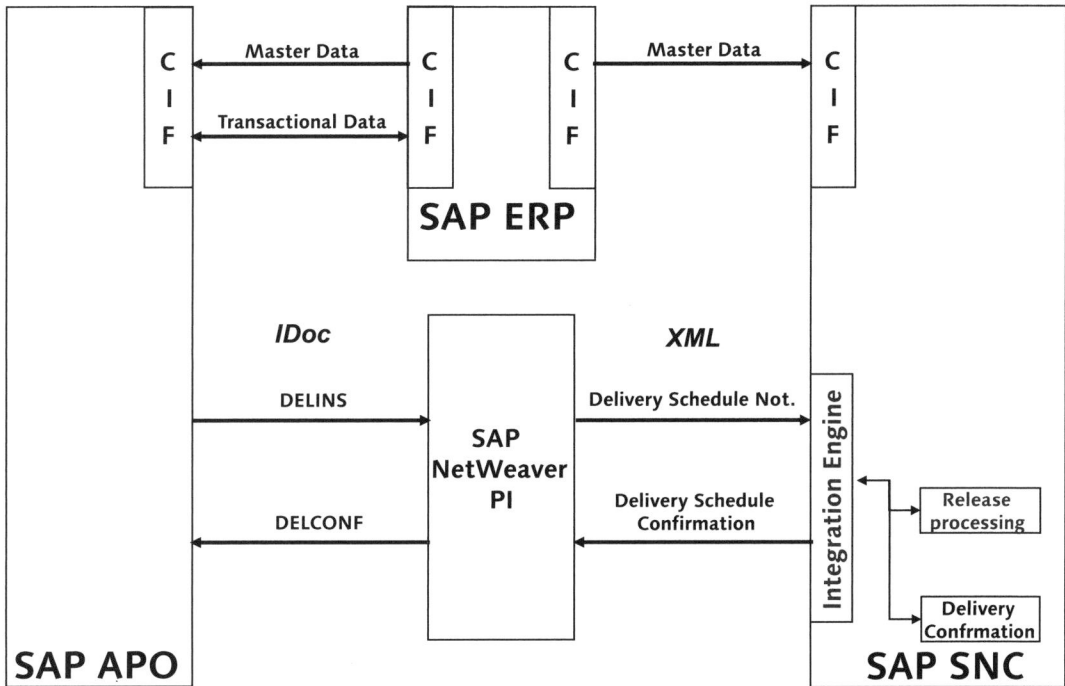

Figure 5.5 Integration of SAP SNC with SAP APO

For transaction data, both systems depend to a large extent on different data sources. Transaction data is often exchanged indirectly by means of the connected SAP ERP system. It is, however, exchanged directly in forecast delivery schedule processing with SAP APO (see Figure 5.5). A forecast delivery schedule is created on the basis of the result of distribution requirements planning in an SAP APO system and transferred in the form of an IDoc of type DELINS.DELFOR02. The IDoc is converted in SAP NetWeaver PI into an XML message of type *DeliverySchedule Notification*, which can be processed as an inbound message by SAP SNC. In SAP SNC, the supplier can respond to the forecast delivery schedule with delivery confirmations that, in turn, are sent to SAP NetWeaver PI as XML messages of type *DeliveryScheduleConfirmation*. These XML messages are converted into IDocs of type DELCONF.DELFOR01, which can be processed as inbound messages in SAP APO. In all of the processes described below, for example, ASNs, goods receipt, and stock updates, both systems are synchronized by means of the connected SAP ERP system.

5.3 Basic Services

This section begins by outlining which master data objects can be transferred from the customer's backend system. It then presents the *Validation Framework*, which verifies the validity of business data. Finally, it describes the ways in which exceptions (alerts) can be displayed as part of the supplier collaboration process with SAP SNC.

5.3.1 Master Data Integration

When SAP SNC is integrated with a customer SAP ERP system, the master data should preferably be transferred using the Core Interface, because this ensures data consistency and prevents unnecessary maintenance effort.

Master data objects

Figure 5.6 shows which master data objects can be transferred using the Core Interface and which objects can be entered using reports or maintained manually in SAP SNC.

When master data is created in SAP SNC, it is important that the order is correct: locations are created first, followed by location products, and finally by external procurement relationships and transportation lanes.

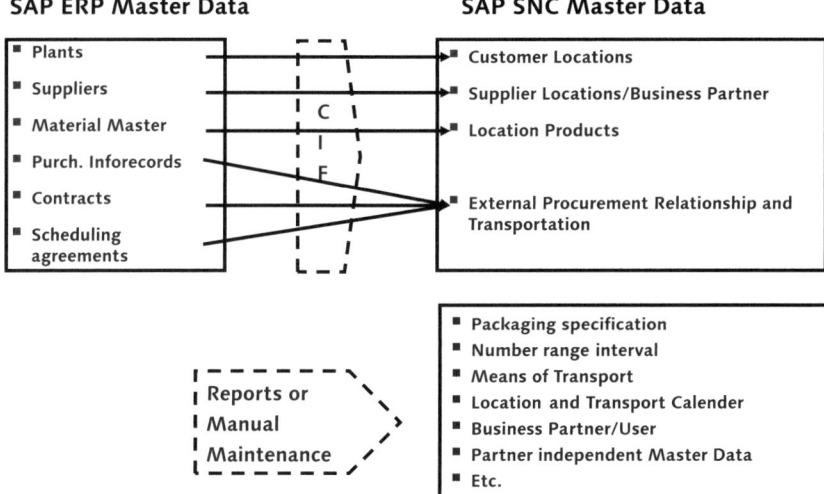

Figure 5.6 Master Data Integration

5.3.2 Validating Business Data

To ensure the validity of the business data to be managed in SAP SNC, predefined *validation checks* are performed when a business object (ASN, forecast delivery schedule, purchase order, delivery confirmation, and so on) is created or modified. The checks establish the completeness and consistency of the business object concerned. They are managed and executed in the Validation Framework.

The validation checks are grouped into *validation profiles* according to business object category. These profiles can be assigned to one of the predefined processes. Furthermore, the profiles define whether SAP SNC should respond to failed validation checks by generating a message or a specific alert (see Figure 5.7). Depending on the severity of an error (ERROR, WARNING, or INFORMATION), SAP SNC can interrupt further processing of the business object and potentially reject it (in Transaction SPRO, follow the menu path SUPPLY NETWORK COLLABORATION • BASIC SETTINGS • VALIDATION • SAP STANDARD SETTINGS • DISPLAY SETTINGS FOR STANDARD VALIDATION PROFILES).

Validation settings

5 | SAP SNC – Architecture

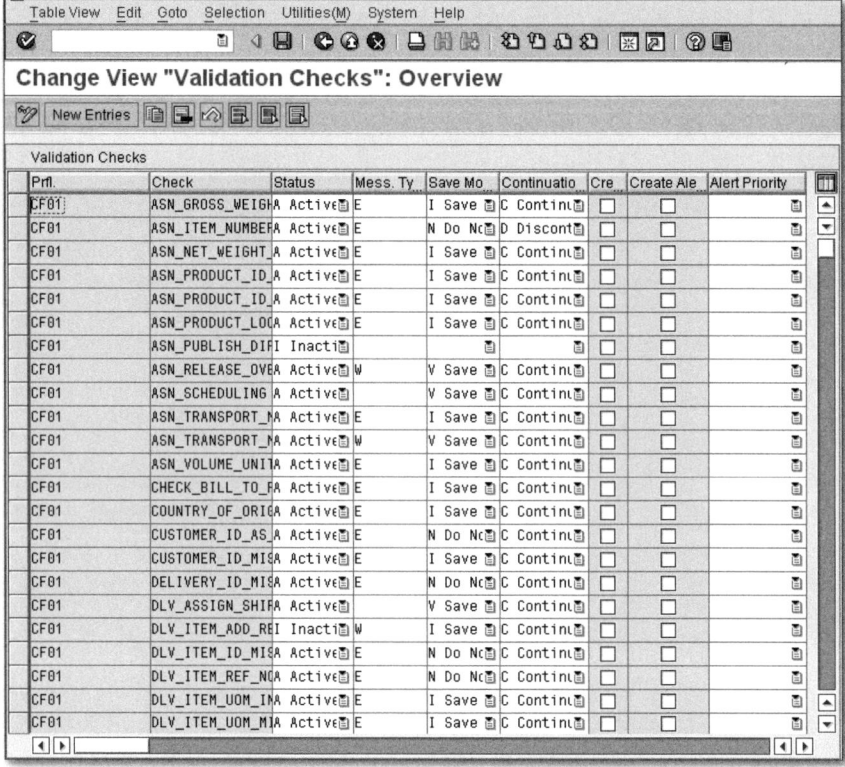

Figure 5.7 Validation Profiles

Validation checks are called when business objects are processed both in the SAP SNC web browser and by the message inbound interfaces.

Customer-specific validation

The validation checks and settings provided in the standard shipment of SAP SNC can be enhanced on a customer-specific basis or overridden completely. The scope of the checks and the system responses can be adapted to meet particular requirements (in Transaction SPRO, follow the menu path SUPPLY NETWORK COLLABORATION • BASIC SETTINGS • VALIDATION • OWN SETTINGS).

In addition, the validation checks for a business object category can be configured on a process-specific basis depending on the values entered for the following supply relationship parameters: customer, customer location, supplier, ship-from location, and product (see Figure 5.8).

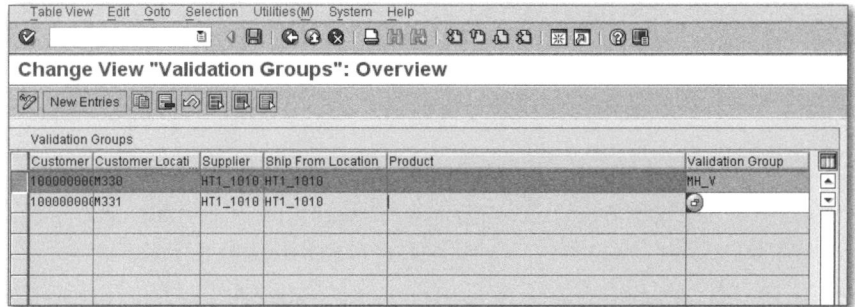

Figure 5.8 Validation Group

First, a validation group is created and assigned to one of the supply relationship parameter values. As shown in Figure 5.9, the validation group is assigned to a process and potentially to a newly defined validation profile. Within the validation profile, you can define a number of new validation checks whose check logic can be implemented with the /SCMB/BOL_VALFRMWRK BAdI.

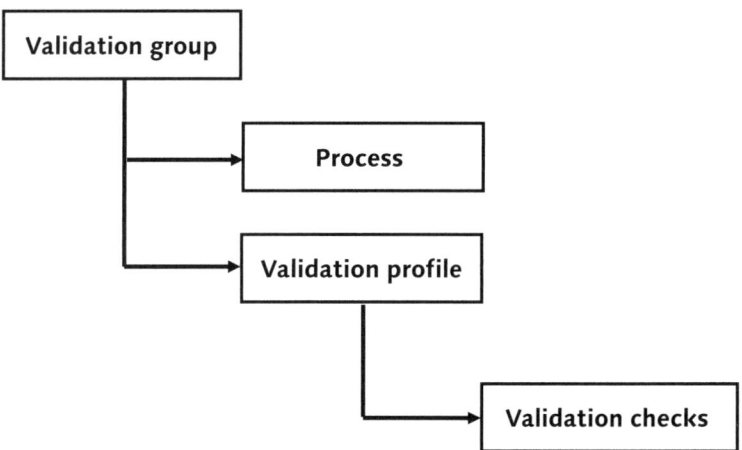

Figure 5.9 Enhancements in the Validation Framework

5.3.3 Managing Exceptions

Alerts are used in SAP SNC to identify exception situations that are relevant for business processes or from a technical perspective. Predefined alert types exist, each of which describes a particular exception situation.

Alerts to map exceptions

If an exception situation is identified, the system generates an alert with the respective alert type. To highlight the significance of the situation that triggered the alert, one of three priority levels—ERROR, WARNING, or INFORMATION—is assigned to each alert.

The alert types relevant for business processes are described for each business process in Chapter 4 Business Processes in SAP SNC 5.1. Technical alert types relate to exception situations that, for instance, might occur when inbound or outbound XML messages are being processed in SAP SNC.

Alert Generation

Subject to the alert type, an exception situation may be identified—and thereby an alert generated—as a result of one of the following:

- **Validation check**

    If the validation of a business object reveals that important data is missing or invalid, SAP SNC generates an alert for the business object concerned. For example, in the standard shipment, an alert is generated if the ship-from location is not specified in an ASN (see Figure 5.10).

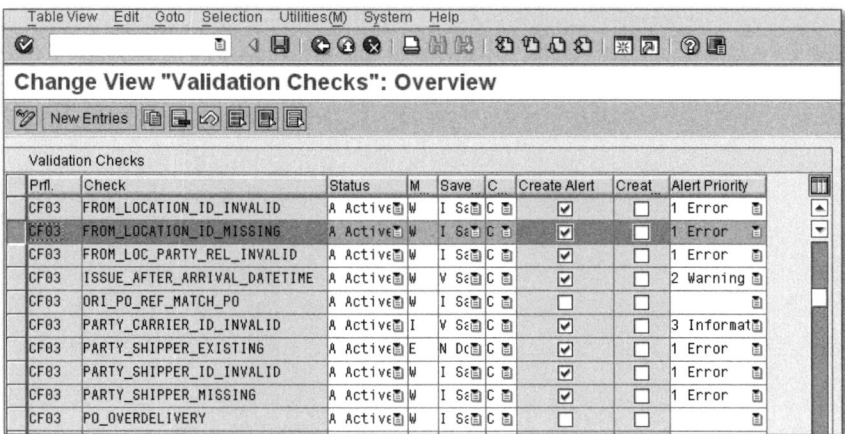

Figure 5.10 Validation Alerts

- **Post Processing Framework (PPF)**
  The Post Processing Framework allows actions to be generated on the basis of conditions. The actions are generated if particular conditions are met for a business object. For instance, the PPF can trigger an alert in response to user actions or inbound XML messages.

- **Generation through particular reports**
  Some alerts are generated in SAP SNC by means of special reports. Depending on the alert to be generated, the reports can be triggered manually for a selection or executed at regular intervals as a background job.

Alert Handling

The central component to manage alerts is the Alert Monitor. Both customers and suppliers can view and manage all of the alerts that are relevant for their products in the Alert Monitor in the SAP SNC web browser (see Figure 5.11).

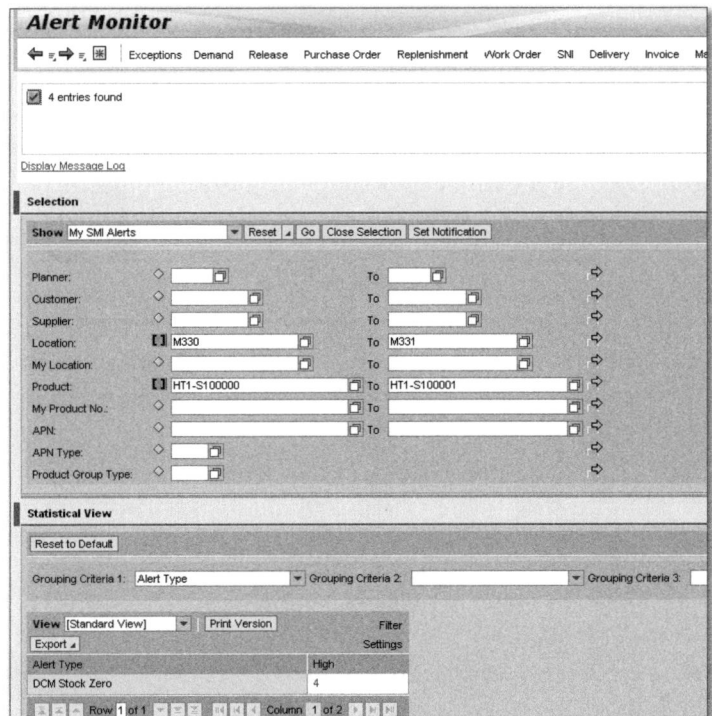

Figure 5.11 Alert Monitor

Alert Monitor in the SAP SNC web browser

The Alert Monitor consists of three screen areas:

In the SELECTION area, you can restrict the number of alerts displayed according to particular criteria. Furthermore, you can create selections using predefined criteria and assign them to a business partner organization or a particular user. Selections assigned to a business partner organization can be viewed by all of the users in that organization.

The STATISTICAL VIEW in the Alert Monitor displays the number of alerts found that match the criteria specified in the selection. The number of alerts can be broken down into four grouping criteria: ALERT TYPE, ALERT PRIORITY, LOCATION, and PRODUCT.

From the STATISTICAL VIEW, you can call up the DETAILS VIEW (see Figure 5.12). Here, detailed information is displayed for each alert, allowing you to analyze the alert trigger. In this view, you can confirm the alert and, in doing so, document the fact that you are aware of what caused the alert. Furthermore, you can enter a note for the alert or delete it if you want.

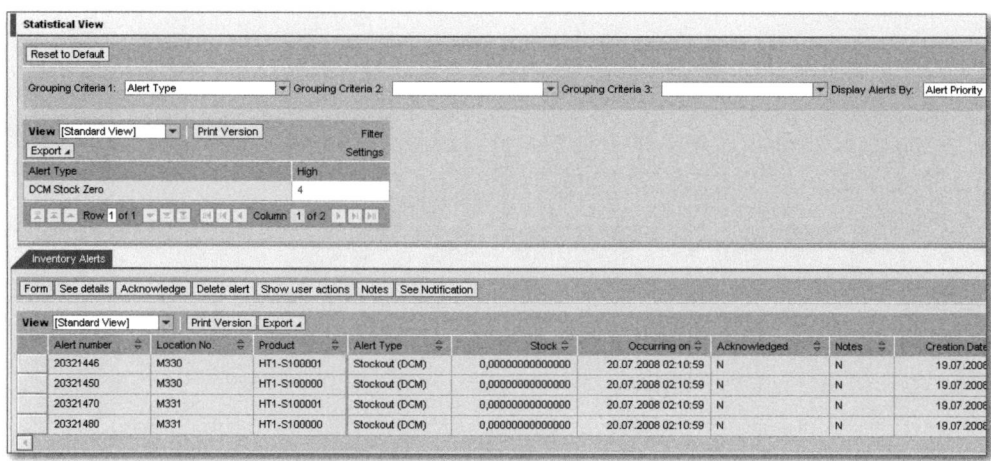

Figure 5.12 Alert Monitor – Details View

Sending Alerts

Alerts can be sent by email, SMS, fax, or pager both to the customer and the supplier. All users with authorization to do so can arrange to receive their assigned alerts through these channels. However, it is important to clarify at the outset whether the customer wants to define selection criteria for suppliers and set up the notification channel centrally. In this way, the customer can ensure that the supplier actually receives all relevant alerts.

The following steps must be performed to enable alerts to be sent:

1. **Set up message profile**
   In a message profile (Transaction /SCMB/ANOTMP), you define whether SAP SNC sends a notification (individual message) for each alert, bundles several alerts together in a notification (collective message), or sends alert statistics (aggregated message) for the alerts that occur. In addition, the message parameters in the message profile allow you to define the alert information that you want to be included in the notification. This means information relevant for business processes can be included in the alert, for instance, product, location, document number, and document item.

2. **Create alert selection**
   In the Alert Monitor, an alert selection must be created for the alerts to be sent. A range of criteria can be used here (alert type, product, ship-to location, ship-from location, and so on). However, only the ALERT TYPE, SHIP-TO LOCATION, and PRODUCT fields are taken into account when alerts are sent. All other selection criteria are only used to restrict output in the Alert Monitor.

3. **Maintain notification profile**
   A notification profile can be set up in the SAP SNC web browser on the basis of an alert selection (see Figure 5.13).

The parameters in the notification profile control when and how the alerts in an alert selection are sent to the recipient. The fields in the notification profile have the following meanings:

Settings in the notification profile

- VALID-FROM DATE and VALID-TO DATE: Define the period in which the profile is valid.

- RECIPIENT TYPE: If C-CHANNEL is selected, the email address provided in the E-MAIL ADDRESS field is used; if U-USER IN SYSTEM is selected, the email address of the user entered in the RECIPIENT field is taken from the user master (Transaction SU01).

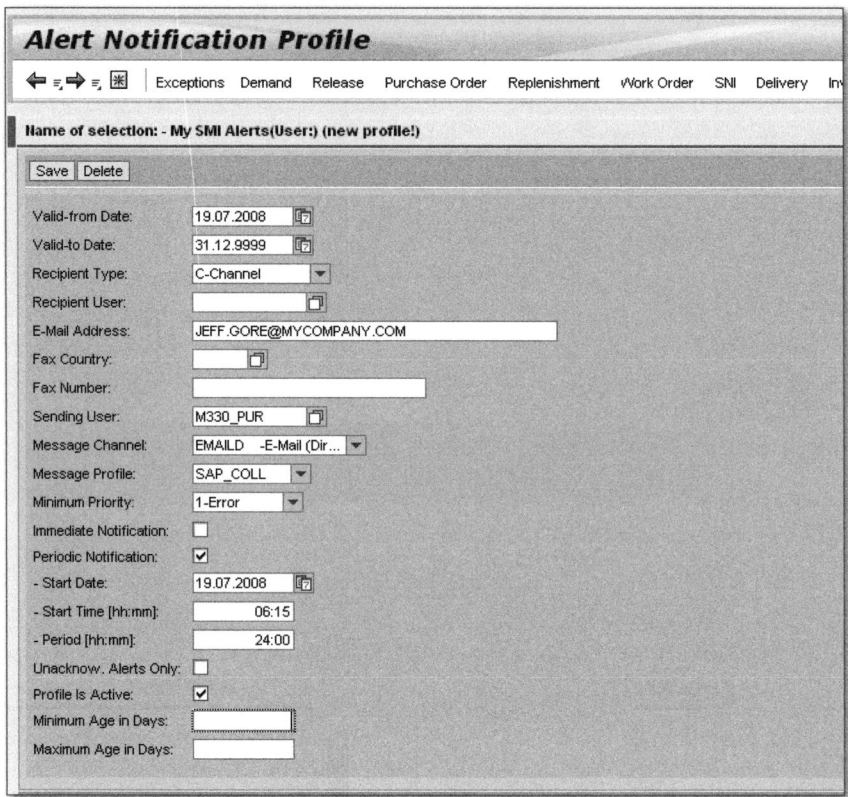

Figure 5.13 Maintaining a Notification Profile

- RECIPIENT USER: Only relevant if U-USER IN SYSTEM has been selected as the recipient type.

- E-MAIL ADDRESS: Only relevant if C-CHANNEL has been selected as the recipient type.

- FAX COUNTRY and FAX NUMBER: Country and number of the fax connection.

- SENDING USER: User whose email address is obtained from the user master as the sending address.

- MESSAGE CHANNEL: Here, you define whether an alert is sent by fax, email, SMS, or pager.

- MESSAGE PROFILE: Here, you select the message profile that controls the structure of an alert notification.

- MINIMUM PRIORITY: The minimum priority an alert must have to be sent.
- IMMEDIATE NOTIFICATION: Notification is provided immediately if the conditions are met.
- PERIODIC NOTIFICATION: All of the relevant alerts are gathered at regular intervals.
- START DATE and START TIME: If the PERIODIC NOTIFICATION indicator has been set, you can specify a start date and time here.
- PERIOD [HH:MM]: If the PERIODIC NOTIFICATION indicator has been set, you can enter the interval here.
- UNACKNOW. ALERTS ONLY: Only alerts that have not yet been acknowledged in the Alert Monitor are sent.
- PROFILE IS ACTIVE: Indicates whether the notification profile is active.
- AGE: Minimum and maximum age of alerts to be included in the notification.

If you use periodic notification, you must schedule report /SCMB/ANOTPULL regularly to create the alert mail.

Alert History

A change history can be recorded in SAP SNC for an alert. If an alert is created, changed, or deleted, the system automatically creates a new data record in the alert history of the alert type. Transaction /SCMB/ALENCFG can be used to define whether the system records a history for each of the alert types. Obsolete data records can be deleted from the alert history with report /SCMB/ALERTHOUSECLEAR.

Alert-Based Rating

Alert-based rating can be used to rate business partners, locations, and products on the basis of alerts. The alert types that are taken into account in the rating are stored in a rating profile (Transaction /SCMB/AMEACFG). First, the relevant alert types are assigned to an alert group. A basic score is defined for each alert type. The basic score for an alert denotes the score when the alert priority or the time at which the alert situation occurs are not relevant. Next, the level of detail with which rating records are generated is defined for each alert type. The customer, supplier, customer location, ship-from location, or product parameters can be used here for control purposes. Additionally, priority-dependent and alert-time-dependent scores can be determined for each alert type.

An alert group and rating period are assigned to the rating profile. In alert-based rating, the system subdivides the evaluation period into rating periods. In addition, the way in which the overall score for each characteristics combination is calculated from the scores for each of the alerts in a rating period is defined in the rating profile.

Report /SCMB/AMEA_REC_CREATE must be executed to perform alert-based rating. The results of the rating are displayed in the customer view in the SAP SNC web browser.

5.4 Enterprise SOA Concepts

This section begins by offering a broad outline of a service-oriented architecture approach in the SAP environment. It then explores the supplier collaboration services in SAP SNC in greater detail.

5.4.1 From SOA to Enterprise SOA

Service-oriented architecture

Service-oriented architecture (SOA) is a concept that joins business aspects with system-related architectural aspects, thereby bridging the gap between business processes and information technology. The business part of the SOA concept is aimed at achieving an IT infrastructure geared toward the required business processes that can react rapidly to changing requirements in the business world. The system architecture concept caters to the provision of technical services and functions. In this context, *services* means self-contained, reusable (business) functions that can be made available via standardized interfaces. Communication is ensured through use of appropriate infrastructure components. These infrastructure components call the services in a defined sequence and, in this way, map a complete business process (*composite applications*). It is also possible for the information determined in one service to be transferred to another service called at a later time (see Hack and Lindemann, *Enterprise SOA Roadmap*, SAP PRESS 2007, p. 25).

Enterprise service-oriented architecture (Enterprise SOA) is the SAP service-oriented architecture for adaptive business solutions. Enterprise SOA lays the foundation for a process-oriented software architecture that allows process applications to be composed and restructured rapidly thanks to its flexible process and service layer. On the basis of *SAP NetWeaver*, the SAP open integration and application platform, *enterprise services* can be realized and made available using the directory and search service in the *Enterprise Services Repository* (ES Repository).

Enterprise SOA

In its *enterprise services bundles* (ES bundles), SAP brings together a range of enterprise services and their accompanying documentation to respond to one common business situation. These bundles describe solution approaches and scenarios to highlight the benefits Enterprise SOA brings to your business. For example, Enterprise SOA for Supply Chain Management includes ES bundles for product availability checks, demand planning, service parts management, and SAP Supply Network Collaboration.

Enterprise services bundles

Information about ES bundles can be found in interactive wiki in the SAP Developer Network (*https://wiki.sdn.sap.com/wiki/display/ESpackages/home*), which also provides customers and SAP partners with a platform on which exchange experiences.

Wiki in the SDN

5.4.2 Enterprise SOA in Supplier Collaboration

The enterprise services for SAP SNC are already used for supplier collaboration in the standard business scenarios shipped by SAP. They make it possible to realize business processes that extend across the entire company and beyond, on the one hand by integrating SAP SNC with the company's internal SAP ERP systems, and on the other by exploiting the option of connecting to the backend systems of associated business partners. They are based on well-defined interfaces compliant with the industry standard that use the XML format and can be called using SAP NetWeaver PI.

Enterprise SOA in SAP SNC

The following section presents the enterprise services in the ES bundle for Supply Network Collaboration that are relevant for supplier collaboration. The enterprise services are grouped in process components depending on the business object to be processed. Detailed technical documentation about the interfaces (structure, input and output parameters, how they are called, and so on) of the enterprise services can be found in the *ES Workplace* (*https://www.sdn.sap.com/irj/sdn/explore-es*). The technical relationships described there are used here.

Process Component: Delivery Collaboration

Delivery collaboration is composed of enterprise services for processing ASNs and showing delivery progress in SAP SNC.

- **DispatchedDeliveryNotification_In**
  This can be used to create ASNs in SAP SNC. When incoming data is processed, a validation check is first performed to verify the consistency of the data before it is posted. With *DispatchedDeliveryNotification_In*, ASNs from a supplier's backend system or an internal legacy system can be transferred to SAP SNC.

- **DispatchedDeliveryNotification_Out**
  Once an ASN has been published in SAP SNC, an XML message is created with *DispatchedDeliveryNotification_Out* and sent to SAP ERP. SAP NetWeaver PI converts this XML message into IDoc format DESADV.DELVRY03 or DESADV.DELVRY05 so that a corresponding delivery can be created in SAP ERP. Goods receipt can be posted against this delivery at a later time.

- **DeliveryInformation_In**
  With *DeliveryInformation_In*, the ASN can be updated in SAP SNC with information from SAP ERP about the planned execution or status of the inbound delivery. In the service parts scenario, *DeliveryInformation_In* is used to confirm the results of the (external) validation of an inbound delivery in SAP ERP to SAP SNC.

- **ReceivedDeliveryNotification_In**
  ReceivedDeliveryNotification_In represents the inbound interface for proof of delivery messages for an ASN in SAP SNC. If, for instance, goods receipt or partial goods receipt is posted in SAP ERP for an

inbound delivery, the respective ASN item is updated accordingly in SAP SNC.

Process Component: Delivery Schedule Collaboration

Delivery schedule collaboration consists of enterprise services for forecast delivery schedule processing in SAP SNC.

- **DeliveryScheduleNotification_In**
  With *DeliveryScheduleNotification_In*, forecast delivery schedules and JIT delivery schedules from the backend system can be maintained in SAP SNC. Forecast delivery schedules and JIT delivery schedules can be generated from both SAP APO and SAP ERP. Delivery schedules from SAP APO are generated with an IDoc of type DELINS.DELFOR02. Forecast delivery schedules from SAP ERP are generated with an IDoc of type DELINS.DELFOR01. If an SAP ERP DIMP system is in use, IDocs of type DELFOR.DELFOR02 can be used for forecast delivery schedules, and type DELJIT.DELFOR02 can be used for JIT delivery schedules.

- **DeliveryScheduleConfirmation_Out**
  If a supplier creates and publishes a confirmation for a forecast delivery schedule line, an XML message can be created and sent to the backend system with *DeliveryScheduleConfirmation_Out*. If the receiver system is SAP APO, the XML message is converted into IDoc format DELCONF.DELFOR01. In SAP APO, the quantities and dates/times confirmed by the supplier can be compared with those originally requested.

Process Component: Replenishment Order Collaboration

Replenishment order collaboration consists of enterprise services for purchase order handling in SAP SNC.

- **ReplenishmentOrderNotification_In**
  ReplenishmentOrderNotification_In is the inbound interface for maintaining normal purchase orders and subcontract orders in SAP SNC. Purchase orders are created in the company's own SAP ERP system and can be sent via SAP NetWeaver PI to SAP SNC as IDocs of type ORDERS.ORDER05 in the case of normal purchase orders or

PORDCR1.PORDCR102 in the case of subcontract orders. In the service parts scenario, ReplenishmentOrderNotification_In is used to maintain third-party purchase orders that are sent from SAP ERP using an IDoc of type ORDNTF.ORDINT01.

- **ReplenishmentOrderConfirmation_In**
  Confirmations of quantities and dates/times that a supplier makes in an external system can be transferred to SAP SNC using the *ReplenishmentOrderConfirmation_In* interface.

- **ReplenishmentOrderConfirmation_Out**
  The *ReplenishmentOrderConfirmation_Out* interface enables supplier confirmations for purchase order items to be exported from SAP SNC. The XML message created here is converted in SAP NetWeaver PI into IDoc format ORDRSP.ORDERS05 and can then be processed in SAP ERP.

- **ReplenishmentOrderNotification_Out**
  The quantities and dates/times confirmed by a supplier for a purchase order item and the confirmations for component requirements for a subcontract order item can be made subject to an approval process in SAP SNC. If approved, the confirmations can be transferred to the company's internal SAP ERP system with the *ReplenishmentOrderNotification_Out* interface, where they are then included in the purchase order as request schedule lines or component requirements.

- **OrderIDAssignmentNotification_In**
  OrderIDAssigmentNotification_In is the inbound interface for maintaining purchase order number intervals in SAP SNC.

- **VendorGeneratedOrderNotification_Out**
  Suppliers can create a purchase order on the basis of planned receipts in SAP SNC. The *VendorGeneratedOrderNotitification_Out* interface can be used to notify the company's internal SAP ERP system of the new purchase order. The XML message created here is converted in SAP NetWeaver PI into IDoc format ORDRSP.ORDERS05 and can then be processed in SAP ERP.

- **VendorGeneratedOrderConfirmation_In**
  VendorGeneratedOrderConfirmation_In is the inbound interface for maintaining supplier confirmations for a purchase order created by a supplier in SAP SNC.

Process Component: Inventory Collaboration

ProductActivityNotification_In is the inbound interface for maintaining product-related stock information in SAP SNC. It makes it possible to create the company's own stock (unrestricted-use, blocked, and quality inspection), subcontracting stock, consignment stock, and stock at suppliers and third parties.

Process Component: Demand Collaboration

Demand collaboration consists of enterprise services for demand processing in SAP SNC.

- **ProductActivityNotification_In**
  In addition to being used to maintain stock information, *ProductActivityNotification_In* can receive product-related stock and receipt information. Requirements are prepared in the form of product-related quantities and dates/times. This means that requirements—for instance, sales orders, forecast demands, planned independent demands, dependent demands, and dependent reservations—can be extracted from an SAP ERP system and transferred to SAP SNC. A distinction is made between planned and firm receipts. Planned receipts can be represented in SAP ERP in the form of purchase order requests, planned orders, manual reservations, stock transfer reservations, and scheduling agreement delivery schedule lines (from planning). Firm receipts are purchase orders, production orders, and forecast delivery schedule lines with production go-ahead or material go-ahead as their levels of commitment.

- **ProductActivityNotification_Out**
  ProductActivityNotification_Out is the outbound interface for product-related stock information. It can be used, for example, to pass on stock information to the supplier's backend system.

Process Component: Invoice Collaboration

Invoice collaboration consists of enterprise services for invoice processing in SAP SNC, in particular, for exchanging invoice data and invoice confirmation data between the invoicing party and the invoice recipient.

- **InvoiceRequest_In**

  InvoiceRequest_In is the inbound interface for maintaining invoices in SAP SNC, for example, from the backend system of an invoicing party or supplier. If self-billing is used to process invoices (for evaluated receipt settlement, for example), invoice data can also be transferred from a company's own SAP ERP system.

- **InvoiceConfirmation_In**

  InvoiceConfirmation_In is used to maintain a confirmation or rejection of an invoice on the part of the invoice recipient in SAP SNC.

- **InvoiceRequest_Out**

  InvoiceRequest_Out is the outbound interface for sending an invoice from SAP SNC to the invoice recipient. If a supplier creates and publishes an invoice manually in SAP SNC with reference to a purchase order or ASN, an XML message can be generated from it with *Invoice Request_Out*. The XML message is converted in SAP NetWeaver PI into an IDoc of type INVOIC.INVOIC01 and can then be processed by the SAP ERP system of the invoice recipient (customer).

- **PaymentAdviceNotification_In**

  The *PaymentAdviceNotification_In* inbound interface enables payment advices to be maintained for invoices in SAP SNC. A payment advice is created in SAP ERP on the basis of a payment run and transferred via SAP NetWeaver PI to SAP SNC with an IDoc of type REMADV. PEXR2002. When a payment advice is received, the payment status of the corresponding invoice is updated in SAP SNC.

Process Component: Manufacturing Work Order Collaboration

Manufacturing work order collaboration consists of enterprise services for processing work orders in SAP SNC.

- **ManufacturingWorkOrderRequest_Out**

  ManufacturingWorkOrderRequest_Out is the outbound interface for transferring new or modified work orders from SAP SNC to the backend system of a supplier.

- **ManufacturingWorkOrderConfirmation_In**

  ManufacturingWorkOrderConfirmation_In is the inbound interface that enables a supplier to confirm, reject, or change a work order in SAP SNC.

- **ManufacturingWorkOrderWorkInProcessNotification_In**
  ManufacturingWorkOrderWorkInProcessNotification_In allows the production progress being made on a work order at the supplier to be entered in SAP SNC. The supplier can confirm actual quantities once production has begun and thereby update the work order status in SAP SNC.

- **ManufacturingWorkOrderWorkInformation_Out**
  Information about the status of a work order in SAP SNC can be created using the *ManufacturingWorkOrderWorkInformation_Out* interface.

Process Component: Supply Chain Exception Collaboration

Supply chain exception collaboration makes it possible to exchange information about exceptions in the business process between SAP SNC and other systems.

- **SupplyChainExceptionReportNotification_In**
  With the *SupplyChainExceptionReportNotification_In* inbound interface, information about exceptions in SAP SNC can be processed and mapped to predefined alerts in SAP SNC as required.

- **SupplyChainExceptionReportNotification_Out**
  The *SupplyChainExceptionReportNotification_Out* interface allows information about exceptions in the business process identified in SAP SNC to be created and sent to other systems.

This chapter deals with the optional integration of SAP SNC with other SAP solutions. It introduces SAP solutions that are beneficial for comprehensive supplier collaboration.

6   Integrating SAP SNC with Other SAP Solutions

This chapter illustrates the individual business processes of supplier collaboration and explains the business processes for which the SAP SNC solution can be implemented. It also introduces other SAP solutions that can be integrated with SAP SNC to enable comprehensive supplier collaboration.

6.1   Classifying SAP SNC into Various Supplier Collaboration Business Processes

Supplier collaboration is divided into five areas:

- Strategic purchasing
- Design and product lifecycle management
- Procurement planning
- Procurement processing
- Billing and dispute management

Areas of supplier collaboration

As shown in Figure 6.1, SAP SNC 5.1 supports supplier collaboration predominantly in the areas of procurement planning, procurement processing, and billing.

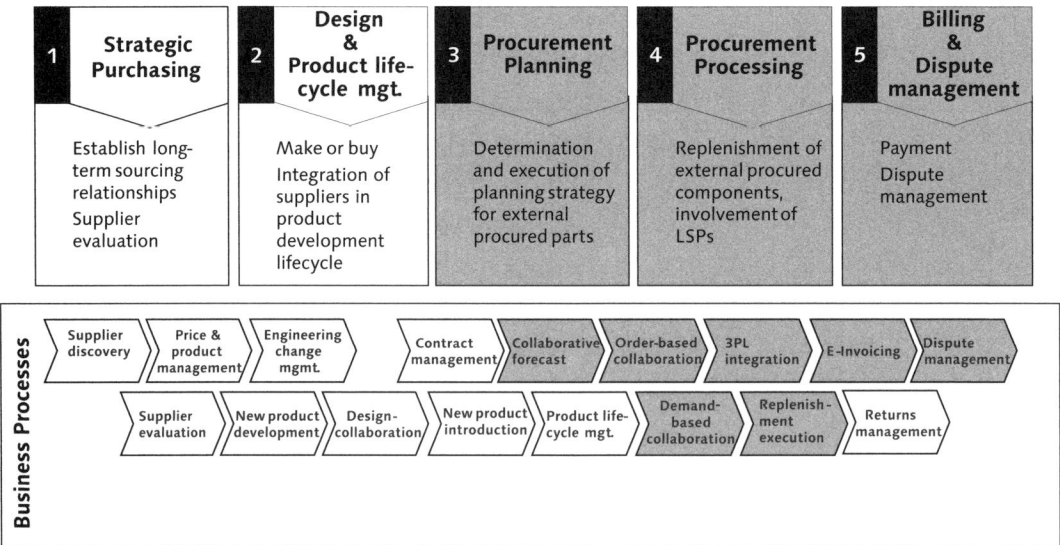

Figure 6.1 Classification of the SAP SNC Solution in Supplier Collaboration Business Processes

The SAP SNC solution supports the individual areas within procurement planning, procurement processing, and billing as follows:

Collaborative forecasting

Collaborative forecasting arises in procurement planning if the customer allows the supplier access to planning figures. These figures are used purely for information and can change at any time. The supplier can use this information to adjust his capacity promptly and therefore avoid unnecessary stock on hand. Collaborative forecasting is supported by various business processes in SAP SNC:

- Displaying gross demand in the SMI process
- Long-term forecasting in forecast delivery schedule processing
- Transferring requirement coverage requests (purchase requisitions) and planned orders for medium-term and long-term planning in the dynamic replenishment process

Order-related collaboration

In *order-related collaboration*, the customer uses individual orders to inform the supplier about net demands. This is covered by the following processes:

- Ordering process
- Work order cooperation processing
- Forecast delivery schedule processing
- Dynamic replenishment
- Kanban process

Unlike order-related collaboration, in *demand-related collaboration* the customer transfers the gross demands to the supplier using *time series* with a temporal aggregation of at least one day. Demand-related collaboration takes place through:

- Replenishment planning with SMI
- Delivery Control Monitor

Replenishment execution is carried out by creating an ASN in SAP SNC and integrating the *third-party logistics provider* using the Supply Network Inventory (SNI) functionality.

Replenishment execution

Invoices can be covered independently for all business processes within SAP SNC using invoice collaboration in SAP SNC. Either the supplier manually creates an invoice in SAP SNC or the customer carries out automatic receipt settlement.

Dispute management is supported both by the approval process in purchase order handling and by alert management.

Dispute management

These standard business processes require at least the following components to be integrated in the system landscape (see Section 5.2 System Landscape):

Required components

- SAP SNC
- SAP NetWeaver PI
- SAP ERP

The optional integration of SAP SNC with other SAP solutions enables the other business process areas within supplier collaboration to be orchestrated optimally.

6 Integrating SAP SNC with Other SAP Solutions

6.2 Collaboration Folders

cFolders

SAP *Collaboration Folders* (cFolders) are a web-based collaboration platform in *SAP Product Lifecycle Management* (PLM) that allows virtual teams to work on documents simultaneously.

SAP SNC 5.1 is already closely integrated with cFolders. This allows you to navigate directly to cFolders from different monitors. The button for navigating to the cFolders system must be activated and is visible only to users with the relevant authorization.

Product lifecycle management

Optimizing supplier collaboration requires *design and product lifecycle management* to be clearly integrated with procurement planning, because collaboration in product innovation, design collaboration, and the introduction of new products is essential due to decreasing levels of in-house production and the outsourcing of production to external partners. Figure 6.2 shows the areas of the main business processes covered by the cFolders solution.

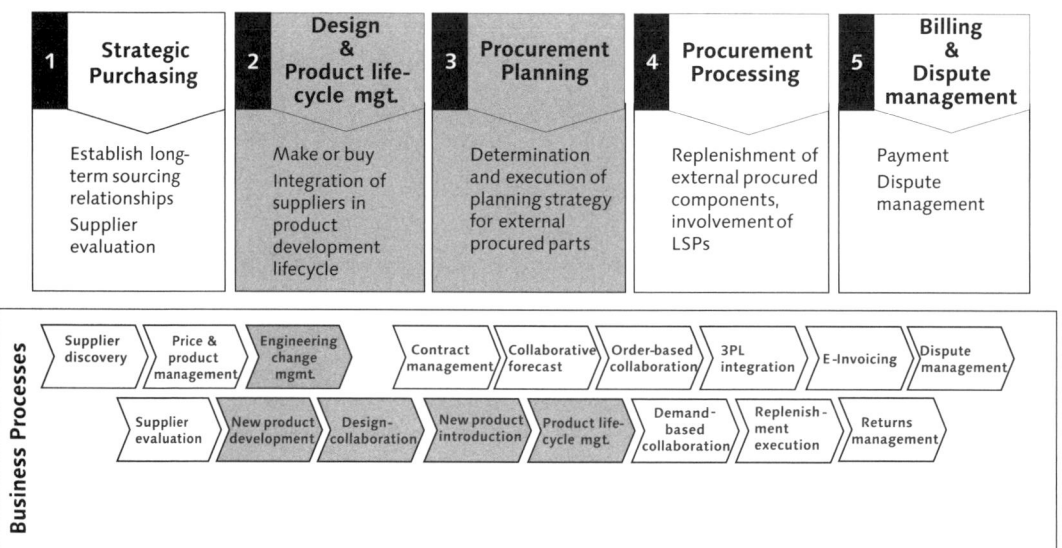

Figure 6.2 Classification of the cFolders Solution in Supplier Collaboration Business Processes

Typical examples of collaboration using cFolders as part of procurement processes are:

- Publishing the latest bill of material information, packaging instructions, and drawings
- Close collaboration in design changes between the affected departments at different partner locations

Figure 6.3 shows the design collaboration for new packaging in the consumer products industry:

1. The engineering department enters the master data in SAP ERP and publishes the packaging specifications in cFolders ❶.

   Packaging design

2. Both the external design partner and the partner for legal issues are automatically informed that cFolders contains new specifications. The design company checks the specifications for marketing-specific criteria. The legal department ensures that legal requirements are met. Both parties consult closely with the engineering department. Because all relevant parties have access to the same information, the collaboration process is accelerated compared to the earlier process, which relied on traditional means of communication such as fax, mail, and phone ❷.

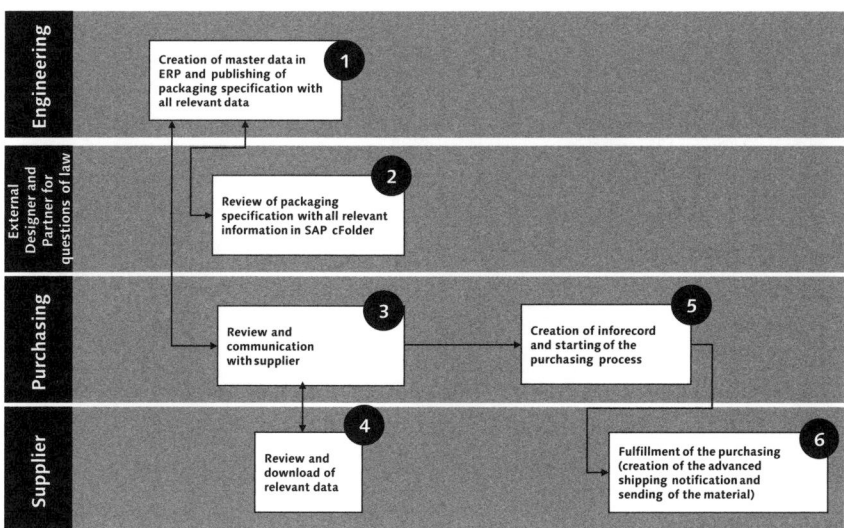

Figure 6.3 Sample Process Flow for Collaborative Design Management with cFolders and SAP SNC

3. cFolders automatically informs purchasing once the design and legal departments have completed their work. Purchasing then carries out

a review and clarifies any outstanding points with the engineering department ❸.

4. Once these points have been clarified, purchasing uses cFolders to contact the supplier in question. In turn, the supplier can check the specifications and negotiate with purchasing ❹.

5. Once this process is complete, the purchasing department enters any missing master data (info record, contract, and so on) in SAP ERP and triggers the ordering process ❺.

6. The supplier can then view the purchase order in SAP SNC ❻.

The supplier can use the same Internet link to access both cFolders and the information relevant for SAP SNC.

6.3 SAP NetWeaver Business Intelligence

SAP NetWeaver Business Intelligence (SAP NetWeaver BI) enables you to evaluate data from different SAP applications. SAP SNC is already integrated with SAP NetWeaver BI. Alerts generated in SAP SNC can be read using extractor /SCMB/BWEX_ALERT_BASED_RATING.

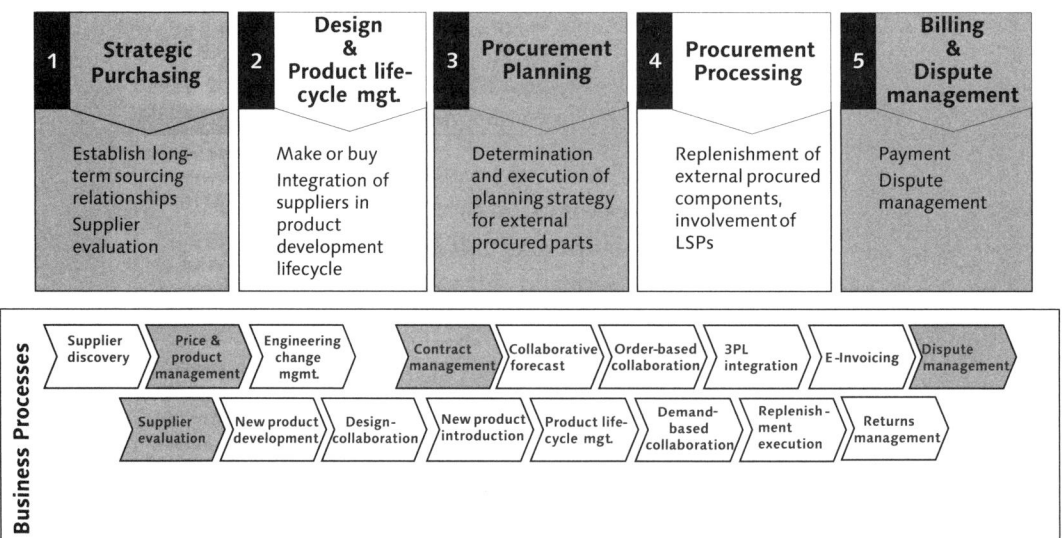

Figure 6.4 Classification of the SAP NetWeaver BI Solution to Support Supplier Collaboration Business Processes

Figure 6.4 shows which areas of the main business processes can be supported by SAP NetWeaver BI.

Evaluations

Figure 6.5 graphically illustrates the SAP systems from which, for example, key figures for evaluating suppliers can be read and displayed in SAP NetWeaver BI.

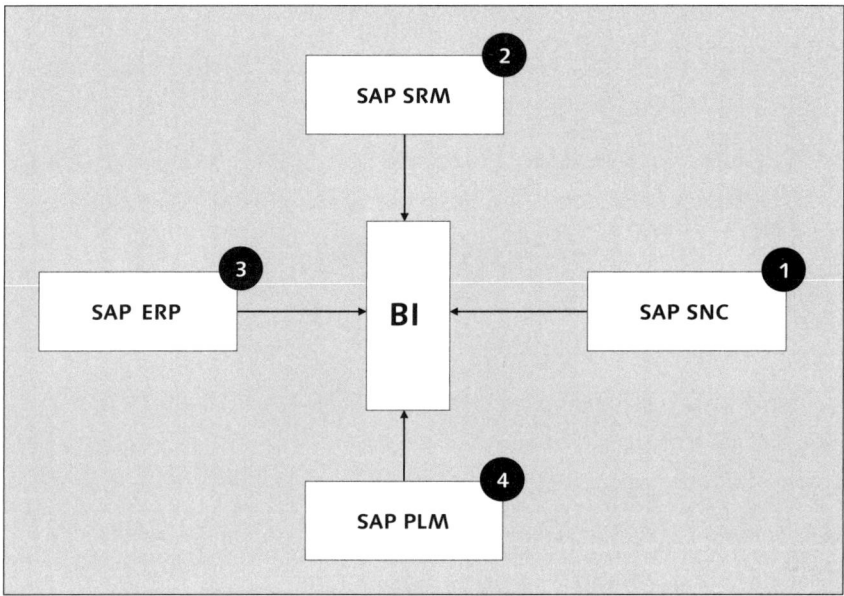

Figure 6.5 Example – Sources for Supplier Evaluation

The standard SAP SNC system contains alert-based rating to assess the performance of the supplier. Points, which can be defined freely by the customer in Customizing, are assigned for each alert type. It is advisable to allocate more points to alerts with a higher priority than to those with a lower priority ❶.

Alert-based rating in SAP SNC

For example, an alert that indicates a stockout in replenishment planning should be allocated more points than an alert that indicates that the customer's actual stock has reached the reorder point. Alert-based rating analyzes alerts that occurred for an evaluation period in the past and calculates the points value. The higher the number of points, the more alerts occurred or the higher the priority of the alerts. Besides the key figures that can be obtained from alerts in SAP SNC, customers should also use key figures from other sources to obtain the broadest possible impression of a supplier. A centralized SAP NetWeaver BI system is ideally suited to this purpose.

SAP SRM *SAP Supplier Relationship Management* (SAP SRM) can be used to analyze a report on the group-wide spending at different suppliers. This analysis helps the customer identify low-cost procurement options and provides a basis for negotiating prices with suppliers ❷.

SAP ERP SAP ERP can be used to evaluate on-time delivery performance, quality audits, or complaints, for example ❸.

SAP PLM SAP Product Lifecycle Management can be used, for example, to include the results of a completed supplier audit in the overall rating of the supplier ❹.

6.4 SAP Event Management

SAP Event Management (SAP EM) provides transparency along the entire supply chain. This allows messages about events, for example, in procurement, to be processed and those involved in the supply network to be informed in different ways. A typical example of a procurement event is when a customer expects a product to arrive within a specified period of time. If this does not occur, an alert is generated automatically. The alert can then be sent to the responsible person (such as the procurement manager) so that he knows to contact the supplier.

Logistics events Automatically checking the events that must take place to ensure a smooth flow along the supply chain means that any delay or nonoccurrence of these events can be identified immediately. Steps can then be taken more quickly to correct the problem.

SAP Event Management supports all supplier collaboration business processes.

The standard shipment of SAP EM 5.1 already contains a number of integration points with the SAP SNC solution:

1. **Expected confirmation of an order in the ordering process**
   The supplier is expected to confirm an order within a specific period. This event is automatically generated in SAP SNC when a new order is received (inbound message). A check is then carried out to ensure that the order confirmation was published or sent to SAP ERP within the relevant period (see Figure 6.6).

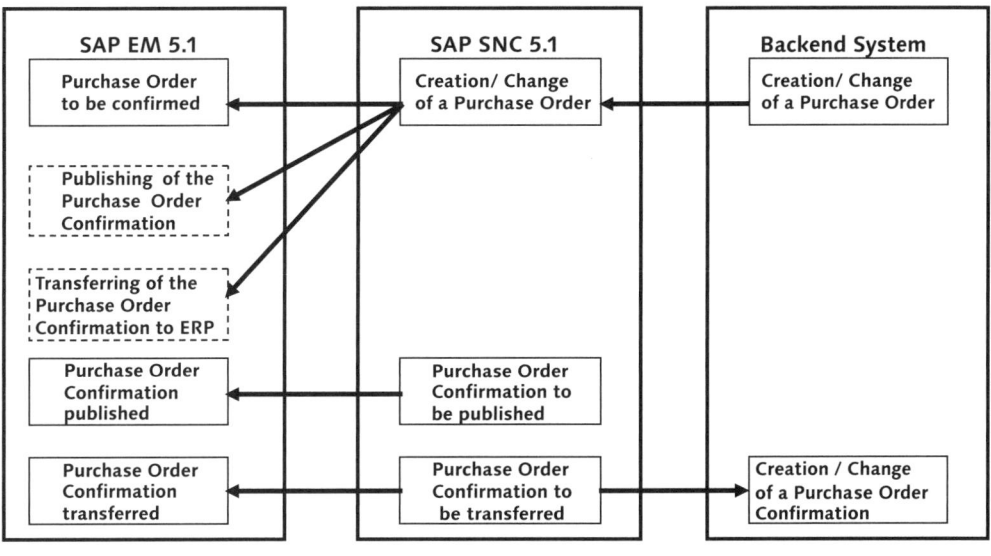

Figure 6.6 Integration with SAP EM – Expected Confirmation of an Order

The period in which the order must be confirmed can be defined flexibly in *Configurable Process Scheduling* (in Transaction SPRO, follow the menu path SCM BASIS • CONFIGURABLE PROCESS SCHEDULING).

2. **Expected XML message for the SMI process**
   The customer's SAP ERP system is expected to send the XML message *ProductActivityNotification* to SAP SNC within a specific period in a day. This event is generated with report /SCA/EM_MSG_EE_CREATE. If the event does not take place, the Event Manager generates an alert that is also displayed in the SAP SNC Alert Monitor of (see Figure 6.7).

6 Integrating SAP SNC with Other SAP Solutions

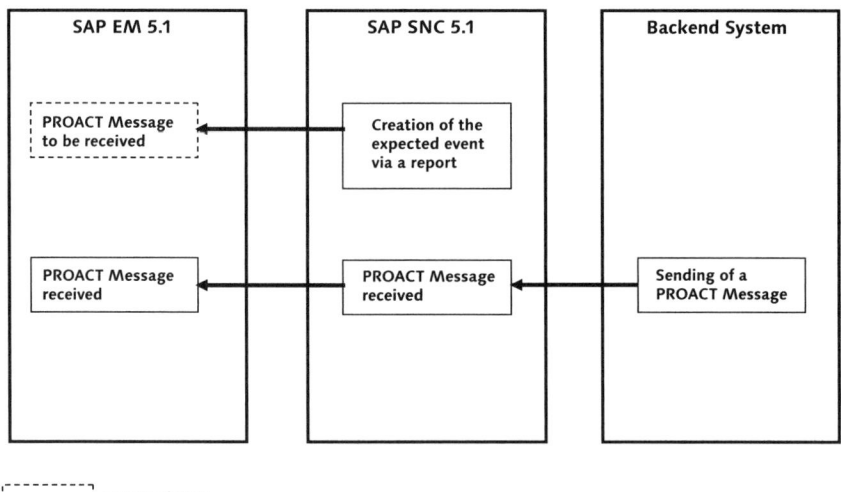

Figure 6.7 Integration with SAP EM – Expected XML Message in the SMI Process

6.5 SAP NetWeaver Portal

Cross-system processes

The *SAP NetWeaver Portal* enables you to use small programs, known as iViews, to call data from information sources in your company and from the Internet. You collate a personalized overview of all elements that, for example, are relevant for a supplier's activities.

If you want to allow a supplier access to other customer systems besides SAP SNC using an external link, you can add these systems to an SAP NetWeaver Portal.

The SAP NetWeaver Portal can therefore group together process steps that are required for the complete process flow but that are actually carried out in different systems.

For example, it is of considerable benefit if the subcontractor can post the goods receipt for parts provided by a third-party supplier (third-party order processing) for a subcontract order. However, this transaction is still part of the customer's SAP ERP system. Integrating the goods receipt transaction of SAP ERP and the relevant iViews of SAP SNC would simplify the subcontracting process for both parties (that is, the customer and the supplier) because the subcontractor would no longer be required to phone or fax the customer to confirm receipt of the components so that the customer, in turn, can enter the data in the backend system in accordance with the supplier's specification.

You can also include SAP NetWeaver BI reports in the same portal so that the supplier also has access to this information from a central point of entry.

Figure 6.8 shows an example of how different customer systems can be integrated to ensure a smooth flow of the process steps required for the supplier.

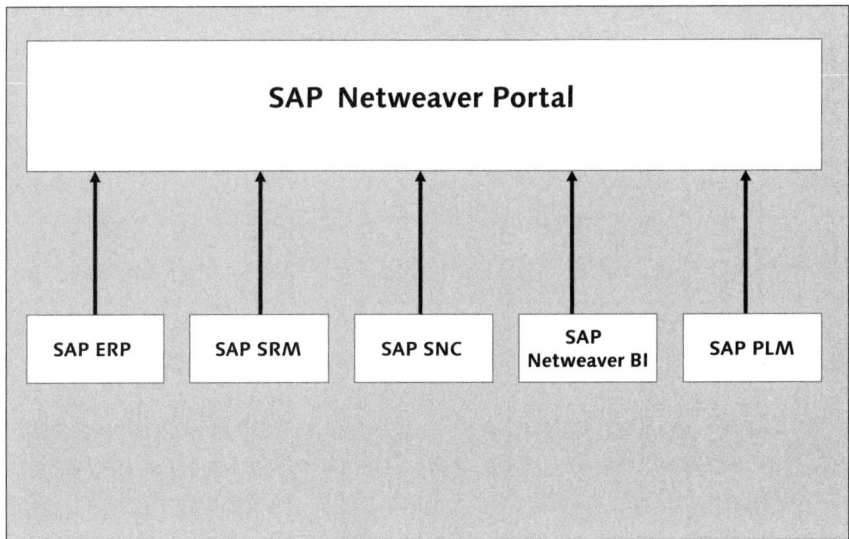

Figure 6.8 Example of Integrating Different SAP Solutions in the SAP NetWeaver Portal to Optimize Supplier Collaboration

6.6 SAP Advanced Planning & Optimization

SAP Advanced Planning & Optimization (SAP APO) offers a fully integrated range of functions for cross-company interaction on the strategic, tactical, and operational level of your logistics processes.

Planning tool

253

The standard shipment of SAP APO already contains a number of integration points with the SAP SNC solution. For example, SAP APO and SAP SNC share some basic services, including master data management, exceptions (alerts), and validation checks.

In master data management, for example, locations (plants or suppliers), products, transportation lanes, and external procurement relationships (contracts, scheduling agreements, and info records) are transferred from the customer's backend system using the same Core Interface (CIF) and written to the same master data tables.

In exception management, alerts are generated and displayed in the Alert Monitor, and in the validation checks, business objects (ASNs, purchase orders, and so on) are checked for completeness and consistency (see Section 5.3 Basic Services).

In the standard system, transaction data is directly integrated in forecast delivery schedule processing only if scheduling agreement releases are generated in SAP APO instead of the customer's SAP ERP system. In this case, an IDoc is sent directly from SAP APO to SAP SNC using SAP NetWeaver PI (see Section 4.3 Forecast Delivery Schedule Processing).

6.7 SAP Supplier Relationship Management

SAP Supplier Relationship Management allows you to align your business processes with your suppliers and manage them more effectively. It helps you optimize your procurement strategy and examine and forecast purchasing behavior.

Integrating SAP SNC with strategic purchasing and contract management from the SAP SRM solution completes the picture of successful and comprehensive supplier collaboration.

Figure 6.9 shows which areas of the main business processes can be supported by SAP SRM.

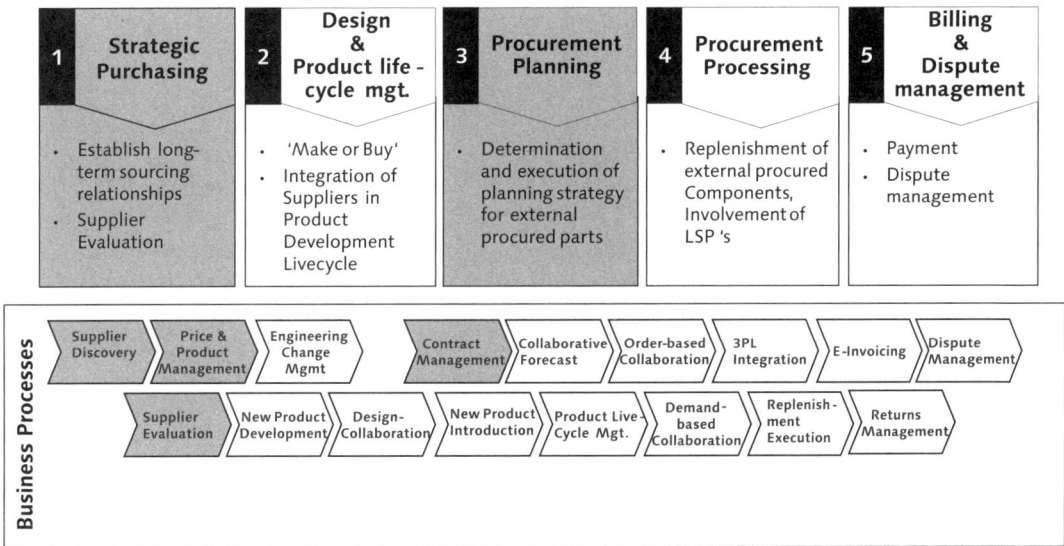

Figure 6.9 Classification of the SAP SRM Solution to Support Supplier Collaboration Business Processes

Typical examples of collaboration with SAP SRM in strategic purchasing and procurement planning are:

▶ **Automated bid invitations and auctions**
The bid invitation and auction functionality in SAP SRM allows you to expand your supplier base more easily and supports price and product management. It also facilitates the evaluation of received offers.

▶ **Central contract management**
Outline agreements can be negotiated in SAP SRM and provided for operational use. SAP SRM also enables you to manage contract documents.

Data reorganization helps you delete or archive data from a system that is obsolete or no longer required on a daily basis. This maximizes system performance.

7 Data Reorganization

This section first explains the basic procedure for reorganizing data in SAP SNC. It then describes how you can reorganize transaction data and master data. The final part concentrates on the archiving of specific transaction data.

7.1 Procedure

To avoid data inconsistency, you should ensure that specific conditions are fulfilled before data is reorganized. Before you delete master data, the respective transaction data must be removed. If necessary, you should check and delete the assignment to model *000*.

Conditions for reorganization

When deleting master data, note the order of assignments. Start with the highest level of detail. For example:

1. Delete the product assignment for a transportation lane.
2. Delete the transportation lanes and external procurement relationships.
3. Set the deletion indicator for (location) products and execute the deletion report.
4. Delete the business partner data.
5. Delete the location data.

Before you remove master data, you should check thoroughly whether it is still in use. You can use the where-used list (Transaction WUF) in SAP SNC to determine whether a product is in use. In this way, you can find

Where-used list

out, for example, the locations to which a product is assigned or which transaction data relates to a specific product.

7.2 Reorganizing Transaction Data

To maximize system performance, you should reorganize transaction data at regular intervals. Transaction data for business processes is stored in SAP SNC in the form of time series data (such as demands and planned receipts), order document data (such as purchase orders, forecast delivery schedules, work orders, and ASNs), and tables (such as alerts and alert history). This data is managed using the SCM Basis functions for managing time series data and order document data.

Time series data Reorganize time series data: You delete time series data from SAP SNC using report /SCA/TSDM_TS_DELETE. If you have activated the change history for the time series, use report /SCA/TSDM_TS_HIST_DELETE to remove changes made to the time series before a specific date.

Stock Create, delete, and reset stock: Stock in SAP SNC can be used with the SNI and SMI business processes for test and simulation purposes.

- You can create and update stock using report /SCA/CREATE_INV.
- You can reset stock using report /SCA/RESET_INV.
- You can delete stock using report /SCA/DELETE_INV.

Invoice data Reorganize invoice data: You delete invoices using report /SCA/INVOICE_DELETE. This removes invoices with the following statuses:

- Invoice status DRAFT
- Invoice status PUBLISHED
- Invoice status PAID
- Acceptance status ACCEPTED

ASN data Reorganize ASN data: You delete ASNs using report /SCA/DLV_DELETE. This removes ASNs with the following header statuses:

- DRAFT
- GOODS RECEIPT COMPLETE

- CLOSED
- CANCELED
- For ASNs with Published or Goods Receipt Partial status, you assign Closed status using report /SCA/DM_BOL_DLV_CLOSE
- Note that the manual completion or deletion of ASNs in SAP SNC is not integrated with the customer's backend system

Reorganize forecast delivery schedule data: You remove forecast delivery schedules from the SAP SNC system using report /SCA/DM_BOL_REL_DELETE. Deletion is not integrated with the customer's backend system. | Forecast delivery schedule data

- Reorganize purchase orders and replenishment orders: You delete purchase orders and replenishment orders with DELIVERY COMPLETED or CLOSED status using report /SCA/PO_DELETE. For purchase orders and replenishment orders that do not have one of the statuses specified, you assign CLOSED status using report /SCA/PO_SET_CLOSED. | Purchase orders and replenishment orders

- Reorganize work order data: You delete work orders from the SAP SNC system that have CLOSED or EXECUTION COMPLETED status using report /SCA/WO_DELETION. For work orders that do not have one of the statuses specified, you assign CLOSED status using report /SCA/WO_SET_STATUS_CLOSED. | Work order data

- Reorganize kanban data: You delete kanbans with CLOSED status in SAP SNC using report /SCA/DM_KNBN_DEL_CLOSED. This only deletes kanban data from the SAP SNC system, not from the customer's backend system. If you update the master data in the customer's backend system and transfer it to SAP SNC, the kanbans deleted from the customer's backend system are also removed from SAP SNC. | Kanban

Reorganize alerts and alert history: You delete alerts from the alert tables using report /SCMB/ALEN_ALERT_DELETE. If you have specified that the alert history is to be recorded, the deleted alert data records are transferred to the alert history tables. You remove the alert history from the database using report /SCMB/ALERTHOUSECLEAR. | Alerts and alert history

7.3 Reorganizing Master Data

When reorganizing master data, note the order and dependencies of the master data objects.

Product relationship/ transportation lane

Remove assignment for product relationship/transportation lane: You can remove the assignment of one or more products to the transportation lane using Transactions /SAPAPO/SCC_TL1 and /SAPAPO/TR_DELTRPR.

External procurement relationship

Reorganize external procurement relationships: You reorganize external procurement relationships in two steps. First, you deactivate the relationships. In the second step, you can delete the deactivated external procurement relationships. You can deactivate and remove individual external procurement relationships using Transactions /SAPAPO/PWBSRC1 and /SAPAPO/PWBSRC2. You can also carry out mass processing (Transaction MASSD) when reorganizing external procurement relationships.

You can transfer information about deleted purchasing info records, scheduling agreements, and contracts in the customer's backend system via the Core Interface (CIF). This deactivates the relevant external procurement relationship.

Transportation lane

Reorganize transportation lanes: A transportation lane is deleted automatically as soon as no more products are assigned to it.

Products and location products

Reorganize (location) product data: Before you can delete a product or location product, a deletion flag must be set in the product master or location product master. You can remove the product from active model 000 so that it no longer appears in the SAP SNC web browser.

You can set the deletion flag for one (location) product (Transaction /SAPAPO/MAT1) or multiple (location) products (Transaction MASSD). You can then remove products or location products from the SAP SNC system that are flagged for deletion using report /SAPAPO/DELETE_PRODUCTS.

Business partners

Reorganize business partners: Before you delete business partners, you should check whether all business partner–dependent assignments such as selections and time bucket profiles have been removed. You can also check whether the business partner is assigned to a location using report /SCA/USRPRTLOC.

You flag one or more business partners for deletion or archiving using Transaction BUPA_PRE_DA. To delete business partners, use Transaction BUPA_DEL. You can archive business partner data using Transaction SARA and archiving object CA_BUPA.

Reorganize location data: Before you can delete a location, a deletion flag must be set in the location master. You can remove the location from active model 000 so that it no longer appears in the SAP SNC web browser.

Location data

You can set the deletion flag for one location (Transaction /SAPAPO/ LOC3) or multiple locations (Transaction MASSD). You can then remove locations from the SAP SNC system that are flagged for deletion using report /SAPAPO/DELETE_LOCATIONS.

7.4 Archiving Transaction Data

In SAP SNC, you can archive old transaction data for work orders and supplier confirmations that you no longer require on a daily basis. The archived data records are moved from the database and can be displayed in the archive history. Archiving reduces the volume of transaction data and maximizes database performance.

Archiving old data

Archive supplier confirmations: You archive supplier confirmations using archiving object ICH_SCON (Transaction SARA).

Archiving supplier confirmations

Report /SCA/SCON_ARC_PREPROC is used to preprocess the supplier confirmations to be archived. If the selected supplier confirmations fulfill the conditions for archiving, the system sets the archiving status of the confirmation to 0. From this point, no more changes can be made to the supplier confirmations.

Report /SCA/SCON_ARC_WRITE reads all of the supplier confirmations for which the archiving status is set to 0 and writes the data to the archive file.

Report /SCA/SCON_ARC_DELETE deletes the archived supplier confirmations from the database.

You can display the archived supplier confirmations in the SAP SNC web browser by selecting DELIVERY • SUPPLIER CONFIRMATIONS • HISTORY.

Archiving work orders

Archive work orders: You archive work orders using archiving object ICH_WO (Transaction SARA).

Report /SCA/WO_ARC_PREPROC is used to preprocess the work orders to be archived. If the selected work orders fulfill the conditions for archiving, the system sets the archiving status of the work order to 0. From this point, no more changes can be made to the work orders.

Report /SCA/WO_ARC_WRITE reads all of the work orders for which the archiving status is set to 0 and writes the data to the archive file.

Report /SCA/WO_ARC_DELETE deletes the archived work orders from the database.

You can display the archived work orders in the SAP SNC web browser by selecting WORK ORDER HISTORY.

Appendices

A Glossary 265

B SAP Consulting Services Portfolio 271

C The Authors 283

A   Glossary

Adaptive Supply Chain Network   An approach that allows all of the companies involved in the supply chain network to share information and resources so they can adjust to changing market conditions with greater agility.

Advanced Planning & Optimization (APO)   Part of SAP SCM. A software solution that enables dynamic supply chain management; it includes applications for detailed planning, optimization, and scheduling, allowing the supply chain to be accurately and globally monitored even beyond a company's boundaries.

Advanced Planning and Scheduling (APS)   A software solution for planning processes (information, cash, and material flow) beyond company boundaries. External partners are involved in planning, and it is carried out across three planning horizons (short term, medium term, and long term).

Advanced Shipping Notification (ASN)   Notification of goods receipt that is sent from the supplier to the customer before the goods are delivered; it informs the customer of the time of the goods receipt so that any necessary arrangements can be made.

Alert Monitor   An SAP SNC component that processes alerts for all SNC business processes. The Alert Monitor displays information about the causes of alerts.

Alert   An alert notifies the user about a critical situation that has already occurred or will occur in the future. The user must take manual action to resolve the problem that caused the alert.

Available-to-Promise (ATP)   A function that uses certain basic methods to check whether a product can be confirmed. A binding delivery date is confirmed to the customer when the order is received.

Bill of Material   A complete, structured list of the components of a product or assembly that specifies the description, quantity, and unit of measure of the individual components.

Bottleneck Resource   Potential shortages of materials, raw materials, or staff that threaten to limit throughput in production or the supply chain.

Business Application Programming Interface (BAPI)   A standard interface that can be used to integrate different components, such as SAP APO and an external system. BAPIs provide an object-oriented view of the business components of the SAP system. They are implemented and stored as RFC-enabled function modules in the Function Builder of the ABAP Workbench.

Capable-to-Match (CTM)   Performs a quick check of production capacities and transportation capabilities; used to plan multiplant production processes taking into account time-dependent factors, such as the lead time.

Capacity Leveling   Allocation of work during a time period so that a process can be completed successfully and employees and computers are not overloaded.

Collaboration   Collaboration between companies that goes beyond simply cooperating: Different users, employees, customers, suppliers, and business partners can work together across company boundaries, sharing resources and data.

Collaborative Planning, Forecasting, and Replenishment (CPFR)   Business partners collaborate using the Internet. The demand planning (DP) component is the only one used to carry out CPFR. Process optimization achieves improved forecasting accuracy and reduces the stock on hand, for example.

Compliance   A procedure applied in the company to ensure compliance with statutory obligations and regulations, such as the Sarbanes-Oxley Act or labor protection laws.

Consignment   Indicates the transfer of ownership of a material (consignment material) when it is delivered to vendor consignment stores; the materials are stored at the customer but remain the property of the supplier until the customer withdraws them.

Contract Management   A function in the SAP system for managing outline agreements.

Core Interface (CIF)   The Core Interface is an interface between SAP SNC and the standard ERP system. The Core Interface provides SAP SNC with master data in real time.

Days' Supply   The days' supply is calculated as follows: Stock on hand is divided by the daily requirement. If the stock on hand or the requirement is zero, 9999 is calculated as the days' supply.

Electronic Data Interchange (EDI)   Electronic exchange of structured business data between the applications of cooperating companies using standardized data exchange formats and communication protocols via telecommunications networks.

Enterprise Resource Planning (ERP)   A software application for integrating all the data and processes in a company. See SAP ERP.

Enterprise Service (ES)   A web service that is used to carry out a step in a business process; Enterprise services can be used to create business applications and can be combined.

Enterprise Service-oriented Architecture (Enterprise SOA)   The SAP approach for implementing a service-oriented architecture in which services are used as building blocks for business processes based on open standards. See Enterprise service.

ES Bundle   A grouping of various SAP enterprise services and their documentation to address one common area of business (for example, requirements planning).

Forecast Delivery Schedule   Used to transfer demand fluctuations (order quantity, order time) to the supplier, who sometimes takes on responsibility for stockholding; the demand for goods is released within an outline agreement.

Handling Uunit   A handling unit is composed of packaging materials and the material they contain (for example, cases or pallets). It is delivered, processed, or shipped in the production process. A handling unit is often composed of several handling units.

IDoc   (Intermediate document) An SAP standard format for electronic data interchange between systems.

Incoterms   (International Commercial Terms) International rules for interpreting specific trade conditions in foreign trade; provided by the International Chamber of Commerce (IC) as a basis for foreign trade and to regulate the delivery of goods (www.incoterms.com).

Invoice Verification   An SAP ERP Materials Management component used to create and check the supplier invoice for accuracy in terms of content, price, and calculations and to authorize payment.

iView   An SAP NetWeaver Portal component used to display data from applications, documents, and the Internet.

Kanban   A procedure for controlling production in accordance with the pull principle; based on the demand of the consuming location in production; used to reduce stock and increase flexibility. See Pull principle.

Key Figure   See Key performance indicator

Key Performance Indicator (KPI)   Key figures such as sales, delivery time, and capacity utilization for evaluating the company objectives.

Lifecycle Management   Takes into account all of the stages in the lifecycle of a product: design, launch, growth, maturity, saturation, and discontinuation.

Location   Place or organizational unit in SAP APO/SNC at which quantities of products or resources are managed. The following standard location types exist: production plant, distribution center, transportation zone, stock transfer point, storage location MRP area, customer, supplier, subcontractor, transportation service provider, terminal, geographical area, and store.

Make or Buy   The question of whether in-house production (that is, manufacturing a product in-house) or external procurement (that is, purchasing products from a supplier) is less expensive for the company.

Master Data   Data that remains relatively constant over a period of time, such as customer address. See Transaction data.

Multisourcing   Sourcing goods or services from multiple sources.

A | Glossary

Outsourcing Transferring tasks to external service providers.

Post Processing Framework (PPF) An interface for SAP applications; when a defined condition is met, a particular operation is triggered (for example, delivery notes are printed, order confirmations faxed, or approval processes initiated).

Part Provided A material that a customer supplies to a subcontractor so that the subcontractor can fulfill the subcontract order for the customer.

Payment Advice Advance notice of payment.

Production Order An order for the production of a specific quantity of a part or product; triggered by a sales order or an internal event (for example, stock falls below the defined reorder point).

Pull Principle Demand-based production control

Resource Machine, person, facility, warehouse, means of transportation, and so on that has a limited capacity and fulfills a particular function.

SAP cFolders (Collaboration Folders) An SAP PLM application that enables internal employees and external suppliers to work on the same documents and share information. Because they are not able to access the backend system, confidential data is protected.

SAP Dispute Management An SAP ERP Financials application that supports the handling of dispute cases in invoice processing.

SAP ERP A suite of software applications from SAP that focuses on the core business requirements of midsize and large companies, including Human Capital Management, Financials, Operations, and Corporate Services.

SAP Event Management (EM) An SAP SCM component used to track business processes; triggers notifications and alerts to control and monitor business processes along the entire supply chain.

SAP Extended Warehouse Management (EWM) An SAP SCM component used to extend and enhance storage processes in the SAP system.

SAP Inventory Collaboration Hub Former name of SAP SNC (up to Release 5.0). See SAP Supply Network Collaboration.

SAP NetWeaver Business Intelligence (BI) An SAP NetWeaver component that offers data warehousing functionality and tools for information integration and analysis as well as reporting.

SAP NetWeaver Exchange Infrastructure (SAP NetWeaver XI) A function in SAP NetWeaver that allows you to integrate processes, thereby enabling applications to communicate with each other.

SAP NetWeaver Portal An SAP NetWeaver component that can be used to integrate SAP applications and applications from other providers; the users can access data and applications via the user interface or a web browser.

SAP NetWeaver Process Integration (PI)   See SAP NetWeaver Exchange Infrastructure.

SAP NetWeaver   A technology platform for most SAP solutions; used to integrate processes, data, and users.

SAP Product Lifecycle Management (PLM)   An SAP Business Suite software solution that supports companies with product development, project management, product structures, and quality management.

SAP Supplier Relationship Management (SRM)   Part of the SAP Business Suite. This application helps companies manage the procurement process (strategic purchasing and operational purchasing, for example, self-service procurement).

SAP Supply Chain Management (SCM)   An application that is part of the SAP Business Suite used to cover all processes from planning to networking the supply chain.

SAP Supply Network Collaboration (SNC)   An SAP SCM component that provides enhanced functions for collaboration in the entire supply chain network.

Service-Oriented Architecture (SOA)   A software architecture that allows interchangeable services to be used to map business processes. See Enterprise SOA.

Single Sourcing   Purchasing particular goods or services from just one supplier; associated with certain benefits (low prices, long-term business relationships, and so on) and drawbacks (default risk, less flexibility, stronger dependencies).

Subcontracting   The supplier (subcontractor) receives components from a customer or third-party supplier (subcontracting components) that are required to manufacture the product ordered.

Supplier-Managed Inventory (SMI)   Scenario in which a customer outsources replenishment planning to the supplier. Planning is based on the gross demand and stock that the customer provides.

Supply Network Inventory (SNI)   Business scenario in SAP SNC that supports the customer, subcontractor, supplier (and supplier's suppliers), and other partners (such as logistics service provider) to monitor the stock/requirements situation of selected location products in the supply chain.

Total Demand   The total quantity of a particular product that is required. In Supply Network Planning, projected total demand is equal to the sum of the forecast, sales orders, dependent demand, and distributed demand (planned and firmed).

Total Receipts   Sum of production (planned and firmed), distribution receipts, and in-transit receipts.

Transaction Data   Dynamic data, such as order or invoice data. See Master data.

Vendor-Managed Inventory (VMI) The supplier takes on the provision of goods and replenishment for the customer.

Warehouse Management An SAP ERP component used to organize and manage warehouses, stock transfers, stock movements, inventories, and so on.

B   SAP Consulting Services Portfolio

This section of the appendix is aimed at customers who want to initiate a project in the area of supplier collaboration with SAP SNC. SAP Consulting offers a number of best practice consulting services for this purpose. For more information, please refer to SAP Note 1000565.

In the following sections, we begin by identifying the parties who might call for a supplier collaboration project and their motivations. We then look at the questions a company needs to ask itself to achieve a successful supplier collaboration implementation with SAP SNC.

This is followed by a detailed look at the various consulting services offered by SAP Consulting and the related customer benefits.

B.1   Implementing an SAP SNC Solution

Several factors determine whether a company can implement supplier collaboration with SAP SNC successfully. Before initiating a project, a company should ask itself a few questions:

What are the main incentives, who is calling for such a project, and why?

A supplier collaboration project can be required from a business or IT perspective.

The business motivation may be to reduce procurement and logistics costs, innovate existing processes, improve quality, push for optimum capacity and stock utilization, automate purchasing processes, optimize the flow of information, or introduce centralized cost and supplier analysis.

The IT-related motivation might be the desire for *one* central platform for purchasing, planning, *and* the supplier or one integrated system landscape.

Central platform

Which business processes in supplier collaboration are relevant for the company?

Optimizing supplier collaboration can be regarded as particularly important and urgent in strategic purchasing, design and product lifecycle management, procurement planning and processing, and dispute management. A defined project roadmap with prioritized business processes is recommended.

What potential has already been exploited in the past in terms of supplier collaboration?

Certain business process areas in supplier collaboration may have already been optimized as part of earlier projects. For example, planned independent requirements are already being transferred to the supplier electronically.

To ensure swift success in the implementation of supplier collaboration, SAP Consulting offers consulting service packages for best practice implementation. For an overview of the consulting services offered by SAP, see Figure B.1.

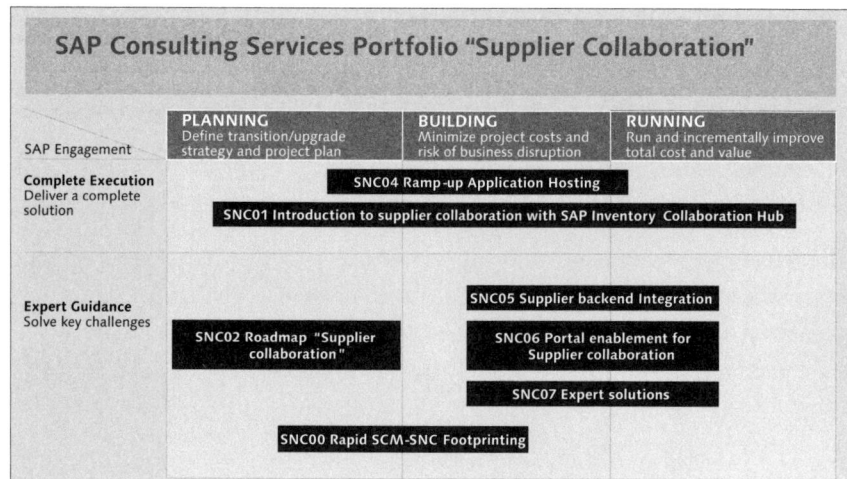

Figure B.1 Consulting Services Portfolio of SAP Consulting

B.2 SNC02 – Strategic Roadmap Development for Supplier Collaboration

This consulting service is aimed at customers who have already introduced supplier collaboration processes to a certain level and now want to increase the scope by taking into account new supplier collaboration processes, and customers who are still defining supplier collaboration processes and want to establish a medium-term and long-term project roadmap together with SAP Consulting to implement supplier collaboration.

This consulting service is structured as follows:

Project roadmap

1. **Preparation**
   A one-day workshop is held to define the scope and organization of roadmap development and agree on the schedule for subsequent workshops.

2. **Identification**
   Two-day workshops are held (up to three times) to pinpoint trends in supplier collaboration, verify the customer's actual processes, identify who is calling for supplier collaboration, analyze the potential of the actual processes in supplier collaboration, define the relevant *key performance indicators* (KPIs), and determine how the IT landscape is affected.

3. **Focus**
   Two-day workshops are held (twice or up to six times if necessary) to map the customer's actual processes in supplier collaboration to the SAP solutions, analyze how the SAP solutions affect the actual processes, analyze the organization and applications, determine the value added by supplier collaboration processes, identify the strategic relevance of supplier collaboration processes, and evaluate the future IT architecture and its alternatives.

4. **Roadmap development**
   Two-day workshops are held (twice if necessary) to define the roadmap content, identify the dependencies between the roadmap blocks, determine the sequence of roadmap blocks, define the organization

that will implement the roadmap, and gather relevant change management topics.

5. **Realization coaching**
   Workshops can be held two days a month or three days every quarter as required to assess and adapt the roadmap according to business, IT, and external factors. The coaching also covers quality assurance in roadmap implementation.

The aim of this consulting service is to identify the areas set to benefit most from supplier collaboration so that these can be examined more closely. Furthermore, it helps to structure the implementation project and identify dependencies between the various roadmap blocks in the strategic roadmap.

B.3 SNC00 – Rapid SAP SNC Footprinting

This consulting service is aimed at customers who have already purchased SAP SCM but have not yet started a project. They cannot afford to implement a complete SAP SCM-SNC solution but want to develop project know-how. Alternatively, the customers are unable to confirm the exact extent to which they want to use SAP SNC functions in their collaboration processes with suppliers. However, they want to use this pilot project as a reference in other organizational units (sales organizations, production locations, and so on) to establish common best practice standards internally.

This consulting service is structured as follows:

1. **Preparatory discussion**
   A preparatory discussion lasting approximately half a day is held to define the level of detail at which supplier collaboration processes are to be developed, check the system requirements, schedule the next workshops, allow SAP Consulting to check the installation, and define the master data that the customer has to provide to create a prototype.

2. **Analysis of supplier collaboration processes**
   A one-day workshop is held to discuss actual processes, present the SAP SNC system architecture, provide an overview of SAP SNC processes, and activate and check the SAP SNC content in SAP NetWeaver Process Integration.

3. **SAP SNC implementation workshops**
   Over a period of five to ten days (as required), master data is structured in preparation for integration of the customer's SAP ERP system and SAP SNC. The SAP SNC processes are established based on the predefined level of detail. Test users are set up, configuration steps documented with the customer, and a demonstration guide written.

4. **Joint presentation of pilot**
   A one-day workshop is held to present a demonstration to all persons involved, internal business partners, and suppliers. The processes presented are discussed and the fit and gaps of the standard SAP SNC system verified.

5. **Project development of supplier collaboration**
   A two-day workshop is held to create a fit and gap analysis of the standard SAP SNC functions based on the customer's target processes, determine the scope of the SAP SNC implementation project, and develop a project plan for implementing and rolling out SAP SNC.

This consulting service enables customers to acquire knowledge of SAP SNC functions and target processes to be mapped with the appropriate SAP SNC solution. Customers are given an overview of the project complexity and work packages within the implementation project, which enables them to market the SAP project internally.

B.4 SNC01 – Introduction to Supplier Collaboration with SAP SNC

This consulting service is aimed at small and medium-sized companies that are trying to establish collaboration processes with their suppliers quickly and with minimum effort using SAP SNC. The customer wants to make a quick start with a small number of suppliers and products.

This consulting service is structured as follows:

Fast implementation

1. **Scoping workshop**
   A two-day workshop is held to define the scope of the SNC processes to be implemented, determine the system requirements in SAP ERP and SAP SNC with the focus on existing procurement processes, and identify potential gaps in the standard SAP SNC system that are to be closed.

2. **Project start and installation of system landscape**
   If necessary, SAP SNC, SAP NetWeaver PI, and the required plug-in for the customer's SAP ERP system are installed according to the engagement model agreed on in the scoping workshop. Both the customer and SAP Consulting form a project team, and customer-specific knowledge is transferred to SAP SNC applications by an SAP Consulting team. The project is then planned in detail (to set milestones, define the scope of suppliers, plants, and materials).

3. **Blueprint phase**
   A technical and business blueprint is created with support from SAP Consulting, a development landscape prepared, test scenarios defined, and training materials created. In the case of customer-specific enhancements, the technical specifications are written.

4. **Implementation and test phase**
   This phase is for configuring SAP SNC, SAP NetWeaver PI, and the customer's SAP ERP systems, testing functions and integration, and creating test documentation.

5. **Preparation and go-live**
   Preparations are made for the go-live phase, and support is provided (also for any additional rollouts required).

Once the project has started, it takes approximately three to four months to reach the go-live phase, depending on the project scope.

This consulting service enables customers to implement the solution quickly at a fixed price and roll out SAP SNC independently.

Figure B.2 shows a proposal from SAP Consulting for a project plan created with the help of SAP consulting services.

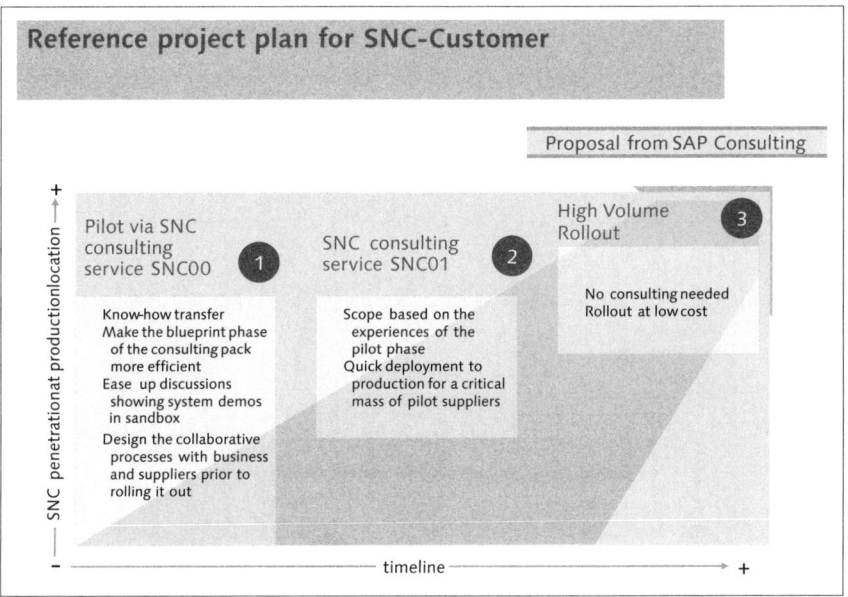

Figure B.2 Proposal for Best Practice Implementation of SAP SNC

B.5 SNC04 – Ramp-Up Application Hosting

This consulting service is aimed at customers who want to evaluate the options provided by SAP SNC applications for a specific period using their own data (SAP ERP) but want the SAP SNC solution to be hosted. They should also have the option to transfer the (Customizing) settings made in SAP SNC to their own system landscape at a later time.

Two variants are offered:

Variant 1: The entire system landscape (SAP ERP, SAP NetWeaver PI, and SAP SNC) is hosted, while the current copy of the customer's SAP ERP system is sent to SAP on a USB drive. The customer can access the system landscape via Citrix VMware.

Variant 2: Only parts of the system landscape (for example, SAP SNC, SAP NetWeaver PI) are hosted. The customer's SAP ERP system is linked with the hosted systems, and the customer can access the hosted systems through a firewall configuration via the SAP Logon.

Figure B.3 shows the two hosting variants graphically.

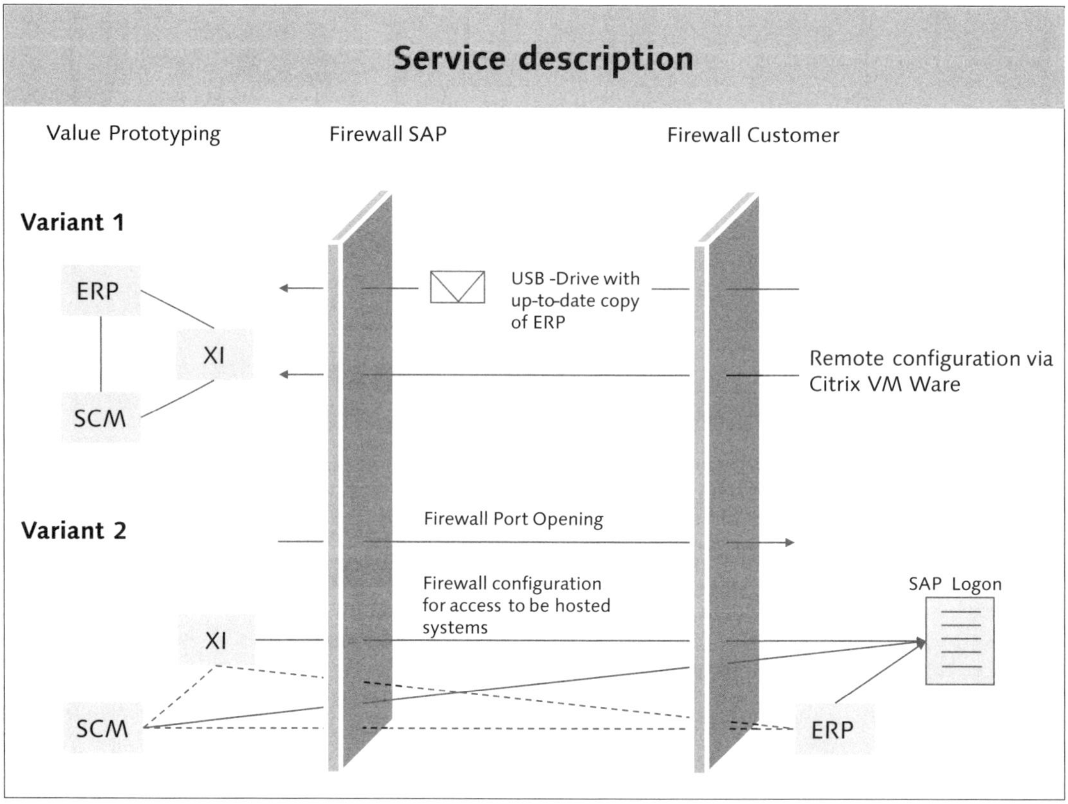

Figure B.3 SAP SNC Application Hosting Variants

In both variants, SAP implements the hosted solution. The solution can be configured by SAP or the customer, and the hosting period is determined by SAP together with the customer. The hosted solution (configuration) can be transferred to the customer's own hardware after the hosting period has come to an end.

This consulting service enables customers to evaluate the SAP SNC solution with data from their own SAP ERP system without investing in new hardware. Customers can decide how long the solution should be hosted before it is transferred to their own system landscape. Short-term hosting is also possible.

B.6 SNC05 – Supplier Backend Integration in the SAP SNC-SMI Process

As of SAP SNC 5.1, data published in SAP SNC can be transferred to the supplier electronically as part of the standard business process for SMI planning (see Section 4.2.16 Downloading SMI Data).

To enhance the standard solution, this consulting service is aimed at customers who implement the SMI business process (see Section 4.2 Supplier Managed Inventory (SMI)) to organize the way replenishment deliveries are planned and processed. In this process, the customer publishes information about stock and gross demand in SAP SNC at regular intervals, and the supplier ensures that the customer's stock always remains between the agreed minimum and maximum limits.

Integrated solution

This consulting service enables customers to provide their supplier with various SMI-Monitor-related data as XML files in SAP NetWeaver PI, which are not downloaded by default (for example, additional fields). This data is compiled in the same form that would be shown to defined supplier users in the SMI Monitor. The data can be read from SAP SNC and configured in SAP NetWeaver PI in two ways:

- Explicitly by report
- Automatically in response to updates from the customer's SAP ERP system (at times defined by the supplier)

To process the data in the supplier's backend system, the format may need to be mapped. Planned receipts can also be uploaded from SAP NetWeaver PI to SAP SNC. In this case, the supplier provides the data in a suitable format. Figure B.4 provides a technical overview of how data can be downloaded and uploaded.

This consulting service benefits customers by automating the backend integration to the supplier, which greatly reduces the amount of work for suppliers by eliminating the need to maintain data twice (in SAP SNC and their own backend system) which, in turn, prevents potential errors. An integrated supplier backend system enables suppliers to compare capacities in their system before communicating planned receipts in SAP SNC to the customer.

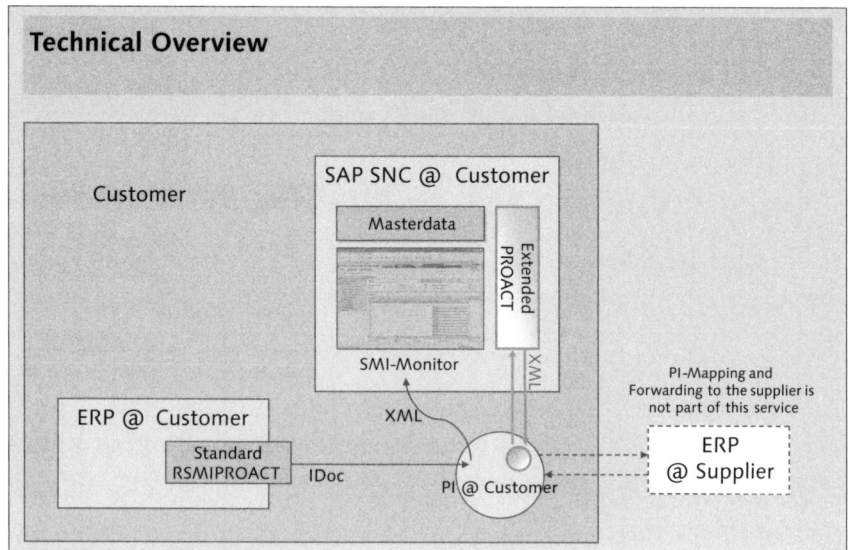

Figure B.4 Back-End Integration for Suppliers in the SMI Process

B.7 SNC06 – SAP SNC with SAP NetWeaver Portal

This consulting service is aimed at customers who have already installed an SAP SNC system and now want to attend a workshop to find out what options are offered by a supplier portal.

This consulting service is structured as follows:

In a five-day customer workshop, an SAP NetWeaver Portal is installed and configured to a basic level so that a prototype can be created. This prototype includes the integration of fully functional SAP SNC iViews for one supplier. For this purpose, the following functions are set up in the portal:

- Information page for the supplier
- Alert Monitor in SAP SNC
- SMI Monitor in SAP SNC
- Forecast Delivery Schedule Monitor in SAP SNC
- ASN Monitor in SAP SNC

- Quick Poll

Once the prototype has been set up, the following processes can be evaluated in the customer's system:

- Start of Enterprise Portal in browser
- Logon
- Navigation in the Enterprise Portal
- General and customer-specific information on the start page
- Single Sign-On to SAP SNC within the portal environment
- Example transactions (such as MIGO and so on) from SAP ERP (Web GUI or WinGUI)

As part of the workshop, minor adjustments can be made to the user interface; for example, the customer logo can be integrated or the layout of the start page changed. Once SAP SNC has been configured in the SAP NetWeaver Portal, the results should be discussed in a workshop with all departments concerned.

This consulting service benefits customers by facilitating their decision about using a supplier portal with SAP SNC. Customers can also access the prototype after the workshop is over because the portal is implemented on their own hardware. The supplier portal is evaluated on the basis of customer-specific data. The processes and functions that are important to customers and their system landscape are integrated.

B.8 SNC07 – Expert Solutions in SAP SNC

This consulting service is aimed at new and existing SAP SNC customers who want to realize requirements that are not covered by the standard SAP SNC solution by implementing additional enhancements. The expert consulting service is composed of a one-day workshop (two days if required) to define customer requirements and identify suitable enhancement blocks. The SAP SNC enhancements are then implemented, tested, and transferred.

Expertise

C   The Authors

Dr. Mohamed Hamady is a senior consultant in the field of supply chain management at SAP Deutschland AG. After studying computing and obtaining a doctorate in business informatics, he was involved in a range of SAP SCM implementations for industry customers in both a consulting and a project management capacity. He has been working on SAP ICH/SNC since 2004.

Anita Leitz is a principal consultant in the field of supply chain management at SAP Deutschland AG. She has 19 years of professional experience, seven of which were spent working abroad in Europe, the United States, and Latin America. She has served as a solution consultant and business solution architect for topics relating to inbound processes in numerous projects. Anita Leitz's specialist fields include high tech, automotive, and consumer industries. She has been working on SAP ICH/SNC since 2004.

Index

A

Adapter Engine, 221
Adaptive supply chain network, 19, 21
Advanced Planning & Scheduling (APS), 265
Advanced shipping notification, 56
Alerts, 77, 171
  exception, 227
  generation, 228
  handling, 229
  history, 233
  monitor, 230, 265
  profile, 190
  reorganize, 259
  selection, 231
  sending, 230
  type, 77, 172, 227
Analysis of potential, 39, 273
Analytics, 23
Application hosting, 277
Approval process, 31, 109, 121
  consensus finding, 111
  without tolerances, 110
Approval profile, 110, 121
Approval status, 111
Archiving
  supplier confirmations, 261
  work orders, 262
Archiving object
  CA_BUPA, 261
  ICH_SCON, 261
ASN
  confirmation, 112
  data, 258
  header, 194
  item, 194
  processing, 193
  status, 199, 259
Automatic packing, 196
Available-to-Promise (ATP), 265

B

Basic service, 224, 254
Billing, 26, 243
Billing and dispute management, 32, 35, 37, 39
Bill of material, 247, 269
Binning, 144
Bottleneck resource, 266
Business Application Programming Interface, 265
Business partner, 54
  reorganize, 260
Business process, 30, 39, 53
Business process analysis, 43, 45, 47, 49

C

Capable-to-Match (CTM), 265
Capacity leveling, 267
Collaboration, 19, 265
  demand-related, 245
  order-related, 245
Collaborative Planning, Forecasting and Replenishment (CPFR), 266
Color profile, 190
Components, 36
  assignment rules, 143
  requirement, 119
  supplier, 36
Condition technique, 111
Confirmation, 48
Confirmation request, 95
Consensus finding, 111, 184
Consignment stock, 128
Consulting service, 271
Contract management, 254
Control cycle, 162
Core Interface (CIF), 221, 254, 260, 266
Credit memo processing, 203
Cumulative quantity, 100
Custom production, 33

D

Database performance, 261
Data inconsistency, 257
Data reorganization, 257
Days' supply, 268
Degree of automation, 35
Delivery
   collaboration, 236
   control monitor (DCM), 45, 46, 173
   costs, 212
   overview, 148
   schedule collaboration, 237
Demand collaboration, 239
Demand forecast, 32, 34
Demand Monitor, 184
Design and product lifecycle management, 25, 31, 34, 37, 39, 243
Design change, 247
Design collaboration, 247
Dispute management, 26, 243, 245
Distribution status, 105
Drawing, 247
Due list
   planned receipts, 64, 73
   purchasing documents, 74
Dynamic replenishment, 28, 44, 183

E

Electronic Data Interchange (EDI), 26, 266
Enterprise Resource Planning (ERP), 266
Enterprise SOA, 234, 235
ES bundle, 235
Expert solution, 281

F

Firm and trade-off zone, 92
Firm demands, 187
Forecast delivery schedule, 89
   compare, 94
   data, 259
   processing, 27, 89

Forecasting
   collaborative, 244

G

Gross demand, 55

H

Handling unit, 195
Header status, 105

I

ICH_WO, 262
IDoc, 223
Inbound delivery control, 28
Incoterms, 206
Input components, 142
Integration, 222, 243
Interface mapping, 222
Inventory collaboration, 239
Invoice
   collaboration, 28, 200
   confirmation, 209
   data, 258
   processing, 201
   status, 258
   verification, 209
Item status, 107
iView, 252

J

JIT delivery schedule, 89

K

Kanban, 28, 38, 49, 158
   board, 165
   late response, 172
   process, 45

reorganize data, 259
request, 165
status, 168
Key figure, 62, 70, 178
Key Performance Indicator (KPI), 267

L

Lifecycle management, 267
List
　receipts/requirements, 102
　stock/requirements, 61
Location, 53, 267
　assigned, 126
　delete, 261
　product data, 260
　reorganize data, 261

M

Make-or-buy, 25
Manual effort for consultation, 37
Manual packing, 196
Manufacturing work order collaboration, 240
Master data, 221, 257
　generic, 53
　integration, 224
　object, 224, 260
　reorganize, 260
Material analysis, 41
Material investigation, 43, 46, 48
Message profile, 231
Min/max replenishment, 79
Model, 55
Monitoring, 76, 171, 181, 216
Multisourcing, 60

N

Negotiation status, 147
Notification profile, 231

O

Order Forecast Monitor (OFM), 184
Outline supply agreement, 34, 36
Output components, 142
Outsourcing, 38

P

Packaging instruction, 247
Partner
　assigned, 126
　data, 126
Part provided, 37, 49
Payment advice, 211
Phase, 141
　status, 154
　structure, 141
Planned demands, 187
Planning
　automatic, 81
　offset, 79
　profile, 81
　responsibility, 46
　version, 55
　zone, 92
Platform
　central, 271
Post Processing Framework (PPF), 229
Prioritization, 50
Process block, 84
Process scheduling
　configurable, 251
Procurement
　planning, 26, 32, 34, 37, 39, 243
　process, 30, 31
　processing, 26, 32, 34, 37, 39, 51, 243
　responsibility, 30
　strategy, 30
　type, 105
Product, 54
Product data
　reorganize, 260
Product data structure (PDS), 141

Production
 order, 37
 process model (PPM), 141
 supply area, 161
Product relationship/transportation lane, 260
Progress report code, 153
Pull principle, 38
Purchase order, 259
 handling, 27
Purchasing
 strategic, 243

Q

Quantity profile, 112
Quota arrangement rule, 34

R

Rating
 alert-based, 233
RCMPROACT2, 128
Receipt
 planned, 55
Relationship
 external procurement and transportation lane, 54
Release creation profile, 91
Release upgrade, 30
Replenishment
 alternatives, 57
 execution, 245
 method, 79
 net-demand-based, 79
 order collaboration, 237
 planning, 55
 process, 173
 reorganize, 259
 service profile, 78
 strategy, 161
 variant 1, 61
 variant 2, 69

Report
 /SAPAPO/DELETE_LOCATIONS, 261
 /SCA/CREATE_INV, 258
 /SCA/DELETE_INV, 258
 /SCA/DLV_DELETE, 258
 /SCA/DM_BOL_DLV_CLOSE, 259
 /SCA/DM_KNBN_DEL_CLOSED, 259
 /SCA/INVOICE_DELETE, 258
 /SCA/PO_DELETE, 259
 /SCA/PO_SET_CLOSED, 259
 /SCA/RESET_INV, 258
 /SCA/SCON_ARC_DELETE, 261
 /SCA/SCON_ARC_PREPROC, 261
 /SCA/SCON_ARC_WRITE, 261
 /SCA/TSDM_TS_DELETE, 258
 /SCA/TSDM_TS_HIST_DELETE, 258
 /SCA/USRPRTLOC, 260
 /SCA/WO_ARC_DELETE, 262
 /SCA/WO_ARC_PREPROC, 262
 /SCA/WO_ARC_WRITE, 262
 /SCA/WO_DELETION, 259
 /SCA/WO_SET_STATUS_CLOSED, 259
 /SCMB/ALEN_ALERT_DELETE, 259
 /SCMB/ALERTHOUSECLEAR, 233, 259
 /SCMB/AMEA_REC_CREATE, 234
 /SCMB/ANOTPULL, 233
Required actions, 156
Resource, 268
Revaluation, 204
Roadmap development
 strategic, 273
ROEMPROACT, 128
ROEMPROACT2, 128
RPRTPROACT, 128
RSMIPROACT, 59, 186
RSMIPROACT2, 60

S

SAP Advanced Planning & Optimization (APO), 217, 253
SAP cFolder, 246
SAP Consulting, 271
SAP Event Management (EM), 217, 250

SAP Extended Warehouse Management
(EWM), 217
SAP NetWeaver Portal, 252, 280
SAP NetWeaver Process Integration (PI),
220
SAP Supply Chain Management (SCM)
2007, 217
   SCM 5.1 full version, 219
SAP Supply Network Collaboration
(SNC), 39, 44, 47, 49
   architecture, 217
   lean, 219
   SNC 5.1 version
SAP Supplier Relationship Management
(SRM), 254
Self-billing, 35, 46
Serial number, 196
Series production part, 38
Service list, 84
Single sourcing, 60
SMI data
   download, 86
SNI
   alert rules, 138
   audit trail, 139
   details, 133
   details - product view, 136
   history comparison, 139
   monitor, 124
   overview, 135
Source determination, 34
Stock, 55
   create, 258
   data, 176
   delete, 258
   of material provided to vendor, 119
   owner, 126
   projected, 55, 77
   reset, 258
Strategic purchasing, 25, 31, 34, 37, 39
Subcontracting, 27, 36, 116
Subcontracting component, 37
Subcontract order, 116
Subsequent debit or credit, 202
Supplier
   analysis, 33, 40
   backend integration, 279

collaboration, 25, 29
confirmation archive, 261
history, 262
introduction, 275
investigation, 45, 48
Managed Inventory (SMI), 26, 27, 45, 55
Supply chain exception collaboration, 241
Supply Chain Management (SCM), 22, 269
Supply Network Inventory (SNI), 27, 122, 269
SXMB_MONI, 88
System landscape, 40, 50, 220
   integrated, 271

T

Tax code, 205
Time profile, 112
Time series data, 258
Total demand, 266
Total receipts, 266
Tracking, 147
Trade-off zone, 92
Transaction
   BUPA_PRE_DA, 261
   MASSD, 260
   /SAPAPO/DELETE_PRODUCTS, 260
   /SAPAPO/LOC3, 261
   /SAPAPO/MAT1, 260
   /SAPAPO/PWBSRC1, 260
   /SAPAPO/PWBSRC2, 260
   /SAPAPO/SCC_TL1, 260
   /SAPAPO/TR_DELTRPR, 260
   SARA, 261
   /SCMB/ALENCFG, 233
   /SCMB/AMEACFG, 233
   /SCMB/ANOTMP, 231
   SU01, 231
   WUF, 257
Transaction data, 222, 258
   archive, 261
Transparency, 23

Transportation lane
   reorganize, 260
Transportation phase, 142

V

Validation, 225
   check, 225, 254
   Framework, 224
   profile, 225
Vendor-managed inventory (VMI), 270
View
   purchase order worklist, 108
   release details, 93
Visibility concept, 124
Visibility control
   profile, 126
   profile-based, 124

W

Where-used list, 257
Workaround, 38
Work order, 141
   collaboration, 27, 139
   data, 146, 259
   details, 146
   generation, 143
   overview, 146
   proposal, 146
   reorganize, 259
   status, 155
   types, 144

Find the tools and techniques you need to deliver fast and successful SAP SRM implementations

512 pp., 2008, 79,95 Euro / US$ 79.95
ISBN 978-1-59229-154-0

Consultant's Guide to SAP SRM

www.sap-press.com

PadmaPrasad Munirathinam,
Ramakrishna Potluri

Consultant's Guide to SAP SRM

Find the tools and techniques you need to deliver fast and successful SAP SRM implementations

Consultants hold many roles during an SAP implementation, from business consultant during the blueprint phase, and product specialist during the realization phase, to trainer after go-live, and this book provides the information a consultant needs to hold these roles effectively.
Based on SAP SRM 6.0, each chapter covers a specific process of supplier relationship management, ensuring that implementation teams can utilize their time efficiently. Going beyond standard SRM scenarios, the book arms consultants with practical tips for enabling complex customer requirements, and provides insightful troubleshooting tips and techniques.
The authors use their years of experience implementing SAP applications to make this a must-have resource for SAP SRM implementation teams.

Provides a comprehensive overview of the entire delivery process

Teaches functions, processes, and customization

Covers dangerous goods management, availability checks, user exits, and much more

574 pp., 2008, 79,95 Euro / US$ 79.95
ISBN 978-1-59229-169-4

Transportation Management with SAP LES

www.sap-press.com

Othmar Gau

Transportation Management with SAP LES

This in-depth reference provides readers with practical and detailed knowledge on all aspects of shipping and transportation with SAP Logistics Execution System (LES). Using this book, employees in the warehouse and shipping departments, as well as consultants, can benefit from proven best practices for working successfully with the Transportation Management module. The author describes the entire shipping and delivery process, from the creation of a delivery in the SAP system, to mapping the internal supply chain, and from transportation planning to invoicing and settlement with forwarding agencies – and everything in between. Plus, readers also learn how to master system configuration, and much more.

Master real-life business processes and the structuringof plant maintenance technical systems

Discover tips and tricks for implementing daily operations

Explore interfaces, reporting, and new EAM technologies – MAM, RFID, Enterprise SOA, NetWeaver Portal, and more

552 pp., 2008, with CD, 69,95 Euro / US$ 69.95
ISBN 978-1-59229-150-2

SAP Enterprise Asset Management

Karl Liebstückel

SAP Enterprise Asset Management

This is a must-have guide for anyone interested in learning about the implementation and customization of SAP EAM. Consultants, managers, and administrators will learn about the plant maintenance process, how to evaluate which processes work best for them, and then go on to review the actual configuration steps of these processes. This book includes practical tips and best practices for implementation projects. The companion DVD contains examples, practice tests, presentations, and more. This book is up-to-date for SAP ERP 6.0.

Master inventory optimization using SAP ERP and SCM APO with this updated & expanded new edition

Explore inventory factors such as inventory controlling, demand planning, MRP, and much more

Learn how to improve your forecast accuracy and planning

705 pp., 2. edition 2008, 79,95 Euro / US$ 79.95
ISBN 978-1-59229-205-9

Inventory Optimization with SAP

www.sap-press.com

Marc Hoppe

Inventory Optimization with SAP

This new edition provides a completely up-to-date reference to teach users how to manage inventory to increase profitability and operational efficiency using SAP ERP 6.0 and/or SAP SCM 5.1. New and updated topics include additional sections on Material Requirements Planning, Controlling with SAP NetWeaver BI, Vendor Managed Inventory and Supplier Managed Inventory, and much more. This is the one-stop, must-have reference for anyone who needs to improve and maximize inventory management with SAP.

Teaches how to integrate MDM data into everyday business processes

Covers the benefits of integrating business partner master data processes throughout an enterprise

Provides practical, real-world case studies and solution examples

Up-to-Date for MDM 5.5 SP06

approx. 400 pp., 69,95 Euro / US$ 69.95
ISBN 978-1-59229-223-3, Sept 2008

Effective Master Data Management with SAP NetWeaver MDM

www.sap-press.com

Andy Walker, Jagadeeshwaren Ganapathy

Effective Master Data Management with SAP NetWeaver MDM

This book describes the key business benefits of implementing business partner master data processes in SAP MDM. Users learn the business drivers for MDM, as well as the value of integrating with Dun & Bradstreet services. The book covers the complete process of planning for and understanding master data management and how it can specifically affect business processes. Users will understand what MDM is and what it can do for their business, and you'll develop the practical skills necessary to integrate SAP MDM effectively.

- Discover the power and potential of SAP for Retail
- Explore SAP's various software offerings for retailers
- Understand the concepts, functionality, and software architecture

approx. 300 pp., 69,95 Euro / US$ 69.95
ISBN 978-1-59229-213-4, Dec 2008

SAP for Retail

www.sap-press.com

Heike Rawe

SAP for Retail

This must-have guide presents the 20 individual products in SAP for Retail, illustrating what each do for retailers, and how they fit together. This is the first complete and comprehensive review of SAP for Retail that explains how business processes and general business concepts fit into its solution. The book is written in an easy-to-follow style, with applied real-world examples and graphics throughout. Topics covered include planning, merchandising and buying, supply chain and fulfilment, and store and multi-channel retailing.

Interested in reading more?

Please visit our Web site for all
new book releases from SAP PRESS.

www.sap-press.com